Pro JavaScript Development

Coding, Capabilities, and Tooling

Den Odell

Apress®

Pro JavaScript Development: Coding, Capabilities, and Tooling

ISBN-13 (pbk): 978-1-4302-6268-8

ISBN-13 (electronic): 978-1-4302-6269-5

Publisher: Heinz Weinheimer
Lead Editor: Louise Corrigan
Technical Reviewers: Ben Howdle and Zach Inglis
Editorial Board: Steve Anglin, Mark Beckner, Ewan Buckingham, Gary Cornell, Louise Corrigan, Jim DeWolf,
    Jonathan Gennick, Jonathan Hassell, Robert Hutchinson, Michelle Lowman, James Markham,
    Matthew Moodie, Jeff Olson, Jeffrey Pepper, Douglas Pundick, Ben Renow-Clarke, Dominic Shakeshaft,
    Gwenan Spearing, Matt Wade, Steve Weiss
Coordinating Editor: Christine Ricketts
Copy Editor: Laura Lawrie
Compositor: SPi Global
Indexer: SPi Global
Artist: SPi Global
Cover Designer: Anna Ishchenko

Distributed to the book trade worldwide by Springer Science+Business Media New York, 233 Spring Street, 6th Floor, New York, NY 10013. Phone 1-800-SPRINGER, fax (201) 348-4505, e-mail orders-ny@springer-sbm.com, or visit www.springeronline.com. Apress Media, LLC is a California LLC and the sole member (owner) is Springer Science + Business Media Finance Inc (SSBM Finance Inc). SSBM Finance Inc is a Delaware corporation.

For information on translations, please e-mail rights@apress.com, or visit www.apress.com.

Apress and friends of ED books may be purchased in bulk for academic, corporate, or promotional use. eBook versions and licenses are also available for most titles. For more information, reference our Special Bulk Sales–eBook Licensing web page at www.apress.com/bulk-sales.

Any source code or other supplementary material referenced by the author in this text is available to readers at www.apress.com. For detailed information about how to locate your book's source code, go to www.apress.com/source-code/.

This book is dedicated to my wife, Maria

Contents at a Glance

About the Author xv

About the Technical Reviewers xvii

Acknowledgments xix

Introduction xxi

■Chapter 1: Object-Oriented JavaScript 1

■Chapter 2: Documenting JavaScript...37

■Chapter 3: Writing High-Quality JavaScript 65

■Chapter 4: Boosting JavaScript Performance 91

■Chapter 5: Design Patterns: Creational 119

■Chapter 6: Design Patterns: Structural..137

■Chapter 7: Design Patterns: Behavioral...163

■Chapter 8: Design Patterns: Architectural 199

■Chapter 9: Managing Code File Dependencies 223

■Chapter 10: Mobile JavaScript Development 237

■Chapter 11: Building Games with Canvas API...261

■Chapter 12: Using WebRTC for Video Chat...321

■Chapter 13: Using Client-Side Templates 341

■Chapter 14: The Node.js Application Platform..369

■Chapter 15: Build Tools and Automation 391

■Chapter 16: Browser Developer Tools 423

Index...439

Contents

About the Author xv

About the Technical Reviewers xvii

Acknowledgments xix

Introduction xxi

■Chapter 1: Object-Oriented JavaScript 1

Objects in JavaScript 1

Custom Objects 1

Classes 2

Coding Conventions And Naming 23

Rule 1: Use descriptive names 24

Rule 2: Begin with a lowercase letter 24

Rule 3: Use camel-case to represent word divisions 25

Rule 4: Use all uppercase characters to represent universal constants 25

Rule 5: Group together variable declarations in one statement at the top of every function block 26

ECMAScript 5 28

JSON Data Format Parsing 28

Strict Mode 29

Function binding 30

Array Methods 31

Object Methods 33

Summary 36

■**Chapter 2: Documenting JavaScript** **37**

Inline and Block Comments...37

Structured JavaScript Documentation 38

The YUIDoc Documentation Format..38

Documenting "Classes", Constructors, Properties and Methods 39

Documenting Events.. 47

Documenting Code Examples 48

Other YUIDoc Documentation Tags 48

Expressive Documentation Formatting – Markdown 48

Grouping Content Under Headings 49

Breaking Lines And Creating Paragraphs 49

Creating Lists... 50

Emphasizing Text 53

Displaying Code 54

Adding Quotes 54

Linking To URLs 55

Inserting Images.. 56

Creating Horizontal Rules 56

Using Backslash To Insert Reserved Characters 57

For Everything Else, There's HTML 57

Creating a Documentation Website Using YUIDoc 58

Taking It Further 63

Summary...63

■**Chapter 3: Writing High-Quality JavaScript** **65**

Performing Static Code Analysis 65

JSLint... 65

JSHint 69

Google Closure Compiler and Linter 70

Choosing a Static Code Analysis Tool 71

Unit Testing In JavaScript 71

    Unit Testing Frameworks For JavaScript 72

    Using Jasmine For JavaScript Unit Testing...72

Handling Runtime Errors 79

    JavaScript's Native Error Types 79

    Wrap Code That May Error In A try-catch Statement..80

    Detecting The Type Of Error Thrown 81

    Creating Custom Error Types 82

Measuring Code Quality 83

    Unit Test Code Coverage 83

    Measuring Code Complexity 86

Summary...89

■Chapter 4: Boosting JavaScript Performance 91

Improving Page Loading Time 91

    HTML Tag Order Matters..91

    GZip Encode Delivery Of Your JavaScript Files 91

    Minification, Obfuscation, and Compilation 92

    Lazy Loading JavaScript Files On Demand...97

Optimize Document Object Manipulation 98

    Minimise Access to Page Elements...98

    Close Existing Elements Where Possible 99

    Utilise The Offline DOM 100

    Use CSS To Manipulate Page Styles Rather Than JavaScript 100

Improving DOM Event Performance 101

    Delegate Events To Parent Elements 101

    Handle Rapid-Fire Events With Framing 103

Improving Function Performance 104

    Storing Previous Function Return Values With Memoization 104

Faster String Manipulation With Regular Expressions 106

Faster Use Of Arrays 110

    Fast Array Creation 110

    Fast Array Looping 110

Offload Intensive Tasks To Web Workers 113

    Using a Web Worker to Process Image Data 114

Basic Performance Measurements 117

Summary 118

■Chapter 5: Design Patterns: Creational 119

What Are Design Patterns? 119

Creational Design Patterns 120

    The Factory Pattern 120

    The Abstract Factory Pattern 122

    The Builder Pattern 127

    The Prototype Pattern 129

    The Singleton Pattern 132

Summary 135

■Chapter 6: Design Patterns: Structural 137

The Adapter Pattern 137

The Composite Pattern 140

The Decorator Pattern 141

The Façade Pattern 143

The Flyweight Pattern 145

The Mixin Pattern 152

The Module Pattern 155

The Proxy Pattern 159

Summary 161

■Chapter 7: Design Patterns: Behavioral 163

The Chain of Responsibility Pattern 163

The Command Pattern..166

The Iterator Pattern 169

The Observer Pattern 172

The Mediator Pattern..177

The Memento Pattern..181

The Promises Pattern 183

The Strategy Pattern 194

Summary...198

■Chapter 8: Design Patterns: Architectural 199

The Model-View-Controller (MVC) Pattern 199

The Model-View-Presenter (MVP) Pattern..209

The Model-View-ViewModel (MVVM) Pattern..214

Architectural Pattern Frameworks 220

Summary...221

■Chapter 9: Managing Code File Dependencies 223

Using RequireJS to Manage Code File Dependencies...223

Loading and Initializing RequireJS 228

Using Aliases For Module Names 230

Content Delivery Networks and Fallbacks...230

Creating Modules 231

Loading Additional Scripts On Demand 232

The RequireJS Code Optimizer Tool 234

Additional Plugins for RequireJS..234

Alternatives To RequireJS 235

Summary...235

■ Chapter 10: Mobile JavaScript Development 237

The Constraints of Mobile Web Development 237

Battery Life 237

Network Bandwidth Speeds And Latency 238

On-Board Memory Size 238

Operating System Responsiveness 239

Accessing Mobile Device Sensors with JavaScript 239

Accessing The Geolocation Sensor 240

Accessing The Touch Sensor 243

Accessing The Orientation and Direction Sensors 245

Accessing The Motion Sensor 248

The Missing Sensors 249

Event Framing For Sensor Data 250

Taking Sensor Data Further 250

Network Connection Failures And Offline States 251

Detecting Online and Offline States 251

Persisting Data With The Web Storage API 253

The HTML5 Application Cache 256

JavaScript For Responsive Design 258

Summary 259

■ Chapter 11: Building Games with Canvas API 261

Basic Drawing Operations in Canvas 261

High-Definition Canvas Elements 264

Building Games Using Canvas 265

Drawing Images onto a Canvas 265

Animation in Canvas 267

Game Control 268

Collision Detection 269

The Game Loop 270

Layering Canvases for Better Performance 272

Building a "Frogger" Game in Canvas 272

Summary 319

■**Chapter 12: Using WebRTC for Video Chat** **321**

The WebRTC Specification 321

Accessing the Webcam and Microphone 322

Creating a Simple Video Chat Web Application 325

    Connection and Signalling 325

Building the Video Chat Client 328

Summary 339

■**Chapter 13: Using Client-Side Templates** **341**

Dynamically Updating Page Content 341

Loading HTML Dynamically Via Ajax 342

Client-Side Templating 343

    Client-Side Templating without a Library 344

    Client-Side Templating with Mustache.js 345

    Client-Side Templating with Handlebars.js 353

    Alternative Client-Side Templating Libraries 364

Consider Progressive Enhancement 367

Summary 368

■**Chapter 14: The Node.js Application Platform** **369**

Installing Node.js 369

Writing Node.js Applications 370

    The Console 371

    Loading Modules 372

Node.js Packages 374

Splitting a Node.js Application across Multiple Files 380

Node.js Frameworks for Web Applications 382

    Express 382

    Socket.IO 384

Node.js Hosting 389

Summary 390

■Chapter 15: Build Tools and Automation 391

Build Tools 391

Grunt—The JavaScript Task Runner 392

Gulp.js—The Streaming Build System 400

Using Build Tools to Automate Common Tasks 404

Managing Third-Party Libraries and Frameworks 419

Project Setup and Scaffolding 420

Summary 422

■Chapter 16: Browser Developer Tools 423

Locating the Hidden Browser Developer Tools 423

The JavaScript Console 425

Outputting Messages to the Console Window 425

Using the Console for Performance Measurement 427

Remove Code References to the Console Object for Release 428

Debugging Running JavaScript Code 428

Working with Minified Code 428

Pause and Observe Running JavaScript Code 430

Profiling JavaScript Code 432

Locating Memory Leaks 432

Identifying Performance Bottlenecks 435

Summary 437

Index 439

About the Author

Den Odell is Head of Web Development at ideas and innovation agency AKQA, where his skill and passion for user interface development has led to launch of some of the web's most impressive websites and apps for clients such as Nike, Audi, and Heineken. He uses his role to train other web developers in the art of building sites and apps that are scalable, efficient, responsive, and beautiful.

Den is also an avid author and public speaker, writing numerous articles for technology publications alongside a previous book for Apress, and presenting talks at conferences and meetup events around the world.

In his spare time, Den dabbles in digital photography and has a passion for music that has led him to run nightclub events and DJ at venues around the world.

About the Technical Reviewers

Zach Inglis has been a web designer and developer hybrid for the last thirteen years. With a passion for creating, he has loved working on a wide variety of new and well-known companies. When he isn't freelancing at Superhero Studios (superhero-studios.com), he organizes HybridConf (hybridconf.net), a conference dedicated to bridging the gap between designers and developers.

Ben Howdle is a freelance developer, working with Node.js, JavaScript, and the whole front-end stack. Recently he is more and more excited by iOS and the new opportunities it brings.

Acknowledgments

I would like to thank my wife, Maria, who supported me throughout what must have seemed like endless evenings and weekends spent apart as I wrote this book. Thank you so much for your encouragement and for your love that kept me motivated to see this project through to completion. You are the most beautiful, wonderful, and intelligent person. I love you so very much.

Thank you to the whole team at Apress: to Louise Corrigan for seeing the potential in my idea; to Christine Ricketts, who coordinated and ensured that everything ran to schedule; to Ben and Zach for their invaluable feedback; and to Laura, Anna, and the rest of the team for turning my source material into the quality product you have in front of you. Thanks to the whole team at AKQA—particularly Ben Jones for his leadership, and the web development team for being the smartest group of engineers I have ever come across in my career. You rock!

Finally, I would like to thank you, dear reader, for taking the time to read the words, study the code, and generally engross yourself in this book. I hope that you take something away from its contents that will help you work, with me, to build a better web for the world.

Introduction

I wrote this book for the benefit of developers who have familiarized themselves with the JavaScript language and who want to take their knowledge to the next level, to become professional JavaScript developers. As I see it, there are three aspects to modern JavaScript development: *Coding, Capabilities,* and *Tooling*. Because I believe that these topics are intertwined, rather than divide the book into three distinct sections, these threads run through every chapter. My mission is to help you create the highest quality, most maintainable, scalable, and efficient code you can, taking advantage of modern coding techniques, capabilities, and tooling to help you get there.

As you follow through the material in this book, your coding skills should improve; you'll learn the details of JavaScript objects, about context, scope, prototypes, and inheritance, as well as the latest updates to the language that have landed in the major browsers. You'll also learn all about design patterns, how to comment your code in the best way for your project team, and how to boost the performance of your running code.

You'll discover capabilities of the language that you may not have been familiar with previously, including native APIs for drawing and building games that run in the browser, that allow for plugin-free video chat, and others specifically for mobile device development.

Developers are taking advantage of tools and automation more than ever to help their development workflow and improve the quality of the code that they produce. In this book, you'll discover how to check code quality, how to auto-generate a documentation website from your code, how to run a series of tasks on your code to improve your day-to-day workflow and to package your code up for release to the public, and, finally, how to use the developer tools built into the major browsers to help debug and profile your code as it runs in place.

By the end of this book, you should have the knowledge and experience to be a professional JavaScript developer, capable of building applications that are high-quality, maintainable, scalable, and efficient.

Let's get started!

CHAPTER 1

■ ■ ■

Object-Oriented JavaScript

If you've been developing websites for some time, you may have heard other programmers decree that JavaScript is not an object-oriented programming language, and often in the same sentence write off the language as a result. As JavaScript developers, it's up to us to educate each other and any naysayers about the JavaScript language, for it is indeed an object-oriented language, and a very powerful one at that.

In reality, when other programmers dismiss JavaScript, they are often belittling it for the fact that it does not adhere to all the same structures and conventions of classical languages, such as C++, Java, PHP, and Objective-C. This is not necessarily a negative, in my opinion, as JavaScript, if written in the right way, actually provides more flexibility by not having such a rigid structure enforced upon it.

In this chapter, I will explain how you can harness the power of JavaScript to write code using object-oriented programming principles adopted by other languages, emphasizing the ways in which this is made more flexible through JavaScript. I will also cover some of the built-in objects contained in the language itself, and some lesser-known facets of these.

■ **Note**   A classical programming language is one that defines and creates objects through blueprints or templates known as classes, hence the name.

Objects in JavaScript

An object in JavaScript is a standalone entity consisting of one or more related variables and functions, known as properties and methods, respectively. Objects are used to group together related concepts or functionality, often things that tie back to the real world or to specific software behavior. They make code easier to understand for developers, and so ultimately they make code easier to read and write.

Custom Objects

The simplest way of creating your own object for use in your JavaScript code is to use object literal notation, denoted by curly braces, when defining a variable. Properties and methods can then be attached to the object by encapsulating their names and values within the braces, using the format shown in Listing 1-1. Here we create a new object to represent a house, with two properties and two methods. Once created, we can read and write properties and methods within the object through dot notation, where the object name is separated by the property or method name with a dot (.) character.

Listing 1-1. Creating an object using object literal notation

```
var house = {
 rooms: 7,
 sharedEntrance: false,
 lock: function() {},
 unlock: function() {}
};

// Read out the values of the two properties
alert(house.rooms); // 7
alert(house.sharedEntrance); // false

// Execute the 'lock' method of the object
house.lock();

// Update the value for the 'rooms' property
house.rooms = 8;

// Add a completely new property dynamically
house.floors = 2;

// Read out the 'rooms' property again - notice it has now changed
alert(house.rooms); // 8
```

Let's imagine we want to represent another type of property, an apartment. It is similar to a house yet often has fewer rooms and is spread out over a single floor, probably with a shared entrance to the street. Let's represent this in a new variable as an object literal:

```
var apartment = {
 floors: 1,
 rooms: 4,
 sharedEntrance: true,
 lock: function() {},
 unlock: function() {}
};
```

Conceptually, an apartment is like a house but with different properties. If we chose to represent even more types of accommodation in the same way, we'll soon get into the position where it will be difficult or frustrating to alter the name of a property that we want to share between all these objects, or to add a new property or method to them all. Ideally, we would want to create a template or blueprint that represents the properties and methods of our objects, such that if we wanted to change a property name or add a new method then we could do this with ease. JavaScript allows us to create this kind of object template through constructors, which in other classical languages are commonly known as classes.

Classes

A class is a template or blueprint for similar creating objects that share a set of properties and methods. Programming languages such as Java and Objective-C allow developers to define classes through specific keywords and structures used for just that purpose. In JavaScript, defining a simple function creates some of the same behavior as a class. What makes it different from any other function is not how it is defined, but how objects are created from it.

■ **Note**   JavaScript has always had a reserved word called `class` in its language, which means you cannot create your own variable by that name. It has never actually been used in the language for anything; the name was simply reserved for later use. It appears that this keyword may finally get some usage in a forthcoming revision of the language, known as ECMAScript 6, which is currently being drafted.

Let's create a constructor function which we'll use as a blueprint for our house and apartment objects. We'll add the properties and methods later.

```
function Accommodation() {};
```

This looks no different from any other function we could have created in JavaScript. Creating objects using this as a template involves the use of the new keyword followed by the execution of the function.

```
var house = new Accommodation();
var apartment = new Accommodation();
```

Any object created using the new keyword is said to be an object instance of the structure represented by the function, essentially it's been created as an instance of this template or blueprint. Each object instance created in this way is not connected to any other created from the same template; they are treated as entirely separate variables that merely share an identical blueprint structure. Although the template structure resembles a class in classical programming languages, it is not strictly the same.

We'll take a closer look at the constructor function tlater in this chapter.

Detecting An Object's Constructor

Any object literal created from a template in this way has an extra property, called `constructor`, which points back to the JavaScript constructor function used to create it with. Armed with this knowledge, you can check to see if any object literal in your application matches one of your constructors by comparing the `constructor` properly directly with the constructor function.

```
house.constructor === Accommodation;      // true
apartment.constructor === Accommodation; // true
```

You can perform a similar comparison using the `instanceof` keyword, which compares an object literal with the constructor function used to create it.

```
house instanceof Accommodation;      // true
apartment instanceof Accommodation; // true
```

In fact, because the `constructor` property maps directly to the function used to create the instance, you could theoretically create new instances using this property directly, together with the new keyword. This is an uncommon usage, but still interesting to be aware of.

```
var apartment = new house.constructor();
apartment instanceof Accommodation; // true
```

Because we defined our "class" with an empty function, it has none of the properties and methods that we want to use as the template for each object instance. There are two ways of assigning properties and methods to a "class", through its prototype and through its scope. Let's look at each now, in turn.

Assigning Properties And Methods Using Prototype

Every function, and therefore every constructor, created in JavaScript has a prototype property. This is an object containing the properties and methods associated with any object instance created from that "class" with the new keyword. We can use dot notation on this prototype object to add our own properties and methods to all associated object instances. Each property we specify, we give a default value to so no value is left undefined. Listing 1-2 shows how we could define the properties and methods of our template, or "class", using the prototype keyword.

Listing 1-2. Assigning properties and methods to a constructor using the prototype keyword and dot notation

```
// Define a constructor called Accommodation
function Accommodation() {}

// Assign properties to our "class" blueprint
Accommodation.prototype.floors = 0;
Accommodation.prototype.rooms = 0;
Accommodation.prototype.sharedEntrance = false;

// Assign methods to our "class" blueprint
Accommodation.prototype.lock = function() {};
Accommodation.prototype.unlock = function() {};

// Create object instances from our Accommodation "class"
var house = new Accommodation();
var apartment = new Accommodation();

// Read properties from object instances
alert(house.floors); // 0
alert(house.sharedEntrance); // false

// Write properties to object instances to set the correct values
house.floors = 2;
accommodation.sharedEntrance = true;

// Execute methods on object instances
house.unlock();
apartment.lock();
```

Because the prototype is an object property associated with the function that we're using as a "class", we can also use object literal notation instead of dot notation. Listing 1-3 shows how we would do this.

Listing 1-3. Assigning properties and methods to a constructor using an object literal

```
// Define a constructor called Accommodation
function Accommodation() {}

// Assign properties and methods to our "class" blueprint with an object literal
Accommodation.prototype = {
 floors: 0,
 rooms: 0,
 sharedEntrance: false,
 lock: function() {},
 unlock: function() {}
};

// Create object instances from our Accommodation "class"
var house = new Accommodation();
var apartment = new Accommodation();

// Read properties from object instances
alert(house.floors); // 0
alert(house.sharedEntrance); // false

// Write properties to object instances to set the correct values
house.floors = 2;
accommodation.sharedEntrance = true;

// Execute methods on object instances
house.unlock();
apartment.lock();
```

One powerful feature of the prototype keyword is that you can add properties and methods to it, even after object instances have been created, and those new properties and methods will be automatically added to all object instances, both created previously and created afterward, as shown in Listing 1-4.

Listing 1-4. Dynamically adding properties and methods to preexisting object instances

```
// Define a constructor called Accommodation
function Accommodation() {};

// Assign properties and methods to our "class" blueprint with an object literal
Accommodation.prototype = {
 floors: 0,
 rooms: 0,
 sharedEntrance: false,
 lock: function() {},
 unlock: function() {}
};

// Create an object instance
var house = new Accommodation();
```

```
// Dynamically add a new method to the "class" prototype
Accommodation.prototype.alarm = function() {};

// The existing object instance gains the new method automatically
house.alarm();
```

Assigning Properties And Methods Using Scope

Any variable or function defined within a function is scoped to that function, meaning it cannot be accessed outside of that function—the function acts like a sandboxed development environment, or closure, for variables and methods declared within it. This is great for developers as it means the variables declared within one function don't impact on those within another; the same variable names can even be used within different functions without conflict.

Declaring a variable or function outside of any other function, just straight within a JavaScript or HTML file, places that variable or function within the global scope, which means it can be used anywhere throughout your code, even within another function. In fact, a nested function of any kind has access to the variables declared in its parent function because of scoping. This principle is demonstrated in Listing 1-5.

Listing 1-5. Variable Scope

```
// Variable declared outside of any function is in global scope and available to access anywhere
var myLibrary = {
 myName: "Dennis"
};

function doSomething() {
 // Variable declared within a function is not accessible outside that function
 var innerVariable = 123;

 // The global variable is accessible from within the function
 myLibrary.myName = "Hello";

 function doSomethingElse() {
  // Variables declared in a surrounding scope are accessible
  innerVariable = 1234;
 }

 doSomethingElse();

 alert(innerVariable); // 1234
}

doSomething();

// This property was overridden within the doSomething function
alert(myLibrary.myName); // "Hello"

// Trying to access a variable declared within a function from outside results in an error
alert(innerVariable); // ERROR!
```

Context and the `this` keyword

The JavaScript reserved keyword this is used to represent the context of a function, which in most cases represents the object encapsulating the function when it's run. When used outside of an object, it takes on the global window object. Using this within an object's method refers to the surrounding object, in this case the house object. The beauty is that by referring to this rather than the object's variable name, you can easily change the variable name at any time without affecting the behavior of the methods it contains. Because the this keyword becomes synonymous with the object that surrounds the function it's within, you can use dot notation on the keyword itself, as you would on the object. The code in Listing 1-6 demonstrates context and the this keyword.

Listing 1-6. Using dot notation with the this keyword

```
// Outside of any function, 'this' represents the global 'window' object
alert(this === window); // true

// Because the doSomething function is called outside of an object, the keyword this adopts
// the global JavaScript window object in the browser.
function doSomething() {
 alert(this === window); // true
}

doSomething();

var house = {
 floors: 2,
 isLocked: false,
 lock: function() {
  alert(this === house); // true, as the this keyword represents the object containing this method

  // We can treat 'this' as equivalent to the 'house' object, including using dot notation
  this.isLocked = true;
 }
};

house.lock();

alert(house.isLocked); // true
```

Nested functions within an object take on the global window object rather than the surrounding object, which is probably not the behavior you were expecting and catches many people out. Get around this by creating a variable to store the value of the this keyword at the point at which it contains the surrounding object, then use the variable in place of the surrounding object name. Many developers choose to use a variable named that to store the object's reference, as demonstrated in Listing 1-7.

Listing 1-7. Storing the value of the this keyword into a variable

```
var apartment = {
 isLocked: false,
 lock: function() {
  var that = this;

  // Set the isLocked property
  this.isLocked = true;
```

```javascript
 function doSomething() {
  alert(this === apartment); // false
  alert(this === window); // true
  alert(that === apartment); // true

  // Overwrite the isLocked property of the object,
  // accessing it through the stored variable
  that.isLocked = false;
 }

 doSomething();
 }
};

apartment.lock();

alert(apartment.isLocked); // false
```

The this keyword takes on a different value when used alongside the new keyword. In this case, it refers to the object instance created from the constructor function. It's this behavior, therefore, that we can harness to set properties and methods on our construction for use on all object instances, rather than using the prototype keyword, as shown in Listing 1-8.

Listing 1-8. Using the this keyword within a constructor function

```javascript
// Define a new constructor to represent a type of accommodation
function Accommodation() {

 // The 'this' keyword refers to the individual object instance created from this "class"
 this.floors = 0;
 this.rooms = 0;
 this.sharedEntrance = false;
 this.isLocked = false;
 this.lock = function() {

  // Using this within a function refers to its surrounding object, which in this
  // case refers to the object instance, since it's that which calls the method
  this.isLocked = true;
 };
 this.unlock = function() {
  this.isLocked = false;
 };
}

// Create object instances from the constructor
var house = new Accommodation();
var apartment = new Accommodation();

// Read and write properties and execute methods as normal with these object instances
alert(house.floors); // 0
house.floors = 2;
apartment.lock();
```

The most common way JavaScript developers declare the properties and methods for their object instances is through a combination of the prototype keyword and the this keyword, using the former for methods and the latter for properties. Each time a new object instance is created from a constructor, the constructor function gets executed. This combination approach is used to avoid needing to execute the code to initialize the methods each time an object is instantiated. By defining the methods on the prototype keyword, they're defined only once and available for every object created from that constructor making object creation more efficient. Methods assigned to the prototype can refer to this to get a reference to the instantiated object, as demonstrated in Listing 1-9.

Listing 1-9. Using a combination of the this and prototype keywords to create an efficient constructor

```
// Create a constructor function to represent types of accommodation
function Accommodation() {

  // Use the this keyword to set properties on the instantiated object
  this.floors = 0;
  this.isLocked = false;
}

// Define methods for instantiated objects using the prototype keyword
Accommodation.prototype.lock = function() {

  // Methods can refer to the this keyword to reach those properties created
  // in the constructor function
  this.isLocked = true;
};

Accommodation.prototype.unlock = function() {
  this.isLocked = false;
};

// Instantiate an object of the Accommodation type
var house = new Accommodation();

// Execute the 'lock' method
house.lock();

// Check that the 'isLocked' property was set as expected
alert(house.isLocked); // true
```

Another reason developers prefer to set properties using this within the constructor function is that it permits the initialization of certain properties based on values passed into the constructor function at the time of its execution. I personally prefer to use the this keyword for those properties that I may wish to initialize on creation, and to set other properties using prototype, together with my methods. This way the constructor function remains clear of any code that doesn't actually need to be executed at the time of object instantiation making the code more efficient, as demonstrated in Listing 1-10.

Listing 1-10. Initializing properties using the this keyword within a constructor function

```
// Define a constructor function with three parameters representing values to initialize
// properties of the instantiated object with
function Accommodation(floors, rooms, sharedEntrance) {

  // Initialize three properties with values passed in when an object is instantiated
  // from this "class". The Logical OR operation - || - allows a default value to be specified
  // in case no value is passed in
  this.floors = floors || 0;
  this.rooms = rooms || 0;
  this.sharedEntrance = sharedEntrance || false;
}

// Properties that don't need values set at instantiation time should be set with prototype
// as these are then defined and executed only once.
Accommodation.prototype.isLocked = false;

Accommodation.prototype.lock = function() {
  this.isLocked = true;
};

Accommodation.prototype.unlock = function() {
  this.isLocked = false;
};

// Instantiate an object from the "class", passing in two out of the possible three values
// for initialization. Arguments are passed in the order defined on the constructor function
var house = new Accommodation(2, 7);

alert(house.floors); // 2
alert(house.rooms); // 7

// A value for sharedEntrance wasn't passed into the constructor function, so its value
// defaults to false because of the Logical OR operation in the constructor function - see above
alert(house.sharedEntrance); // false
```

As your "class" grows, you may find the need to pass in a number of arguments to the constructor function in order to set the initial values of properties in your object instances. Although listing each argument in turn works fine for a small number of function inputs, it soon becomes unwieldy and confusing once the number of arguments gets beyond three or four. Fortunately, there is a solution in the form of object literals. By passing in a single argument to the constructor function consisting of an object literal containing all the initial values to set the properties to, we not only remove the confusion of multiple function arguments but also improve the understanding of our code since an object literal describes name-value pairs rather than unnamed function inputs. This is my preferred way of passing arguments to any function that requires more than two or three inputs; you can see this in action in Listing 1-11.

Listing 1-11. Using an object literal as the input to a constructor function

```
function Accommodation(defaults) {

  // If no argument is passed, default to an empty object literal
  defaults = defaults || {};
```

```
    // If the defaults object contains a named property, set the property of the
    // same name in the object instance to the supplied value, otherwise resort to a default
    this.floors = defaults.floors || 0;
    this.rooms = defaults.rooms || 0;
    this.sharedEntrance = defaults.sharedEntrance || false;
}

Accommodation.prototype.isLocked = false;

Accomodation.prototype.lock = function() {
    this.isLocked = true;
};

Accommodation.prototype.unlock = function() {
    this.isLocked = false;
};

// Instantiate two objects from the Accommodation "class", passing in named arguments
// through an object literal
var house = new Accommodation({
    floors: 2,
    rooms: 7
});

var apartment = new Accommodation({
    floors: 1,
    rooms: 4,
    sharedEntrance: true
});
```

Chaining Methods

We've defined methods that have been adopted by our object instances, and these methods are executed as any function would, with open and closing braces following the method name. To execute a number of methods on our object instance consecutively, we currently need to execute each one in turn on a new line, specifying the object literal's name each time.

```
house.lock();
house.alarm();
house.unlock();
```

By making a small change to each method, we can allow method chaining, meaning that one method call can directly follow another. You may have seen similar behavior if you've used the jQuery library (http://bit.ly/jquerycom), which allows for this same type of method chaining.

```
house.lock().alarm().unlock();
```

We do this by simply returning a reference to the object instance through the this keyword at the end of each method in the "class", as shown in Listing 1-12, which returns the object instance ready for immediate use again.

Listing 1-12. Chaining method calls using the this keyword

```
function Accommodation() {}

Accommodation.prototype.isLocked = false;

Accommodation.prototype.lock = function() {
 this.isLocked = true;

 // By returning the context, we are in fact returning an instance of the object instance
 // which called this function. Since that object contains all the methods, we're able to
 // call the other methods immediately after calling this one
 return this;
};

Accommodation.prototype.unlock = function() {
 this.isLocked = false;
 return this;
};

Accommodation.prototype.alarm = function() {
 alert("Sounding alarm!");
 return this;
};

// Create an object instance
var house = new Accommodation();

// Because each method returns its context, which in this case is the object instance, we can
// chain method calls one after another
house.lock().alarm().unlock();
```

Inheritance

A key facet of classical programming languages is the ability to create new classes that inherit, or extend, properties and methods from a parent class with which they share a similar logical connection. These are called child classes, or subclasses. This same kind of inheritance is possible in JavaScript, though not in quite the same way as in classical languages. Here it's known as *prototypal inheritance* and it takes advantage of a JavaScript object's so-called prototype chain, as demonstrated in Listing 1-13.

Listing 1-13. Creating a subclass using prototypal inheritance

```
// Define a "class" with two methods
function Accommodation() {}

Accommodation.prototype.lock = function() {};
Accommodation.prototype.unlock = function() {};

// Define a constructor function for what will become our subclass
function House(defaults) {
 defaults = defaults || {};
```

```javascript
    // Initialize the floors property to '2' for all instances of this "class"
    this.floors = 2;

    // If a 'rooms' property is passed within an object literal to this constructor, use its
    // value, otherwise default to 7 rooms
    this.rooms = defaults.rooms || 7;
}

// Map an instance of the Accommodation "class" to the prototype of the House "class".
// This executes the constructor function for Accommodation with the 'new' keyword, which
// creates and returns an object containing all its properties and methods. This is passed into
// the prototype of the House "class", making that "class" inherit everything from Accommodation
House.prototype = new Accommodation();

// The 'constructor' property of an object instance points to the constructor function that
// created it. However, by mapping everything from Accommodation to House, we also copied over
// the 'constructor' value, which we now need to reset to point to the new subclass instead.
// If we miss this step, object literals created from the House "class" will report that they
// were created from the Accommodation "class" instead.
House.prototype.constructor = House;

// Create an instance of a House, inheriting properties and methods from Accommodation, also
var myHouse = new House();

// Pass in a value for 'rooms' to set that value at the point of object instantiation
var myNeighborsHouse = new House({
 rooms: 8
});

alert(myHouse.rooms); // 7 (the default value set in the House constructor function)
alert(myNeighborsHouse.rooms); // 8

// Methods that were set on Accommodation are also available to objects created from House
myHouse.lock();
myNeighborsHouse.unlock();

// Objects created from House report that fact, thanks to us fixing the 'constructor'
// property earlier
alert(myHouse.constructor === House); // true
alert(myHouse.constructor === Accommodation); // false, since we pointed the constructor to House

// The instanceof keyword looks up the prototype chain, so can also be used to check if an
// object instance is derived from a particular parent "class"
alert(myNeighborsHouse instanceof House); // true
alert(myNeighborsHouse instanceof Accommodation); // true, since House inherits Accommodation
```

We've used the prototype keyword to add methods and properties to a constructor that will then be available to object instances created from that. If we attempted to refer to a method or property on our object that wasn't present on that constructor's prototype, instead of immediately raising an error, JavaScript will first try to check to see if a method or property of that name exists on any parent constructor that the current constructor is inherited from.

■ **Caution** When creating a subclass, ensure to point its `constructor` property at its own constructor function, as by default this will be pointing at the parent's constructor function, having been copied directly from its prototype.

Observe that the `instanceof` keyword follows the prototype chain, meaning it can identify if a particular object instance is created from a particular constructor, as well as from any constructor that constructor was inherited from. The prototype chain goes all the way up to the built-in `Object` type in JavaScript, as every variable in the language is ultimately inherited from this.

```
alert(myHouse instanceof House); // true
alert(myHouse instanceof Accommodation); // true, since House inherits Accommodation
alert(myHouse instanceof Object); // true, since objects are inherited from JavaScript's
        // built-in Object type
```

Encapsulation

When using inheritance to create variations or specializations of existing classes, all the properties and methods of the parent "class" are available to the child. You do not need to declare or define anything extra within the subclass to be able to use properties and methods of the parent. This ability is termed encapsulation; the subclass needs to contain definitions only for the properties and methods that are in addition to those of the parent.

Polymorphism

When inheriting and extending a "class" to form a new subclass, you may find you need to replace a method with another of the same name to perform a similar purpose, but with specific alterations for that subclass. This is termed polymorphism and is possible in JavaScript simply by rewriting the function and giving it the same name as the original method, as shown in Listing 1-14.

Listing 1-14. Polymorphism

```
// Define our parent Accommodation "class"
function Accommodation() {
 this.isLocked = false;
 this.isAlarmed = false;
}

// Add methods for common actions to all types of accommodation
Accommodation.prototype.lock = function() {
 this.isLocked = true;
};

Accommodation.prototype.unlock = function() {
 this.isLocked = false;
};

Accommodation.prototype.alarm = function() {
 this.isAlarmed = true;
 alert("Alarm activated");
};
```

```javascript
Accommodation.prototype.deactivateAlarm = function() {
 this.isAlarmed = false;
 alert("Alarm deactivated");
};

// Define a subclass for House
function House() {}

// Inherit from Accommodation
House.prototype = new Accommodation();

// Redefine the 'lock' method specifically for the House "class" - known as Polymorphism
House.prototype.lock = function() {

 // Execute the 'lock' method from the parent Accommodation "class". We can access this
 // directly through the prototype property of the "class" definition. We pass our context
 // to the function using the 'call' method of the function, ensuring that any references to
 // 'this' within the 'lock' method refer to the current object instance of House
 Accommodation.prototype.lock.call(this);

 alert(this.isLocked); // true, showing that the call to the lock method above worked as expected

 // Call the alarm method, inherited from Accommodation
 this.alarm();
};

// Redefine the 'unlock' method in the same way
House.prototype.unlock = function() {
 Accommodation.prototype.unlock.call(this);
 this.deactivateAlarm();
};
```

Observe the way in which we can refer to the original method we're polymorphing within our new method by simply referring directly to it within the prototype property of the parent "class" definition. Because that method contains references to its context, this, we need to ensure that it refers to the context of the object instance created from this subclass. We do this by executing the call method, which is available to any function in JavaScript and used for the purpose of applying context from one function to another.

The JavaScript Function's apply and call Methods

We took a look at context earlier; the keyword this in JavaScript refers to the object surrounding the current method, and in the case of object-oriented JavaScript programming, it refers to a specific object instance created from a "class."

If you call a method from another object than that which is your current context, any references to this in that method will refer to the object surrounding that, rather than the one in which you are executing your code—you've jumped to a different context. We need a way to maintain our original this context when calling methods from other objects. JavaScript provides a means to do this through two similar methods available to any function—apply and call.

We saw the call method in use in the previous section on Polymorphism as a way of calling a function from a parent "class" within a subclass. In that, we passed the context of the object instance created from the subclass directly into a method called on the parent's prototype. Any use of this in that method refers to the object instance, so we have a way of applying context from one place to another. If you need to also pass parameters to the function, you list these parameters after the context. The difference between call and apply is that with apply, the parameters should be contained within a single array parameter whereas they should be listed serially with call, separated by commas, as shown in Listing 1-15.

Listing 1-15. The apply and call methods on a function

```
// Define a simple "class"
function Accommodation() {
 this.isAlarmed = false;
}

// Create an object whose functions can be used in conjunction with an object in your code
// - also known as a 'mixin'
var AlarmSystem = {
 arm: function(message) {
  this.isAlarmed = true;
  alert(message);
 },
 disarm: function(message) {
  this.isAlarmed = false;
  alert(message);
 }
};

var myHouse = new Accommodation();

// Pass the object instance context into the 'arm' function using 'call'.
AlarmSystem.arm.call(myHouse, "Alarm activated");

// The 'arm' function's 'this' value was the object instance, therefore the 'isAlarmed' property
// of myHouse was changed
alert(myHouse.isAlarmed); // true

// The same effect can be achieved using 'apply', this time the parameters are sent as an array
AlarmSystem.disarm.apply(myHouse, ["Alarm deactivated"]);
alert(myHouse.isAlarmed); // false
```

The arguments object

When a function is executed, we pass any parameters within brackets that are then available as variables to use within that function. In addition, there is a reserved keyword, arguments, available in JavaScript that is present within functions and acts like an array containing a list of the arguments passed to the function in order.

Imagine that you have a function that you wish to use to add together all the numbers passed to it as parameters. Because you don't wish to specify the exact number of arguments, you can leave these empty and instead rely on the arguments pseudo-array, as demonstrated in Listing 1-16. We call it a pseudo-array because it can be iterated over in a for loop, but does not exhibit the other methods available for standard arrays, such as sorting, which you should not need when dealing with it in your code.

Listing 1-16. The arguments object

```
// Create a function to add together any parameters ('arguments') passed to it
var add = function() {

 // Create a variable to store the total of the addition in
 var total = 0;

 // The 'arguments' pseudo-array contains the arguments passed into this function.
 // Loop through each and add them together to form a total
 for (var index = 0, length = arguments.length; index < length; index++) {
  total = total + arguments[index];
 }

 return total;
};

// Try the function out with different numbers of parameters
alert(add(1, 1)); // 2
alert(add(1, 2, 3)); // 6
alert(add(17, 19, 12, 25, 182, 42, 2)); // 299
```

The arguments pseudo-array comes into its own when used with the function apply method. Because this method takes the parameters to pass to the function as an a array, we have a simple way of calling a function from any other that has the same input parameters—we effectively pass-on the arguments from one function call to another. This comes in useful with object inheritance and polymorphism, allowing us to pass arguments from a method of a subclass to a similar method on its parent, as shown in Listing 1-17.

Listing 1-17. Using the arguments pseudo-array within subclasses

```
// Define our parent Accommodation "class"
function Accommodation() {
 this.isAlarmed = false;
}

Accommodation.prototype.alarm = function(note, time) {
 var message = "Alarm activated at " + time + " with the note: " + note;

 this.isAlarmed = true;

 alert(message);
};

// Define a subclass for House
function House() {
 this.isLocked = false;
}

// Inherit from Accommodation
House.prototype = new Accommodation();
```

```
// Redefine the 'alarm' method specifically for the House "class". No need to list the arguments
// in the function definition here since we're going to simply pass them through to the same
// method on the parent "class"
House.prototype.alarm = function() {

  // Set the 'isLocked' property on this object instance to 'true'
  this.isLocked = true;

  // Execute the 'alarm' method from the parent Accommodation "class", passing all the
  // arguments from the execution of this method onto the parent method - no need to
  // explicitly list the arguments!
  Accommodation.prototype.alarm.apply(this, arguments);
};

// Create an object instance from the subclass and try it out
var myHouse = new House();
myHouse.alarm("Activating alarm", new Date()); // Alerts "Alarm activated at Fri Feb 14 2014
            // 13:02:56 GMT+0100 (BST) with the note:
            // Activating alarm"

alert(myHouse.isLocked); // true
```

Public, Private, and Protected Access To Properties And Methods

In our examples so far, we've created "class" templates that bind properties and methods to the prototype property of a constructor function or to the scope of the object instance created from that "class" with the this keyword. Every property and method created in either of these ways is said to be public, that is all the properties and methods are available to all the object instances created from that "class" and hence to any other part of the code base that can access that object instance.

There may be cases, however, where you wish to limit the exposure of certain properties and methods so that they can't be freely accessed, directly manipulated or called from the object instance itself. Many classical programming languages feature the ability to restrict access to properties and methods by defining them as either public, private, or protected. A private variable or function is one that cannot be read or written at all from outside the class definition, and a protected variable is one that cannot be accessed directly but can be read or written through a wrapper method. Such wrapper methods are typically called getters and setters, they allow you from the object instance to get the value from the variable and/or set its value. By only creating a getter function, you make the variable read-only from outside of the class definition. We don't have a specific notation for private or protected variables or functions in JavaScript, however we can reduce access to properties and methods by making some changes to the way we declare our "classes."

Declaring a variable with var within a constructor function keeps that variable scoped to that function only— any method then placed on the prototype object would not have access to it since that method would have its own scope. To allow us to access private variables through public methods we need to create a new scope that encompasses both. We do this by creating a self-executing function, called a closure, which completely contains the definition for the "class", its private variables and its prototype methods, as shown in Listing 1-18.

A good convention to follow, though not required in the JavaScript language, is to prefix any private variable or function name with an underscore character (_) to denote the fact that it is private. This will help you and other developers on your project understand better the intention of the developer of each "class."

Listing 1-18. Public, private, and protected properties and methods

```
// We wrap our "class" definition code in a self-executing function which returns the "class" we
// create and places it into a variable for use throughout the rest of our code.
var Accommodation = (function() {

  // Create our constructor function for our "class". Since we are inside a new function, we
  // have a new scope, therefore we can use the same name as the variable we are returning
  // our "class" to, for use in the rest of our code
  function Accommodation() {}

  // Any variable defined here is considered 'private', it isn't available outside this scope
  // We can denote it as such by prefixing its name with an underscore.
  var _isLocked = false,
   _isAlarmed = false,
   _alarmMessage = "Alarm activated!";

  // Any function defined in this scope only (not on the prototype of the constructor
  // function), is considered 'private' also
  function _alarm() {
   _isAlarmed = true;
   alert(_alarmMessage);
  }

  function _disableAlarm() {
   _isAlarmed = false;
  }

  // Any method placed on the prototype is going to be 'public', accessible outside this scope
  // once the "class" is returned later on in this closure
  Accommodation.prototype.lock = function() {
   _isLocked = true;
   _alarm();
  };

  Accommodation.prototype.unlock = function() {
   _isLocked = false;
   _disableAlarm();
  };

  // Create a 'getter' function to allow public read-only access to the value inside the
  // private variable 'isLocked' - effectively making this variable 'protected'
  Accommodation.prototype.getIsLocked = function() {
   return _isLocked;
  };

  // Create a 'setter' function to allow public write-only access to the '_alarmMessage'
  // private variable - effectively making it 'protected'
  Accommodation.prototype.setAlarmMessage = function(message) {
   _alarmMessage = message;
  };
```

```
// Return the "class" we created in this scope to make it available to the surrounding scope
// and hence the rest of our code. Only the public properties and methods will be available
return Accommodation;
}());

// Create an object instance
var house = new Accommodation();
house.lock();  // Alerts "Alarm activated"

house._alarm();  // error! The '_alarm' function was never exposed publicly so it's not
      // available directly to any object instance created from the "class"

alert(house._isLocked);// undefined ('_isLocked' is private and cannot be accessed outside
      // the closure)

house.getIsLocked(); // true (returns the value of the '_isLocked' variable, but doesn't allow
      // direct access to it, so it's a read-only value)

house.setAlarmMessage("The alarm is now activated!");
house.lock();  // Alerts "The alarm is now activated"
```

As a general rule, you should declare all variables and functions as private unless you specifically need to expose them publicly. Even then, consider using getter and/or setter methods for accessing variables to restrict what others can do with your "class" to just what's strictly required, which should reduce the chance of errors in their code.

Simplifying Inheritance

We can take steps to simplify object construction and inheritance by defining a base "class" from which all other "classes" can be created. By giving this "class" a method for inheriting from itself and allowing subclass access to the parent through a property, we make the task of creating and using subclasses a lot simpler. We can also wrap up all the code for setting methods on the prototype within a single object literal, and can even include our constructor function within that literal, making "class" creation a breeze. Study the code in Listing 1-19 and feel free to use it on your own projects to simplify the creation of your "classes."

Listing 1-19. A base "class" for simplifying the creation of other "classes"

```
// Define an object called Class with a create() method for use creating "classes".
// Use a closure to maintain inner functions without exposing them publicly.
var Class = (function() {

    // The create() method defines and returns a new "class" when called, based on an object
    // literal representing the public properties and methods for its prototype. A method named
    // initialize() will be executed as the constructor function. If an optional
    // 'parentPrototype' property is passed in, representing a parent "class", it creates the
    // new "class" as a subclass of that.
    function create(classDefinition, parentPrototype) {

        // Define the constructor function of a new "class", using the initialize() method from
        // the 'classDefinition' object literal if it exists
```

```javascript
    var _NewClass = function() {
            if (this.initialize && typeof this.initialize === 'function') {
                this.initialize.apply(this, arguments);
            }
        },
        _name;

    // If a 'parentPrototype' object has been passed in (when inheriting from other
    // "classes"), inherit everything from the parent to this subclass
    if (parentPrototype) {
        _NewClass.prototype = new parentPrototype.constructor();

        for (_name in parentPrototype) {
            if (parentPrototype.hasOwnProperty(_name)) {
                _NewClass.prototype[_name] = parentPrototype[_name];
            }
        }
    }

    // Define a function to create a closure and return a function to replace the one
    // passed in, wrapping it and providing a __parent() method which points to the
    // method of the same name from a parent "class", to enable support for polymorphism
    function polymorph(thisFunction, parentFunction) {
        return function () {
            var output;

            this.__parent = parentFunction;

            output = thisFunction.apply(this, arguments);

            delete this.__parent;

            return output;
        };
    }

    // Apply the newly provided "class" definition, overriding anything that already exists
    // from the parentPrototype
    for (_name in classDefinition) {
        if (classDefinition.hasOwnProperty(_name)) {

            // If we're attempting polymorphism, creating new methods named the same as
            // ones from the parent "class", then we want to expose a way of calling the
            // parent function of the same name in a simple way
            if (parentPrototype && parentPrototype[_name] &&
                    typeof classDefinition[_name] === 'function') {
                _NewClass.prototype[_name] = polymorph(classDefinition[_name], parentPrototype[_name]);
            } else {
```

```
                    // If we're not attempting polymorphism, just map over the entry from the
                    // 'classDefinition' object literal to the prototype directly
                    _NewClass.prototype[_name] = classDefinition[_name];
            }
        }
    }

    // Ensure the constructor is set correctly, whether inherited or not (in case a
    // 'constructor' property or method was passed in the 'classDefinition' object literal)
    _NewClass.prototype.constructor = _NewClass;

    // Define an extend() method on the "class" itself, pointing to the private extend()
    // function, below, which allows the current "class" to be used as a parent for
    // a new subclass
    _NewClass.extend = extend;

    return _NewClass;
}

// The extend() method is the same as the create() method but with an additional parameter
// containing the prototype from the parent "class" for inheriting from
function extend(classDefinition) {
    return create(classDefinition, this.prototype);
}

// Expose the private create() method publicly under the same name
return {
    create: create
};
}());
```

We can use this base "class" creator to create and inherit classes in an easy-to-understand way, as demonstrated in Listing 1-20.

Listing 1-20. The base "class" creator in action

```
// Define a "class" using Class.create, passing an object literal representing the public
// properties and methods to be made available to that "class". The 'initialize' method will
// become the constructor function of the new "class"
var Accommodation = Class.create({
 isLocked: true,
 isAlarmed: true,
 lock: function() {
  this.isLocked = true;
 },
 unlock: function() {
  this.isLocked = false;
 },
 initialize: function() {
  this.unlock();
 }
});
```

```javascript
// Create a subclass of Accommodation, using the 'extend' method that Class.create adds to any
// "classes" it creates, for simple inheritance. All the public properties and methods from the
// parent "class" are available to the subclass, with those of the same name overriding those
// from the parent.
var House = Accommodation.extend({
 floors: 2,
 lock: function() {

  // Even though we're using polymorphism to replace the parent "class" of the same name,
  // we can still access that parent "class" method using 'this.parent()'
  this._parent();
  alert("Number of floors locked: " + this.floors);
 }
});

// Create object instances from the new "classes"
var myAccommodation = new Accommodation();
alert(myAccommodation instanceof Accommodation); // true
alert(myAccommodation instanceof House); // false

var myHouse = new House();
alert(myHouse.isLocked); // false (set by the parent "class"'s initialize method,
     // inherited by House)
myHouse.lock(); // Alerts "Number of floors locked: 2"
alert(myHouse.isLocked); // true
alert(myHouse instanceof House); // true
alert(myHouse instanceof Accommodation); // true
```

Coding Conventions And Naming

Now we've covered the intricacies of object-oriented programming in JavaScript, let's look at coding conventions and the way that we name our variables and functions to imply meaning and to ensure that all developers in a larger team code in a similar way.

JavaScript permits you to store variables in memory for reuse throughout your code by using the reserved word var followed by the name of your variable and an optional initial value. Similarly functions can be stored in memory for repeated execution by preceding the name with the function keyword. You can name your variables and functions as you like provided they adhere to the following rules:

Its name must start with either:

- a letter, e.g. a-z, A-Z

- an underscore character, _

- the dollar symbol, $

After the first character in the variable name, numbers (0-9) are permitted alongside those mentioned above.

The following are all examples of valid variable and function names in JavaScript:

```
var a;
function A() {};
var a1;
function _() {};
var _a;
function $() {};
var $_$;
```

In addition to these fixed rules, as developers we wish to ensure our code is readable and understandable while we're working and maintaining it, so we use conventions for naming which are common to many developers and programming languages. By sticking to these rules for variable naming, you will understand how the variable is used in your code and you will better understand code written by others, too.

Rule 1: Use descriptive names

This rule is the most important so I've chosen to highlight it first. Variable names are there to represent the data stored within them, so choosing a name that best describes its use will help make your code more readable and hence more understandable, as shown in the following example:

```
var greeting = "Hello, world";
```

Rule 2: Begin with a lowercase letter

Use a lowercase letter to start your variable name and continue in lower case with the rest of your variable name as much as possible. Doing so avoids confusion with JavaScript's built-in types and objects, which all begin with uppercase letters, for example, String, Object, Math. For example:

```
var age = 35;
```

There are some specific exceptions to this rule that I use in my coding. First, when using jQuery I prefer to store located DOM elements in variables to avoid the need to look them up again from the page later in my code. In this case, I precede these variable names with $ to distinguish between DOM nodes and other variables in my code. The remainder of the variable name after the $ character then follows the same rules as for other variables, for example:

```
var $body = $(document.body);
```

The second exception is when naming functions that are to be used as constructors in your code. We'll come on to look at constructors in more detail shortly, but essentially the built-in types in JavaScript are constructors, e.g. String, Number, Boolean, and so on. Essentially these are any functions that are expected to be used with the new keyword. These should be named with an initial uppercase letter, as shown here:

```
function MyType() {};
var myTypeInstance = new MyType();
```

The third exception, as mentioned previously, is when naming variables and functions within a constructor function which are designed to be private, to prefix their name with an underscore (_) character to mark these apart from those intended to be made public.

```
function MyType() {
 var _myPrivateVariable;
};
var myTypeInstance = new MyType();
```

Rule 3: Use camel-case to represent word divisions

Rule 1 instructs us to use descriptive names, but if we're to only use lower case characters the variable names we create will be hard to read when we reach the boundaries of words, for example.

```
var myemailaddress = "den.odell@me.com";
```

On the first letter of words in your variable name, besides the first word, use an uppercase character as this makes the name much easier to read, as shown here.

```
var myEmailAddress = "den.odell@me.com";
```

Rule 4: Use all uppercase characters to represent universal constants

This rule concerns what are known as magic numbers, which are often used in calculations. These are those stray numbers used often when working with dates and times, or with calculations based on real-world constant values such as Pi. Many developers simply use these numbers at the point at which they're needed, which works but often leads to confusion. Take a look at the following example, which demonstrates this point.

```
var today = new Date(),
 todayInDays = today * 1000 * 60 * 60 * 24;
```

Without closer inspection, a quick glance at this code example reveals a series of numbers whose purpose is unclear. By creating variables and naming each of these numbers, the code becomes a lot more understandable. We use all uppercase characters to denote that these are fixed numerical values, also known as constants—which, although a feature of many other programming languages, are not in JavaScript—with word separations achieved using the underscore (_) character, as shown in the updated example given here:

```
var today = new Date(),
 MILLISECS_IN_1_SEC = 1000,
 SECS_IN_1_MIN = 60,
 MINS_IN_1_HOUR = 60,
 HOURS_IN_1_DAY = 24,
 todayInDays = today * MILLISECS_IN_1_SEC * SECS_IN_1_MIN * MINS_IN_1_HOUR * HOURS_IN_1_DAY;
```

Admittedly, this produces more code, however I believe it is worth the tradeoff in exchange for the readability it provides. Each declared constant could then be reused throughout the code, making calculations easier to understand.

Rule 5: Group together variable declarations in one statement at the top of every function block

JavaScript allows a shorthand way of declaring multiple variables at the same time using the var keyword, by splitting each variable declaration with a comma (,) character. It is wise to ensure that your variables are declared before attempting to use them so as to avoid errors when running your code. I advise you, therefore, to declare all the variables you use as the top of any function block or JavaScript file, and to combine them together into a single statement. Note that you do not have to initialize values into any variable that you will initialize later, but simply declare all variables up front. Separate each variable with a comma and a line break and align the start of each variable name with the preceding one to ensure readability, as shown in the following example:

```
var myString = "Hello, world",
 allStrongTags = /<strong>(.*?)<\/strong>/g,
 tagContents = "&1",
 outputString;

outputString = myString.replace(allStrongTags, tagContents);
```

Variable and Function Name Hoisting

In many other common programming languages, variables can be defined within any code block such as a for loop or any block typically denoted by being wrapped in curly braces { and }, and their scope be limited to that code block. In JavaScript, however, we know that scope is restricted at function-level only, yet this can trip up some developers who are used to programming in other languages; this is demonstrated in Listing 1-21.

Listing 1-21. Code blocks and scope

```
function myFunction() {
 var myArray = ['January', 'February', 'March', 'April', 'May'],
  myArrayLength = myArray.length,
  counter = 0;

 for (var index = 0; index < myArrayLength; index++) {
  // Increment counter each time around the loop
  counter = index + 1;
 }

 // The values of the variables should be as expected
 alert(counter); // 5
 alert(index); // 5 (since the loop increments before testing its condition)
 alert(myArrayLength); // 5

 if (myArrayLength > 0) {

  // In many languages, defining variables in a code block like this keeps their scope
  // locked to that code block. Not so in JavaScript, so beware defining variables locally
  // to code blocks in this way
  var counter,
   index = 0,
   myArrayLength;
```

```
  counter = 0;
}


// The values of 'counter' and 'index' were altered within the 'if' statement, regardless of
// the use of the 'var' statement in that code block
alert(counter); // 0
alert(index); // 0

// Note that the value of 'myArrayLength' has not changed, despite it being redefined within
// the code block with the 'var' statement. This is because variable names are 'hoisted' to
// the top of functions by JavaScript before the function executes
alert(myArrayLength); // 5
}

// Execute the defined function
myFunction();
```

JavaScript exhibits an interesting behavior commonly known as hoisting, in which variable and function declarations are internally raised, or hoisted, to the top of the function block in which they're defined. This means that any variable name definition is effectively available, though not necessarily initialized to a value, from the very top of its surrounding scope, usually a function. In order to minimize any odd effects that this may cause, it is advisable to begin any function with a list of all the variables to be used within that function, initialized or otherwise, as this mimics best the internal behavior of JavaScript hoisting and reduces the chance of confusion within unknown variable definitions and values your code; this is shown in Listing 1-22.

Listing 1-22. Begin all functions with variables used within that function

```
function myFunction() {

// All variables defined up front in the function to avoid being tripped up by hoisting
var myArray = ['January', 'February', 'March', 'April', 'May'],
 myArrayLength = myArray.length,
 counter = 0,
 index = 0;

// The first statement within the for loop definition, which would normally be used to
// initialize a variable can be skipped now we've moved all variable declarations to
// the top of the function
for (; index < myArrayLength; index++) {
 counter = index +1;
}

// The values of the variables should be as expected
alert(counter); // 5
alert(index); // 5
alert(myArrayLength); // 5
}

// Execute the function
myFunction();
```

The same applies to functions, whose names are available anywhere in their current scope, thanks to hoisting, even before their definition, as shown in Listing 1-23.

Listing 1-23. Hoisting of functions

```
function myFunction() {

 // Executing a function before its definition is possible due to 'hoisting' in JavaScript
 doSomething(); // The function below is executed

 function doSomething() {
  alert("Doing something");
 }
}

myFunction();
```

ECMAScript 5

In 1996, Brendan Eich, the creator of JavaScript from the company that was then Netscape submitted his language to Ecma international, a standards body, for review and standardization, from where the first official version of the language, known as ECMAScript, was launched in 1997. JavaScript is not the only implementation of ECMAScript; Adobe has been using a flavor known as ActionScript in their Flash and Flex products for a number of years.

Ecma International did very little work in the ten years from 1999, when they launched the third version of the language, and no changes were seen in the language itself during this time, largely due to disagreements over language complexity; a planned fourth edition was dropped for just those reasons. That changed in the end of 2009, when the organization revealed a fifth version of the language (they needed to be consistent with their internal numbering, even though the fourth version was dropped). A sixth version is planned, though release dates are unknown at the time of writing.

Because browser manufacturers have moved to more regular release schedules, the browser support for ECMAScript 5, despite being just two years old, is surprisingly good, being supported in the latest version of each of the major browser manufacturers' products. You can see the latest support matrix for features by visiting http://bit.ly/ecma_compat.

I will highlight a couple of the major features of this specification in this section as a taster, but I encourage you to read more in detail on the official ECMAScript site via http://bit.ly/ecma_5.

JSON Data Format Parsing

The majority of professional JavaScript developers will have come across JSON-formatted data before. This is data stored as a string, or within a text file, in a format that closely resembles an object literal, such as the JSON-formatted data structure shown here:

```
{
 "success": false,
 "error_message": "The wrong parameters were passed to this web service."
}
```

Converting such a string to a JavaScript object literal for use within functions used to involve downloading and including Doug Crockford's JSON parsing library, json.js from `http://bit.ly/crock_json`. ECMAScript 5, however, embeds this library right into the JavaScript language, making the following functions available for converting JSON data to object literals and vice versa:

```
JSON.parse(stringOfJSONFormattedData); // returns an object literal
JSON.stringify(objectLiteral); // returns a string of JSON-formatted data
```

Strict Mode

ECMAScript 5 introduces the ability to place a function or an entire JavaScript file in a new strict coding mode by simply placing the following string within that file or function.

```
"use strict";
```

Any code within the file or function containing that string will be subject to tighter language rules that should help avoid potential errors and pitfalls. Now if you attempt to use a variable that hasn't been defined, JavaScript will throw an error when executing code placed in this strict mode. It will also complain if you attempt to use an object literal which has two of the same named properties within it (something that's tripped me up, personally, before), and also if you attempt to use the delete keyword on a variable or function, instead of on an object property where that keyword is intended to be used. Strict mode will also prohibit the use of eval for executing strings containing JavaScript code, as these might be a security hazard and take the control of your code away from what you write yourself.

The beauty of strict mode being enforced by a simple string means that older browsers won't trip up when they come across the statement in your code, they'll simply execute it as a string and, because it isn't assigned to a variable value, will effectively ignore it. Compare the two functions shown in Listing 1-24, one in normal mode and one in strict mode. I have started using this new strict mode in all my code in order to assure myself that my code quality is sufficiently high, and I commend it to you also.

Listing 1-24. Demonstrating ECMAScript 5 strict mode

```
// Define a function
function myFunction() {

  // Using a previously undefined variable will implicitly create it as a global variable
  counter = 1;

  // Executing strings of JavaScript code using eval() throws no errors
  eval("alert(counter)");

  // The delete keyword is for removing properties and methods from an object, but
  // calling it on a variable throws no error
  delete counter;
}

// Execute the function
myFunction();

// Redefine the same function using ECMAScript 5 strict mode
function myFunction() {
```

```
// Enforce strict mode for the code within this function
"use strict";

counter = 1; // Throws an error when executed, since the 'counter' variable was not defined

eval("alert(counter)"); // Throws an error as 'eval' is to be avoided for security reasons

delete counter; // Throws an error since the 'delete' keyword is only to be used for
    // removing named properties and methods from object literals
}

// Execute the function
myFunction();
```

Function binding

We've already looked at the apply and call methods available to all functions in JavaScript. ECMAScript 5 adds another method, bind, which doesn't execute the function but rather returns a new function with the context of the function set to whichever object is passed into the first parameter of the call to bind.

You may have come across a need for this in your own code, particularly with reference to event handlers. If your event handler function is a method on an object instance, you may have been tempted to use this with your handler to execute another method or access a property on the object instance. If you tried this, you might have realized that the context of an event handler is a reference to the event that occurred rather than the object instance of the method. The function's new bind method allows you to alter this behavior to pass in your own context as needed to the handler, as shown in Listing 1-25.

Listing 1-25. The function bind method

```
var header = document.createElement("header"),
 mouseState = "up",

 // Define an object containing three methods
 eventHandlers = {
  onClick: function() {

   // If the context is wrong when 'onClick' is called, the next two calls will fail
   this.onMouseDown();
   this.onMouseUp();
  },
  onMouseDown: function() {
   mouseState = "down";
  },
  onMouseUp: function() {
   mouseState = "up";
  }
 };
```

```
// Force the correct context for 'eventHandlers.onClick' by using 'bind' to return a new
// function, bound to the context we require
header.addEventListener("click", eventHandlers.onClick.bind(eventHandlers), false);

// Add the <header> element to the page
document.body.appendChild(header);
```

Array Methods

Most professional JavaScript developers use arrays on a day-to-day basis for looping, sorting and organizing data. ECMAScript 5 provides some much needed new methods to the JavaScript developers' toolkit for working with these kinds of data structures.

First, and probably most important, is the ability to easily determine whether a variable contains array data. This may sound strange, but to detect whether a variable actually contained array data involved casting it to an object type and reading out its value as a string—madness! To detect whether a variable contains array data in ECMAScript 5, you simply call the Array.isArray method, as shown in Listing 1-26.

Listing 1-26. ECMAScript 5 isArray method

```
var months = ["January", "Febraury", "March", "April", "May"],
 items = {
  "0": "January",
  "1": "February",
  "2": "March",
  "3": "April",
  "4": "May"
 };

alert(Array.isArray(months)); // true
alert(Array.isArray(items)); // false
```

Looping through arrays currently involves creating a for loop and iterating through some type of index counter. ECMAScript 5 introduces a new forEach method that allows for far simpler looping; supply the method a function and it executes that function once for each item in the array, passing in the current value of the iteration, the index, and, finally, a reference to the entire array, as shown in Listing 1-27.

Listing 1-27. ECMAScript 5 forEach method

```
var months = ["January", "February", "March", "April", "May", "June", "July", "August", "September",
"October", "November", "December"];

// The forEach method allows you to loop through each item in an array, executing a function
// each time
months.forEach(function(value, index, fullArray) {
 alert(value + " is month number " + (index + 1) + " of " + fullArray.length);
});
```

If you've ever needed to determine whether every element in an array meets a specific condition, defined by a function, you've been waiting far too long for ECMAScript 5's new every method. A similar some method returns true if at least one of the items in the array matches the given condition. Both the every and some methods take the same parameters as the forEach method, as shown in Listing 1-28.

Listing 1-28. ECMAScript 5 every and some methods

```
var months = ["January", "February", "March", "April", "May", "June", "July", "August", "September",
"October", "November", "December"],

// The every method loops through each item in an array, comparing it to a
// condition. If the condition returns true for every item in the array, the
// every method returns true, otherwise it returns false
everyItemContainsR = months.every(function(value, index, fullArray) {

  // returns a true or false value indicating whether the current
  // iteration matches your condition, in this case whether the value contains
  // the letter 'r'
  return value.indexOf("r") >= 0;
}),

// The some method loops through each item in an array, comparing it to a
// condition. If the condition returns true for any item in the array, the
// some method returns true, otherwise it returns false
someItemContainsR = months.some(function(value, index, fullArray) {
  return value.indexOf("r") >= 0;
});

// Not every item contains the letter 'r'…
alert(everyItemContainsR); // false

// …but some do!
alert(someItemContainsR); // true
```

The new map method allows you to create a whole new array from an existing one, executing a function once per item as the new array is formed, as demonstrated in Listing 1-29.

Listing 1-29. ECMAscript 5 map method

```
var daysOfTheWeek = ["Monday", "Tuesday", "Wednesday"],

// The map method allows a whole new array to be created by looping through an existing one,
// executing a function for each item to determine the equivalent item in the new array
daysFirstLetters = daysOfTheWeek.map(function(value, index, fullArray) {
  return value + " starts with " + value.charAt(0);
});

alert(daysFirstLetters.join(", ")); // "Monday starts with M, Tuesday starts with T,
        // Wednesday starts with W"
```

ECMAScript 5's new filter array method creates a new array, like map, but the only items that match a certain condition are permitted into the new array, as shown in Listing 1-30.

Listing 1-30. ECMAScript 5 filter method

```
var months = ["January", "February", "March", "April", "May"],

  // The filter method creates a cut-down array from an original array, only permitting those
  // items that match a certain condition into the new array
  monthsContainingR = months.filter(function(value, index, fullArray) {

    // return a true or false value indicating whether the current array item should be
    // included in your filtered array, i.e. whether its value contains the letter 'r'
    return value.indexOf("r") >= 0;
  });

// The only month that didn't contain the letter 'r' was 'May'
alert(monthsContainingR.join(", ")); // "January, February, March, April"
```

Object Methods

ECMAScript 5 introduces a raft of extensions to the native `Object` type, bringing to JavaScript abilities present in many other programming languages. Firstly, if using strict mode, it introduces the ability to lock-down an object so that no additional properties or methods can be added after a certain point in your code through a new `Object.preventExtensions` method and an associated `Object.isExtensible` method which allows you to detect whether an object is able to be added to, as shown in Listing 1-31.

Listing 1-31. ECMAScript 5 Object methods

```
// Define a simple object with two properties
var personalDetails = {
 name: "Den Odell",
 email: "den.odell@me.com"
};

alert(Object.isExtensible(personalDetails)); // true, as by default all objects can be extended

// Prevent the 'personalDetails' object being added to
Object.preventExtensions(personalDetails);

alert(Object.isExtensible(personalDetails)); // false, as the object is now locked down

// Attempt to add a new property to the 'personalDetails' object
personalDetails.age = 35; // Throws an exception if using 'strict' mode as the object is locked
```

If you wish to lock down an object so that not even its existing properties can be altered, you have the ability through ECMAScript 5's new `Object.freeze` method, as shown in Listing 1-32.

Listing 1-32. ECMAScript 5 Object freeze method

```
// Define a simple object with two properties
var personalDetails = {
 name: "Den Odell",
 email: "den.odell@me.com"
};

// Lock down the object so that not even its existing properties can be manipulated
Object.freeze(personalDetails);

alert(Object.isFrozen(personalDetails)); // true

personalDetails.name = "John Odell"; // Throws an error if using strict mode as the object
         // cannot be altered once frozen
```

Each property of an object now has a set of options that determine how it can be used in the rest of your code, known as a property descriptor, represented as an object literal with four properties. To read the descriptor for a property, use the new `Object.getOwnPropertyDescriptior` method, as shown in Listing 1-33. All properties in the descriptor default to `true` apart from the `value` property.

Listing 1-33. ECMAScript 5 Object getOwnPropertyDescriptor method

```
// Define a simple object with two properties
var personalDetails = {
 name: "Den Odell",
 email: "den.odell@me.com"
};

Object.getOwnPropertyDescriptor(personalDetails, "name");
// Returns the following object literal representing the 'name' property:
// {
//   configurable: true,
//   enumerable: true,
//   value: "Den Odell",
//   writable: true
// }
```

Using ECMAscript 5, you can create properties and define their property descriptors at the same time, as demonstrated in Listing 1-34.

Listing 1-34. ECMAScript 5 property definitions

```
// Define a simple object with two properties
var personalDetails = {
 name: "Den Odell",
 email: "den.odell@me.com"
};

// Define a new individual property for the object
Object.defineProperty(personalDetails, "age", {
 value: 35,
 writable: false,
```

```
 enumerable: true,
 configurable: true
});

// Define multiple new properties at the same time
Object.defineProperty(personalDetails, {
 age: {
  value: 35,
  writable: false,
  enumerable: true,
  configurable: true
 },
 town: {
  value: "London",
  writable: true
 }
});
```

If you ever need to generate an array of the property names used in an object, ECMAScript 5 has your back with its new Object.keys method, as shown in Listing 1-35.

Listing 1-35. ECMAScript 5 Object keys method

```
// Define a simple object with two properties
var personalDetails = {
  name: "Den Odell",
  email: "den.odell@me.com"
 },
 keys = Object.keys(personalDetails);

alert(keys.join(", ")); // "name, email"
```

A powerful new method for creating a new object from the properties of another object is provided in ECMAScript 5's Object.create method. One possible usage of this method would be to duplicate an existing object, as shown in Listing 1-36.

Listing 1-36. ECMAScript 5 Object create method

```
// Define a simple object with two properties
var personalDetails = {
  firstName: "Den",
  lastName: "Odell"
 },

 // Create a duplicate of this object
 fathersDetails = Object.create(personalDetails);

// Customize the duplicated object
fathersDetails.firstName = "John";

// The properties set via the original object are still intact
alert(fathersDetails.lastName); // "Odell"
```

If there were one new method in ECMAScript 5 you should research more, it's the `Object.create` method as it can open up a whole new world of object inheritance in advance of what we've covered in this chapter. The opportunities opened up to use to greatly simplify the running and readability of our code are present in ECMAScript5, it's just a case of learning how to use it best.

Summary

In this chapter, we've covered the basics of object-oriented JavaScript programming, including objects, "classes," inheritance, and other programming features prevalent in other classical programming languages. I've shared some of my experience with variables and function naming conventions and those I've found to work best. Finally, we concluded with an introduction to ECMAScript 5, the latest version of JavaScript fast being supported by browser manufacturers.

In the next chapter, we will look into how best to aid yourself and other developers by documenting your code in a consistent and readable manner, making it easier to understand and therefore easier to work with.

CHAPTER 2

■ ■ ■

Documenting JavaScript

In the previous chapter, we looked at object-oriented JavaScript and coding conventions. The purpose of writing OO code and establishing conventions is to ensure that the code is legible and understandable for a developer. A JavaScript engine in a browser isn't concerned about how neatly your code is written, or whether it makes sense to you—it merely follows a set of rules on whatever it's been given. It's more important for you and your team to understand the code you've written and how to work with it as this simplifies the task of maintaining your code base. Code maintainability means that teams of any size can collaborate on the same set of files with a common understanding of how to add, amend, and remove parts of that code with consistent results. In addition to the code itself being understandable, you will find you need to add small comments or larger blocks of documentation to explain to other developers, including yourself if you don't remember your reasoning in future, what task a particular section of code performs and how it is to be used.

There are two groups of users who benefit from good documentation, which depends on the intended audience for your code. The first group is yourself and your fellow project collaborators. Good documentation keeps everyone aware of what your code does, how it does it, and why it does it, reducing the chance of confusion and errors being introduced.

The second group is other developers, unrelated to your project. If your project exposes public functions as some kind of API (Application Programming Interface) then you will need to ensure that your documentation is up-to-date, readable, and understandable, preferable with working examples to aid its adoption by other developers. Imagine if jQuery had poor documentation, it certainly wouldn't have been adopted as quickly as easily as it has been. Good, thorough documentation is key to getting adoption of your code to a wider group of developers.

Documentation can take many forms from a few key comments in a code file to an entire website dedicated to describing a code base; each suits different situations more appropriately. This chapter will focus largely on a structured form of documentation using specially formatted tags within comments in JavaScript code files, and will use this structure to generate a fully working documentation website without writing a line of HTML or CSS.

Inline and Block Comments

Sometimes code itself doesn't explain exactly what's going on and you just can't get away from adding comments to your code to make that code more understandable. It's fine to comment code but as a general rule, try to let the code do the talking. If you can avoid adding a comment by better naming a variable, then do that. If you need to add a comment to add value to your code, use either an inline comment, which is designed for use on a single-line of your JavaScript code:

```
// JavaScript recognises this line a comment because of the double slashes at the start
```

Or use a block comment, which is designed to span multiple lines of code:

```
/*
 * JavaScript recognises this as a block comment because of the slash / asterisk combination
 * at the start and the asterisk / slash combination at the end. Many developers choose to
 * begin each line of commented text with an asterisk and apply spacing such that each
 * asterisk lines up with the one from the previous line.
 */
```

Structured JavaScript Documentation

We could simply create a separate documentation file containing the usage notes and examples that describe our code, however, we'd have to ensure that this file was kept up to date whenever changes were made to the code itself, which can be time-consuming and most likely will not be done, meaning that it will forever be out of sync with the code it was written to describe.

In my opinion, the best way to create documentation is to add the usage notes and examples straight into block comments within the code file itself, right where the code is. In that way, it's clear to a developer adding or changing the code that the documentation they see surrounding it needs updating too, giving a better chance of the documentation staying up to date.

We've got a strategy, therefore, for ensuring that documentation is kept relevant, however it's not so easy to read if it's right with the source code and all you want to read is the documentation itself. We need a way of extracting the documentation out of the source code, therefore, into a more presentable form—ideally, this will be a simple case of running a program to do this for us, as we don't want to perform the extraction ourselves manually – we're developers and we just don't have the patience for that!

Fortunately, several programs exist to extract specially formatted documentation from source code files and present it within a simple webpage, in an easy to use format. Such programs include JSDoc (http://bit.ly/jsdoc_3), dox (http://bit.ly/d_o_x), and YUIDoc (http://bit.ly/yui_doc). Industry preference seems to be moving toward the latter and that's what we'll use to generate our documentation throughout the rest of this chapter.

The YUIDoc Documentation Format

YUIDoc does not process and understand any code in your source files; rather, it observes only the specially formatted block comments that you write yourself around your code. In my experience of using other documentation processors, some automatic processors often miss important factors that I understand about my code but they don't. You're then forced to add extra documentation manually in order to override its automatic processor. My preference is, therefore, for a processor that understands only what I tell it, so that I can be clear and explicit about my code in my documentation without any spurious information finding its way into my documentation.

YUIDoc will read only block comments from a file, and even then will ignore all that do not begin with the combination /**, as shown below. You can optionally add extra asterisk (*) characters to the beginning of each line of the comment to continue to denote that each line is part of the same comment and to line each up. Code editors such as Sublime Text (http://bit.ly/sublime_text) will do this automatically for you:

```
/**
 * This will be read by YUIDoc
 */

/*
 * This will not
 */
```

```
/***
 * Neither will this
 */
```

Now we know how to get YUIDoc to read a comment block, we need to know what to put inside the block in a format that YUIDoc can understand. YUIDoc supports @-tags, small labels that each start with the @ character followed by other names and information as relevant. YUIDoc has two sets of tags in its vocabulary, primary tags and secondary tags. Each comment block that describes some surrounding code must include one, and only one, primary tag, followed by as many or as few secondary tags as necessary.

Rather than list out every tag and its definition, let's look at some real-life use cases and see which tags are appropriate for which case.

Documenting "Classes", Constructors, Properties and Methods

We looked closely at object-oriented JavaScript coding in Chapter 1, in which we covered the creation of "classes" and associating methods and properties to them. Let's take one of our examples from that chapter and add some basic documentation comments to it in YUIDoc format.

Listing 2-1 defines a "class" named `Accommodation` using the `Class.create` method from Listing 1-19, with a constructor function named `initialize`, two public properties, `isLocked` and `isAlarmed`, and two public methods, `lock` and `unlock`.

Listing 2-1. A simple JavaScript "class" that needs documenting

```
var Accommodation = Class.create({
    isLocked: true,
    isAlarmed: true,
    lock: function() {
        this.isLocked = true;
    },
    unlock: function() {
        this.isLocked = false;
    },
    initialize: function() {
        this.unlock();
    }
});
```

We'll start our documentation at the top, using YUIDoc's `@class` tag for marking up a "class". The tag is preceded by a definition of the "class", and followed by the name of the "class". We include the name since YUIDoc's parser only reads these formatted comments and doesn't execute or parse your code for variable names. First, we describe the "class", leave an empty line, then we place the YUIDoc tags.

```
/**
 * A "class" defining types of accommodation
 *
 * @class Accommodation
 * @constructor
 */
```

We start the specially formatted comment with a simple text description of the "class" we're defining. This could be as long or as short as we like, spanning multiple lines if needed. We then start each new line with a YUIDoc tag, the first being @class followed by the "class" public variable name, and then adding a new line with the @constructor tag, which indicates that the variable is a constructor function from which object instances can be created. The beauty of YUIDoc, I believe, lies in the fact that it doesn't try and parse your code to extrapolate documentation by usage of variables and functions. In this case, the fact we created a constructor function and "class" using Class.create instead of defining a simple function won't matter to YUIDoc as long as the correct @-tags are used to describe it. Another documentation engine might have been thrown by this approach to declaring a "class" and might have returned different documentation altogether to what we'd expect.

You may have a "class" in your code that is not intended to be instantiated with the new keyword each time but, rather, is instantiated itself after definition, and the rest of your code should use that single instantiation. This is known as a singleton, or static "class", and can be denoted in your documentation by using the @static tag instead of the @constructor tag with your "class" definition, as shown in Listing 2-2.

Listing 2-2. Documentating a static "class"

```
/**
 * A static "class" containing methods for reading and writing browser cookies
 *
 * @class Cookies
 * @static
 */

// A self-instantiating "class" such as this is known as a singleton or static "class"
var Cookies = (function() {
    // Properties and methods to get and set cookie values go here…
}());
```

Documenting a property follows a similar pattern to the "class" itself; we create the formatted comment immediately above the property we're documenting in our code.

```
/**
 * Denotes whether the accommodation is currently locked
 *
 * @property {Boolean} isLocked
 */
```

After our property definition, we define our property by name to YUIDoc using the @property tag. Note that we can declare the type within curly braces between the @-tag and the property name. This is useful for other developers to be aware of the correct value types to use for your properties, so it's especially important that you remember to add this into your documentation. You can use any of the default types available in JavaScript, such as Boolean, String, Number, Object, Array, Date, Function, as well as any custom "class" types you create yourself within your code.

Documenting methods works in a very similar way to properties except that we use the @method tag and don't need to specify the data type, because methods are always of the Function type.

```
/**
 * Unlocks the accommodation
 *
 * @method unlock
 */
```

Listing 2-3 shows the full documented version of the `Accommodation` "class" from Listing 2-1.

Listing 2-3. A simple, fully-documented JavaScript "class"

```
/**
 * A "class" defining types of accommodation
 *
 * @class Accommodation
 * @constructor
 */

var Accommodation = Class.create({

    /**
     * Denotes whether the acommodation is currently locked
     *
     * @property {Boolean} isLocked
     */

    isLocked: true,

    /**
     * Denotes whether the acommodation is currently alarmed—thieves beware!
     *
     * @property {Boolean} isAlarmed
     */

    isAlarmed: true,

    /**
     * Locks the accommodation
     *
     * @method lock
     */

    lock: function() {
        this.isLocked = true;
    },

    /**
     * Unlocks the accommodation
     *
     * @method unlock
     */

    unlock: function() {
        this.isLocked = false;
    },
```

```
/**
 * Executed automatically upon creation of an object instance of this "class".
 * Unlocks the accommodation.
 *
 * @method initialize
 */

initialize: function() {
    this.unlock();
    }
});-
```

Specifying Inputs Parameters and Return Values of Methods

The methods we documented in Listing 2-3 contained no inputs or outputs, so documenting them was as simple as describing the purpose of the function. To mark up a method with a description of its inputs and outputs, which are essential if other developers are to understand how your method should be used, you add the @param and @return tags to the @method tag we've seen already. Take a look at the following method, which we'll add into our Accommodation "class" from Listing 2-1.

```
alarm: function(message) {
    this.isAlarmed = true;
    alert("Alarm is now activated. " + message);
    return this.isAlarmed;
}
```

We would add documentation to this method, detailing what the method does, along with its inputs and outputs, each listed on a separate line.

```
/**
 * Activates the accommodation's alarm and displays a message to that effect
 *
 * @method alarm
 * @param {String} message The message to display once the alarm is activated
 * @return {Boolean} The current activation state of the alarm
 */
```

Note that @param is similar to @property in that the type of the input parameter should be specified; unlike @property, however, the description of the parameter should immediately follow its name. The @return tag requires that we also specify the data type of the returned value within curly braces, followed by a description of what that value represents.

You may have written your code to group together the inputs to one of your methods into a single object literal parameter, as recommended in Chapter 1. This can be documented by listing each property in the object literal as a separate parameter, using dot notation to indicate each as part of the same object.

```
/**
 * Set all object instance properties in one shot
 *
 * @method setProperties
 * @param {Object} options Properties object
 * @param {Boolean} options.isAlarmed Denotes whether the accommodation is alarmed
```

```
 * @param {Boolean} options.isLocked Denotes whether the accommodation is locked
 * @param {String} options.message Message to display when alarm is activated
 */

Accommodation.prototype.setProperties(options) {
    options = options || {};

    this.isAlarmed = options.isAlarmed || false;
    this.isLocked = options.isLocked || false;
    this.message = options.message || "Alarm activated!";
};
```

Documenting Optional Method Input Parameters

If you have methods containing optional parameters, you can denote these in YUIDoc format by surrounding the parameter name in square brackets.

```
/**
 * Activates the accommodation's alarm, optionally displaying a custom message
 *
 * @method alarm
 * @param {String} [message] Custom message to display once the alarm is activated
 * @return {Boolean} The current activation state of the alarm
 */
```

Certain optional input parameters might have default values if the optional value is not provided. In our example, we may wish to default the optional message input parameter to a specific text string. We can denote this in YUIDoc format by following the parameter name with = and then by the default value for that parameter.

```
/**
 * Activates the accommodation's alarm, optionally displaying a custom message
 *
 * @method alarm
 * @param {String} [message=Alarm activated!] Custom message to display when alarm is activated
 * @return {Boolean} The current activation state of the alarm
 */
```

Documenting a Property Containing a Constant Value

In Chapter 1, we looked at denoting "constant" variables, or *magic numbers*, using capital letters. We can denote constants in our YUIDoc format documentation using the @final tag:

```
/**
 * The mathemtical constant Pi
 *
 * @property PI
 * @final
 */

var PI = 3.1415;
```

Documenting Private, Protected and Public Methods and Properties

For the benefit of yourself and other developers, you should document the public, protected and private properties and methods in your code. A method or property can be denoted as being private simply by adding the @private tag on a line by itself in your documentation, and protected properties can be marked with the @protected tag. Listing 2-4 shows a full documented "class" with public, protected and private properties and methods, taken from code we wrote in Chapter 1.

Listing 2-4. Fully documented "class" containing private and public methods and properties

```
/**
 * A "class" defining types of accommodation
 *
 * @class Accommodation
 * @constructor
 */

var Accommodation = (function() {
    function Accommodation() {}

    /**
     * Denotes whether the property is currently locked
     *
     * @property {Boolean} _isLocked
     * @protected
     */

    var _isLocked = false,

        /**
         * Denotes whether the property is currently alarmed
         *
         * @property {Boolean} _isAlarmed
         * @private
         */

        _isAlarmed = false,

        /**
         * Message to display when the alarm is activated
         *
         * @property {String} _alarmMessage
         * @protected
         */

        _alarmMessage = "Alarm activated!";
```

```
/**
 * Activates the alarm
 *
 * @method _alarm
 * @private
 */

function _alarm() {
    _isAlarmed = true;
    alert(_alarmMessage);
}

/**
 * Disables the alarm
 *
 * @method _disableAlarm
 * @private
 */

function _disableAlarm() {
    _isAlarmed = false;
}

/**
 * Locks the accommodation
 *
 * @method lock
 */

Accommodation.prototype.lock = function() {
    _isLocked = true;
    _alarm();
};

/**
 * Unlocks the accommodation
 *
 * @method unlock
 */

Accommodation.prototype.unlock = function() {
    _isLocked = false;
    _disableAlarm();
};

/**
 * Returns the current lock state of the accommodation
 *
 * @method getIsLocked
 * @return {Boolean} Indicates lock state, 'true' indicates that the accommodation is locked
 */
```

```javascript
    Accommodation.prototype.getIsLocked = function() {
        return _isLocked;
    };

    /**
     * Sets a new alarm message to be displayed when the accommodation is locked
     *
     * @method setAlarmMessage
     * @param {String} message The new alarm message text
     */

    Accommodation.prototype.setAlarmMessage = function(message) {
        _alarmMessage = message;
    };

    return Accommodation;
}());
```

Documenting Inherited "Classes"

From the material covered in Chapter 1, we know how to exhibit inheritance through our code, but we need to represent relationships between parent and subclasses in our documentation also. We can use the YUIDoc @extends tag to denote which "class" is the parent of the currently documented "class".

```javascript
/**
 * Define a "class" representing a house
 *
 * @class House
 * @constructor
 * @extends Accommodation
 */

function House() {};
House.prototype = new Accommodation();

/**
 * Locks the house and activates the alarm
 *
 * @method lock
 */

House.prototype.lock = function() {
    Accommodation.prototype.lock.call(this);
    this.alarm();
};
```

Documenting Chained Methods

Your documentation can be marked up to denote that certain methods in your code can be chained together, using the @chainable tag. As we saw in Chapter 1, this simply involved returning the context of the method call at the end of the method so the same methods are available to be immediately called:

```
/**
 * Locks the house and activates the alarm
 *
 * @method lock
 * @chainable
 */

House.prototype.lock = function() {
    Accommodation.prototype.lock.call(this);
    this.alarm();
    return this;
};
```

Documenting Groups of Related "Classes"

Your code files may contain several "classes", all of which share a similar grouping or related meaning to each other. In many cases, this grouping will be form naturally as a set of inherited "classes" from a single parent "class". You can denote this grouping to YUIDoc using the @module tag and the name of the grouping, of which at least one such tag should exist within your code base, even if that grouping contains only a single "class".

```
/**
 * Group of accommodation-related "classes"
 *
 * @module Accommodation-related
 */
```

Should you wish to refine your groupings further, you can use the @submodule tag together with @module to represent a subgrouping module of "classes" in your code.

```
/**
 * House-specific "classes"
 *
 * @module Accommodation-related
 * @submodule House-specific
 */
```

Documenting Events

If you're writing code that triggers custom events in your code, with listener functions to be called when such events are triggered, you should document your events by name using the @event tag, and describing any parameters that get passed to any functions listening for that event to trigger, using the @param tag:

```
/**
 * Fired when the accommodation is alarmed
 *
```

```
 * @event accommodationAlarmed
 * @param {String} message The message that was shown when the accommodation was alarmed
 */
```

Documenting Code Examples

Sometimes text-based documentation is no substitute for a code example. That's why YUIDoc contains the ability to mark up code within your structured documentation comments as an example usage of the code that follows, by using the @example tag. You can specify as many examples as you like, separating each with another @example tag. Example code should be indented by four spaces or one tab character, for reasons that will become clear further in this chapter when we discuss Markdown formatting.

```
/**
 * Sets a new alarm message to be displayed when the accommodation is locked
 *
 * @method setAlarmMessage
 * @example
 *     var myAccommodation = new Accommodation();
 *     myAccommodation.setAlarmMessage("My alarm is enabled - thieves beware! ");
 *     myAccommodation.alarm(); // Alerts "My alarm is enabled - thieves beware! "
 *
 * @example
 *     var myAccommodation = new Accommodation();
 *     myAccommodation.setAlarmMessage(); // Leave message blank
 *     myAccommodation.alarm(); // Alerts an empty box with no message
 */
```

Other YUIDoc Documentation Tags

In this chapter, we've covered the documentation tags that you'll need in probably 90 percent of real-life cases. As you become more familiar with documenting your own code, however, you may find you need to document aspects of your code that haven't been explained in this chapter. To see the full list of available tags for use with YUIDoc, visit the official syntax reference site via http://bit.ly/yuidoc_syntax.

Expressive Documentation Formatting – Markdown

Rather than writing longer-form "class", method and property descriptions and usage documentation in HTML markup, where as a developer it becomes fairly difficult read, it's possible to use a more developer-friendly format, known as Markdown— http://bit.ly/markdown_format.

John Gruber and Aaron Swartz developed Markdown in 2004 as a simple way for developers to write documents in plain text that can be easily read as plain text but just as easily transformed into HTML for easier reading. It uses conventions already present in plain text messages of the time, notably in emails and on newsgroups. It has become popular for generating rich text on sites such as GitHub, Stack Overflow, and SourceForge without the need to write HTML.

Using Markdown in your structured documentation will help your documentation be rich and expressive without overbloating your source code files or making them any harder to read. YUIDoc supports the Markdown format for free-form documentation within descriptions and examples, allowing for very expressive and thorough documentation to be produced. It is therefore important to become familiar with the format in detail. Let's take a look through some of the most common ways of writing Markdown and the HTML outputs these produce when run through a Markdown processor, such as the one present within YUIDoc.

Grouping Content Under Headings

The HTML heading tags <h1> through <h6> can be produced as the output of a block of markdown text using the forms shown in the example below:

```
A Main Heading
==============

A Secondary Heading
-------------------

# Alternative Form Of Main Heading, aka Header Level 1
## Alternative Form Of Secondary Heading, aka Header Level 2
### Header Level 3
#### Header Level 4 ####
##### Header Level 5
###### Header Level 6 ######
```

This block of Markdown produces the following when processed into HTML:

```
<h1>A Main Heading</h1>
<h2>A Secondary Heading</h2>
<h1>Alternative Form Of Main Heading, aka Header Level 1</h1>
<h2>Alternative Form Of Seconday Heading, aka Header Level 2</h2>
<h3>Header Level 3</h3>
<h4>Header Level 4</h4>
<h5>Header Level 5</h5>
<h6>Header Level 6</h6>
```

Visually comparing the markdown input to the HTML output should reveal to you just how simple to read and write Markdown is compared to the relatively tricky-to-scan HTML output.

Note the two possible forms for main and secondary headings, and also the obsolete end markers on the level 4 and 6 headers in the original Markdown. These both are purely to allow easier to read input without affecting the output, feel free to use any approach you see fit according to which appearance you prefer.

Breaking Lines And Creating Paragraphs

Creating paragraphs of text using markdown requires no special symbols; simply add two line breaks between one block of text and another to produce a <p> tag around each block in the resulting HTML.

```
80 days around the world, we'll find a pot of gold just sitting where the rainbow's ending.
Time—we'll fight against the time, and we'll fly on the white wings of the wind.

Ten years ago a crack commando unit was sent to prison by a military court for a crime they didn't
commit. These men promptly escaped from a maximum-security stockade to the Los Angeles underground.
```

The markdown shown in the example here will be converted to the following HTML output.

```
<p>80 days around the world, we'll find a pot of gold just sitting where the rainbow's ending.
Time—we'll fight against the time, and we'll fly on the white wings of the wind.</p>
```

```
<p>Ten years ago a crack commando unit was sent to prison by a military court for a crime they
didn't commit. These men promptly escaped from a maximum-security stockade to the Los Angeles
underground.</p>
```

You might assume from this that to create a line break in the HTML output rather than a paragraph break you would simply include a single line break in your Markdown file, but this is not the case. A single line break on its own in Markdown will flow the output text together into a single paragraph.

```
80 days around the world, we'll find a pot of gold just sitting where the rainbow's ending.
Time—we'll fight against the time, and we'll fly on the white wings of the wind.
```

The example here produces the following HTML output after processing.

```
<p>80 days around the world, we'll find a pot of gold just sitting where the rainbow's ending.
Time—we'll fight against the time, and we'll fly on the white wings of the wind.</p>
```

To generate a HTML line break <br /> in the output, you must precede your line break in Markdown with two or more spaces. This will be at the end of the line before so won't be seen visually when reading the input file.

```
80 days around the world, we'll find a pot of gold just sitting where the rainbow's ending.
Time—we'll fight against the time, and we'll fly on the white wings of the wind.
```

The ⌴ symbols at the end of the first line in the example here denote the use of the space character, so ensure that you do not use the ⌴ character itself. Processing this Markdown input produces the following HTML output.

```
<p>80 days around the world, we'll find a pot of gold just sitting where the rainbow's
ending.<br />Time—we'll fight against the time, and we'll fly on the white wings of the wind.</p>
```

Creating Lists

Both ordered and unordered lists can be represented through markdown and interpreted into their correct HTML tags.

An unordered, or bulleted, list can be represented using asterisks (*), hyphens (-), or pluses (+) as bullet points, each followed by one or more space characters, or tab characters, meaning it's very flexible and you can use whichever feels most natural to you.

```
* Monkey
* Donkey
* Wonky


-       Monkey
-       Wonky
-       Donkey


+ Donkey
+ Monkey
+ Wonky
```

The example shown produces the following HTML output once processed. Observe that the HTML for each list is identical, despite the different bullets used in the original markdown list.

```
<ul>
    <li>Monkey</li>
    <li>Donkey</li>
    <li>Wonky</li>
</ul>

<ul>
    <li>Monkey</li>
    <li>Wonky</li>
    <li>Donkey</li>
</ul>

<ul>
    <li>Donkey</li>
    <li>Monkey</li>
    <li>Wonky</li>
</ul>
```

Ordered lists can be generated by beginning each line with a number, followed by a period then one or more tabs or space characters. The actual numbers used in the markdown file don't matter; they will be processed as a single ordered number list starting from the number 1. This is actually beneficial to the person writing the markdown text as they need only set all numbers to the same digit, meaning they don't have to reorder the numbers if they add an extra item to the list.

```
1. Monkey
2. Donkey
3. Wonky

1.      Monkey
1.      Wonky
1.      Donkey

1. Donkey
2. Monkey
3. Wonky
```

The example produces the following HTML output once processed. Observe that the HTML for each list is identical, despite the different numbers used in the original markdown list.

```
<ol>
    <li>Monkey</li>
    <li>Donkey</li>
    <li>Wonky</li>
</ol>
```

```
<ol>
    <li>Monkey</li>
    <li>Wonky</li>
    <li>Donkey</li>
</ol>

<ol>
    <li>Donkey</li>
    <li>Monkey</li>
    <li>Wonky</li>
</ol>
```

Not all lists are flat like the examples we've seen so far; you may wish to nest lists inside each other to create hierarchy. Fortunately, this can be achieved using markdown by simply indenting a child list item by four spaces, or one tab character.

```
* Monkey
    * Wonky
* Donkey

1. Monkey
    1. Wonky
1. Donkey
```

The code in the example generates the following HTML output once processed. Notice the nesting of the list items.

```
<ul>
    <li>Monkey
        <ul>
            <li>Wonky</li>
        </ul>
    </li>
    <li>Donkey</li>
</ul>

<ol>
    <li>Monkey
        <ol>
            <li>Wonky</li>
        </ol>
    </li>
    <li>Donkey</li>
</ol>
```

Paragraphs can be placed around list item text simply by adding a line break between items in the list. You can include multiple paragraphs of text per list item simply by indenting each extra paragraph by four spaces, or one tab character.

*   Monkey

    A monkey is a primate of the Haplorrhini suborder and simian infraorder.

*   Donkey

    The donkey or ass, Equus africanus asinus, is a domesticated member of the Equidae or horse family.

This example produces the following HTML output once processed.

```
<ul>
    <li>
        <p>Monkey</p>
        <p>A monkey is a primate of the Haplorrhini suborder and simian infraorder.</p>
    </li>
    <li>
        <p>Donkey</p>
        <p> The donkey or ass, Equus africanus asinus, is a domesticated member of the Equidae or
horse family.</p>
    </li>
</ul>
```

Emphasizing Text

Using markdown, you can emphasize text within a sentence by using either asterisk (*) or underscore (_) characters around the text to be emphasized.

```
Donkeys are *not* monkeys.##
I repeat, Donkeys are _not_ monkeys.
```

The example produces the following HTML output once processed. Note the italicized text when emphasis is used.

```
<p>Donkeys are <em>not</em> monkeys.<br />
I repeat, Donkeys are <em>not</em> monkeys.</p>
```

You can add extra emphasis by doubling up the asterisk or underscore characters.

```
Donkeys are **really** not monkeys.##
I repeat, Donkeys are __really__ not monkeys.
```

This example produces the following HTML output once processed. Note the use of embolded text when stronger emphasis is used in the markdown document.

```
<p>Donkeys are <strong>really</strong> not monkeys.<br />
I repeat, Donkeys are <strong>really</strong> not monkeys.</p>
```

Displaying Code

There are two ways to demark snippets of code in Markdown format: an inline method and a block method. The former is denoted by backtick (`) characters surrounding the code and is for use where you wish to include a small portion of code as part of a line of text. The latter is for use to show one or more lines of code together and is denoted by simply indenting each line of code by four space characters or one tab character. This is the reason why when we use the @example YUIDoc tag, we indent the code listed alongside it.

```
Simply install Grunt by typing `npm install grunt` at the command line.
```

```
    <!doctype html>
    <html>
        <head></head>
    </html>
```

The example shown produces the following output HTML once processed. Note that any HTML tags have some of their characters replaced with entities so they render as text instead of attempting to parse as the tags they represent.

```
<p>Simply install Grunt by typing <code>npm install grunt</code> at the command line.</p>
```

```
<pre><code>&lt;!doctype html&gt;
&lt;html&gt;
    &lt;head&gt; &lt;/head&gt;
&lt;/html&gt;</code></pre>
```

Adding Quotes

To quote a citation within a paragraph of its own, simply precede the text with a right-facing angle bracket followed by one or more spaces or tab characters. Multiple paragraphs can be nested within a block quote by including empty quote lines to delimit each paragraph.

```
> Little Henry took his book one day and went into the garden to study. He sat where the arbor cast
a pleasant shade, and he could smell the fragrance of the flowers that he himself had planted.
>
> At times, he would forget his book while listening to the music of the birds, or gazing at the
peonies and tulips, but he would soon think again of his lesson, and commence studying with new
zeal.
```

This example produces the following output once processed to HTML.

```
<blockquote>
    <p>Little Henry took his book one day and went into the garden to study. He sat where the arbor
cast a pleasant shade, and he could smell the fragrance of the flowers that he himself had planted.
</p>
    <p>At times, he would forget his book while listening to the music of the birds, or gazing at
the peonies and tulips, but he would soon think again of his lesson, and commence studying with new
zeal.</p>
</blockquote>
```

Linking To URLs

Linking to a URL is as simple as including that URL in your Markdown-formatted content. The URL can be written as-is, or by wrapping it within angle brackets, < and >. Both absolute and relative URLs are permitted.

```
For more, see http://www.google.com or <http://www.bing.com>
```

This example produces the following HTML once processed.

```
For more, see <a href="http://www.google.com">http://www.google.com</a> or
<a href="http://www.bing.com">http://www.bing.com</a>
```

More often than not, however, you will want to link specific text to a URL. This is achieved by wrapping the text to be linked within square brackets, [and], and then including the link URL within standard brackets immediately after.

```
One popular search engine is [Google](http://www.google.com)
```

This example produces the following HTML output once processed.

```
One popular search engine is <a href="http://www.google.com">Google</a>
```

Finally, Markdown supports the use of reference links, a sort-of look up table of links used throughout a document. This allows the author of the markdown file to move all link URLs to another point in the document, commonly at the end, to make the rest of the document easier to read. Each link is then assigned a reference name or number within square brackets, separated from the URL by a colon character (:) and one or more spaces or tab characters. The link can then be referred to by this same name of number within square brackets throughout the rest of the markdown content. Reference names themselves may contain any combination of letters, numbers, spaces and punctuation, but note that they are not case sensitive.

```
Popular search engines include [Google][1], [Bing][2], and [Yahoo][yahoo], but the most popular
today is [Google][1].

[1]: http://www.google.com
[2]: http://www.bing.com
[yahoo]: http://www.yahoo.com
```

The following HTML is produced after processing. Note that the reference list itself is not displayed in the output.

```
Popular search engines include <a href="http://www.google.com">Google</a>,
<a href="http://www.bing.com">Bing</a>, and <a href="http://www.yahoo.com">Yahoo</a>, but the most
popular today is <a href="http://www.google.com">Google</a>.
```

If you would prefer to add a title attribute to the link tag in the HTML output, you can supply this to the markdown content with the use of quotation marks following the link URL. This applies to both inline and reference links.

```
The most popular search engine today is [Google](http://www.google.com "Visit Google"), followed by
[Bing][1] and [Yahoo][2].

[1]: http://www.bing.com "Visit Bing"
[2]: http://www.yahoo.com "Visit Yahoo"
```

The example shown produces the following HTML output once processed.

```
The most popular search engine today is <a href=http://www.google.com title="Visit Google">Google</a>,
followed by <a href=http://www.bing.com title="Visit Bing">Bing</a> and <a href=http://www.yahoo.com
title="Visit Yahoo">Yahoo</a>.
```

Inserting Images

The syntax for adding images to markdown content is very similar to the link syntax seen already. The main difference is that it is denoted as an image by a preceding exclamation point (!) character with no extra spaces or tab characters. This is then followed by a name placed within square brackets, which will produce an `alt` attribute containing that text in the resulting HTML output. The image URL itself is then placed within brackets, and providing an optional title in quotation marks after the URL adds a title attribute in the resulting HTML output, once processed.

```
![A squirrel](/path/to/squirrel-image.jpg)
![Homepages](http://www.homepages.com/image.jpg "Image from homepages.com")
![Company Logo][logo]
![Main Image][1]

[logo]: /path/to/logo.png
[1]: /path/to/main.jpg "The Main Page Image"
```

The example shown produces the following HTML output once processed.

```
<img src="/path/to/squirrel-image.jpg" alt="A squirrel" />
<img src="http://www.homepages.com/image.jpg" alt="Homepages" title="Image from homepages.com" />
<img src="/path/to/logo.png" alt="Company Logo" />
<img src="/path/to/main.jpg" alt="Main Image" title="The Main Page Image" />
```

Creating Horizontal Rules

To divide up sections in your markdown content, you insert a horizontal divider. This can be achieved in markdown using three or more asterisks (*), hyphens (-) or underscores (_) together on their own line. Unlike some other markdown rules, you can use spaces between these characters without affecting the output, but you may not mix the three types of characters on the same line.

```
***

---

___

* * *

- - - -

_____
```

Each example shown produces exactly the same HTML output once processed, as shown below.

```
<hr />
```

Using Backslash To Insert Reserved Characters

You will have seen that certain characters have specific meanings in markdown and get converted into HTML. If you want to use one of these characters in your markdown without it being converted, markdown provides a mechanism to do that—simply insert a backslash (\) character before the character that would otherwise be replaced. This works for the following characters:

```
\   backslash
`   backtick
*   asterisk
_   underscore
{}  curly braces
[]  square braces
()  parentheses
#   hash
+   plus
-   minus (hyphen)
.   dot
!   exclamation point
```

For Everything Else, There's HTML

If you find you need to represent something that just isn't supported by Markdown's set of formatting rules, you needn't be downhearted. Markdown supports the addition of HTML tags as needed to provide additional formatting. Note that HTML blocks will be processed as-is, which means that any Markdown-formatted content within the HTML block will be ignored.

```
Markdown doesn't support tables, but *HTML* does!

<table>
    <tr>
        <td>Hello</td>
        <td>World</td>
    </tr>
</table>

And now we're back into __Markdown__ again!
```

The example above produces the following HTML output once processed.

```
<p>Markdown doesn't support tables, but <em>HTML</em> does!</p>

<table>
    <tr>
        <td>Hello</td>
        <td>World</td>
    </tr>
</table>

<p>And now we're back into <strong>Markdown</strong> again!</p>
```

Creating a Documentation Website Using YUIDoc

Now we've written some documentation for our code, it's time to surface this in an easy-to-use format for others to digest. We've been writing our documentation in YUIDoc format, so we'll use the associated YUIDoc tool to generate us a site.

This YUIDoc tool is a JavaScript application designed to work with Node.js, an application framework that runs files written entirely in JavaScript on a command line. We'll look in greater detail at Node.js in a future chapter but for now all you need to do is install it.

Visit http://bit.ly/node_js and download Node.js from there, following the instructions to install it; this also installs a tool called Node Package Manager (NPM) which allows you to quickly and easily download applications (known as packages) from a central repository.

Next we need to download the YUIDoc package itself. On the command line, execute the following command, which will automatically install the YUIDoc tool and make it available to run within any folder on your computer:

```
npm -g install yuidocjs
```

For those on a Mac or other Unix-based system, you may need to precede the command with sudo to allow the code to execute with sufficient privileges to install the tool system-wide.

Now we have YUIDoc installed, let's run it. Use the command line to navigate to the folder containing your documented JavaScript code files and run the following command (without leaving off the period character at the end):

```
yuidoc .
```

When executed, YUIDoc will look through all the JavaScript files in the current folder and any sub folders within, and extract out the structured documentation from it. It will not attempt to execute any of your code, it merely reads each file as if it were plain text, looking for its specific set of tags and specially formatted opening comment block characters. It then takes the information it gleans from your documentation and generates a JSON-formatted file representing that data in a structured form, along with a full click-through HTML site generated using a default template style.

If you wish YUIDoc to only look in the current folder and no subfolders, supply the –n argument to the command.

```
yuidoc -n .
```

Now we can run YUIDoc to generate documentation for us, we need some code to generate the documentation for. Let's use the code in Listing 2-5, which you should save into a file named Listing2-5.js within a folder on your computer. You can take a pre-written copy for youself from the code for this chapter hosted in GitHub at http://bit.ly/pro_js_dev. This code defines a parent "class" and a subclass, together with methods and properties, some public, some protected.

Listing 2-5. Documented code to use to generate a site using YUIDoc

```
/**
 * Accommodation-related "classes"
 *
 * @module Accommodation-related
 */
```

```
/**
 * A "class" defining types of accommodation
 *
 * @class Accommodation
 * @constructor
 * @example
 *      var myAccommodation = new Accommodation();
 */

var Accommodation = Class.create((function() {

    /**
     * Denotes whether the accommodation is currently locked
     *
     * @property {Boolean} _isLocked
     * @protected
     */

    var _isLocked = true,
        publicPropertiesAndMethods = {

            /**
             * Locks the accommodation
             *
             * @method lock
             * @example
             *      var myAccommodation = new Accommodation();
             *      myAccommodation.lock();
             */

            lock: function() {
                _isLocked = true;
            },

            /**
             * Unlocks the accommodation
             *
             * @method unlock
             * @example
             *      var myAccommodation = new Accommodation();
             *      myAccommodation.unlock();
             */

            unlock: function() {
                _isLocked = false;
            },
```

```
            /**
             * Establishes whether the accommodation is currently locked or not
             *
             * @method getIsLocked
             * @return {Boolean} Value indicating lock status—'true' means locked
             * @example
             *     var myAccommodation = new Accommodation();
             *     myAccommodation.getIsLocked(); // false
             *
             * @example
             *     var myAccommodation = new Accommodation();
             *     myAccommodation.lock();
             *     myAccommodation.getIsLocked(); // true
             */

            getIsLocked: function() {
                return _isLocked;
            },

            /**
             * Executed automatically upon creation of an object instance of this "class".
             * Unlocks the accommodation.
             *
             * @method initialize
             */

            initialize: function() {
                this.unlock();
            }
        };

    return publicPropertiesAndMethods;
}()));

/**
 * "Class" representing a house, a specific type of accommodation
 *
 * @class House
 * @constructor
 * @extends Accommodation
 * @example
 *     var myHouse = new House();
 */

var House = Accommodation.extend({

    /**
     * Indicates whether the house is alarmed or not—'true' means alarmed
     *
     * @property {Boolean} isAlarmed
     */
```

```
isAlarmed: false,

/**
 * Activates the house alarm
 *
 * @method alarm
 */

alarm: function() {
    this.isAlarmed = true;
    alert("Alarm activated!");
},

/**
 * Locks the house and activates the alarm
 *
 * @method lock
 */

lock: function() {
    Accommodation.prototype.lock.call(this);
    this.alarm();
}
});—
```

Navigate to the folder you saved the code within from the command line, and execute YUIDoc to generate the documentation website for this code listing:

```
yuidoc -n .
```

This will have produced a subfolder named out within the current folder and filled it with HTML and CSS representing your documentation. Open the file named index.html in your web browser to view the generated website. This will reveal a page looking much like that shown in Figure 2-1.

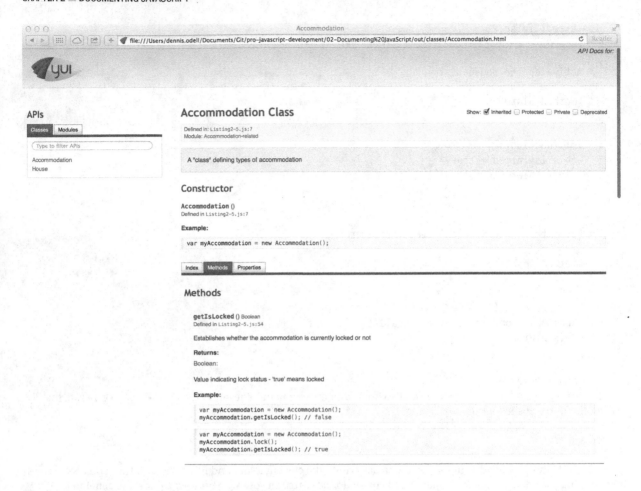

Figure 2-1. *YUIDoc generates a full HTML site automatically from your documented JavaScript code*

Two tabs on the left-hand side of the page allow you to jump between the lists of "classes" and modules that have been documented—we documented two "classes" and one module. Click on a module name to see a description of that module in the center of the page, together with a listing of all the "classes" grouped together into that module. Clicking on a "class" name here or in the left-hand side bar will display the full documentation for that "class" within the center area of the page.

The "class" documentation shows the "class" description together with the constructor function and the example code we declared within our documentation, complete with syntax highlighting. Three tabs beneath allow you to view an index list of all the methods and properties, or a detailed look at either the methods or the properties for that "class". Clicking a method or property name takes you straight to the appropriate tab, scrolling the page to its definition and documentation. All the documentation from our code is here, formatted as easy-to-read text.

By default, the generated site only displays public properties and methods. To view or hide protected and private properties and methods, toggle the appropriate checkbox on the top-right of the page. When viewing the documentation for the House subclass, you can use the inherited checkbox on the top-right of the page to toggle between displaying all the methods and properties available to this "class," or only those that were defined on the "class" definition itself. This can be a useful way of checking specific documentation for an inherited "class" or just viewing those methods and properties unique to that "class."

Taking It Further

YUIDoc supports all sorts of customization, from setting the logo in the top-left of the page, to full prebuilt themes for an entirely different look to your documentation. To learn more about customizing YUIDoc, visit the project documentation page via `http://bit.ly/yui_doc`. For a good alternative theme, try Dana, available via `http://bit.ly/yuidoc_dana`. If you want to learn how to create your own custom themes, full documentation is available via `http://bit.ly/yuidoc_themes`. Have fun experimenting with YUIDoc and remember to make sure you document your code, both for the benefit of other developers and for your own sanity.

Summary

In this chapter, we've covered JavaScript code documentation, both casual and structured, which allow you to benefit yourself, your project team, and any members of the general public who interface with your code. We've covered YUIDoc and the Markdown format, and automatically produced a fully-fledged documentation website based on structured documentation in code without writing a single line of HTML or CSS.

In the next chapter, we will be looking into how to write the highest quality JavaScript code we can using a combination of tricks, tips and techniques, making our code run well and with as few errors as possible.

CHAPTER 3

Writing High-Quality JavaScript

There is no such thing as bug-free software, and the more unknowns about the system running your software, the greater the likelihood of errors occurring. As JavaScript developers, we write code to be run within at least five major web browsers, the majority of which have fairly rapid release schedules. Couple this moving target with the fact that a single error in JavaScript code within a browser has the potential to stop all other JavaScript within that page functioning, and you can see the challenge we have to write high-quality, bug-free code.

The purpose of this chapter is to help you write high-quality JavaScript code and show you how to have confidence in the code that you execute in your pages. I'll introduce you to code analysis tools, the principle of unit testing, and how to handle runtime errors. Finally, I'll show you how to measure the quality of your code with a view to making continuous improvements to it.

Performing Static Code Analysis

The best first pass at finding potential errors in your code is to check your code using a code analysis tool before you've even run it for the first time. This type of analysis is referred to as static, as the code is checked as a static text file rather than in the context of being executed.

Using this approach, common sources of errors and coding pitfalls can be highlighted to you so they don't end up in your running code, potentially introducing bugs. The range of problems this form of code analysis can detect include missing semicolons, the use of undefined variables, and, importantly, the use of the JavaScript eval method for executing strings as if they were JavaScript code—a big no-no when it comes to code security, as it potentially allows malicious code to be executed within the context of your code. By ensuring that none of these potentially risky operations occur in your code, you can have increased confidence that you are reducing the chance of bugs appearing in your software. Let's take a look at a few of the more common static code analysis tools for JavaScript now.

JSLint

Static code analysis tools have existed for some time in other programming languages. With the advent of the C language in the early 1970s came fairly basic compilers that converted the code written in C into machine code for running on a computer's processor. Some programmers were writing code that could potentially introduce errors, and the compilers weren't picking up those errors. This led to a static code analysis tool called lint being released in 1979 to allow developers to check their code before compiling, in order to reduce this risk of releasing buggy software.

Douglas Crockford of Yahoo created a tool to do something similar for JavaScript code, allowing it to be checked for known errors before releasing that code into the wild, and he named this tool JSLint after the original tool for the C language. He made this tool available via an online form, into which you can copy and paste your JavaScript code, at http://www.jslint.com.

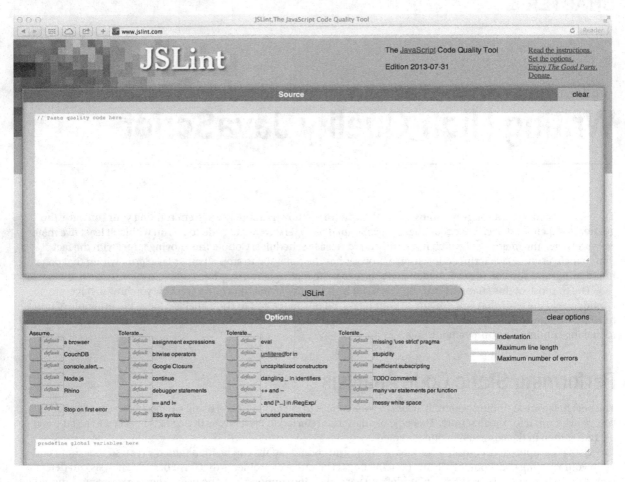

Figure 3-1. *The JSLint homepage. Paste your JavaScript code into the box to check its quality*

Chances are if you try to analyze some of your code in JSLint, you have found yourself chastised for writing code it considers to be of poor quality. In fact, using the code from Listing 2-5 reveals a total of 16 errors out of the 29 lines of JavaScript code that were checked. The project homepage declares that JSLint "will hurt your feelings," and it doesn't take many attempts at checking your code quality before that statement starts to ring true.

A closer look at the list of errors produced, shown in Figure 3-2, reveals that the majority are due to the fact that there is no space character between the `function` keyword and the opening bracket character that follows. Personally, I prefer not to leave any spaces after my use of the `function` keyword; however, it is how Douglas Crockford, who created the tool, prefers to write his code. Therefore, that particular rule is enabled by default. We'll look shortly at how to alter the applied rules so as to ignore this particular constraint.

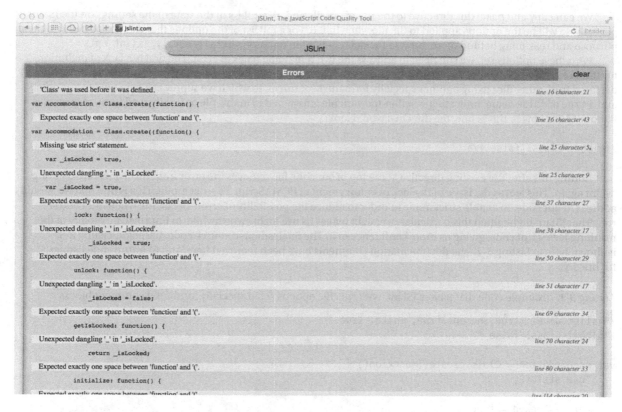

Figure 3-2. *The results of running code from Listing 2-4 in JSLint don't make for happy reading*

Other errors include the fact that we've not defined the Class object before using it, that there are missing `"use strict"` statements to enforce the preferred ECMAScript strict mode, that we've used an underscore character at the beginning of variable names, and that the `alert` method is called before it was defined. The latter error might seem strange as alerts work in any browser. The reason that it's flagged is because it isn't a part of the official JavaScript language specification; it's merely added by browser manufacturers to their software to allow developers to provide popup messages. JSLint prefers your code to contain no browser-specific JavaScript so that it could run without error in any environment that supports the language.

Beneath the list of errors on the JSLint site, there is a section titled Options, which contains a number of checkboxes, allowing the default set of rules to be overridden for your code. Try setting the options console, alert, . . . , dangling _ in identifiers, and messy white space to `true`, and then running the JSLint tool again; you should find the list of errors has shortened now. Scroll down to the very bottom of the page and you will find a section title JSLint Directive, containing a specially formatted JavaScript comment. You can set different rules on a per-file basis in your code, by placing one of these directives at the top of your files. The directive begins with `/*jslint` and there follows a list of the options to apply to the file when it is run through JSLint, followed by a `true` or `false` value, indicating whether that option should be enabled or disabled, respectively; multiple options are separated by a comma. For the options that we have selected, we are given the following directive:

```
/*jslint devel: true, nomen: true, white: true */
```

We can copy and paste this directive to the top of our file and, regardless of the state of the settings on the JSLint page, these will be the options applied to the file when linted. For a full list of the options that can be applied and their purpose and reasoning behind them, browse the documentation online via http://bit.ly/jslint_opts.

With these options set, we still need to address the two remaining types of error. The first is a lack of definition for the Class object, which in this case would exist in a separate file. We can instruct JSLint about global variables declared from other files using another specially formatted comment, to which we supply the name of our variable and a true or false value, indicating whether the variable is assigned to in this file or is only read from, respectively. For our Class object, this is how the directive would look:

```
/*global Class: false */
```

Adding this after the existing directive at the top of our code file removes the error from the list when executing JSLint again. This leaves the issue of the lack of enforcement of ECMAScript 5's strict mode. This is one that we should address in our code, to enable strict mode in order to reduce the possibility of errors occurring when our code is run. That JSLint highlighted this particular oversight makes its use highly worthwhile, to improve the quality of the resulting JavaScript code, giving us more confidence in it. The final, adapted source code, based on Listing 2-5, is shown here in Listing 3-1. The documentation comments have been removed here, and in future code listings, for brevity.

Listing 3-1. Example code that passes JSLint, with specific options set in specially formatted comment blocks

```javascript
/*jslint devel: true, nomen: true, white: true */
/*global Class: false */

var Accomodation = Class.create((function() {
    "use strict";

    var _isLocked = true,
        publicPropertiesAndMethods = {
            lock: function() {
                _isLocked = true;
            },
            unlock: function() {
                _isLocked = false;
            },
            getIsLocked: function() {
                return _isLocked;
            },
            initialize: function() {
                this.unlock();
            }
        };

    return publicPropertiesAndMethods;
}()));

var House = Accomodation.extend({
    isAlarmed: false,
    alarm: function() {
        "use strict";
```

```
        this.isAlarmed = true;
        alert("Alarm activated!");
    },
    lock: function() {
        "use strict";

        Accomodation.prototype.lock.call(this);
        this.alarm();
    }
});
```

It's not always convenient for a large project to run your code through the JSLint homepage for each file, as this would add considerable overhead time to your workflow. Fortunately, developer Reid Burke of Yahoo has developed a version of JSLint for the Node.js application framework that can be run from a command prompt on your own machine. We'll look in greater detail at Node.js in a future chapter but, for now, if you do not have it installed, visit the site at `http://nodejs.org` to download and install the framework.

With Node.js and its associated NPM tool installed, run the following from your command prompt to install the JSLint tool onto your machine. Note that Mac and Linux users may have to precede the command with `sudo` to apply administrator privileges to the command:

```
npm install jslint -g
```

You can now run the tool within any directory from the command prompt; simply navigate to the directory containing your code files and run the following command to lint every JavaScript file in the folder:

```
jslint *.js
```

To learn how to configure the tool with custom options and other settings, visit the GitHub project for the tool online via `http://bit.ly/jslint_node`.

JSHint

The JSHint code analysis tool shares more in common with JSLint than just a similar name; it is actually a fork of the original JSLint code to allow for greater customization of options for analyzing JavaScript code. It is organized and contributed to as a community-driven effort via its site at `http://jshint.com`. As with JSLint, you can check your code by copying and pasting into the online form on their homepage and configuring the options for how you want your code to be analyzed.

The JSHint project was started in 2011 as a reaction to feeling from within the community that JSLint, the original static code analysis tool for JavaScript, was becoming far too opinionated. Some of the rules that JSLint attempts to enforce are really just code style rules preferred by Douglas Crockford, its creator, and it was felt that a code analysis tool should focus more on finding syntax and other errors that would stop code from functioning correctly rather than refusing to let code pass because of formatting issues.

Submitting the code from Listing 2-5 into the form on the JSHint homepage produces a series of errors, many of which are similar to those reported by JSLint previously. There are two notable differences between the errors reported with JSHint and those reported with JSLint. First, JSHint does not complain about the use of a space character between the `function` keyword and the opening bracket that follows, which was purely a coding preference by the JSLint tool's author. Second, JSHint produces an additional error, letting us know that we are defining a new variable, `House`, which is not used anywhere in the rest of the file.

To let JSHint know that we're happy with the fact we're declaring a variable that's not used within the same file, and that it's okay that we're using the alert method in our code, we can place a specially formatted comment at the top of the file, in a similar way to JSLint, to set the options to use in its analysis:

```
/*jshint devel:true, unused:false */
```

The full list of options, and there are numerous, are available on the documentation site online via http://bit.ly/jshint_opts.

To let JSHint know of our global Class object variable, declared elsewhere, we can use the same comment as with JSLint:

```
/*global Class */
```

Including the appropriate "use strict" commands as in Listing 3-1, together with these specially formatted comments at the top of the file, allows the code to pass the JSHint static code analysis.

You can use JSHint on the command line, as with JSLint. To install, simply ensure that Node.js is installed and execute the following command on the command prompt:

```
npm install jshint -g
```

You can then run JSHint from within any folder in just the same way as with JSLint:

```
jshint *.js
```

In addition to the command line tool, the team behind JSHint has made available a whole raft of other possible ways to use the tool, including as plugins for common text editors and IDEs, such as Sublime Text and Visual Studio, to provide live code checking as you type. The full list of plugins is available on their site online via http://bit.ly/jshint_install.

Google Closure Compiler and Linter

Google open-sourced a number of tools they use internally for JavaScript development at the end of 2009 under the general name Closure Tools. These included a JavaScript UI library called Closure Library, a JavaScript templating solution called Closure Templates, and a complete optimization and code checking tool called Closure Compiler. In 2010, they added a fourth tool, the Closure Linter, which is used to validate JavaScript code against a set of style rules. The first two of these tools we will cover in later chapters. For now, we're interested in the latter two.

The Closure Compiler's primary objective is to make JavaScript code download and run faster. It parses and analyses, removes unused code, and rewrites what it can to reduce the size of the resulting code. It is one of the best tools around for optimizing JavaScript files to the smallest possible size, meaning that it can be downloaded and executed faster in the end user's browser. Because of its parsing ability, it can also identify syntax errors in JavaScript, as well as highlight potentially dangerous operations, which is what makes it useful as a static code analysis tool.

To use the Closure Compiler to analyze and optimize your code, try coping and pasting your code into the online form via http://bit.ly/closure_compile and pressing the Compile button. The optimized code will appear on the right-hand side of the page within the Compiled Code tab. Any JavaScript syntax errors or potential coding hazards discovered through the analysis are listed within the Errors and Warnings tabs, respectively, for you to action. If you prefer, the tool is available to run on the command line using Java (installation instructions online via http://bit.ly/closure_install) as well as via a REST-based Web Service API, for integration into your own systems (usage instructions online via http://bit.ly/closure_api).

The Closure Linter's primary objective is to analyze and compare the way that code files are written against Google's own style guide for JavaScript, the latest version of which is available online via http://bit.ly/google_style. As well as reporting back the issues that it finds, it also contains a tool to automatically fix the errors that it finds, if possible. It is used internally by Google to ensure the code for Gmail and Drive, and their other products, adhere to same set of coding style rules.

To use the Closure Linter to check your code against Google's JavaScript style guide, you must first download and install the application framework Python to your computer via http://bit.ly/dl_py. Mac and Linux users will likely have this installed already as part of their operating system. Windows users will also need to install the Easy Install package for Python via http://bit.ly/py_easy. Once installed, execute the following command to install the Closure Linter to your machine. Note that Mac and Linux users may have to precede the command with sudo to grant administrative privileges to the installation:

```
easy_install http://closure-linter.googlecode.com/files/closure_linter-latest.tar.gz
```

To run the tool on all JavaScript files in a directory to report on your adherence to Google's style guide, execute the following at the command prompt:

```
gjslint *.js
```

You can also replace *.js with a specific file name if you wish to target just a single file. The tool then lists the issues it finds in the command window. If you'd like to then attempt to automatically fix these issues, execute the following command to overwrite your files with their fixes:

```
fixjsstyle *.js
```

By simply running this latter command on a directory of files, you can update your code to adhere to Google's style guide with minimal effort. If you'd like to know more about the tool, visit the documentation site online via http://bit.ly/linter_howto.

Choosing a Static Code Analysis Tool

We've taken a look at a few of the more common static code analysis tools for JavaScript in this chapter. Choosing which tool is right for your project depends on what specifically you wish to check for. By simply selecting to use any of the tools covered in this chapter, you will ensure that syntax errors and common programming mistakes are caught, improving the quality of your code and the confidence you can have that fewer errors will occur when it runs. In addition, you need to decide how much or how little of your code style and formatting you wish to have scrutinized, as this is where the decision really lies. I personally prefer JSHint, as it focuses more on syntax checking than specific coding style, and I know that it's not going to get in the way of me writing and releasing my code. Your needs may differ. Research and try out each tool to discover which works best for your needs, those of your team members, and those of your projects.

Unit Testing In JavaScript

Once you're in the habit of using static code analysis to give you confidence that your JavaScript is of a high quality, it's time to move to the next level of ensuring high-quality JavaScript code: unit testing. If you write each function in your JavaScript files to be an individual unit of behavior, consisting of inputs and outputs, and performing a clear, documented operation, then a unit test is a JavaScript function that executes each function you have written in turn using different inputs and checking that the output matches what was expected.

The JavaScript function in Listing 3-2 adds together all numbers passed to it as arguments.

Listing 3-2. A simple function to add together any numbers passed to it

```
var add = function() {
    var total = 0,
        index = 0,
        length = arguments.length;

    for (; index < length; index++) {
        total  = total + arguments[index];
    }

    return total;
};
```

A unit test for such a function would run that function with several different inputs, including edge cases such as leaving inputs blank, ensuring that the original function behaves in an expected way and produces appropriate results for each combination of inputs. By rigorously testing each function in your code base in this way, you increase the quality of that code and you can have increased confidence that your system will function as expected when these unit tested functions are run within it.

Unit Testing Frameworks For JavaScript

Although you could probably write the code yourself to unit test your own code, it makes sense to benefit from the work of others in this area and employ an established unit testing framework to test your code. There are several such frameworks available at the time of writing, including QUnit (`http://bit.ly/q_test`), Mocha (`http://bit.ly/mocha_test`) and Jasmine (`http://bit.ly/jas_test`). Each works in a similar way, consisting of a JavaScript library file containing the framework code that is designed to be used within an HTML page that needs to include the framework library file, the file containing your JavaScript code to be tested, and the file containing your unit tests to be run against that code. Tests are run automatically when the HTML page is opened within a browser, showing the detailed results, including test passes and failures, on screen. Because the frameworks are similar to each other, I'll take you through how to write unit tests for your code using just the Jasmine framework, my personal choice for this task.

Using Jasmine For JavaScript Unit Testing

The Jasmine unit testing framework allows you to group together a series of individual tests for an individual function or method within a group; sets of groups can then be grouped together again to allow for related code to be tested together. Groups of tests are known as suites, and individual tests are known as specs. Each file in your code base should typically have an associated test suite file, grouped together into a separate folder, which I usually name `spec`.

■ **Tip** Try naming your test spec files by the same name as their associated code file, with the addition of –spec. For example, a code file named `add.js` might have an associated test suite file named `add-spec.js`.

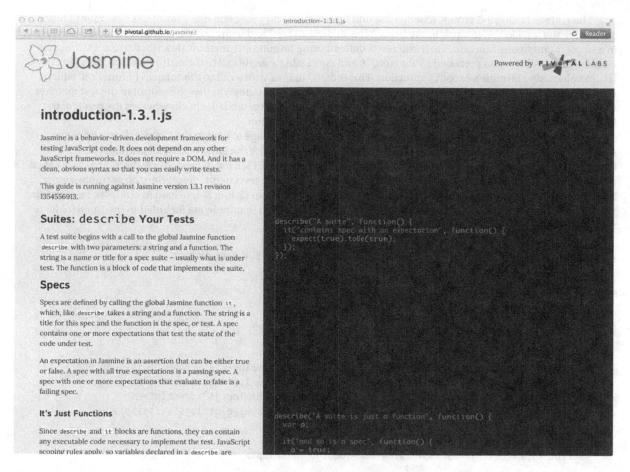

Figure 3-3. The Jasmine unit testing framework project homepage features extensive documentation

A simple suite file might look like Listing 3-3, which executes two individual tests against the add() function, defined previously in Listing 3-2.

Listing 3-3. A simple test spec file

```
describe("The add function", function() {
    it("Adds 1 + 2 + 3 together correctly", function() {
        var output = add(1, 2, 3);
        expect(output).toEqual(6);
    });

    it("Adds negative numbers together correctly", function() {
        var output = add(-1, -2, -3);
        expect(output).toEqual(-6);
    });
});
```

The code in Listing 3-3 groups together the unit tests for the add() function using Jasmine's describe() function, describing the tests in the group with the string "The add function" and wrapping the group's individual unit tests in a single, anonymous function. Each unit test is defined using Jasmine's it method, described using a string that would read sensibly when preceded by the word it, and containing a single call to the add() function, checking its return value using Jasmine's expect() function. This is then chained with a call to the toEqual() function, which is an example of a matcher, a Jasmine function which detects and compares whether the output of the test matches the expected result. The matcher function we are using in Listing 3-3, toEqual(), checks whether the result of the function call exactly matches our specific known values for the operation.

To run the test spec in order to test our function, we need a web page to load in the Jasmine framework, the source files, and the test files, before executing the tests. By downloading the latest release of Jasmine via http://bit.ly/jas_dl you get the framework itself and an example HTML file named SpecRunner.html and called a spec runner, which contains some example source files and example tests to run. Replacing the example source files and tests with our own, we can update the HTML page, as shown in Listing 3-4, to load in our tests. I assume that you've named your source file add.js and your spec add-spec.js, and that these are included in the same folder as the spec runner itself.

Listing 3-4. A Jasmine spec runner HTML file, configured to load and run our unit tests

```
<!DOCTYPE HTML PUBLIC "-//W3C//DTD HTML 4.01 Transitional//EN"
    "http://www.w3.org/TR/html4/loose.dtd">
<html>
<head>
    <title>Jasmine Spec Runner</title>

    <link rel="shortcut icon" type="image/png" href="lib/jasmine-1.3.1/jasmine_favicon.png">
    <link rel="stylesheet" type="text/css" href="lib/jasmine-1.3.1/jasmine.css">
    <script type="text/javascript" src="lib/jasmine-1.3.1/jasmine.js"></script>
    <script type="text/javascript" src="lib/jasmine-1.3.1/jasmine-html.js"></script>

    <script type="text/javascript" src="add.js"></script>
    <script type="text/javascript" src="add-spec.js"></script>

    <script type="text/javascript">
        (function() {
            var jasmineEnv = jasmine.getEnv();
            jasmineEnv.updateInterval = 1000;

            var htmlReporter = new jasmine.HtmlReporter();

            jasmineEnv.addReporter(htmlReporter);

            jasmineEnv.specFilter = function(spec) {
                return htmlReporter.specFilter(spec);
            };

            var currentWindowOnload = window.onload;

            window.onload = function() {
                if (currentWindowOnload) {
                    currentWindowOnload();
                }
```

```
                execJasmine();
            };

            function execJasmine() {
                jasmineEnv.execute();
            }
        })();
    </script>
</head>

<body>
</body>
</html>
```

Loading this HTML page in a web browser will automatically execute the unit tests, showing the results on screen, indicating a pass or fail. The output of running the spec runner from Listing 3-4, indicating that all tests passed, is shown in Figure 3-4.

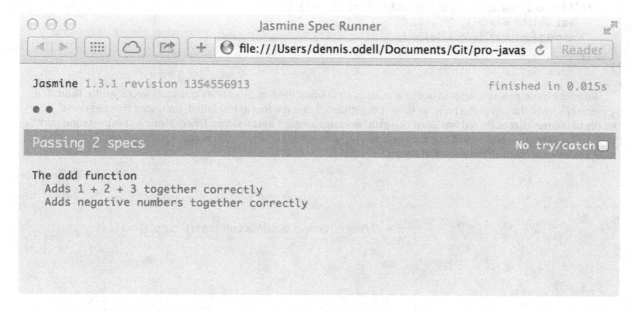

Figure 3-4. *Running the spec runner from Listing 3-4 indicates that all tests passed*

When writing unit tests, it's important to only write as many tests as are necessary to prove your code is functioning correctly; this will involve at least one test for a normal, expected set of inputs. You should also test edge cases, those instances in which unusual or unexpected inputs are provided, as these will force you to consider what happens in your code if such as condition occurred, allowing to capture potential errors before they affect the end user. In the case of our add() function, we would be wise to test what would happen when no inputs are provided, or when non-numeric inputs are provided. We know that our function would not be willingly used in this way; however, with edge cases we're trying to protect our code from accidental, as well as deliberate, misuse.

Let's extend our test spec from Listing 3-3, adding a test for when no inputs are provided, and another for when non-numeric inputs are provided. In the former case, we want the output to be 0 when no inputs are provided, and in the latter case, we want all the provided numeric inputs to be added, and any non-numeric inputs ignored.

Listing 3-5. Unit tests for the add() function from Listing 3-2

```
describe("The add function", function() {
    it("Adds 1 + 2 + 3 together correctly", function() {
        var output = add(1, 2, 3);
        expect(output).toEqual(6);
    });

    it("Adds negative numbers together correctly", function() {
        var output = add(-1, -2, -3);
        expect(output).toEqual(-6);
    });

    it("Returns 0 if no inputs are provided", function() {
        var output = add();
        expect(output).toEqual(0);
    });

    it("Adds only numeric inputs together", function() {
        var output = add(1, "1", 2, "2", 3, "3");
        expect(output).toEqual(6);
    });
});
```

Running these new unit tests in our spec runner shows that the first three tests complete successfully, indicated by green circles at the top of the page, as shown in Figure 3-5, but the fourth test failed, indicated by a red cross. Details of failures that occurred are listed beneath headings for each unit test that failed. Here, our expectation that the function output would be 6 in our final unit test was incorrect, and the actual output produced was "112233", a string concatenation of all the provided inputs.

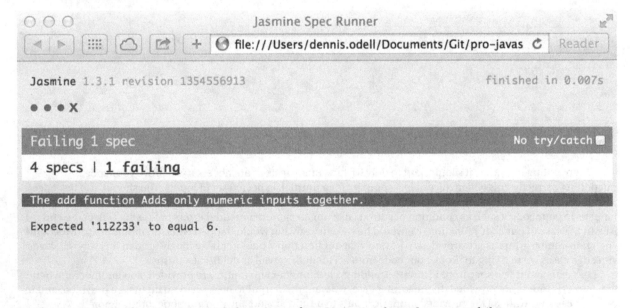

Figure 3-5. *Running the spec runner with the unit tests from Listing 3-4 shows that one test fails*

Now our unit test has revealed a potential issue in our code, which might result in errors occurring when that code is used in a real-world web page, we need to go back and amend our original add() function from Listing 3-2 in order to produce the output we expect for non-numeric inputs. We wrap the addition in an if statement that checks whether the input parameter is a number, permitting the addition if it is, and denying it if it is not.

Running the spec runner again against the updated add() function from Listing 3-6 produces a pass for each of the tests, giving us confidence in that errors are unlikely to occur when it's used within a page.

Listing 3-6. Updating the add function from Listing 3-2 handle non-numeric inputs

```
var add = function() {
    var total = 0,
        index = 0,
        length = arguments.length;

    for (; index < length; index++) {
        if (typeof arguments[index] === "number") {
            total  = total + arguments[index];
        }
    }

    return total;
};
```

■ **Tip**   Only write unit tests for code that you, yourself, have written. You should not write tests for third-party libraries or other scripts for which you are not responsible; that is the responsibility of the library code's authors.

When running your code within your web page with differing inputs, you may come across other cases that reveal unexpected outputs for given inputs. If this happens, before amending your function to correct the issue, you should create a unit test using the exact set of inputs that you find cause an error in your page so as to reproduce the issue. You should then rewrite your code until all your unit tests, including the new test, pass. By leaving this new unit test in the spec from that point onward, you can ensure that you catch the error again should the code of the original function be updated in future.

■ **Tip**   When choosing a third-party library for use in your page, consider giving extra weight to those that adopt the principle of unit testing. This will give you the confidence that all the code in your page has been unit tested and the chance of errors occurring become slimmer.

Online virtual machine-based testing services Browserstack (http://bit.ly/brow_stack) and Sauce Labs (http://bit.ly/sauce_labs) feature the ability to run your unit tests automatically over a number of different web browsers and operating systems simultaneously, reporting their results back to you. You might consider this as a worthwhile alternative to manually running your tests. Both services offer basic, free options for you to get started with.

Other Matchers

The unit tests that we've written so far are based on a given set of inputs producing an exact, numerical output. For those, we've used the Jasmine matcher toEqual(). It's quite likely that a function you may be testing will require other, more specific types of comparison to take place, and Jasmine provides many other matches for you in that case.

To find out if the result of a function call is the opposite of a specific case, you can combine the property not together with another matcher, as shown here:

```
expect(output).not.toEqual(6);
```

To compare a function result against a regular expression, use the toMatch() matcher. This is especially useful if the output might not be the same each time it's run:

```
expect(output).toMatch(/[a-s]/);
expect(output).not.toMatch(/[t-z]/);
```

If you would like to compare against a truthy, falsy, or null value, use the toBe(), toBeTruthy(), toBeFalsy() or toBeNull() matchers:

```
expect(output).toBe(true);
expect(output).not.toBe(null);
expect(output).toBeTruthy();
expect(output).not.toBeNull();
expect(output).toBeFalsy();
```

If you need to find out if a unit test output value has an undefined value, use the toBeDefined() matcher:

```
expect(output).toBeDefined();
expect(output).not.toBeDefined();
```

If you need to find out if the array result of your function contains or does not contain a particular value, you should use the toContain() matcher:

```
expect(output).toContain("Monday");
expect(output).not.toContain("Sunday");
```

When testing functions that contain mathematical operations that do not always result in identical outputs for the same inputs, you can use the matchers toBeGreaterThan() or toBeLessThan():

```
expect(output).toBeGreaterThan(2);
expect(output).not.toBeLessThan(3);
```

A third mathematical matcher, toBeCloseTo(), allows you to determine whether the floating point (a number with decimal places) output of your function is close to an expected number up to a certain number of decimal places, passed as the second parameter to the matcher:

```
expect(3.1415).toBeCloseTo(3.14, 2); // true
expect(3.1415).toBeCloseTo(3, 0); // true
```

If your function throws an error if its input parameters are invalid, you can check for this in your unit test with the `toThrow()` matcher:

```
expect(output).toThrow();
expect(output).not.ToThrow();
```

Finally, if none of Jasmine's core matchers do what you need, you can write your own custom matcher function to meet your particular needs. Documentation for this is available online via `http://bit.ly/new_matchers`.

You should have noticed from these examples that Jasmine's core matcher functions are named in such a way that the statement can be read as if it's written almost in plain English. This means that, with a little practice, it becomes simple to write unit tests for your code, and you find yourself doing that more and more, increasing the confidence you have in your code that it is written to the highest quality and is unlikely to cause errors when run on a page.

Additional Features Of Jasmine

In this chapter, we've looked at the basics of using Jasmine, getting unit testing up and running on your functions, and checking that their outputs match expectations based on a given set of inputs. Jasmine is capable of so much more than we've been able to cover here, including the ability to run specific setup and tear-down code before and after each test is run, the support for asynchronous operations including JavaScript timers, the ability to mock objects from other locations that you're not explicitly testing, and much more. I encourage to experiment and investigate for yourself, using the full online documentation for this impressive unit testing framework via `http://bit.ly/jas_test`.

Handling Runtime Errors

So far, we've seen how to use static code analysis and unit testing to improve the quality of your code, and the confidence you can have that it will not produce errors when run. There will be times, however, when an error does occur when the code is run on a page that wasn't anticipated by your unit tests. As mentioned previously, if this does occur you need to add a new unit test to cover this case so it can be caught in future, but this doesn't help the user attempting to use your page who is becoming frustrated that it has stopped functioning correctly. Fortunately, JavaScript allows us a way to catch errors when they occur at runtime, allowing us to handle them in such a way as to ensure the rest of the code does not choke as a result. By writing your code to catch and work around potential errors, you ensure a greater confidence in your code, that it will not produce unexpected errors when run, avoiding user frustration and meaning that your code quality can be considered at a very high level.

JavaScript's Native Error Types

There are six types of error that can occur in running JavaScript code: syntax errors, type errors, range errors, eval errors, reference errors, and URI errors.

A syntax error occurs when JavaScript code can't be parsed correctly, possibly due to misuse of the rules of the language or more likely that stray characters found their way into the wrong part of your code, meaning it no longer made sense to the browser:

```
var PI = ; // throws a syntax error as JavaScript was expecting a value between = and ;
```

A type error will occur when a value used in an operation isn't of a type—for example, String, Number, Boolean—that was expected to be used by that operation, or when a method is used against a value of the wrong data type. In many cases, this occurs because the value being used is unexpectedly `null` or has an `undefined` value:

```
var PI = 3.1415;
PI.concat(9); // throws a JavaScript type error - the concat method only applies to Strings
```

A range error occurs when one of JavaScript's core functions expects a number within a certain range to be provided and you provide it with a number outside of that range. For example, when using the toFixed() method on a number, a range error will be thrown if the number of digits supplied as a parameter to the function is outside of the range 0 to 20, inclusive:

```
var PI = 3.1415;
PI.toFixed(21); // throws a JavaScript range error
```

An eval error was designed to occur if you attempt to call the JavaScript eval() method in an improper way, either by attempting to instantiate it with the new keyword or by attempting to set it as a variable. However, most browsers throw a type error instead for the former case, and permit it to be overwritten as a variable in the latter case, so you will unlikely come across this error in your day-to-day coding. You should avoid using eval() at all costs, however, as it is a security risk to your code:

```
new eval(); // Should throw a JavaScript eval error, commonly throws a type error instead
eval = "var PI = 3.1415"; // Should throw a JavaScript eval error, but lets it run anyway
```

A reference error occurs when you attempt to access data from a variable that hasn't yet been declared. Ensure that you declare your variables at the top of each function you create that you wish to use within the scope of that function:

```
alert(PI); // throws a JavaScript reference error since PI has not yet been defined
```

A URI error will occur if you supply a malformed URL to one of JavaScript's URI functions: decodeURI(), encodeURI(), decodeURIComponent(), encodeURIComponent(), escape(), and unescape():

```
decodeURIComponent("%"); // throws a JavaScript URI error - the parameter contains an invalid
                         // URI escape sequence
```

Wrap Code That May Error In A try-catch Statement

If you suspect a particular line of your JavaScript code may throw one of the six native error types when executed, you should wrap it in a try block, which will capture the error, preventing it from stopping the rest of your code from running. If you have multiple statements within your try block and an error occurs in one of them, the statements following the one that threw the error will not run. Control will instead pass to an associated catch block, which must immediately follow, from where you can choose how to handle the error gracefully. The catch block is passed a parameter containing details of the error that occurred, including its type; this allows you to handle different types of errors in different ways within that block. Once the catch block has executed, control flows to the code following that block, outside of the try-catch statement.

Listing 3-7. A try-catch block

```
var PI = 3.14159265358979323846264338327950288419,
    decimalPlaces = Math.floor((Math.random() * 40) + 1), // random number between 1 and 40
    shortPi;

// Wrap any code you suspect might cause an error in a try-catch statement
try {
    shortPi = PI.toFixed(decimalPlaces); // Throws a range error if decimalPlaces > 20
} catch (error) {

    // This block is executed only if an error occurs within the try block, above
    alert("An error occurred!");
}
```

Whereas the catch block only executes if an error occurs in the try block, you can add an optional finally block to the statement if you wish to execute code whether an error occurred or not. This is rarely used because the code immediately following a try-catch statement is executed regardless, whether an error occurred or not, however you might find it useful to use finally to group together related code within the full try-catch-finally statement.

Listing 3-8. A try-catch-finally block

```
var PI = 3.14159265358979323846264338327950288419,
    decimalPlaces = Math.floor((Math.random() * 40) + 1),
    shortPi;

try {
    shortPi = PI.toFixed(decimalPlaces);
} catch (error) {
    decimalPlaces = 20;
    shortPi = PI.toFixed(decimalPlaces);
} finally {
    alert("The value of PI to " + decimalPlaces + " decimal places is " + newPi);
}
```

■ **Note** A try block can be used without a catch block, but only if a finally block is included. In this case, an error is still thrown in the browser but before it is, the finally block is executed, allowing you to tie up any loose ends in your code before the error is thrown.

Detecting The Type Of Error Thrown

The parameter passed to the catch block is an object instance of a "class", or type, relating to one of the JavaScript language's six native error types; these are named SyntaxError, TypeError, RangeError, EvalError, ReferenceError, and URIError, respectively, for the six error types described previously. Each of these error types is inherited from a JavaScript native base Error type. Within your catch block, you can determine the type of error that occurred by using the instanceof keyword, as we covered in Chapter 1.

Listing 3-9. Detecting the type of error caught within a catch block

```
try {
    // Code that might throw an error to go here
} catch (error) {
    if (error instanceof SyntaxError) {
        // A syntax error was thrown
    } else if (error instanceof TypeError) {
        // A type error was thrown
    } else if (error instanceof RangeError) {
        // A range error was thrown
    } else if (error instanceof EvalError) {
        // An eval error was thrown
```

```
    } else if (error instanceof ReferenceError) {
        // A reference error was thrown
    } else if (error instanceof URIError) {
        // A URI error was thrown
    }
}
```

The error object contains a property called message, which contains a text description of the error that occurred. Depending on your browser, the object may also contain details of the line number the error occurred on and other information, though this is a nonstandard addition to the language. You would be wise to avoid reading browser-specific properties, instead relying on the error type to determine what action to take in your catch block.

Creating Custom Error Types

If a specific type of error occurs in your project, you may wish to handle it with your own custom code rather than repeat yourself with code based around the six native error types. Fortunately, creating a custom error type is as simple as creating a new "class" in JavaScript.

Listing 3-10. Creating a custom error type, using Class.create() from Listing 1-19

```
var ElementNotFoundError = Class.create({
    id: "",
    message: "The element could not be found by the given ID",
    initialize: function(id) {
        this.id = id;
    }
});
```

If you want to then execute this so that it's recognized as an error by the browser, use the throw keyword together with an instance of your error type "class":

```
throw new ElementNotFoundError("header");
```

You could actually throw any value in an error, from a simple string to an object literal to a full-blown object instance, as we've done here. Within your catch block, you will have access to the data thrown so it depends on your project how much data you need when an error occurs. I prefer to create a custom error "class" as I can detect its type and store any properties I may need in order to help me debug errors as they occur.

Let's put this together into a real-world example of custom error handling, demonstrated in Listing 3-11.

Listing 3-11. Defining and throwing custom JavaScript errors

```
var ElementNotFoundError = Class.create({
    id: "",
    message: "The element could not be found by the given ID",
    initialize: function(id) {
        this.id = id;
    }
});
```

```
function findElement(id) {
    var elem = document.getElementById(id);
    if (!elem) {
        throw new ElementNotFoundError(id);
    }
    return elem;
}

try {
    findElement("header");
} catch (error) {
    if (error instanceof ElementNotFoundError) {
        alert("Sorry, the 'header' element was not found");
    }
}
```

■ **Tip** Try creating your own base error "class" that all your custom error types inherit from. You could use that base "class" to use Ajax to post details of any errors that occur in your system to a log on your server, allowing you to actively track and fix bugs in your code, increasing its quality.

By using static code analysis and unit tests, you can restrict the number of runtime errors that will occur in your code when it's executed within a web page. To catch those unknown errors that slip through the net, however, use the `try-catch` statement in your code to prevent such errors causing your code to cease executing in the user's browser.

Measuring Code Quality

The purpose of this chapter has been to help you learn how to improve the quality of your code, and reduce the likelihood of errors, through the use of static code analysis, unit testing, and runtime error handling. But how do you know how good our code is without a means of somehow measuring its quality. By running tools to establish metrics about our code quality, we can take steps to improve it, seeing this reflected in improved metrics with each subsequent run of the same tools.

Unit Test Code Coverage

We saw previously in this chapter that a unit test runs against a function that you've written in order to prove that it produces an expected output given a specific set of inputs. If we could detect which specific lines of code within that function did and did not get executed, we can generate a metric for code quality based on that. Such a metric is known to programmers as code coverage and is possible to generate using JavaScript. It is then possible to use the information gleaned about which lines and code branches were executed to add additional unit tests to ensure that all lines and branches are covered, increasing the metric but—more importantly—increasing the confidence you can have in your code.

To generate a list of which lines of code were executed and which were not, each line of the code for our original function needs to be wrapped in a function call that increments a counter and stores a reference to the line number it corresponds to in the original file. That way, such a function is called as line of code is executed, keeping a tally of which lines were and were not executed. Fortunately, you do not need to write the code to generate these function wrappers yourself, as a well-tested JavaScript library, Istanbul (`http://bit.ly/istanbul_cover`), exists to do this for you.

Istanbul is a JavaScript application designed to work with Node.js, an application framework that runs files written entirely in JavaScript on a command line. We'll look in greater detail at Node.js in a future chapter, but for now all that you need to do is install it.

Visit http://bit.ly/node_js and download Node.js, following the instructions to install it; this also installs a tool called Node Package Manager (NPM), which allows you to quickly and easily download applications (known as packages) from a central repository.

Next, we're going to download Grunt, a JavaScript-based task runner, which will simplify the job of running our Jasmine unit tests with Istanbul. We'll cover Grunt in more detail in Chapter 12, but for now we just need to install it by running the following on the command prompt. This installs the Grunt command line interface, which allows us to install and run different versions of Grunt in different project folders on the same machine. Mac and Linux users will likely need to precede the following command with sudo to run it with the necessary permissions:

```
npm install -g grunt-cli
```

Grunt requires two specially named and formatted files to be created in our project folder for it to run. The first of these is package.json and contains project details such as name, version and code dependencies. We'll add the dependencies later, but for now create a file named package.json using the code from Listing 3-12, which defines the project name and version number only.

Listing 3-12. A package.json file for running Jasmine unit tests with Istanbul through Grunt

```json
{
    "name": "jasmine-istanbul-grunt",
    "version": "1.0.0"
}
```

Now we need to install the specific version of Grunt we require into our project folder, by installing it locally and listing it in our package.json file as a dependency. We can do this in one simple step, by executing the following on the command line:

```
npm install grunt --save-dev
```

Now we have Grunt installed, we need to install the Jasmine and Istanbul tasks to run alongside it. Execute the following on the command line to install these:

```
npm install grunt-contrib-jasmine --save-dev
npm install grunt-template-jasmine-istanbul --save-dev
```

To run our tests from Grunt, we need to create a second file, Gruntfile.js, which will contain the definition of the tasks we wish to run together with the settings we wish to use for them. In this case, that is the Jasmine and Istanbul tasks and the specific locations of the original JavaScript functions to test and their unit tests. We also need to specifiy an output folder location for Istanbul's generated code coverage reports to be saved. Listing 3-13 shows how this file should look to achieve this, assuming the code to be tested is in a src folder within the current directory, and the unit tests are in a spec folder. A reports folder will be created, if it does not already exist, to store the generated coverage reports. Because we will cover Grunt in detail in Chapter 12, I will not attempt to explain the code for Gruntfile.js any further here here. Feel free to jump ahead to fully understand each line of the code here, or simply stick with it for now to see the code coverage reports generated through Istanbul.

Listing 3-13. A Gruntfile.js for tunning Jasmine unit tests with Istanbul through Grunt

```javascript
module.exports = function(grunt) {
    grunt.initConfig({
        jasmine: {
            coverage: {
                src: ["src/*.js"],
                options: {
                    specs: ["spec/*.js"],
                    template: require("grunt-template-jasmine-istanbul"),
                    templateOptions: {
                        coverage: "reports/coverage.json",
                        report: [
                            {
                                type: "lcov",
                                options: {
                                    dir: "reports"
                                }
                            },
                            {
                                type: "text-summary"
                            }
                        ]
                    }
                }
            }
        }
    });

    grunt.loadNpmTasks("grunt-contrib-jasmine");
    grunt.loadNpmTasks("grunt-template-jasmine-istanbul");

    grunt.registerTask("default", ["jasmine:coverage"]);
};
```

The final step is to run Grunt on the command line, which will trigger the tasks listed in Gruntfile.js to execute, wrapping the original functions to be tested in Istanbul's instrumentation code and then running those unit tests in Jasmine on the command line via PhantomJS, a WebKit-based headless web browser that has no user interface yet can be accessed via a JavaScript API through Node.js. Read more about PhantomJS via `http://phantomjs.org`.

```
grunt default
```

Once run, you should notice a new `reports` folder is generated, containing an HTML file, among other files. Opening this HTML file in a browser will show you the code coverage results, shown in Figure 3-6, of running the unit tests in a format known as LCOV. The top of the page shows results indicating how many lines of your original function were executed during the running of your unit tests. Clicking through on file names will reveal your original code listing, highlighting which lines were executed and which were not when all the unit tests were run.

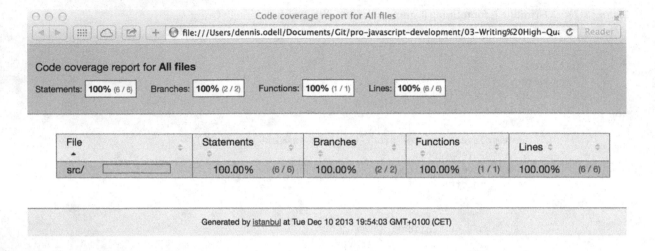

Figure 3-6. *Code coverage results of running Istanbul, in LCOV format*

This gives you a score indicating the quality of, and confidence you can have in, your code. If your unit tests cover every line of code, you can be more certain that your code will behave as expected when run in your application than if fewer lines were covered by your tests. You can then use the information from the Istanbul report to improve and add to your unit tests to attain a higher coverage score when running Istanbul again.

Measuring Code Complexity

Any experienced professional JavaScript developer will tell you that the more complex your code, the harder it is to ensure its quality. Complex code is harder to write unit tests for, is harder to maintain, and is harder to debug when things do go wrong. You can improve the quality of your JavaScript code by reducing its complexity. Design patterns, which we will cover in Chapter 5, can help with this, but there are simpler things that will make a difference, such as breaking down the code in functions longer than a few lines into smaller blocks. Smaller functions are simpler to test, are easier to reuse, and by virtue of the fact that they're assigned readable names, help to make your code easier to read and therefore maintain. You should also attempt to reduce complexity by looking at the number of branches in your code, things like if, else and switch statements, to see if these can't be reduced by breaking down your code into smaller functions, or by rearranging or refactoring your code.

Jarrod Overson's Plato tool (http://bit.ly/plato_tool) can be run against your JavaScript code to produce reports that highlight functions that can be considered to be complex according to its internal complexity rules. You can then work to improve these functions, resulting in code that will be simpler to test and maintain, increasing the confidence you can have in them when executed within your application, thus increasing the quality of that application's code. The generated reports are very creative and I find help to motivate the process of code quality improvement.

The tool produces a report on your code file as a whole, and also on the individual functions contained therein. It's a form of static code analysis, as the code itself doesn't run, it is merely observed. The report contains a number of metrics, including:

- lines of code, where more lines in a function indicates the chance of greater complexity;

- a maintainability score, out of 100, indicating how maintainable your code is estimated to be—the higher the number, the better Plato believes your code to be. Read more information on this maintainability score via http://bit.ly/maintain_score;

- estimated number of errors, based on metrics introduced by Maurice Howard Halstead in 1977, who believed software development could be established as an empirical science. This is not an actual error count value established by running the code, but an estimate based on the complexity of the code. Read more information on how this is calculated via http://bit.ly/halstead_complex;

- difficulty, a measure of how hard the code is to write and understand, based on a formula written by Halstead. The lower the score, the less difficult the code is considered to be to write and understand;

- cyclomatic complexity, a metric indicating the number of code branches, loops, and calls to other functions present within the function being measured, where a lower score indicates less complexity;

- number of JSHint static code analysis errors found; and

- historical results for each metric, for making quality comparisons over time.

To install the Plato tool, you require Node.js and its NPM tool. See instructions previously in this chapter for installing Node.js. Then execute the following on the command prompt to install the tool for access in any folder on your machine. Mac and Linux users may need to precede the command with sudo to grant the necessary installation privileges:

```
npm install -g plato
```

To run the tool, navigate on the command line to the folder containing the code that you wish to run the tool against and execute the following command to generate a report for all files in a folder named src, placing the generated report in a folder named reports:

```
plato -d reports src/*.js
```

You will find a generated report as an HTML file within the reports folder, which was created automatically if it did not already exist. Figure 3-7 shows the top part of this report. Repeated running of the same command results in historical data being shown in reports, indicating the progress of your code towards achieving greater quality.

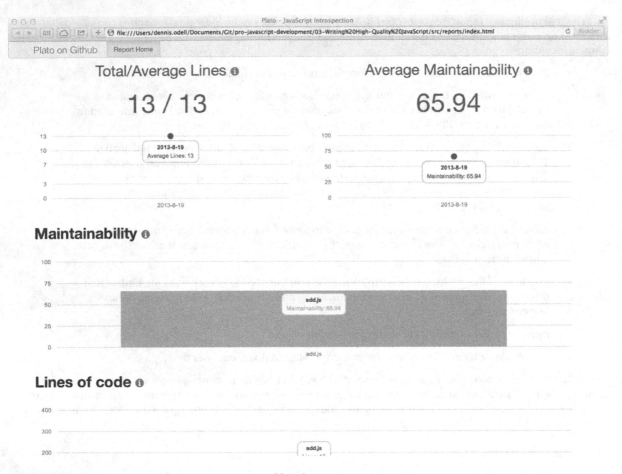

Figure 3-7. *A JavaScript complexity report generated by Plato*

Clicking on individual file names within Plato's overview report jumps to a file-specific report, as shown in Figure 3-8, which details more specific measurements for the code in that file as well as the code itself for the file with any JSHint errors and warnings highlighted.

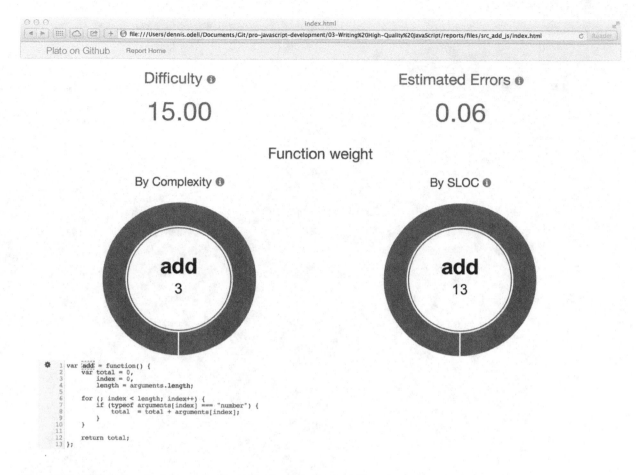

Figure 3-8. *A Plato JavaScript complexity report for an individual file*

Plato is a fantastic tool for measuring the quality of your JavaScript code, and one that I recommend you investigate for thoroughly for use in your own projects.

Summary

The purpose of this chapter has been to help you write high-quality JavaScript code and show you how to have confidence in the code that you execute in your pages. We looked in detail at static code analysis tools, unit testing, runtime error capturing, and handling, as well as how to measure the quality of your code, all with the aim of reducing errors and improving the experience for the end users of your applications. Strive to increase code quality over time and not only will you find your code has fewer errors, but you'll also find it easier to read, write, and understand, making your day-to-day working life that much simpler.

In the next chapter, we'll look at how you can improve the performance of your JavaScript applications through a combination of coding tips, techniques, best practices, and the use of modern APIs.

■ ■ ■

## CHAPTER 4

Boosting JavaScript Performance

In this chapter, we'll look at how to improve the performance of JavaScript applications through coding tips, techniques, best practices, and modern APIs. I take my view on performance holistically, meaning I take the lifecycle of the whole application into account. That means that instead of focusing purely on the number of lines of code executed, I appreciate that the perceived performance of an application can be improved by faster and more efficient JavaScript file loading, as well as more efficient calls, selectors, and even through CSS and HTML optimizations. In this chapter, however, we'll focus specifically on what we can do with JavaScript code and files to improve the performance of our web sites and applications. If you would like to read more about improving rendering performance for your page, take a look at Addy Osmani's excellent case study on this topic, titled "Gone In 60 Frames Per Second" via `http://bit.ly/gone_60`.

Improving Page Loading Time

Before we start altering any JavaScript code in order to improve the performance of our applications, we need to look into the first instance your browser has contact with your JavaScript code, which is through the references to loading it via HTML `<script>` tags. Changes that we can make at this stage will ensure that your code loads quickly and efficiently, meaning that your code is ready to execute sooner and improving the perceived responsiveness of your application.

HTML Tag Order Matters

When the browser encounters a `<script>` tag, in most cases it will stop rendering the page until it's managed to read and parse the contents of that script, just in case that script contained a `document.write()` method call, which would mean a change to the rendering of the page at that point. For this reason, move all the `<script>` tags you can to just before the `</body>` tag in your HTML. That way your entire page will render before your scripts load and are parsed, improving the perceived performance of your page.

GZip Encode Delivery Of Your JavaScript Files

A simple server setting can ensure your JavaScript code files, as well as your HTML, CSS, and any other text-based files, are sent to the browser in the most efficient way possible, by compressing, or "zipping," the data before sending, and decompressing, or "unzipping," when it reaches the browser, resulting in less data transferring across the wire, reaching your browser faster. This setting is known as gzip encoding, and can be enabled on virtually any web server, provided that you have control over your server's settings:

- For websites hosted on an Apache web server, install and configure the mod_deflate module (http://httpd.apache.org/docs/2.2/mod/mod_deflate.html) to enable gzip compression.

- For sites hosted on Microsoft's IIS 7, open up the IIS Manager program and select the Features view. Open the Compression option and check the boxes to enable gzip compression for static and/or dynamic content types. Static content is one that produces the same output every time, for example a CSS or flat HTML file, whereas a dynamic content produces a different output using application server-side code.

- For sites hosts on Node.js and using the Express framework (http://expressjs.com), simply use the compress() method of the Express object as early as possible within your application code. All following responses will then be gzip encoded.

The process of gzip encoding on-the-fly with each request can consume extra resources and CPU time on the server. If you are using a server whose performance you are concerned about, you can compress your JavaScript and other text-based files in advance. Just ensure that you serve those precompressed files with the additional HTTP header Content-Encoding: gzip and you get the same performance improvement without any cost to the performance of the server.

Minification, Obfuscation, and Compilation

The smaller the JavaScript file, the quicker it will download over the wire to your browser and the quicker it can be read and parsed by the browser. We therefore need to do everything we can in order to ensure our code is as small as it can be, and this we achieve through three processes, known as minification, obfuscation, and compilation.

Minification is the removal of all white space and line feed characters from your JavaScript to result in a smaller file size, yet still containing the exact same code statements written by the developer. Because JavaScript execution is based around specific keywords and statements and not about the white space characters that it contains, we can safely remove these to reduce our file size.

Obfuscation is a more advanced form of code optimization that looks at variable and function names, and figures out which are globally accessible and which are restricted only to a specific scope. Any global variable and function names are left as is, but those with limited scope are renamed to be shorter and therefore significantly reduce the amount of space those names take up in the code file. By ensuring that the names get replaced in the right place in the correct way, the code will continue to operate as it did before the obfuscation occurred. The less global variables and functions in your code, which is a good practice to adopt as it reduces the chance of interference between your code and others', the smaller your obfuscated code can become.

Compilation is a more advanced process that studies your code in its entirety and attempts to simplify, reduce, and combine statements of code into others that have the same behavior. Although there are fewer tools available to perform this specific type of optimization, when combined with minification and obfuscation, it is the most effective at producing the smallest file sizes.

Let's take the function in Listing 4-1 and attempt to reduce its size using minification, obfuscation, and compilation, respectively. The code this listing weighs in at 205 bytes, which we need to know in order to discover how much smaller we have made our resulting files.

Listing 4-1. Function to be minified, obfuscated, and compiled

```
var add = function() {
    var total = 0,
        index = 0,
        length = arguments.length;
```

```
for (; index < length; index++) {
    total  = total + arguments[index];
}

return total;
};
```

Using JSMin For Code Minification

Doug Crockford's JSMin tool, available via `http://bit.ly/js_min` and shown in Figure 4-1, was written back in 2001 for the purpose of minifying JavaScript files to reduce file size and therefore improve download times. It is believed to be the first of such tools available, and it essentially removes all unnecessary white space and carriage returns from a file. Originally only available as a MS-DOS command line tool, it is now available as a command line tool for most operating systems using the Node.js application framework, thanks to developer Peteris Krumins, who ported it over to this application platform (download via `http://bit.ly/node_jsmin`).

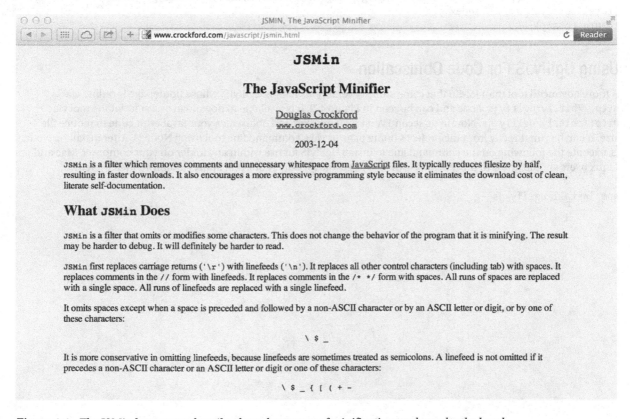

Figure 4-1. *The JSMin homepage describes how the process of minification works under the hood*

After installing Node.js on your computer (from `http://nodejs.org`), execute the following command on your command line to install JSMin for use within any folder on your computer. Mac and Linux users may need to precede the command with `sudo` to execute the command with sufficient priveleges:

```
npm install -g jsmin
```

Minifying a file is then as simple as specifying the output file name preceded by the command line tool's -o option, followed by the file name to minify, as shown here:

```
jsmin -o Listing4-1.min.js Listing4-1.js
```

Running the code from Listing 4-1 through JSMin, the code shown in Listing 4-2 is produced, which weighs in at 136 bytes, a file size reduction of 33.6 percent.

Listing 4-2. The code from Listing 4-1 after minification with JSMin

```
var add=function(){var total=0,index=0,length=arguments.length;for(;index<length;index++)
{total=total+arguments[index];}
return total;};
```

Using UglifyJS For Code Obfuscation

A more advanced tool than JSMin that came along several years later is UglifyJS, whose homepage is online via `http://bit.ly/uglifyjs_home` and can be seen in Figure 4-2. It is available to download as a standalone tool via `http://bit.ly/uglify_js`. Now in its second version, it minifies and obfuscates your JavaScript code to reduce file size. It can be run directly from the project's home page or via a command line tool using Node.js. After installing Node. js, execute the following on the command line to install UglifyJS for use within any folder on your computer. Mac and Linux users should know to precede this with `sudo`, as usual for operations that apply globally to their system:

```
npm install uglify-js -g
```

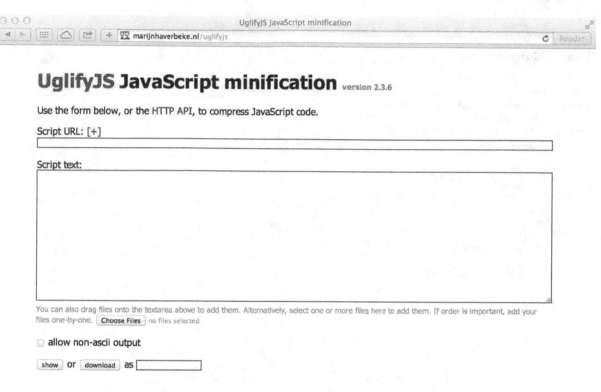

Figure 4-2. *Code can be obfuscated directly from the UglifyJS homepage*

Running the code from Listing 4-1 through UglifyJS produces the code shown in Listing 4-3 below, which weighs in at 88 bytes, a reduction of 57 percent.

Listing 4-3. The code from Listing 4-1 after obfuscation with UglifyJS

```
var add=function(){for(var r=0,n=0,a=arguments.length;a>n;n++)r+=arguments[n]
return r}
```

Using The Google Closure Compiler For Code Compilation

We took a look at Google's Closure Compiler in Chapter 3, using it as a tool for checking your code for errors, but its main purpose is actually to minify, obfuscate, and compile your code into a much smaller file than your original. In my opinion, this is the most effective compression tool for JavaScript available today.

To use the Closure Compiler to optimize your code, try copy and pasting your code into the online form via http://bit.ly/closure_compile, which is shown in Figure 4-3, and pressing the Compile button. The optimized code will appear on the right-hand side of the page within the Compiled Code tab. A link will be present above this box, allowing you to directly download the compiled code as a file. If you prefer to run the compiler standalone rather than via a web browser, the tool is available to run on the command line using a package for Node.js.

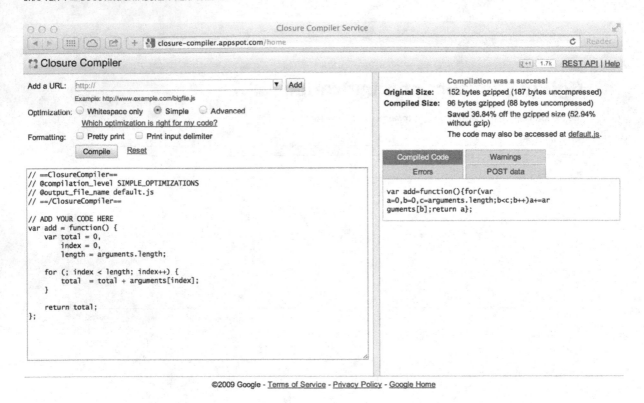

Figure 4-3. *JavaScript code may be compiled through the Google Closure Compiler online service*

Running the code from Listing 4-1 through Google Closure Compiler produces the code shown in Listing 4-4, which weighs in at just 88 bytes, a reduction of 57 percent and a result better than any achieved through minification with JSMin, and virtually identical to the results obtained through obfuscation with UglifyJS.

Listing 4-4. The code from Listing 4-1 after compilation with Google Closure Compiler

```
var add=function(){for(var a=0,b=0,c=arguments.length;b<c;b++)a+=arguments[b];return a};
```

With larger blocks of code, this method can produce large improvements even over and above UglifyJS. This is because, unlike minification and obfuscation tools, Google Closure Compiler actually runs and studies the code, continually seeking the most optimal final code that functions exactly the same as the original. This is in contrast to minification and obfuscation, which use a form of static analysis where the code is not run, simply observed as is.

In the majority of cases, Google Closure Compiler produces the best results and the smallest output file sizes, and I recommend adopting it in your applications to significantly reduce the size of your JavaScript files, making them quicker to load, and resulting in a better experience for your end users.

Avoid Global Variables For Better Compression

Any global variable or function name in your code will keep its name after minification, obfuscation, or compilation, so that the behavior of your code is unaffected by these compression operations. So it follows that the fewer global variables or functions you have, the smaller your code can become as these names can be rewritten during compression with shorter names. A good coding technique to avoid unwittingly creating global variables is to surround your whole code, or sections of your code, in an anonymous, self-executing function closure block, which will then create a new non-global scope for variable and function name definitions, as shown in Listing 4-5. Any of these variable names that actually need to be global can then be explicitly listed outside of the anonymous function, leaving all others to be more efficiently compressed.

Listing 4-5. Minimizing global variables with an anonymous, self-executing function closure

```
// Define a global variable
var myGlobalVariable;

// Create a self-executing, anonymous (unnamed) function to wrap around your code
(function() {
    // Your code, that before was global, goes here with a new, non-global scope,
    // making it easier to generate smaller compressed files via minification,
    // obfuscation, or compilation

    // Define a local variable
    var myLocalVariable = "Local";

    // Set the global variable to a string
    myGlobalVariable = "Global";

// The open-close bracket combination here executes the function straight away
}());
```

Lazy Loading JavaScript Files On Demand

When JavaScript files are loaded normally, using file references within your HTML file, the browser blocks the downloading and parsing of the rest of the page until the script has downloaded and executed. This is not ideal, particularly if there is a lot of code to download. There is a way to overcome this performance bottleneck using JavaScript itself, though you must exercise caution. Scripts usually block the browser loading scripts in parallel to avoid race conditions, where one piece of code completes before another, causing execution to occur in the wrong order. If you are going to load scripts in this way, you need a technique to associate a block of JavaScript code to execute once a file has completed downloading, to prevent such a race condition occurring.

You can create a nonblocking request for a JavaScript file by dynamically creating a new `<script>` tag through JavaScript, setting its `src` attribute to point to the location of the file to load asynchronously. By connecting a function to the tag's `onload` method, we can execute the specific code that depends on this script being loaded. Listing 4-6 shows a function that wraps up this behaviour in a simple function that takes as its parameters a script file location to load and a function to execute once that file has loaded, respectively.

Listing 4-6. Loading a JavaScript file on demand without blocking the browser

```
function loadScript(src, onLoad) {
    var scriptTag = document.createElement("script");

    scriptTag.src = src;

    if (typeof onLoad === "function") {
        scriptTag.onload = onLoad;
        scripTag.onreadystatechange = function() {
```

```
            if (scriptTag.readyState === 4) {
                onLoad();
            }
        }
    }

    document.body.appendChild(scriptTag);
}
```

The `loadScript` method in Listing 4-6 can then be used anywhere in your code, as follows:

```
// Loads my-script.js, then outputs "script loaded and available" when complete
loadScript("my-script.js", function() {
    alert("script loaded and available!");
});
```

```
// Loads my-script.js, which is self-contained and does not require extra code to be
// execute once it has loaded. The second parameter is therefore not passed in.
loadScript("my-script.js");
```

We will look into this topic further in Chapter 6, in which I will introduce the RequireJS library that allows lazy loading of JavaScript files and simple management of code file dependencies using a standardized format.

Optimize Document Object Manipulation

The single biggest cause of sluggish performance in most web sites and applications is inefficient access to HTML page elements through JavaScript. Because the JavaScript engine within any web browser is independent of its rendering engine, getting a reference to a page element through JavaScript involves a jump out of one engine and into another, with the browser acting as an intermediary between the two. To improve performance, we need to reduce the number of times this jump has to occur. In this section, I outline a number of techniques to help avoid unnecessary access from JavaScript to elements on the HTML page.

Minimise Access to Page Elements

Reducing access to page elements is fairly simple in that as soon as you have a reference to a page element in JavaScript, you simply store that reference in a variable and refer to that variable throughout your code rather than going back to the page to get the same reference again, as shown in Listing 4-7.

Listing 4-7. Storing DOM element references in variables for future access

```
var header = document.getElementById("header"),
    nav = document.getElementById("nav");

header.className += " " + nav.className;
```

If you need to access a number of page elements that sit within the same parent element, grab a reference to the parent element only and use JavaScript to locate the child elements from within that reference, which will all be brought across from the page with the single request to access the parent, as shown in Listing 4-8. Avoid the temptation to simply get a reference to the entire page and use this as the memory taken up by the entire DOM tree of a page, plus the additional time taken for JavaScript to locate the desired elements you wish to access further down that tree, could actually have negative performance implications for your applications.

Listing 4-8. Accessing child DOM elements through a reference to a single parent element

```
var wrapper = document.getElementById("wrapper"),
    header = wrapper.getElementsByTagName("header")[0],
    nav = wrapper.getElementsByTagName("nav")[0];

header.className += " " + nav.className;
```

If you need to create and add DOM elements to the page dynamically, apply all attributes and set all necessary properties before adding the new elements onto the page, as shown in Listing 4-9. This way, the browser will not need to keep accessing the live HTML page to make changes.

Listing 4-9. Making DOM changes to new elements before adding them to the live page

```
var list = document.createElement("ul"),
    listItem = document.createElement("li");

// Perform all the DOM manipulation possible within JavaScript first
listItem.innerHTML = "I am a list item";
list.appendChild(listItem);

// Finally, add the element to the page when you are sure you no longer need to alter it
// before display
document.body.appendChild(list);
```

Close Existing Elements Where Possible

Creating DOM elements dynamically is a fairly common requirement in websites and applications, but you pay a performance penalty each time you create an element using the standard document.createElement() method and configure it in a similar way to another existing element. To improve performance, duplicate existing elements rather than creating new ones from scratch, as shown in Listing 4-10. If you are creating multiple elements with similar attributes, create one instance, and then use the DOM element's cloneNode() method to duplicate the element and its associated attributes.

Listing 4-10. Duplicating existing elements to improve performance

```
var list1 = document.createElement("ul"),
    list2,
    listItem1 = document.createElement("li"),
    listItem2,
    listItem3;

listItem1.className = "list-item";
listItem1.innerHTML = "I am a list item";

// The cloneNode method duplicates the element efficiently. Setting the optional parameter
// to 'true' also copies across any child elements and properties. Leaving this property out
// copies just the individual element itself
listItem2 = listItem1.cloneNode(true);
listItem3 = listItem1.cloneNode(true);
```

```
// Add the three list items to the unordered list element
list1.appendChild(listItem1);
list1.appendChild(listItem2);
list1.appendChild(listItem3);

// Duplicate the entire unordered list
list2 = list1.cloneNode(true);

// Add the two identical unordered list elements to the live page
document.body.appendChild(list1);
document.body.appendChild(list2);
```

Utilise The Offline DOM

Instead of always accessing the live page to create and manage elements in JavaScript, an often-overlooked aspect of the DOM specification is the document fragment, or offline DOM, a light version of the DOM for creating and manipulating small element tree structures for later addition to the live page, as shown in Listing 4-11. Manipulating elements using this technique gives better performance than using the live page DOM.

Listing 4-11. Utilising the offline DOM to avoid access to the live DOM

```
// Create a DocumentFragment object as an offline DOM structure, disconnected from the live DOM
var offlineDOM = document.createDocumentFragment(),

    // Create elements for adding to the page dynamically
    header = document.createElement("header"),
    nav = document.createElement("nav");

// Add each element to the offline DOM
offlineDOM.appendChild(header);
offlineDOM.appendChild(nav);

// Add a copy of the offline DOM to the live page
document.body.appendChild(offlineDOM);
```

Use CSS To Manipulate Page Styles Rather Than JavaScript

CSS style properties can be manipulated directly through the DOM by using an element's style property. Updating the style property of a page element that affect its layout causes a reflow in the browser to occur, as shown in Listing 4-12, which calculates the effect of the change made to that and other elements on the page. Reflows take time to complete and so manipulating multiple style properties sequentially causes an unnecessary number of reflows to occur.

Listing 4-12. Demonstrating browser reflows when directly updating DOM element style properties

```
var nav = document.getElementsByTagName("nav");

nav.style.backgroundColor = "#000"; // Causes a reflow in the browser
nav.style.color = "#fff"; // Causes a reflow
nav.style.opacity = 0.5; // Causes a reflow
```

There are two solutions to this problem. The first is to apply a CSS class to the page element through JavaScript instead of individual styles. This causes all the CSS rules to be applied at the same time to the element, causing only a single reflow to occur, as shown in Listing 4-13. This has the added logical benefit of keeping all visual and layout rules together in a single CSS file devoted to this task, instead of muddying the waters with some styles applied via CSS and some via JavaScript.

Listing 4-13. Applying CSS classes to DOM elements to reduce browser reflows

```
var nav = document.getElementsByTagName("nav");

nav.className += " selected"; // The CSS class name "selected" contains multiple style settings
```

The second solution, if the first is unachievable in your particular circumstance, is to set the display style property to none before making your changes to other style properties. This removes the element visually from the page flow, causing a browser reflow, but means that any other style properties altered while the element is out of the page flow don't cause a reflow to occur. Once the changes have been made, the element should be returned to the page flow by setting its display property to block or any other acceptable value for this property, as demonstrated in Listing 4-14.

Listing 4-14. Reducing browser reflows by hiding elements whilst altering their style properties

```
var nav = document.getElementsByTagName("nav");

nav.style.display = "none"; // Causes a browser reflow, hiding the element from display
nav.style.backgroundColor = "#000"; // Causes no reflow since the element is hidden
nav.style.color = "#fff"; // Causes no reflow
nav.style.opacity = 0.5; // Causes no reflow
nav.style.display = "block"; // Causes a browser reflow, bringing the element back on display
```

Improving DOM Event Performance

Since the advent of JavaScript, we've been writing code to connect functionality up to user action on our websites and applications. When the user submits a form clicks a link, or loads a page, we want to be able to intercept these actions and improve the experience of our page through JavaScript. We need these actions to be fast and not to interrupt the behavior of the rest of the page within the browser. Poorly attached or handled events can cause performance problems, although thankfully with proper event delegation and framing, we can minimize the performance impact of event handling.

Delegate Events To Parent Elements

DOM events bubble up from the element they were first triggered, to the very top of the document structure. What that means is that, for example, when a user clicks on a link, JavaScript fires a click event for the link element, followed by a click event on the parent element, and so on for every element up the DOM tree to the very top of the tree structure, finally landing at the root <html> element. This is known as the bubble phase of an event. Before this, there is a capture phase where the event fires on elements from the top of the DOM tree downwards to the element. When setting up an event handler using the addEventListener() method of an element, you supply the event name, the handler function that will execute when the event occurs on the element, and, finally, a third parameter, a Boolean true or false value, which indicates whether you would like to fire the event in the capture or bubble phases of the event's lifecycle, respectively.

We can use the bubble phase to our advantage when it comes to improving performance of our application, as this means we only need add a single event handler that handles events on a number of elements by applying this handler to the parent element of those being acted on by the user. You can then assign actions to occur depending on properties of the element the event occurred on, as shown in Listing 4-15, where a single event handler deals with events fired on a number of child elements. These are called event delegates, as they become logic blocks that delegate actions based on properties of events and page elements. Assume that this listing runs within the context of a HTML page, part of which contains the following markup:

```
<ul id="list">
    <li class="list-item"><a href="/" class="list-item-link">Home</a></li>
    <li class="list-item"><a href="/news" class="list-item-link">News</a></li>
    <li class="list-item"><a href="/events" class="list-item-link">Events</a></li>
</ul>
```

Listing 4-15. Event delegation on a list of links

```
// Get a reference to the list element surrounding all the links we wish to
// assign the event handler to
var list = document.getElementById("list");

// Define a function to execute when either the link or an element within the link
// is executed
function onClick(evt) {

    // Get a reference to the actual element clicked on using the event's 'target' property
    var clickedElem = evt.target,
        tagNameSought = "A";

    // Check to see if the element clicked on is of the type we are looking for, in this
    // case if it is an <a> tag
    if (clickedElem && clickedElem.tagName === tagNameSought) {

        // If it is, we get the link's 'href' value and open this in a new window
        window.open(clickedElem.href);

    }
}

// Assign the event handler to the list item, the parent surrounding all the links. Adding
// one event handler is faster than assigning an event handler to each of the individual
// links. The third parameter is set to 'false', indicating that events should be handled
// in the bubble phase of the event lifecycle, from the element the event occurred on, up the
// tree to the list item itself
list.addEventListener("click", onClick, false);
```

By harnessing event delegates, you ensure that you have only a handful of events to wire up to page elements when your page loads, reducing DOM access and improving performance. This helps achieve the overall goal of reducing the time it takes before the end user is able to interact with the page.

Handle Rapid-Fire Events With Framing

Certain events may fire very quickly and in rapid succession, such as the browser resize event when the page is being actively resized, the mousemove and touchmove events when the mouse or touch screen is actively in use, or the scroll event while the page is being scrolled; these events may occur as frequently as every few milliseconds. Connecting event handlers directly to these events that execute a lot of code or potentially computationally intensive operations could cause performance problems. If the event handler code is being executed while another event fires, the function calls are stacked; only when the code from the first event has completed can the code from the second event begin to execute. If many events are occurring in quick succession, soon the browser will appear to be struggle under load put upon it, causing delays to updates of the user interface for the user, resulting in an unresponsive, poor user experience.

For these types of rapid-firing events, adjust your code so that the event handler function does nothing more than save current value from the event into a variable. This means that on each mousemove, touchmove, resize, or scroll event, the event handler simply stores the mouse position, touch position, browser width and height, and scroll position in variables. This will not cause any performance problems. Move your computationally intensive code to a separate function that then fires on a less frequent timer or interval, running your code and using the value stored in the variable rather than directly from the event handler. This principle, known as event framing, is demonstrated in Listing 4-16.

Listing 4-16. Event framing to improve performance

```javascript
// Create variables to store the scroll position of the page
var scrollTopPosition = 0,
    scrollLeftPosition = 0,
    body = document.body,
    header = document.getElementById("header");

// Create an event handler function that does nothing more than store the current
// scroll position
function onScroll() {
    scrollTopPosition = body.scrollTop;
    scrollLeftPosition = body.scrollLeft;
}

// Add a function to write the current scroll position to the header element of the page
function writeScrollPosition () {
    header.innerHTML = scrollTopPosition + "px, " + scrollLeftPosition + "px";
}

// Connect the event to the handler function as usual
document.addEventListener("scroll", onScroll, false);

// Execute the writeScrollPosition function once every 500 ms rather than every time the
// scroll event fires, improving application performance
window.setInterval(writeScrollPosition, 500);
```

Wherever you can, avoid assigning computationally intensive event handler functions directly to events that could fire in rapid succession. Use event framing instead to improve the performance of your event handling.

Improving Function Performance

Improving performance in JavaScript applications is largely about increasing efficiency of the code being executed. Functions are prime territory for applying efficiencies, where every line executed counts toward the speed and performance of the code. Reducing the number of lines executed is the name of the game, therefore, and we can do this through a technique known as memoization.

Storing Previous Function Return Values With Memoization

When it comes to reducing the number of lines of code executed in our applications, we need to ensure that wherever the same function would be executed twice with the same parameters, we store the result of the first execution in a variable for use in place of a second call to the same function. Listing 4-17 shows a function that computes the mathematical factorial of any number, which might get called numerous times in an application.

Listing 4-17. Function to calculate the factorial of a number

```
// getFactorial calculates the factorial of a number, i.e. the multiplication of each number
// from 1 up to the supplied number. The factorial of 3, for example, is (1 * 2 * 3) = 6
function getFactorial(num) {
    var result = 1,
        index = 1;

    for (; index <= num; index++) {
        result *= index;
    }
    return result;
}

// Example usage
alert(getFactorial(3)); // = (1 * 2 * 3) =  6
alert(getFactorial(4)); // = (1 * 2 * 3 * 4) = 24
alert(getFactorial(5)); // = (1 * 2 * 3 * 4 * 5) = 120
```

Once we'd called the function in Listing 4-17 to calculate the factorial of a number once, it would be beneficial to store the result in a variable for use later in our code to avoid executing the entire function again. However, we'd ideally want a way to do this automatically, as we may not be aware in a large application whether or not a particular function has been called previously or not with the same inputs we would be providing. This is where the concept of a memoizer comes in—if a function can contain a storage mechanism that saves the results of previous executions with specific inputs, then it can call on its storage to return previously executed function outputs instead of reexecuting the entire function again, improving its performance. Listing 4-18 shows how we might add storage to our function that calculates factorials, using an object literal with property names set based on the input provided to the function.

Listing 4-18. Memoizing the function in Listing 4-17 in order to improve its performance

```
function getFactorial(num) {
    var result = 1,
        index = 1;

    if (!getFactorial.storage) {
        getFactorial.storage = {};
    } else if (getFactorial.storage[num]) {
        return getFactorial.storage[num];
    }
```

```
    for (; index <= num; index++) {
        result *= index;
    }

    getFactorial.storage[num] = result;

    return result;
}

// Example usage
alert(getFactorial(50)); // Executes the whole function
alert(getFactorial(50)); // Returns a stored value. Avoids full function execution,
                         // boosts performance
```

The memoization technique can have dramatic results, improving complex function performance by large factors; however, to make it truly worthwhile, we need a way of applying memoization to any function without having to manually add it each time. Listing 4-19 shows how to build a utility function that allows you to add the ability to store result values to any function, automatically returning the result of the function from its internal storage property where possible to boost performance.

Listing 4-19. A generic memoizer function for use with any function to improve its performance

```
// memoize() expects a function as an input and returns the same function
// with storage capabilities added

function memoize(fn) {
    return function() {
        var propertyName;

        // Add a memory object property to this function, if it does not exist
        fn.storage = fn.storage || {};

        // Create a property name to use to store and retrieve function results within
        // the 'storage' object literal. This should be based on a combination of
        // all the arguments passed to the function to ensure it is unique based
        // on all possible combinations of inputs.
        // We borrow the 'join' method from the Array type as 'arguments' isn't a
        // proper array type and doesn't contain this method.
        propertyName = Array.prototype.join.call(arguments, "|");

        // Does the key exist in the memory object?
        if (propertyName in fn.storage) {

            // If it does, then return the associated value to avoid re-execution of
            // the full function
            return fn.storage[propertyName];
        } else {
            // If it doesn't, execute the associated function then save the result
            // to the memory object
            fn.storage[propertyName] = fn.apply(this, arguments);
```

```
        // Return the newly saved value, the result of the function's execution
        return fn.storage[propertyName];
    }
  }
};
```

The code in Listing 4-20 shows how the memorize() function from Listing 4-19 can be used to apply to our original getFactorial() function from Listing 4-17.

Listing 4-20. Applying generic memoization to a function

```
function getFactorial(num) {
    var result = 1,
        index = 1;

    for (; index <= num; index++) {
        result *= index;
    }
    return result;
}

// Add the generic memoize capability to the function
var getFactorialMemoized = memoize(getFactorial);

// Example usage
alert(getFactorialMemoized(50)); // Executes the whole function
alert(getFactorialMemoized(50)); // Returns a stored value. Avoids full function execution,
                                 // boosts performance
```

Adopt the practice of memoization to your own JavaScript functions that return specific outputs based on given inputs, and you should find that the performance of your application improves noticeably, particularly for computationally intensive functions.

Faster String Manipulation With Regular Expressions

Regular expressions provide a useful, powerful, and efficient way to perform string location, manipulation, and pattern matching—faster than any other method, which explains why developers of many programming languages have been using them since their first use in software products in the 1960s!

Within JavaScript, regular expressions can be defined in two different ways, using an object constructor or via a literal expression, as shown in Listing 4-21.

Listing 4-21. Defining a regular expression in JavaScript

```
// Define a regular expression through JavaScript's RegExp constructor, where the expression
// is passed in the first parameter as a string, and any modifiers are passed as a string to
// the second parameter
var caps1 = new RegExp("[A-Z]", "g");

// Define a regular expression literal, where the expression is delimited by slashes (/) and
// any modifiers follow immediately after
var caps2 = /[A-Z]/g;
```

The RegExp constructor takes a string and converts this into a regular expression, whereas the literal form is ready to be used without any extra processing; this makes the literal form the fastest way to create a regular expression. You should therefore avoid using RegExp, except where you absolutely need to dynamically generate a regular expression.

Regular expression syntax involves the use of special characters and character sequences to convey certain meaning and to describe how the expression should be handled. Table 4-1 summarizes some common uses of special characters with regular expressions.

Table 4-1. *Characters commonly used in regular expressions*

Characters	Description
[exp]	Square brackets ([]) surrounding a sequence of characters inform the regular expression processor to match any of the characters within the brackets. For example, [ABC] matches any of the characters A, B, or C.
[^exp]	Placing the ^ character within square brackets will match any character except those listed within the brackets. For example, [^ABC] matches anything but the characters A, B, or C.
[exp1-exp2]	The use of the - character indicates that the expression should match a sequence of characters from the first specified to the last. For example, [A-Z] matches any character from A to Z, inclusive, and [0-9] matches any digit between 0 and 9, inclusive.
(exp)	The use of standard brackets surrounding a sequence of characters indicates the expression should match the exact sequence of characters in the order specified. For example, (great) matches only the character sequence great exactly.
(exp1|exp2)	The use of the pipe character | within brackets indicates the regular expression should match one or other of the supplied expressions. For example, (great|escape) matches either the character sequence great or the character sequence escape.
exp+	The use of the + character after an expression matches only if that expression is contained one or more times. For example, A+ matches only if the character A is present one or more times.
exp*	The use of the * character after an expression matches if that expression is present zero or more times, meaning it may or may not be present at all, which is useful for matching optional parts of an expression. For example, A* matches is the character A is present one or more times, or not at all.
exp?	The use of the ? character after an expression matches if that expression is present zero or once. For example, A? matches only if the character A is present zero or once, not more than one time.
\s	Matches a whitespace character, i.e. a space, tab, carriage return, line feed, tab, or form feed character. For example, A\sB matches if the expression contains an A character followed by a whitespace character, followed by a B character.
\S	Matches everything except a whitespace character.
\d	Matches a digit, 0 to 9.
\D	Matches everything except a digit.
\w	Matches a word character, i.e. a letter.
\W	Matches everything that isn't a word character.

The regular expression modifier is an option that defines how the regular expression should be used. There are three possible values that can be used either individually to apply a single option, or together to apply multiple, as shown in Table 4-2.

Table 4-2. *Regular expression modifiers*

Modifier	Description
g	Applies the regular expression, finding all matches in a string being compared, and not just returning the first match
i	Applies the expression regardless of letter case of the text string
m	Applies the expression over multiple lines of text in a string, rather than just the first

Regular expressions are most often applied to strings to locate or replace substrings within them. There are three String type methods that can use regular expressions—match(), replace(), and search(). The match() method finds the substring(s) that match the regular expression and return these as an array of strings, the replace() method finds the same substring(s) and then replaces them each with another string passed to the method, and the search() method locates only the first instance of the substring found with the regular expression and returns the location of that substring within the full string as an numerical index. Examples of each method are shown in Listing 4-22.

Listing 4-22. Regular expression methods used on strings to find substrings

```
// This regular expression locates all capital letters from A to M, inclusive. The 'g' modifier
// indicates that the expression shouldn't stop when it reaches the first match, but continue to
// search through the rest of the applied string
var regEx = /[A-M]/g,
    string = "The Great Escape",
    match,
    search,
    replace;

// match() returns an array of the characters in the string found by the regular expression
match = string.match(regEx); // = ["G", "E"]

// search() returns the index of the first located character - the 'g' modifier in the regular
// expression is ignored
search = string.search(regEx); // = 4

// replace() switches out any located characters matched by the regular expression with the
// value in the second parameter
replace = string.replace(regEx, "_"); // = "The _reat _scape"
```

The string replace() method is actually a lot more powerful than most developers give it credit for, particularly when used with regular expressions. Specific sequences of characters given in the second parameter have the ability to dynamically add text from the located text into the replaced text, as shown in Table 4-3.

Table 4-3. Special characters for use in the second parameter of the JavaScript string `replace()` method

Character Sequence	Meaning
`$$`	Replaces the located substring with a single $ character. For example: `"Hello World".replace(/o/g, "$$"); // "Hell$ W$rld"`
`$&`	Replaces the located substring with the substring given in the first parameter. For example: `"Hello World".replace(/o/g, "$&"); // "Hello World"`
`` $` ``	Replaces the located substring with the text that came before the located substring. For example: `"Hello World".replace(/o/g, "$`"); // "HellHell WHello Wrld"`
`$'`	Replaces the located substring with the text that came after the located substring. For example: `"Hello World".replace(/o/g, "$'"); // "Hell World Wrldrld"`
`$1, $2, etc.`	When the first parameter contains a regular expression with brackets to group expressions, this notation allows you to extract the substring found in the specific expression. For example: `"Hello World".replace(/(o)(\s)/g, "$1$1$2"); // "Helloo World"`

Another little known fact about the string `replace()` method is that the second parameter can be passed as a function rather than a string value. In this case, the function is executed once for each substring match in the original string, passing the matched substring into the function. The returned value of the function is then used and substituted into the replaced string, as shown in Listing 4-23.

Listing 4-23. Using a function as the second parameter of a string `replace()` method call

```
// Initialize a value to use as a counter
var count = 0;

// Define a function to be executed on each matched substring, where the supplied parameter
// is the matched substring itself
function replaceWithCount(value) {

    // Increment the counter
    count = count + 1;

    // Return to the replaced string the passed in value, with the current value of the
    // counter appended to it
    return value + count;
}

// Example usage
alert("Hello World".replace(/o/g, replaceWithCount)); // Hello1 Wo2rld
alert("Hello World".replace(/\s/g, replaceWithCount)); // Hello 3World
```

Regular expressions can become very complex and very powerful, and can take many years to understand and master. I've only covered the very basics here; should you wish to delve deeper into this fantastic world, you can find a very thorough reference on regular expression use in JavaScript online at Mozilla's Developer Network, via `http://bit.ly/reg_exps`.

Faster Use Of Arrays

Working with large arrays of data can potentially slow down your code as you find you need to create, access, sort, or loop through them, which often involves accessing or manipulating each individual item in the array. The larger the array, therefore, the slower this will be and the more importance you should place on ensuring that your code is the most efficient it can be. There are, however, some tips and tricks for dealing with large arrays of data, which I'll explain in detail in this section.

Fast Array Creation

There are two ways to create an array in JavaScript, as shown here. The fastest way for JavaScript to create and initialize an array is the latter of these, as the former requires an extra step to get the Array type's constructor and execute the new keyword against it:

```
var myArray = new Array();
var myArray = [];
```

Fast Array Looping

Most JavaScript code is full of loops. Often, you will need to process arrays or iterate through object literals to perform calculations or manipulations on the data stored therein. Looping through data is a notoriously slow task in JavaScript, particularly in older browsers. The code in Listing 4-24 shows a typical JavaScript for loop, together with a similar, but incredibly more efficient, version of the same loop.

Listing 4-24. Two types of for loops, one more efficient than the other

```
var myArray = [10, 20, 30, 40, 50, 60, 70, 80, 90, 100];

// The most common type of loop
for (var index = 0; index < myArray.length; index++) {
    // On every iteration through the loop, the value of myArray.length must
    // be recomputed to ensure it has not changed since the last iteration
    // - this is slow
}

// A similar but much faster version of the same loop
for (var index = 0, length = myArray.length; index < length; index++) {
    // The value of myArray.length is computed once and stored in a variable.
    // the value is read back from the variable on each iteration instead of being
    // recomputed - much faster!
}
```

You have two JavaScript commands at your disposal to manage your loops:

- break stops the current loop from executing, continuing to execute the code that follows the loop.

- continue stops the current iteration of the loop and moves onto the next iteration.

You can use these commands to effectively stop your loops from iterating if you have located the value you were seeking, or to skip execution of certain code blocks if they are irrelevant to the current iteration of the loop. The code in Listing 4-25 shows an example of both commands.

Listing 4-25. Using break and continue commands to shorten the number of iterations of a loop

```
var myArray = [10, 20, 30, 40, 50, 60, 70, 80, 90, 100];
for (var index = 0, length = myArray.length; index < length; index++) {
    if (myArray[index] < 50) {
        // Ignore any values in the array below 50
        // continue executes the next iteration immediately, ignoring any other code
        // within the loop
        continue;
    }

    if (myArray[index] == 90) {
        // Ignore any values in the array above 90
        // break stops the loop from iterating immediately, ignoring any other code
        // no other iterations will be performed in the loop
        break;
    }
}
```

The fastest way of looping around large amounts of data is known as the reverse-while loop. In this technique, we use a while loop instead of a for loop and count downward on each iteration through the loop from the last element of the array until we reach the first element. The reason this method is faster than the for loop mentioned previously is that on each iteration around the for loop, the JavaScript interpreter must run a comparison, for example, index < length, to know when to stop looping. In the case of the while loop, the loop will stop running when the parameter passed to the while loop is a falsy value, which happens when its value is 0. It's for this reason that we count downward to 0, the first index of the array, and because it does not need to execute a more complex comparison, that this type of loop is fastest. The reverse-while loop is demonstrated in Listing 4-26.

Listing 4-26. The reverse-while loop

```
var daysOfWeek = ["Monday", "Tuesday", "Wednesday", "Thursday", "Friday", "Saturday", "Sunday"],
    len = daysOfWeek.length,

    // The start index of the loop is the end item of the array
    index = len,
    daysOfWeekInReverse = [];

// Decrement the index each time through the loop, just after it's been compared in the while
// loop parameter. When the index is 0, the while loop will stop executing.
while(index--) {
    daysOfWeekInReverse.push(daysOfWeek[index]);
}

// Because of the decrement in the while loop, at the end of the code, the value of index will
// be -1
alert(index); // -1
```

I feel I should emphasise that although this is the fastest method, we're talking about fractions of a second faster for large arrays, so take this more as a piece of education rather than a coding tip, per se.

Avoid Creating Functions Within Loops

In the drive to be more efficient with arrays, you should be aware of the trap of creating functions within loops. Each time a function is created, memory on the machine is reserved for that function and filled with the object data representing that function. Looping through 100 items and creating an identical function on each iteration of the loop will therefore result in 100 separate, yet identical, functions being created in memory. This principle is demonstrated in Listing 4-27 with a smaller array of seven items, where a function is added on each iteration of the loop to a resulting object literal, which can be used to reverse the string in the original array item.

Listing 4-27. Creating functions within loops

```
var daysOfWeek = ["Monday", "Tuesday", "Wednesday", "Thursday", "Friday", "Saturday", "Sunday"],
    index = 0,
    length = daysOfWeek.length,
    daysObj = {},
    dayOfWeek;

// Loop through each day of the week
for (; index < length; index++) {
    dayOfWeek = daysOfWeek[index];

    // Add a property to the daysObj object literal for each day of the week, adding
    // a function that reverses the name of the day of the week to each
    daysObj[dayOfWeek] = {
        name: dayOfWeek,
        getReverseName: function() {
            return this.name.split("").reverse().join("");
        }
    };
}
```

To avoid the need to create a function on each loop, simply create and define a single function before the loop and refer to that within the loop, as shown in Listing 4-28.

Listing 4-28. Using a single function in loop iterations

```
var daysOfWeek = ["Monday", "Tuesday", "Wednesday", "Thursday", "Friday", "Saturday", "Sunday"],
    index = 0,
    length = daysOfWeek.length,
    daysObj = {},
    dayOfWeek;

// Define a single function to be used within any iteration of the loop
function getReverseName() {

    // When called, the 'this' keyword will refer to the context in which it was called,
    // namely the property in the daysObj object literal which it was called on
    return this.name.split("").reverse().join("");
}
```

```
for (; index < length; index++) {
    dayOfWeek = daysOfWeek[index];
    daysObj[dayOfWeek] = {
        name: dayOfWeek,

        // Simply refer to the existing function here, rather than creating a new function
        getReverseName: getReverseName
    };
}
```

Offload Intensive Tasks To Web Workers

As you are probably already acutely aware, JavaScript only runs in a single thread in the browser. Its handling of asynchronous function calls means the entire user interface doesn't lock up when, for example, making an Ajax call to the server. However, create a loop that does a lot of processing on each iteration and you'll soon see how limiting this is, the entire user interface locks up in some cases.

Web workers, a W3C standardized version of work created by Google under the name Gears, solves this issue by allowing you to spin up a new thread on which to execute specific intensive code, saving the original thread from locking up the browser, essentially running that code in the background. If you're familiar with threads from an operating system standpoint, you'll be glad to hear that each new thread created by a web worker actually starts a whole new thread in the operating system, meaning it really is distinct from the original thread, no virtualization involved. In fact, each thread is so distinct from the original browser code that it does not even have access to the page elements in the DOM, nor to any global variables on the page. In order to use a variable or object in a web worker thread, it must be explicitly passed to it. Web workers are supported in the latest version of all web browsers, and specifically in Internet Explorer from version 10.

Creating a web worker thread is as simple as shown in Listing 4-29, all that needs to be passed to the Worker constructor is the location of the JavaScript file containing the code to run in the worker thread. This creates the worker object and initializes it, but it does not yet run the code in the worker thread. This is to give you time to configure the worker after creating it, before the code has actually run.

Listing 4-29. Creating a web worker is a simple task

```
var workerThread = new Worker("filename.js");
```

Creating a worker is all well and good, but in most cases you'll be wanting to offload some intensive code to a new worker thread with the express interest of getting back the output of the code from that thread to use back in your original browser code. The web worker specification defines two events, message and error, which are called when a message is posted back from the worker or when an error occurs within the worker, respectively. Messages can be posted to the worker thread using the postMessage method of the worker thread object, and you start the worker running in the first place by sending it a message with any input data needed in this way to trigger it into action, as shown in Listing 4-30.

Listing 4-30. Configuring a web worker to listen for messages posted from the worker thread

```
//Create the worker thread
var workerThread = new Worker("filename.js");

// Start listening for messages posted from the code in the thread
workerThread.addEventListener("message", function(e) {

    // The object e passed into the event handler contains the
    // posted message in its data property
    alert(e.data);
}, false);

// Run the code in the worker thread
workerThread.postMessage("");
```

Within the worker thread file itself, you listen for received messages using self.addEventListener and can send a message back to the calling browser script by using self.postMessage, thus completing the communications circle between the two scripts.

If a worker has completed its useful work and needs to be closed, it can be done so either from the browser side or from within the worker itself. In the browser, a call to terminate() method of the worker object will immediately stop the code in the worker from executing, no matter what state it is in at the time, its thread is immediately terminated. In the worker thread itself, a call to the self.close() method will stop the worker from running and terminate its thread, sending a close message back to the calling browser script.

Using a Web Worker to Process Image Data

Let's use a web worker to do some heavy image processing that would otherwise block the user interface of a standard browser script. We'll take the raw image data from an image on a page, process the pixels to create a variant of the same image, and then replace the original image once the processing is complete.

To extract the raw pixel data from an image on the page, we need to take that image and draw it within a HTML5 <canvas> element, used for drawing pixel data in an area on a page, which we can create dynamically using JavaScript. We can then take this raw pixel data and process it, using a web worker to avoid locking up the page whilst processing. This worker will create a new set of image pixel data that we can draw onto the same <canvas> element, replacing the original image with the new processed image, before adding that element to the page. We will cover the HTML5 <canvas> element in more detail in Chapter 8, where I will explain how to build simple games using this powerful, yet simple, new browser addition.

Listing 4-31. Image processing with a web worker

```
<!doctype html>
<html>
    <head>
        <meta charset="utf-8">
        <title>Listing 4-31</title>
    </head>
    <body>
        <img id="image" src="Listing4-31.jpg" alt="">
        <script src="Listing4-32.js"></script>
    </body>
</html>
```

The code in Listing 4-31 shows a simple HTML page containing an image referenced by an id of image, to allow JavaScript to easily locate this DOM element. The page then loads the JavaScript code contained in Listing 4-32, below.

Listing 4-32. JavaScript file to kickstart the image processing

```
// Create a <canvas> element dynamically in JavaScript and get a reference to its
// 2d drawing context
var canvas = document.createElement("canvas"),
    context = canvas.getContext("2d"),

    // Get a reference to the image on the page
    img = document.getElementById("image");

// Define a function to process the image data
function processImage() {

    // Store the image width and height to avoid looking them up each time
    var imgWidth = img.width,
        imgHeight = img.height,

        // Define a new web worker, using the code from the 'Listing4-33.js' file
        workerThread = new Worker("Listing4-33.js");

    // Set the new <canvas> element's dimensions to match that of the image
    canvas.width = imgWidth;
    canvas.height = imgHeight;

    // Copy the image to the canvas, starting in the top-left corner
    context.drawImage(img, 0, 0, imgWidth, imgHeight);

    // Define the code to execute once a message is received from the web worker, which
    // will be fired once the image data has been processed
    workerThread.addEventListener("message", function(e) {

        // Get the image data sent in the message from the event's data property
        var imageData = e.data;

        // Push the new image pixel data to the canvas, starting in the top-left corner
        context.putImageData(imageData, 0, 0);

        // Now add the resulting <canvas> element to the page. By performing all the necessary
        // canvas actions before it's added to the page, we avoid the need for the browser to
        // repaint the canvas element as we added and then replaced the image displayed on it
        document.body.appendChild(canvas);
    }, false);

    // Kick off the web worker, sending it the raw image data displayed on the canvas
    workerThread.postMessage(context.getImageData(0,0, imgWidth, imgHeight));
}

// Execute the processImage function once the image has finished loading
img.addEventListener("load", processImage, false);
```

The code in Listing 4-32 grabs a reference to the image on the page and, once it has loaded, determines its width and height for use to create a similarly sized `<canvas>` element. The raw image pixel data is then extracted and a web worker object created, using the code from Listing 4-33. Using the worker thread object's `postMessage()` method, the pixel data is sent to the worker, which processes the data. Once processing is complete, the worker calls its own `self.postMessage()` method, which is received through the calling script's `message` event listener, where the returned, processed image data is then drawn onto the `<canvas>` element, before that element is finally added to the page.

Listing 4-33. Web worker to process an image—inverting its colors

```
// Call the invertImage method when this worker receives a message from the calling script.
// The 'self' object contains the only methods a web worker can access apart from those it
// defines and creates itself
self.addEventListener("message", invertImage, false);

// Define a function to take an image and invert it, pixel by pixel, using its raw data
function invertImage(e) {

    // The 'data' property of the 'message' event contains the pixel data passed from
    // the calling script
    var message = e.data,

        // The 'data' property of the message passed contains the raw image pixel data
        imagePixels = message.data,
        x = 0,
        len = imagePixels.length;

    // Loop through each pixel, inverting its value within the original pixel data array.
    // Pixel data is arranged in groups of 4 values, representing the red, green, blue, and
    // opacity values of each visible screen pixel. We therefore loop through in jumps of 4
    // on each iteration
    for (; x < len; x += 4) {

        // To invert a pixel's value, subtract it from the maximum possible value, which is 255
        imagePixels[x] = 255 - imagePixels[x];
        imagePixels[x + 1] = 255 - imagePixels[x + 1];
        imagePixels[x + 2] = 255 - imagePixels[x + 2];
    }

    // Finally, post a message containing the updated pixel data back to the calling script
    self.postMessage(message);
}
```

The result of this image processing operation is shown in Figure 4-4, in which the original image is on the left and the inverted image, processed by the web worker and drawn into a `<canvas>` element, is on the right.

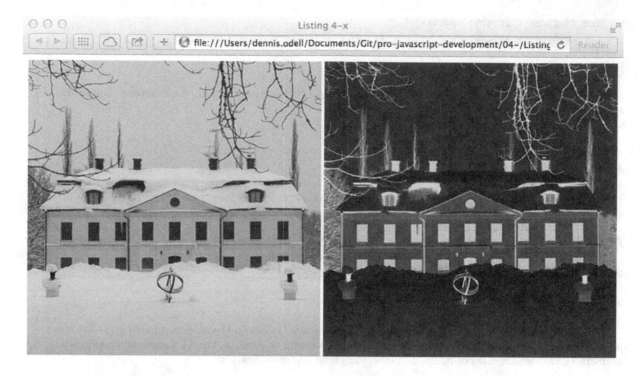

Figure 4-4. *Using a web worker and* `<canvas>` *to invert an image*

Basic Performance Measurements

We've looked at many techniques for improving performance in JavaScript applications in this chapter, but without a means to measure performance, we've only our own senses to rely on to inform us whether performance is improving or not.

   The simplest method for measuring how quickly a section of code is performing is to time it by measuring the difference in the computer clock between when the code execution was started and when it completed, as shown in Listing 4-34.

Listing 4-34. Measuring how long a function took to execute

```
// Define variables to calculate the time taken to execute the function
var startTime,
    endTime,
    duration;

// Function to execute which we wish to measure
function doSomething() {
    var index = 0,
        length = 10000000,
        counter = 0;
```

```
    for (; index < length; index++) {
        counter += index;
    }
}

// Set the initial time to be the current date/time at this exact point, just before execution
// of the function
startTime = new Date();

// Execute the function
doSomething();

// Set the end time to be the current date/time just after execution
endTime = new Date();

// The time taken is the end time minus the first time, with both represented in milliseconds,
// the most precise measurement we have with JavaScript times
duration = endTime.getTime() - startTime.getTime();

alert(duration); // Took ~700 ms on my machine
```

Because JavaScript date objects only represent times down to millisecond level, we're unable to get any more precise measurements using this technique. In Chapter 14, we will see console.time(), a more precise form of JavaScript code measurement using the developer tools built into most browsers.

Summary

In this chapter, we've looked at tips and techniques you can apply to improve the performance of your JavaScript code, from the initial load of the script file through handling DOM elements and events to the best way to work with arrays and strings to boost performance. Finally, we looked at how to offload intensive code tasks to separate operating system threads in order to keep the user interface responsive whilst performing a number of heavy operations in the background, and a simple method for measuring the performance of your JavaScript code. There are potentially thousands more tips that could be written on the subject of JavaScript performance, but implementing those detailed here in this chapter will be all you need to improve the performance of your application in most cases by a noticeable margin.

In the next chapter, we will look at JavaScript design patterns, common ways of solving certain problems with code, and ways to structure your code in order to make them easy to understand for yourself and other developers.

■ ■ ■

## CHAPTER 5

Design Patterns: Creational

In this and the following three chapters, I'm going to explain the priniples of *design patterns* and code architecture pattern for large-scale JavaScript applications that will keep your code sensibly organized and easy to understand, making the job of maintaining and adding to your code a lot simpler. By implementing one or more of the patterns and techniques found in these chapters, you'll find much of your code files look, at a glance, very similar to each other, which breeds instant familiarity for a number of developers working together on the same project. In fact, if you choose to adopt any of these techniques across multiple projects, you'll likely find the same patterns and architecture idioms work across them all, making it easier to get new developers up to speed on different projects and freeing up those developers to concentrate on writing excellent code.

The secret to using design patterns is to consider them like tools in your programming toolbox where each has a specific use. First familiarize yourself with the patterns available and when to use each, and these chapters will help do just that, before you attempt to apply them to your code—applying the wrong tool will cause undue headaches and wasted time. Unless you are a particularly seasoned JavaScript developer, you will start writing the code for your application without a specific design pattern in mind to begin with and, as your code grows, you will find you need to make changes to it in order to make further development more manageable and to give some structure and familiarity to the files in your code base. This process is typically known as *refactoring* and it is often at this stage in development that you will consider applying a particular design or architectural pattern to your code to simplify development going forward. Be wary of anyone who insists starting a new project with a specific pattern in mind or who insists on using a particular prebuilt JavaScript framework at the outset, as, unless they are significantly experienced professionals, this is the equivalent of selecting a new, shiny tool before identifying the problem the tool is needed for.

Each chapter covers design patterns and architectural patterns with which you should familiarize yourself. Study each pattern and understand how it is used, then over time you will start identifying specific patterns in your code that need to be applied to improve the maintainability, and in some cases efficiency, of your code.

What Are Design Patterns?

Design patterns are tried and tested, proven ways of programming and structuring code so that it is easy to understand, easy to maintain, and easy to scale by favoring clarity, removing unnecessary complication for the developer, and by decoupling connections between different parts of a large code base. They are the tools in your programming toolbox.

Design patterns were first introduced in a book titled *Design Patterns: Elements of Reusable Object-Oriented Software*, written by Erich Gamma, Richard Helm, Ralph Johnson, and John Vlissides, collectively known as the *Gang Of Four*, and published in 1994. Their original examples were written in C++ and Smalltalk programming languages, but the principles of most patterns they describe apply to any language, including JavaScript. The authors describe twenty-three different design patterns, split into three distinct categories: *Creational*, *Structural*, and *Behavioral*. In this and the following chapters, we'll cover those that best apply to JavaScript programming, skipping those that aren't relevant, and including some modern patterns missing from the original book that apply equally well to JavaScript. Although many tutorials on design patterns reuse a lot of the same examples over and over again, I have created original examples for each of the patterns featured here that often correlate better to solving real-world coding issues than others that you might find.

Creational Design Patterns

A *creational design pattern* describes a "class" or method that creates objects for you rather than you creating them yourself directly. This layer of abstraction gives you and your code more flexibility in deciding which object or type of object would be most relevant for the specific situation and need you have. Here I will introduce you to five creational patterns that you may find useful in your code, with examples for each.

The Factory Pattern

The *factory* design pattern allows you to create an object without specifying the "class" to use to create it with. When we've covered "classes" in previous chapters, we've used the new JavaScript keyword directly to create an instance of a specific "class" or subclass; with the factory pattern, the object creation process is abstracted, allowing for relatively complex object creation procedures to be masked behind a simple interface that does not require the new keyword. This abstraction means that the underlying "class" types and methods to create them can be completely replaced at any time without changing the interface for "class" creation for other developers—ideal if you know lots of changes may need to be made in future but you don't want to have to rewrite your "class" instantiaton code in a large number of code files.

Listing 5-1 shows an example of the factory pattern for instantiating objects based on a number of different "classes" dependent on the factory method's input parameters.

Listing 5-1. The factory design pattern

```
// Define the factory that will make form field objects for us using the most appropriate
// "class" depending on the inputs
var FormFieldFactory = {

    // The makeField method takes two options:
    // - type, which defines the type of form field object to create, e.g. text, email,
    //    or button
    // - displayText, which defines either the placeholder text for the form field, or the
    //    text to display on the button, depending on the type
    makeField: function(options) {
        var options = options || {},
            type = options.type || "text",
            displayText = options.displayText || "",
            field;

        // Create an object instance using the most appropriate "class" based on the
        // supplied input type
        switch (type) {
        case "text":
            field = new TextField(displayText);
            break;
        case "email":
            field = new EmailField(displayText);
            break;
        case "button":
            field = new ButtonField(displayText);
            break;
```

```
                // If in doubt, use the TextField "class"
                default:
                    field = new TextField(displayText);
                    break;
            }

            return field;
        }
    };

// Define the TextField "class" to be used for creating <input type="text"> form elements
function TextField(displayText) {
    this.displayText = displayText;
}

// The getElement method will create a DOM element using the supplied placeholder text value
TextField.prototype.getElement = function() {
    var textField = document.createElement("input");
    textField.setAttribute("type", "text");
    textField.setAttribute("placeholder", this.displayText);

    return textField;
};

// Define the EmailField "class" to be used for creating <input type="email"> form elements
function EmailField(displayText) {
    this.displayText = displayText;
}

// The getElement method will create a DOM element using the supplied placeholder text value
EmailField.prototype.getElement = function() {
    var emailField = document.createElement("input");
    emailField.setAttribute("type", "email");
    emailField.setAttribute("placeholder", this.displayText);

    return emailField;
};

// Define the ButtonField "class" to be used for creating <button> form elements
function ButtonField(displayText) {
    this.displayText = displayText;
}

// The getElement method will create a DOM element using the supplied button text value
ButtonField.prototype.getElement = function() {
    var button = document.createElement("button");
    button.setAttribute("type", "submit");
    button.innerHTML = this.displayText;

    return button;
};
```

Listing 5-2 demonstrates how the factory created in Listing 5-1 could then be used within an application.

Listing 5-2. The factory design pattern in use

```
// Use the factory to create a text input form field, an email form field, and a submit button.
// Note how we do not need to know about the underlying "classes" or their specific inputs to
// create the form fields - the FormFieldFactory abstracts this away
var textField = FormFieldFactory.makeField({
        type: "text",
        displayText: "Enter the first line of your address"
    }),
    emailField = FormFieldFactory.makeField({
        type: "email",
        displayText: "Enter your email address"
    }),
    buttonField = FormFieldFactory.makeField({
        type: "button",
        displayText: "Submit"
    });

// Wait for the browser's "load" event to fire, then add the DOM elements represented by the
// three newly created objects to the current page
window.addEventListener("load", function() {
    var bodyElement = document.body;

    // Use the getElement() method of each object to get a reference to its DOM element for
    // adding to the page
    bodyElement.appendChild(textField.getElement());
    bodyElement.appendChild(emailField.getElement());
    bodyElement.appendChild(buttonField.getElement());
}, false);
```

The factory pattern is best used when you want to simplify the creation of specific objects throughout the rest of your code by masking a more complex operation to create those objects. To read about the factory pattern in more detail online, take a look at the following resources:

- "JavaScript Design Patterns: Factory" by Joseph Zimmerman on Adobe Developer Connection: (via `http://bit.ly/factory_pattern`)

- "Factory Constructor Pattern" by Ilya Kantor on The JavaScript Tutorial (via `http://bit.ly/factory-pattern`)

The Abstract Factory Pattern

The *abstract factory* pattern takes the factory pattern we just looked at one step further, allowing multiple factories to be created together according to a common use or theme, creating an extra layer of abstraction, if needed by your application. The code in Listing 5-3 demonstrates this pattern, extending the example from Listing 5-1 by treating two factories as instances of a new factory type from which they shame similar behaviors.

Listing 5-3. The abstract factory design pattern

```javascript
// Define a base factory "class" for creating form fields, from which other, more specialised
// form field creation factory "classes" will be inherited.
function FormFieldFactory() {

    // Define a list of supported field types to be applied to all inherited form field
    // factory classes
    this.availableTypes = {
        TEXT: "text",
        EMAIL: "email",
        BUTTON: "button"
    };
}
FormFieldFactory.prototype = {

    // Define a makeField() method which will be overwritten by sub classes using polymorphism.
    // This method should therefore not be called directly from within this parent "class" so
    // we'll throw an error if it is
    makeField: function() {
        throw new Error("This method should not be called directly.");
    }
};

// Define a factory "class", inherited from the base factory, for creating HTML5 form fields.
// Read more about the differences in these form fields from HTML4 at
// http://bit.ly/html5_webforms
function Html5FormFieldFactory() {}
Html5FormFieldFactory.prototype = new FormFieldFactory();

// Override the makeField() method with code specific for this factory
Html5FormFieldFactory.prototype.makeField = function(options) {
    var options = options || {},
        type = options.type || this.availableTypes.TEXT,
        displayText = options.displayText || "",
        field;

    // Select the most appropriate field type based on the provided options
    switch (type) {
    case this.availableTypes.TEXT:
        field = new Html5TextField(displayText);
        break;
    case this.availableTypes.EMAIL:
        field = new Html5EmailField(displayText);
        break;
    case this.availableTypes.BUTTON:
        field = new ButtonField(displayText);
        break;
    default:
        throw new Error("Invalid field type specified: " + type);
    }

    return field;
};
```

```javascript
// Define a factory "class", also inherited from the same base factory, for creating
// older-style HTML4 form fields
function Html4FormFieldFactory() {}
Html4FormFieldFactory.prototype = new FormFieldFactory();

// Override the makeField() method with code specific for this factory
Html4FormFieldFactory.prototype.makeField = function(options) {
    var options = options || {},
        type = options.type || this.availableTypes.TEXT,
        displayText = options.displayText || "",
        field;

    switch (type) {
    case this.availableTypes.TEXT:
    case this.availableTypes.EMAIL:
        field = new Html4TextField(displayText);
        break;
    case this.availableTypes.BUTTON:
        field = new ButtonField(displayText);
        break;
    default:
        throw new Error("Invalid field type specified: " + type);
    }

    return field;
};

// Define the form field "classes" to be used for creating HTML5 and HTML4 form elements
function Html5TextField(displayText) {
    this.displayText = displayText || "";
}
Html5TextField.prototype.getElement = function() {
    var textField = document.createElement("input");
    textField.setAttribute("type", "text");
    textField.setAttribute("placeholder", this.displayText);

    return textField;
};

// Since the placeholder attribute isn't supported in HTML4, we'll instead create and return a
// <div> element containing the text field and an associated <label> containing the
// placeholder text
function Html4TextField(displayText) {
    this.displayText = displayText || "";
}
Html4TextField.prototype.getElement = function() {
    var wrapper = document.createElement("div"),
        textField = document.createElement("input"),
        textFieldId = "text-field-" + Math.floor(Math.random() * 999),
        label = document.createElement("label"),
        labelText = document.createTextNode(this.displayText);
```

```
    textField.setAttribute("type", "text");
    textField.setAttribute("id", textFieldId);

    // Associate the <label> with the <input> using the label 'for' attribute and the input 'id'
    label.setAttribute("for", textFieldId);
    label.appendChild(labelText);

    wrapper.appendChild(textField);
    wrapper.appendChild(label);

    return wrapper;
};

function Html5EmailField(displayText) {
    this.displayText = displayText;
}
Html5EmailField.prototype.getElement = function() {
    var emailField = document.createElement("input");
    emailField.setAttribute("type", "email");
    emailField.setAttribute("placeholder", this.displayText);

    return emailField;
};

// We define the button form element to be identical for both HTML5 and HTML4 form field types,
// so no need for two separate "classes". If we ever needed to create a different HTML5 version
// in future, we'd only need to update the relevant factory "class" with the change, and the
// rest of the code in our full application will adapt accordingly
function ButtonField(displayText) {
    this.displayText = displayText;
}
ButtonField.prototype.getElement = function() {
    var button = document.createElement("button");
    button.setAttribute("type", "submit");
    button.innerHTML = this.displayText;

    return button;
};
```

We can use the abstract factory from Listing 5-3 as shown in Listing 5-4 to produce the correct type of form fields based on the support of the browser the code is being run within.

Listing 5-4. The abstract factory design pattern in use

```
// Establish if the browser supports HTML5, and select the appropriate form field factory
var supportsHtml5FormFields = (function() {

        // This self-executing function attempts to create a HTML5 form field type:
        // <input type="email">
        var field = document.createElement("input");
        field.setAttribute("type", "email");
```

```
        // If the new form field returns the corrent field type then it was created correctly
        // and is a browser that supports HTML5. If not, the browser is HTML4-only
        return field.type === "email";
    }()),

    // Use the value returned previously to select the appropriate field field creation factory
    // "class" and create an instance of it
    formFieldFactory = supportsHtml5FormFields ? new Html5FormFieldFactory() : new
Html4FormFieldFactory(),

    // Use the factory to create a text input form field, an email form field, and a submit
    // button, which will now use the most appropriate field type and attributes for the
    // current browser
    textField = formFieldFactory.makeField({
        type: "text",
        displayText: "Enter the first line of your address"
    }),
    emailField = formFieldFactory.makeField({
        type: "email",
        displayText: "Enter your email address"
    }),

    // Notice how we can harness the availableTypes property containing the list of supported
    // field types from the factory "class" instead of using a hard-coded text string for the
    // form field type. This is preferred, just as variables are preferable over
    // hard-coded values.
    buttonField = formFieldFactory.makeField({
        type: formFieldFactory.availableTypes.BUTTON,
        displayText: "Submit"
    });

// Wait for the browser's "load" event to fire, then add the DOM elements represented by the
// three newly created objects to the current page
window.addEventListener("load", function() {
    var bodyElement = document.body;

    // Use the getElement() method of each object to get a reference to its DOM element for.
    // adding to the page
    bodyElement.appendChild(textField.getElement());
    bodyElement.appendChild(emailField.getElement());
    bodyElement.appendChild(buttonField.getElement());
}, false);
```

The abstract factory pattern is best used when you need to create an extra layer of abstraction away from more than one "class" in your existing code according to a shared purpose or common theme between them, so as to make development in the rest of your application less complex. To read about the abstract factory pattern in more detail online, take a look at the following resources:

- "Abstract Factory Pattern" on Wikipedia (via http://bit.ly/abstract_factory)

- "JavaScript Design Patterns: Factory and Abstract Factory" by Rob Dodson
  (via http://bit.ly/factory_and_abstract)

The Builder Pattern

Like the factory and abstract factory patterns we've seen so far, the *builder* pattern abstracts the creation of objects. In this pattern, we only need supply the content and type of the object we wish to create, with the process of deciding which "class" to use to create it abstracted away by the builder. We effectively construct a complete object by splitting its creation down into a series of smaller steps, finally calling an operation that "builds" the resulting object, returning it to the calling code. A builder can potentially contain a fair amount of code, all with the express intention of making object creation as pain-free as possible for developers.

The builder pattern is demonstrated in Listing 5-5, which defines a builder for creating simple HTML forms containing any number and type of form fields in any order and added at any time; the <form> element is only created and returned at such point as it is needed, using the getForm() "build" method once all of the fields have been added.

Listing 5-5. The builder pattern

```
// Define a builder "class" for constructing simple forms which can be configured according to
// the end developer's needs. The end developer will instantiate the builder and add fields to
// the form as needed throughout the course of their application, finally calling a method to
// return a <form> element containing all the fields added
function FormBuilder() {}
FormBuilder.prototype = {

    // Define a property for storing fields created
    fields: [],

    // Define a method for adding fields to the form instance
    addField: function(type, displayText) {
        var field;

        // Use the supplied form field type and display text to instantiate the relevant form
        // field "class"
        switch (type) {
        case "text":
            field = new TextField(displayText);
            break;
        case "email":
            field = new EmailField(displayText);
            break;
        case "button":
            field = new ButtonField(displayText);
            break;
        default:
            throw new Error("Invalid field type specified: " + type);
        }

        // Add the created field object to the storage array
        this.fields.push(field);
    },

    // Define a method for returning the resulting <form> element, containing the fields added
    // using the addField method
    getForm: function() {
```

```javascript
        // Create a new <form> element
        var form = document.createElement("form"),
            index = 0,
            numFields = this.fields.length,
            field;

        // Loop through each field in the fields property, getting the DOM element from each and
        // adding it to the <form> element
        for (; index < numFields; index++) {
            field = this.fields[index];
            form.appendChild(field.getElement());
        }

        // Return the populated <form> element
        return form;
    }
};

// Define the underlying form field "classes", as in Listing 5-1
function TextField(displayText) {
    this.displayText = displayText || "";
}
TextField.prototype.getElement = function() {
    var textField = document.createElement("input");
    textField.setAttribute("type", "text");
    textField.setAttribute("placeholder", this.displayText);

    return textField;
};

function EmailField(displayText) {
    this.displayText = displayText || "";
}
EmailField.prototype.getElement = function() {
    var emailField = document.createElement("input");
    emailField.setAttribute("type", "email");
    emailField.setAttribute("placeholder", this.displayText);

    return emailField;
};

function ButtonField(displayText) {
    this.displayText = displayText || "";
}
ButtonField.prototype.getElement = function() {
    var button = document.createElement("button");
    button.setAttribute("type", "submit");
    button.innerHTML = this.displayText;

    return button;
};
```

The form builder in Listing 5-5 can then be used in an application as shown in Listing 5-6, in which a number of fields are added to a form without having to directly instantiate any form or field "classes," nor having to manually create any DOM elements. The final object is then "built" using the getForm() method, returning it for use in the calling code.

Listing 5-6. The builder pattern in use

```
// Instantiate the form builder
var formBuilder = new FormBuilder(),
    form;

// Add fields in any order and at any time required in the application - only the type and
// content is required, the actual object creation is abstracted away in the builder
formBuilder.addField("text", "Enter the first line of your address");
formBuilder.addField("email", "Enter your email address");
formBuilder.addField("button", "Submit");

// When the final form is required, call the builder's getForm method to return a <form> element
// containing all the fields
form = formBuilder.getForm();

 window.addEventListener("load", function() {
    document.body.appendChild(form);
}, false);
```

The builder pattern is best used when you need to create a large object in your code through a series of smaller steps, returning the created object at a specific point as required by your application. To read about the builder pattern in more detail online, check out the following resources:

- "Builder Pattern" on Wikipedia (via `http://bit.ly/builder_wiki`)

- "A Builder Pattern Implementation In JavaScript" by Pat Kua (via `http://bit.ly/builder_pattern`)

- "GoF Design Patterns And JavaScript: The Builder Pattern" by Sergey Mozgovoy (via `http://bit.ly/gof_builder`)

The Prototype Pattern

The *prototype* pattern creates new objects by cloning existing objects using prototypal inheritance. This will be familiar to you after reading Chapter 1 as prototypal inheritance is the type of inheritance JavaScript was created around, and can be enforced using either the `prototype` property of an existing object, as we have seen when creating "classes" in JavaScript, or by using ECMAScript 5's `Object.create()` method, which is the preferred method but still requires better web browser support to be used exclusively. Listing 5-7 shows the prototype pattern in action using the first of these techniques, whereas Listing 5-8 demonstrates the pattern using the latter.

Listing 5-7. The prototype pattern using the prototype keyword

```
var textField,
    emailField;

// Define a Field "class" to be used for creating <input> form elements
function Field(type, displayText) {
    this.type = type || "";
    this.displayText = displayText || "";
}

// Use the prototype property to adopt the Prototype pattern of defining methods that will be
// applied to any object instantiated from this "class"
Field.prototype = {
    getElement: function() {
        var field = document.createElement("input");
        field.setAttribute("type", this.type);
        field.setAttribute("placeholder", this.displayText);

        return field;
    }
};

// Create two object instances, both of which receive the getElement method from the prototype
textField = new Field("text", "Enter the first line of your address");
emailField = new Field("email", "Enter your email address");

// Add the elements stored in these objects to the current page once loaded
window.addEventListener("load", function() {
    var bodyElement = document.body;

    bodyElement.appendChild(textField.getElement());
    bodyElement.appendChild(emailField.getElement());
}, false);
```

Listing 5-8. The prototype pattern using ECMAScript 5

```
// Define a base object with two properties, type and displayText, and a getElement() method
// which creates a HTML <input> element, configuring it using the values from the two properties
var field = {
        type: "",
        displayText: "",

        getElement: function() {
            var field = document.createElement("input");
            field.setAttribute("type", this.type);
            field.setAttribute("placeholder", this.displayText);

            return field;
        }
    },
```

```javascript
    // Create a new object based upon the base object, using ECMAScript 5's Object.create()
    // method to clone the original object and apply values to the two properties type and
    // displayText, in order to create an object capable of creating a <input type="text">
    // element when the object's getElement() method is called
    textField = Object.create(field, {

        // The second parameter of Object.create() allows values from the first parameter to be
        // overwritten using the format described in Chapter 1
        'type': {
            value: "text",
            enumerable: true
        },
        'displayText':{
            value: 'Enter the first line of your address',
            enumerable: true
        }
    }),

    // Create another new object based upon the base object, using different property values in
    // order to allow the creation of a <input type="email"> element when the object's
    // getElement() method is called
    emailField = Object.create(field, {
        'type': {
            value: "email",
            enumerable: true
        },
        'displayText':{
            value: 'Enter your email address',
            enumerable: true
        }
    });

// Call the getElement() method of both objects, appending the created <input> DOM elements to
// the current page once loaded
window.addEventListener("load", function() {
    var bodyElement = document.body;

    bodyElement.appendChild(textField.getElement());
    bodyElement.appendChild(emailField.getElement());
}, false);
```

The prototype pattern is best used when you want to create new objects on the fly as clones of existing objects, alternatively to create objects based on "class" templates. To read about the prototype pattern in more detail online, take a look at the following resources:

- "Using The JavaScript Prototype Pattern" by Dan Wahlin on Pluralsight (via http://bit.ly/prototype_pattern)

- "JavaScript Object Creation: Learning To Live Without new" by Keith Peters on Adobe Developer Connection (via http://bit.ly/object_creation)

The Singleton Pattern

The *singleton* pattern, when applied to JavaScript, defines the creation of an object that has only a single instance. In its simplest form, a singleton could therefore be a simple object literal encapsulating specific, related behaviors, as shown in Listing 5-9.

Listing 5-9. The singleton pattern

```
// Group related properties and methods together into a single object literal, which
// we call a Singleton
var element = {

        // Create an array for storage of page element references
        allElements: [],

        // Get an element reference by its ID and store it
        get: function(id) {
            var elem = document.getElementById(id);
            this.allElements.push(elem);
            return elem;
        },

        // Create a new element of a given type, and store it
        create: function(type) {
            var elem = document.createElement(type);
            this.allElements.push(elem);
            return elem;
        },

        // Return all stored elements
        getAllElements: function() {
            return this.allElements;
        }
    },

    // Get and store a reference to a page element with ID of "header"
    header = element.get("header"),

    // Create a new <input> element
    input = element.create("input"),

    // Contains id="header", and new <input> elements
    allElements = element.getAllElements();

// Check to see how many elements are stored
alert(allElements.length); // 2
```

There are cases, however, in which you may wish to execute some initialization code as part of the creation of a singleton. For these, use a self-executing function, as shown in Listing 5-10, and use the return keyword to surface the object structure that you wish to make available to the rest of your code. I'll look further at the use of self-executing functions in this way when I cover the *module* pattern in the next chapter.

Listing 5-10. The singleton pattern with a self-executing function

```
// Define a singleton containing cookie-related methods. Initialization code is achieved by
// using a self-executing function closure, which allows code to be executed at creation which
// is then unavailable publicly to the rest of the application
var cookie = (function() {

    // Cookies are stored in the document.cookie string, separated by semi-colons (;)
    var allCookies = document.cookie.split(";"),
        cookies = {},
        cookiesIndex = 0,
        cookiesLength = allCookies.length,
        cookie;

    // Loop through all cookies, adding them to the "cookies" object, using the cookie names
    // as the property names
    for (; cookiesIndex < cookiesLength; cookiesIndex++) {
        cookie = allCookies[cookiesIndex].split("=");

        cookies[unescape(cookie[0])] = unescape(cookie[1]);
    }

    // Returning methods here will make them available to the global "cookie" variable defined
    // at the top of this code listing
    return {

        // Create a function to get a cookie value by name
        get: function(name) {
            return cookies[name] || "";
        },

        // Create a function to add a new session cookie
        set: function(name, value) {

            // Add the new cookie to the "cookies" object as well as the document.cookie string
            cookies[name] = value;
            document.cookie = escape(name) + "=" + escape(value);
        }
    };
}());

// Set a cookie using the "set" method exposed through the "cookie" singleton
cookie.set("userID", "1234567890");

// Check that the cookie was set correctly
alert(cookie.get("userID")); // 1234567890
```

Many developers use the singleton patten like this to encapsulate and group together related code into a hierarchical structure, known as *namespacing*, which is popular in other programming languages such as Java. By keeping everything together within a single global variable like this, you reduce the risk of conflicting with any third-party code used within your application. Take a look at Listing 5-11, which shows a basic namespaced structure for keeping relating code together in named sections to reduce developer confusion and to simplify maintenance and development, making code easier to read and understand.

Listing 5-11. Namespacing using the singleton pattern

```javascript
// Use an object literal to create a hierarchy of grouped properties and methods,
// known as a "namespace"
var myProject = {
    data: {

        // Each nested property represents a new, deeper level in the namespace hierarchy
        ajax: {

            // Create a method to send an Ajax GET request
            get: function(url, callback) {
                var xhr = new XMLHttpRequest(),
                    STATE_LOADED = 4,
                    STATUS_OK = 200;

                xhr.onreadystatechange = function() {
                    if (xhr.readyState !== STATE_LOADED) {
                        return;
                    }

                    if (xhr.status === STATUS_OK) {
                        callback(xhr.responseText);
                    }
                };

                xhr.open("GET", url);
                xhr.send();
            }
        }
    }
};

// Add to the namespace after creation using dot notation
myProject.data.cookies = {

    // Create a method for reading a cookie value by name
    get: function(name) {
        var output = "",
            escapedName = escape(name),
            start = document.cookie.indexOf(escapedName + "="),
            end = document.cookie.indexOf(";", start);

        end = end === -1 ? (document.cookie.length - 1) : end;

        if (start > = 0) {
            output = document.cookie.substring(start + escapedName.length + 1, end);
        }

        return unescape(output);
    },
```

```
        // Create a method for setting a cookie name/value pair
        set: function(name, value) {
            document.cookie = escape(name) + "=" + escape(value);
        }
    };

// Execute methods directly through the "namespace" hierarchy using dot notation
myProject.data.ajax.get("/", function(response) {
    alert("Received the following response: " + response);
});

// Note how using the hierarchy adds clarity to the final method call
myProject.data.cookies.set("userID", "1234567890");
myProject.data.cookies.set("name", "Den Odell");

// Read back the cookie valus set previously
alert(myProject.data.cookies.get("userID")); // 1234567890
alert(myProject.data.cookies.get("name")); // Den Odell
```

The singleton pattern is best used when you need to create a single instance of an object for use throughout your code, or to *namespace* your code, dividing it into named sections with a hierarchy defined under a single global object. To read about the singleton pattern in more detail online, check out the following resources:

- "JavaScript Design Patterns: Singleton" by Joseph Zimmerman on Adobe Developer Connection (via `http://bit.ly/singleton_pattern`)

- "Essential JavaScript Namespacing Patterns" by Addy Osmani (via `http://bit.ly/namespacing`)

Summary

In this chapter, I have introduced the concept of design patterns and shown how to use creational design patterns to abstract away object creation within your own JavaScript applications. Design patterns are tools in your Swiss Army knife of JavaScript development but, like all tools, you need to know when and where to use them best. Familiarize yourself with the patterns in this chapter, and ensure that you don't use a design pattern before you recognize the need for it in your code.

In the following chapter, I will continue to look at design patterns with a focus on structural design patterns that you can use in your JavaScript code to combine objects together into a larger, more structured form.

CHAPTER 6

■ ■ ■

Design Patterns: Structural

In this chapter, we will continue our look at design pattern, focusing on *structural design patterns*. Where the creational design patterns we looked at in the previous chapter center on object creation, structural design patterns help you combine objects together into a larger, more structured code base. They are flexible, maintainable, extensible, and ensure that if one part of your system changes, you do not need to completely rewrite the rest to suit. Structural design patterns can also be used to help interface with other code structures that you need to work together easily with in your application. Let's look together at eight structural design patterns you may find useful in your code, together with examples.

The Adapter Pattern

The *adapter* pattern is a useful design pattern that can be used when you need to connect together two or more code components that otherwise wouldn't normally connect together; similarly, it comes in useful when an API you have developed is updated such that it is no longer called in the same way—an adapter is provided that interfaces between the old and new versions, helping migration for users of your API who can take advantage of other improvements in your code without breaking theirs. The example shown in Listing 6-1 shows how to use this pattern to create an adapter for your code to map a new API interface to an older one.

Listing 6-1. The adapter pattern

```
// Imagine the following interface exists deep in your large code base for making Ajax requests
// over HTTP
var http = {
    makeRequest: function(type, url, callback, data) {
        var xhr = new XMLHttpRequest(),
            STATE_LOADED = 4,
            STATUS_OK = 200;

        xhr.onreadystatechange = function() {
            if (xhr.readyState !== STATE_LOADED) {
                return;
            }

            if (xhr.status === STATUS_OK) {
                callback(xhr.responseText);
            }
        };
```

```javascript
            xhr.open(type.toUpperCase(), url);
            xhr.send(data);
    }
};

// The http.makeRequest() method defined above could be called as follows, for getting and
// updating user data in a system for a user with an ID of "12345":
http.makeRequest("get", "/user/12345", function(response) {
    alert("HTTP GET response received. User data: " + response);
});

http.makeRequest("post", "/user/12345", function(response) {
    alert("HTTP POST response received. New user data: " + response);
}, "company=AKQA&name=Den%20Odell");

// Now imagine in a refactor of your project, you decide to introduce a new structure using a
// namespace and splitting out the makeRequest() method into separate methods for HTTP GET
// and POST requests
var myProject = {
    data: {
        ajax: (function() {
            function createRequestObj(callback) {
                var xhr = new XMLHttpRequest(),
                    STATE_LOADED = 4,
                    STATUS_OK = 200;

                xhr.onreadystatechange = function() {
                    if (xhr.readyState !== STATE_LOADED) {
                        return;
                    }

                    if (xhr.status === STATUS_OK) {
                        callback(xhr.responseText);
                    }
                };

                return xhr;
            }

            return {
                get: function(url, callback) {
                    var requestObj = createRequestObj(callback);

                    requestObj.open("GET", url);
                    requestObj.send();
                },

                post: function(url, data, callback) {
                    var requestObj = createRequestObj(callback);
```

```
                    requestObj.open("POST", url);
                    requestObj.send(data);
                }
            };
        }())
    }
};

// These new get() and post() methods could be called as follows:
myProject.data.ajax.get("/user/12345", function(response) {
    alert("Refactored HTTP GET response received. User data: " + response);
});

myProject.data.ajax.post("/user/12345", "company=AKQA&name=Den%20dell", function(response) {
    alert("Refactored HTTP POST response received. New user data: " + response);
});

// To avoid rewriting every call to the http.makeRequest() method in the rest of your code
// base, you could create an adapter to map the old interface to the new methods. The adapter
// needs to take the same input parameters as the original method it is designed to replace,
// and calls the new methods internally instead
function httpToAjaxAdapter(type, url, callback, data) {
    if (type.toLowerCase() === "get") {
        myProject.data.ajax.get(url, callback);
    } else if (type.toLowerCase() === "post") {
        myProject.data.ajax.post(url, data, callback);
    }
}

// Finaly, apply the adapter to replace the original method. It will then map the old
// interface to the new one without needing to rewrite the rest of your code at the same time
http.makeRequest = httpToAjaxAdapter;

// Use the new adapter in the same way as the original method - internally it will call the
// newer code, but externally it will appear identical to the old makeRequest() method
http.makeRequest("get", "/user/12345", function(response) {
    alert("Adapter HTTP GET response received. User data: " + response);
});

http.makeRequest("post", "/user/12345", function(response) {
    alert("Adapter HTTP POST response received. New user data: " + response);
}, "company=AKQA&name=Den%20dell");
```

The adapter pattern is best used when you need to connect together code that wouldn't otherwise go together, for example, when an external API has been updated—you create an adapter to map the new methods to the old methods to avoid needing to make changes to the rest of your code that relies on these methods.

To read more about the adapter pattern online, look at the following resources:

- "JavaScript Design Patterns: Adapter" by Joseph Zimmerman on Adobe Developer Connection (via http://bit.ly/adapter_pattern)

- "Adapter Design Pattern" on Wikipedia (via http://bit.ly/adapter_wiki)

The Composite Pattern

The *composite* pattern creates an interface for one or more objects without the end user needing to know how many objects they are dealing with. It comes in useful when you want to simplify the way others access your functions; there need be no difference whether they pass a single object or an array of objects to the same method. Listing 6-2 shows a simple example of the composite pattern, allowing the user to add class names to one or more DOM nodes without needing to know whether they need to pass a single or multiple DOM nodes to the method.

Listing 6-2. The composite pattern

```javascript
// Define a singleton containing methods to get references to page elements and to add
// class names to those elements
var elements = {

    // Define a method to get DOM elements by tag name. If one element is found, it is
    // returned as an individual node, or multiple elements are found, an array of those
    // found elements are returned
    get: function(tag) {
        var elems = document.getElementsByTagName(tag),
            elemsIndex = 0,
            elemsLength = elems.length,
            output = [];

        // Convert the found elements structure into a standard array
        for (; elemsIndex < elemsLength; elemsIndex++) {
            output.push(elems[elemsIndex]);
        }

        // If one element is found, return that single element, otherwise return the array
        // of found elements
        return output.length === 1 ? output[0] : output;
    },

    // Define a composite method which adds an class name to one or more elements, regardless
    // of how many are passed when it is executed
    addClass: function(elems, newClassName) {
        var elemIndex = 0,
            elemLength = elems.length,
            elem;

        // Determine if the elements passed in are an array or a single object
        if (Object.prototype.toString.call(elems) === "[object Array]") {

            // If they are an array, loop through each elements and add the class name to each
            for (; elemIndex < elemLength; elemIndex++) {
                elem = elems[elemIndex];
                elem.className += (elem.className === "" ? "" : " ") + newClassName;
            }
        } else {
```

```
            // If a single element was passed in, add the class name value to it
            elems.className += (elems.className === "" ? "" : " ") + newClassName;
        }
    }
};

// Use the elements.get() method to locate the single <body> element on the current page, and
// potentially numerous <a> elements
var body = elements.get("body"),
    links = elements.get("a");

// The composite elements.addClass() method gives the same interface to single elements
// as it does to multiple elements, simplifying its use considerably
elements.addClass(body, "has-js");
elements.addClass(links, "custom-link");
```

The composite pattern is best used when you do not want the developer interacting with your methods to have to worry how many objects they pass as parameters to them, thus simplifying method calls.

To read more about the composite pattern online, check out the following resources:

- "JavaScript Design Patterns: Composite" by Joseph Zimmerman on Adobe Developer Connection (via http://bit.ly/composite_pattern)

- "Composite Pattern" on Wikipedia (via http://bit.ly/composite_wiki)

The Decorator Pattern

The *decorator* pattern acts as a way to extend and customize methods and properties of an object created from a "class" without the need for creating large numbers of subclasses that could become unmanageable. This is achieved by effectively wrapping the object in another that implements the same public methods with the relevant methods overridden according to the behavior that we are trying to augment. The code in Listing 6-3 shows an example that creates several decorators, which each augment an existing object with extra properties and behaviors.

Listing 6-3. The decorator pattern

```
var FormField = function(type, displayText){
    this.type = type || "text";
    this.displayText = displayText || "";
};

FormField.prototype = {
    createElement: function() {
        this.element = document.createElement("input");
        this.element.setAttribute("type", this.type);
        this.element.setAttribute("placeholder", this.displayText);
        return this.element;
    },

    isValid: function() {
        return this.element.value !== "";
    }
};
```

```
// The form field deocorator, which implements the same public methods as FormField
var FormFieldDecorator = function(formField) {
    this.formField = formField;
};

FormFieldDecorator.prototype = {
    createElement: function() {
        this.formField.createElement();
    },

    isValid: function() {
        return this.formField.isValid();
    }
};

var MaxLengthFieldDecorator = function(formField, maxLength) {
    FormFieldDecorator.call(this, formField);
    this.maxLength = maxLength || 100;
};
MaxLengthFieldDecorator.prototype = new FormFieldDecorator();
MaxLengthFieldDecorator.prototype.createElement = function() {
    var element = this.formField.createElement();
    element.setAttribute("maxlength", this.maxLength);
    return element;
};

var AutoCompleteFieldDecorator = function(formField, autocomplete) {
    FormFieldDecorator.call(this, formField);
    this.autocomplete = autocomplete || "on";
};
AutoCompleteFieldDecorator.prototype = new FormFieldDecorator();
AutoCompleteFieldDecorator.prototype.createElement = function() {
    var element = this.formField.createElement();
    element.setAttribute("autocomplete", this.autocomplete);
    return element;
};
```

The decorators created in Listing 6-3 can then be used as shown in Listing 6-4 to generate an object representing a form field in a form, augmenting its properties and behavior using these decorators rather than through subclasses.

Listing 6-4. The decorator pattern in use

```
// Create an empty <form> tag and a new FormField object to represent
// a <input type="search"> field
var form = document.createElement("form"),
    formField = new FormField("search", "Enter your search term");

// Extend the formField object using our decorators to add maxlength and autocomplete properties
// to the resulting form field element. Note how we pass the extended formField object into each
// decorator in turn, which extends it further.
formField = new MaxLengthFieldDecorator(formField, 255);
formField = new AutoCompleteFieldDecorator(formField, "off");
```

```
// Create the HTML form field element and add it to the <form> element
form.appendChild(formField.createElement());

// Add an event handler to the <form> tag's submit event, preventing the form from submitting if
// the form field we added contains no value
form.addEventListener("submit", function(e) {

    // Stop the form from submitting
    e.preventDefault();

    // Test to see if our form field is valid, i.e. that it contains a value
    if (formField.isValid()) {

        // If it does, go ahead and submit the form
        form.submit();
    } else {

        // If it doesn't, alert the user that something is wrong and they need to correct it
        alert("Please correct the issues in the form field.");
    }
}, false);

// Add the <form> field to the current page once it has loaded
window.addEventListener("load", function() {
    document.body.appendChild(form);
}, false);
```

The decorator pattern is best used when you need to quickly and simply augment the behavior of object instances created from a "class" without having to resort to creating a long series of inherited subclasses from it. To read more about the decorator pattern online, check out the following resources:

- "Exploring The Decorator Pattern In JavaScript" by Addy Osmani (via http://bit.ly/decorator_pattern)

- "Decorator Pattern In JavaScript" by Stoyan Stefanov on Dr. Dobbs (via http://bit.ly/decorator_js)

The Façade Pattern

The *façade* pattern is very common; it is simply the act of writing a single function to simplify access to a larger and potentially more complex function or functions. It could be argued that any function that simply calls another function is an example of this pattern, but I find it best to think of it in terms of simplifying something that would otherwise take multiple steps, or to provide a single point of access to a much larger system that would make access to that system a lot easier for other developers. The code in Listing 6-5 demonstrates a simple façade that provides a wrapper to simplify cross-browser Ajax calls.

Listing 6-5. The façade pattern

```javascript
// Define a function which acts as a façade to simplify and facilitate cross-browser Ajax calls,
// supporting browsers all the way back to Internet Explorer 5
function ajaxCall(type, url, callback, data) {

    // Get a reference to an Ajax connection object relevant to the current browser
    var xhr = (function() {
            try {

                // The standard method, used in all modern browsers
                return new XMLHttpRequest();
            }
            catch(e) {}

            // Older versions of Internet Explorer utilise an ActiveX object installed on the
            // user's machine
            try {
                return new ActiveXObject("Msxml2.XMLHTTP.6.0");
            }
            catch(e) {}

            try {
                return new ActiveXObject("Msxml2.XMLHTTP.3.0");
            }
            catch(e) {}

            try {
                return new ActiveXObject("Microsoft.XMLHTTP");
            }
            catch(e) {}

            // If no relevant Ajax connection object can be found, throw an error
            throw new Error("Ajax not supported in this browser.");
        }()),
        STATE_LOADED = 4,
        STATUS_OK = 200;

    // Execute the given callback method once a succesful response is received from the server
    xhr.onreadystatechange = function() {
        if (xhr.readyState !== STATE_LOADED) {
            return;
        }

        if (xhr.status === STATUS_OK) {
            callback(xhr.responseText);
        }
    };

    // Use the browser's Ajax connection object to make the relevant call to the given URL
    xhr.open(type.toUpperCase(), url);
    xhr.send(data);
}
```

The façade pattern from Listing 6-5 can then be used in your code as shown in Listing 6-6, disguising the complexity behind the cross-browser Ajax operation.

Listing 6-6. The façade pattern in use

```
// The ajaxCall() facade function can make cross-browser Ajax calls as follows
ajaxCall("get", "/user/12345", function(response) {
    alert("HTTP GET response received. User data: " + response);
});

ajaxCall("post", "/user/12345", function(response) {
    alert("HTTP POST response received. New user data: " + response);
}, "company=AKQA&name=Den%20Odell");
```

The façade pattern is best used when you wish to provide access to a series of function or method calls through a single function or method in order to simplify the rest of your code base, making it easier to follow and therefore more maintainable and scalable for the future. To read more about the façade pattern online, look at the following resources:

- "JavaScript Design Patterns: Façade" by Joseph Zimmerman on Adobe Developer Connection (via `http://bit.ly/facade_pattern`)

- "The Façade Pattern" by Carl Danley (via `http://bit.ly/facade_js`)

The Flyweight Pattern

The *flyweight* pattern is an optimization pattern; it is useful for code that creates a large number of similar objects that would otherwise consume a large amount of memory. It replaces this multitude of similar objects with a few shared objects making the code lighter and more performant; hence the name, which heralds from the boxing world where it refers to those competitors of the lightest weight class, those who are most nimble. Listing 6-7 shows an example of a problem that the flyweight pattern is designed to address, the inefficient storage of objects.

Listing 6-7. Inefficient object instances

```
// Create a "class" to store data to related to employees working for one or more different
// companies
function Employee(data) {

    // Represent an employee's ID within an organisation
    this.employeeId = data.employeeId || 0;

    // Represent an employee's social security number
    this.ssId = data.ssId || "0000-000-0000";

    // Represent an employee's name
    this.name = data.name || "";

    // Represent an employee's occupation
    this.occupation = data.occupation || "";
```

```javascript
    // Represent an employee's company name, address and country
    this.companyName = data.companyName || "";
    this.companyAddress = data.companyAddress || "";
    this.companyCountry = data.companyCountry || "";
}

// Create three methods to get the employee's name, occupation and company details from the
// stored object
Employee.prototype.getName = function() {
    return this.name;
};

Employee.prototype.getOccupation = function() {
    return this.occupation;
};

Employee.prototype.getCompany = function() {
    return [this.companyName, this.companyAddress, this.companyCountry].join(", ");
};

// Create four employee objects - note that two share the same company information, and two
// share the same ssId and name. As more objects are created, the amount of data repeated will
// grow, consuming more memory due to inefficiency
var denOdell = new Employee({
        employeeId: 1456,
        ssId: "1234-567-8901",
        name: "Den Odell",
        occupation: "Head of Web Development",
        companyName: "AKQA",
        companyAddress: "1 St. John's Lane, London",
        companyCountry: "GB"
    }),
    steveBallmer = new Employee({
        employeeId: 3,
        ssId: "8376-940-1673",
        name: "Steve Ballmer",
        occupation: "Ex-CEO",
        companyName: "Microsoft",
        companyAddress: "1 Microsoft Way, Redmond, WA",
        companyCountry: "US"
    }),
    billGates = new Employee({
        employeeId: 1,
        ssId: "7754-342-7584",
        name: "Bill Gates",
        occupation: "Founder",
        companyName: "Microsoft",
        companyAddress: "1 Microsoft Way, Redmond, WA",
        companyCountry: "US"
    }),
```

```
billGatesPhilanthropist = new Employee({
    employeeId: 2,
    ssId: "7754-342-7584",
    name: "Bill Gates",
    occupation: "Philanthropist",
    companyName: "Gates Foundation",
    companyAddress: "500 Fifth Avenue North, Seattle, WA",
    companyCountry: "US"
});
```

The flyweight pattern is applied by attempting to deconstruct an existing "class" such that any data that might be repeated between object instances is minimized. This is achieved by studying any current object instances for repetitive data and creating separate "classes" to represent that data. A single object instance can then represent the repeated data, which can be refered to from multiple object instances of the original "class," resulting in less data being stored and thus reducing the memory footprint of the application.

Any data core to each current object instance is known as the *intrinsic* data of that "class," and any data that can be extracted, stored separately, and refered to from the object instead is known as its *extrinsic* data. In Listing 6-7, the intrinsic data pertaining to an employee—essentially that which is unique—are its employeeId and its occupation values. The company data, which is currently duplicated on multiple Employee objects, can be extracted and stored separately; so can each individual person's data such as their name and ssId values. An employee can therefore be represented with four properties: employeeId, occupation, company, person. The last two properties reference other object instances.

The flyweight pattern is applied in three stages, as shown in Listing 6-8: first, by creating new "classes" to represent extrinsic data; second, by applying the factory pattern to ensure that objects previously created are not recreated; and, finally, by writing code to enable the creation of objects in the same way as originally, allowing all of the flyweight's heavy lifting to occur behind the scenes.

Listing 6-8. The flyweight pattern

```
// The first stage of applying the flyweight pattern is to extract intrinsic data from
// extrinsic data in the objects we wish to make more memory-efficient
//
// There are two sets of extrinsic data in an Employee object from Listing 6-7 - people data
// and company data. Let's create two "classes" to represent those types of data
//
// A Person object represents an individual's social security number and their name
function Person(data) {
    this.ssId = data.ssId || "";
    this.name = data.name || "";
}


// A Company object represents a company's name, address and country details
function Company(data) {
    this.name = data.name || "";
    this.address = data.address || "";
    this.country = data.country || "";
}
```

```javascript
// The second stage of the flyweight pattern is to ensure any objects representing unique
// extrinsic data are only created once and stored for use in future. This is achieved by
// harnessing the factory pattern for each of the new extrinsic data "classes" to abstract
// away the creation of the object instance so that if a previously-existing object is found,
// that can be returned instead of creating a new instance
var personFactory = (function() {

        // Create a variable to store all instances of the People "class" by their ssId
        var people = {},
            personCount = 0;

        return {

            // Provide a method to create an instance of the People "class" if one does not
            // already exist by the given ssId provided in the data input. If one exists,
            // return that object rather than creating a new one
            createPerson: function(data) {
                var person = people[data.ssId],
                    newPerson;

                    // If the person by the given ssId exists in our local data store, return their
                    // object instance, otherwise create a new one using the provided data
                    if (person) {
                        return person;
                    } else {
                        newPerson = new Person(data);
                        people[newPerson.ssId] = newPerson;
                        personCount++;

                        return newPerson;
                    }
            },

            // Provide a method to let us know how many Person objects have been created
            getPersonCount: function() {
                return personCount;
            }
        };
}()),

    // Create a similar factory for Company objects, storing company data by name
    companyFactory = (function() {
        var companies = {},
            companyCount = 0;

        return {
            createCompany: function(data) {
                var company = companies[data.name],
                    newCompany;
```

```
        if (company) {
            return company;
        } else {
            newCompany = new Company(data);
            companies[newCompany.name] = newCompany;
            companyCount++;

            return newCompany;
        }
    },

    getCompanyCount: function() {
        return companyCount;
    }
};
}()),
```

```
// The third stage of the flyweight pattern is to allow the creation of objects in a
// simliar way to that in Listing 6-7, providing all the handling of data storage in the
// most efficient way in a transparent way to the end user
//
// Create an object with methods to store employee data and to return data from each
// object by their employeeId. This simplifies the end user's code as they do not need to
// access methods on underlying objects directly, they only need interface with this handler
employee = (function() {

    // Create a data store for all employee objects created
    var employees = {},
        employeeCount = 0;

    return {

        // Provide a method to add employees to the data store, passing the provided data
        // to the Person and Company factories and storing the resulting object, consisting
        // of the enployeeId, occupation, person object reference, and company object
        // reference in the local data store
        add: function(data) {

            // Create or locate Person or Company objects that correspond to the provided
            // data, as appropriate
            var person = personFactory.createPerson({
                    ssId: data.ssId,
                    name: data.name
                }),
                company = companyFactory.createCompany({
                    name: data.companyName,
                    address: data.companyAddress,
                    country: data.companyCountry
                });
```

```
            // Store a new object in the local data store, containing the employeeId,
            // their occupation, and references to the company they work for and their
            // unique personal data, including their name and social security number
            employees[data.employeeId] = {
                employeeId: data.employeeId,
                occupation: data.occupation,
                person: person,
                company: company
            };

            employeeCount++;
        },

        // Provide a method to return the name of an employee by their employeeId - the
        // data is looked up from the associated Person object
        getName: function(employeeId) {
            return employees[employeeId].person.name;
        },

        // Provide a method to return the occupation of an employee by their employeeId
        getOccupation: function(employeeId) {
            return employees[employeeId].occupation;
        },

        // Provide a method to return the address of the company an employee works for -
        // the data is looked up from the associated Company object
        getCountry: function(employeeId) {
            var company = employees[employeeId].company;
            return [company.name, company.address, company.country].join(", ");
        },

        // Provide a utlility method to tell us how many employees have been created
        getTotalCount: function() {
            return employeeCount;
        }
    };
}());
```

The flyweight code from Listing 6-8 can then be used as shown in Listing 6-9, which replicates the behavior of Listing 6-7. The more repeated data in the original memory-consuming objects the flyweight pattern is applied to, the more objects will become shared, therefore reducing the memory footprint of the application, proving the usefulness of this design pattern.

Listing 6-9. The flyweight pattern in use

```
// Create four employee objects - note that two share the same company information, and two
// share the same ssId and name. Behind the scenes, the flyweight pattern from Listing 6-8
// ensures that repeated person and company data is stored in the most efficient way possible.
```

```
var denOdell = employee.add({
        employeeId: 1456,
        ssId: "1234-567-8901",
        name: "Den Odell",
        occupation: "Head of Web Development",
        companyName: "AKQA",
        companyAddress: "1 St. John's Lane, London",
        companyCountry: "GB"
    }),
    steveBallmer = employee.add({
        employeeId: 3,
        ssId: "8376-940-1673",
        name: "Steve Ballmer",
        occupation: "Ex-CEO",
        companyName: "Microsoft",
        companyAddress: "1 Microsoft Way, Redmond, WA",
        companyCountry: "US"
    }),
    billGates = employee.add({
        employeeId: 1,
        ssId: "7754-342-7584",
        name: "Bill Gates",
        occupation: "Founder",
        companyName: "Microsoft",
        companyAddress: "1 Microsoft Way, Redmond, WA",
        companyCountry: "US"
    }),
    billGatesPhilanthropist = employee.add({
        employeeId: 2,
        ssId: "7754-342-7584",
        name: "Bill Gates",
        occupation: "Philanthropist",
        companyName: "Gates Foundation",
        companyAddress: "500 Fifth Avenue North, Seattle, WA",
        companyCountry: "US"
    });

// We've created three objects representing people by ssId and name - Den Odell, Steve Ballmer
// and Bill Gates
alert(personFactory.getPersonCount()); // 3

// We've created three objects representing companies by name, address and country - AKQA,
// Microsoft and the Gates Foundation
alert(companyFactory.getCompanyCount()); // 3

// We've created four objects representing employees, with two unique properties and two
// properties linking to existing person and company objects. The more employee objects we
// create with shared person and company data, the less data we're storing in our application
// and the more effective the flyweight pattern becomes
alert(employee.getTotalCount()); // 4
```

The flyweight pattern is best used when you have a large number of objects with similar shared property name-value pairs that could be separated into smaller objects with data shared by reference between them in order to make the memory footprint of your code lighter and your code more efficient. To read more about the flyweight pattern online, check out the following resources:

- "Managing Application Resources With The Flyweight Pattern" by Addy Osmani on MSDN Magazine (via http://bit.ly/flyweight_pattern)

- "Flyweight Pattern" by Gurpreet Singh (via http://bit.ly/flyweight_js)

The Mixin Pattern

The *mixin* pattern avoids the need for extensive subclassing and inheritance chains by quickly and easily applying a set of methods and properties from one object directly to another, or directly to the prototype of a "class" such that all object instances have access to those properties and methods. Although that may sound like a "hack," particularly for those developers approaching JavaScript from a traditional object-oriented background, this pattern plays directly to the strengths of the JavaScript language and its use of prototypes rather than the strict classical inheritance applied by other languages and, provided that it is used carefully, can simplify development and code maintenance. The code in Listing 6-10 shows how to use the mixin pattern to simply and quickly apply a set of common methods to a number of objects.

Listing 6-10. The mixin pattern

```
// Define a mixin which enables debug logging, to be applied to any object or "class"
var loggingMixin = {

        // Define a storage array for logs
        logs: [],

        // Define a method to store a message in the log
        log: function(message) {
            this.logs.push(message);
        },

        // Define a method to read out the stored logs
        readLog: function() {
            return this.logs.join("\n");
        }
    },
    element,
    header,
    textField,
    emailField;

// Function to apply methods and properties from one object to another, which we'll use to apply
// the mixin to other objects
function extendObj(obj1, obj2) {
    var obj2Key;
```

```
        for (obj2Key in obj2) {
            if (obj2.hasOwnProperty(obj2Key)) {
                obj1[obj2Key] = obj2[obj2Key];
            }
        }

        return obj1;
}

// Define a singleton to which we will apply the mixin, though will function fine without it
element = {
    allElements: [],

    create: function(type) {
        var elem = document.createElement(type);
        this.allElements.push(elem);

        // Use the mixin method log(), ensuring it exists first before calling it. If the mixin
        // is not applied, then the method will still function fine
        if (typeof this.log === "function") {
            this.log("Created an element of type: " + type);
        }

        return elem;
    },

    getAllElements: function() {
        return this.allElements;
    }
};

// Define a simple "class" to which we will apply the mixin
function Field(type, displayText) {
    this.type = type || "";
    this.displayText = displayText || "";

    // Ensure the mixin method log() exists before executing
    if (typeof this.log === "function") {
        this.log("Created an instance of Field");
    }
}

Field.prototype = {
    getElement: function() {
        var field = document.createElement("input");
        field.setAttribute("type", this.type);
        field.setAttribute("placeholder", this.displayText);
```

```
        if (typeof this.log === "function") {
            this.log("Created a DOM element with placeholder text: " + this.displayText);
        }

        return field;
    }
};

// Apply the mixin directly to the 'element' object by essentially copying over methods and
// properties from the mixin to the singleton
element = extendObj(element, loggingMixin);

// Apply the mixin to the Field "class" prototype, making its methods available to each object
// instance created from it
Field.prototype = extendObj(Field.prototype, loggingMixin);

// Create a new DOM element using the element.create() method
header = element.create("header");

// Create two object instances, both of which receive the getElement method from the prototype
textField = new Field("text", "Enter the first line of your address");
emailField = new Field("email", "Enter your email address");

// Add the elements stored in these objects to the current page
document.body.appendChild(textField.getElement());
document.body.appendChild(emailField.getElement());

// Output the logs stored via the mixin
alert(loggingMixin.readLog());

// Outputs the following - note how all the logs from each usage of the mixin are
// stored together:
/*
Created an element of type: header
Created an instance of Field
Created an instance of Field
Created a DOM element with placeholder text: Enter the first line of your address
Created a DOM element with placeholder text: Enter your email address
*/
```

If you study the code in Listing 6-10, you may notice something unexpected: despite applying the mixin independently to the singleton and the "class," all of the logged data is stored together. Calling the readLog() method on any object containing that method will output the same result. This happens because when the extendObj() function copies objectlike properties from one object to another, such as the logs array in this example (remember that an array is a type of object in JavaScript), these are copied by reference and are not actual data duplicates. Each time this property is accessed from any object, the same property is used, the original from the loggingMixin object. In the case of this example, we want to see all of the logs together so this is useful; however, this may not be the result you require when using this pattern in your own code. Should you wish to create separate duplicates of the properties copied over, update the extendObj() function to that shown in Listing 6-11.

Listing 6-11. Updated extendObj() function to duplicate properties rather than copying by reference

```
// Update extendObj() to duplicate object-based properties rather than point to them
// by reference
function extendObj(obj1, obj2) {
    var obj2Key,
        value;

    for (obj2Key in obj2) {
        if (obj2.hasOwnProperty(obj2Key)) {
            value = obj2[obj2Key];

            // If the value being copied is an array, then copy a duplicate of that array using
            // the slice() method
            if (Object.prototype.toString.apply(value) === "[object Array]") {
                obj1[obj2Key] = value.slice();

            // Otherwise, if the value being copied in an object, and not an array, then copy
            // across a duplicate of that object using a recursive call to this function
            } else if (typeof obj2[obj2Key] === "object") {
                obj1[obj2Key] = extendObj({}, value);

            // Otherwise, copy across the value as usual
            } else {
                obj1[obj2Key] = value;
            }
        }
    }

    return obj1;
}
```

The mixin pattern is best used when you wish to quickly apply a set of properties and methods directly from one object to another, or to a "class" for use by all its object instances, without resorting to what would otherwise be complicated subclassing and inheritance. To read more about the mixin pattern online, look at the following resources:

- "A Fresh Look At JavaScript Mixins" by Angus Croll (via http://bit.ly/mixin_pattern)

- "JavaScript Mixins: Beyond Simple Object Extension" By Derick Bailey
  (via http://bit.ly/mixins_beyond)

The Module Pattern

The *module* pattern is probably the one most commonly used by professional JavaScript developers. In fact, we've covered the basis of the pattern twice in previous chapters already: first when discussing public, private, and protected variables in Chapter 1, and again when discussing ways of improving JavaScript compression in Chapter 4. It's all based around the self-executing function closure, which allows us to create a sandboxed area of code that can access global variables and functions but that does not expose variables or functions declared within it to the surrounding scope, unless explicitly with a return statement. The simplest example of a self-executing function is shown here:

```
(function() {
    // Any variables or functions declared within this function aren't accessible outside it
}());
```

We can use this pattern to divide up our code base into smaller, related chunks of code, which we call *modules*, hence the name of the pattern. Each of these modules should clearly state their dependencies on other parts of the code, if any, which should be passed in as parameters to the function, as shown here:

```
(function($) {
    // We very clearly define jQuery as a dependency for this 'module', making it available
    // internally through the $ variable
}(jQuery));
```

■ **Tip** Accessing JavaScript parameters within a function is faster than accessing a global variable in the scope outside the function, as the language interpreter does not have to perform the extra step of leaving the scope of the current function to search for variables.

The basic form of the module pattern is completed by using the return statement within the function closure to pass back any declared code that might be of use to other modules, or to the main application itself. Listing 6-12 shows the complete form of the module pattern, based on Listing 5-10 from the previous chapter.

Listing 6-12. The Module Pattern

```
// The module pattern is distinctive as it uses a combination of a self-executing anonymous
// function closure, with any dependencies passed in as parameters, and an optional return
// statement which allows code created within the closure to be made available externally

// Our only dependency is the 'document' object which contains the browser's cookie data. As an
// added security measure, we can include a final listed parameter named 'undefined' to which we
// never pass a value. This ensures that the variable named 'undefined' always contains an
// undefined value provided we always ensure we never pass in a value to this parameter.
// Otherwise it might be possible for other code, whether through malicious reasons or
// otherwise, to overwrite this value as it is not a reserved word in the language causing all
// kinds of havoc to the way our code behaves.
var cookie = (function(document, undefined) {
    var allCookies = document.cookie.split(";"),
        cookies = {},
        cookiesIndex = 0,
        cookiesLength = allCookies.length,
        cookie;

    for (; cookiesIndex < cookiesLength; cookiesIndex++) {
        cookie = allCookies[cookiesIndex].split("=");

        cookies[unescape(cookie[0])] = unescape(cookie[1]);
    }

    // Return any methods, properties or values that you wish to make available to the rest of
    // your code base. In this case, the following two methods will be exposed through the
    // 'cookie' variable, creating a singleton
    return {
        get: function(name) {
            return cookies[name] || "";
        },
```

```
        set: function(name, value) {
            cookies[name] = value;
            document.cookie = escape(name) + "=" + escape(value);
        }
    };

    // Pass in any dependencies at the point of function execution
}(document));
```

In larger code bases that utilize namespacing through singleton object structures, the module pattern is used in a slightly different way than we've seen; in this case, we pass in a dependency that we then return at the end of the function closure, using the module to augment the singleton with new properties and methods. Listing 6-13 shows the module pattern as it applies to the augmentation of namespaces, one of its most common uses.

Listing 6-13. Augmenting namespaces using the module pattern

```
// Define a namespace which we will populate with code modules
var myData = {};

// Ajax module, added to the myData namespace through augmentation
// The namespace is passed in as a parameter and, once it has been augmented with new method, is
// finally returned back, overwriting the original namespace with the new, augmented one
myData = (function(myNamespace, undefined) {

    // Add an 'ajax' object property to the namespace and populate it with related methods
    myNamespace.ajax = {
        get: function(url, callback) {
            var xhr = new XMLHttpRequest(),
                LOADED_STATE = 4,
                OK_STATUS = 200;

            xhr.onreadystatechange = function() {
                if (xhr.readyState !== LOADED_STATE) {
                    return;
                }

                if (xhr.status === OK_STATUS) {
                    callback(xhr.responseText);
                }
            };

            xhr.open("GET", url);
            xhr.send();
        }
    };

    // Return the new, augmented namespace back to the myData variable
    return myNamespace;

// We can use the following defence mecahnism, which reverts to an empty object if the myData
// namespace object does not yet exist. This is useful when you have modules split over several
// files in a large namespace and you're unsure if the namespace passed in has been initialized
// elsewhere before
}(myData || {}));
```

```javascript
// Cookies module, added to the myData namespace through augmentation
// As before, the namespace is passed in, augmented, and then returned, overwriting the original
// namespace object. At this point, the myData namespace contains the Ajax module code
myData = (function(myNamespace, undefined) {

    // Add a 'cookies' object property to the namespace and populate it with related methods
    myNamespace.cookies = {
        get: function(name) {
            var output = "",
                escapedName = escape(name),
                start = document.cookie.indexOf(escapedName + "="),
                end = document.cookie.indexOf(";", start);

            end = end === -1 ? (document.cookie.length - 1) : end;

            if (start >=0) {
                output = document.cookie.substring(start + escapedName.length + 1, end);
            }

            return unescape(output);
        },
        set: function(name, value) {
            document.cookie = escape(name) + "=" + escape(value);
        }
    };

    return myNamespace;
}(myData || {}));

// Execute methods directly through the myData namespace object, which now contains both Ajax
// and Cookies modules
myData.ajax.get("/user/12345", function(response) {
    alert("HTTP GET response received. User data: " + response);
});
myData.cookies.set("company", "AKQA");
myData.cookies.set("name", "Den Odell");

alert(myData.cookies.get("company")); // AKQA
alert(myData.cookies.get("name"));    // Den Odell
```

The module pattern is best used when you wish to break up large code bases into smaller, manageable, self-contained parts, each with a clear set of dependencies and a well-defined purpose. Because of their sandboxed nature, their self-executing function blocks are also prime territory for creating smaller file sizes through obfuscation and compilation, topics that we covered in Chapter 4. In Chapter 9, we will be looking at an alternative approach to defining and loading modules into your JavaScript code using the Asynchronous Module Definition (AMD) API, but for now if you wish to read more about the module pattern online, check out the following resources:

- "JavaScript Module Pattern: In-Depth" by Ben Cherry (via http://bit.ly/module_pattern)

- "JavaScript Design Patterns—The Revealing Module Pattern" by Raymond Camden (via http://bit.ly/revealing_module)

The Proxy Pattern

The *proxy* pattern is one that defines a surrogate, or stand-in, object or method to replace or augment an existing object or method in order to improve its performance or add extra functionality without affecting the other parts of the code that use that object or method already. The most common way that I and a number of other professional JavaScript developers use this pattern is to wrap around an existing method or function without changing the method or function name, as shown in Listing 6-14.

Listing 6-14. The proxy pattern

```
// To proxy the myData.cookies.get() method from Listing 6-13, we begin by storing the current
// method in a variable
var proxiedGet = myData.cookies.get;

// Override the get() method with a new function which proxies the original and augments its
// behavior
myData.cookies.get = function() {

    // Call the proxied (original) method to get the value it would have produced
    var value = proxiedGet.apply(this, arguments);

    // Do something with the value returned from the proxied method
    value = value.toUpperCase();

    // Return the manipulated value with the same type as the proxied method, so that the use of
    // this new method does not break any existing calls to it
    return value;
};
```

A variation of the proxy pattern known as the *virtual proxy* can be used to improve performance and memory usage by delaying object instantiation, and thus the execution of a constructor function, until the point that methods from the object instance are actually called, as demonstrated in Listing 6-15.

Listing 6-15. The virtual proxy pattern

```
// Define a "class" for constructing an object representing a simple form field
function FormField(type, displayText){
    this.type = type || "text";
    this.displayText = displayText || "";

    // Create and initialize a form field DOM element
    this.element = document.createElement("input");
    this.element.setAttribute("type", this.type);
    this.element.setAttribute("placeholder", this.displayText);
}

// Define two methods for object instances to inherit
FormField.prototype = {
    getElement: function() {
        return this.element;
    },
```

```
    isValid: function() {
        return this.element.value !== "";
    }
};

// Now replace the FormField "class" with a proxy that implements the same methods, yet delays
// calling the original constructor function until those methods are actually called, saving on
// memory resources and improving performance
// Optionally, use the module pattern to localise the scope of the proxy "class", passing in the
// original FormField "class" and returning the proxied version of it
FormField = (function(FormField) {

    // Define a proxy constructor, similar to the original FormField "class"
    function FormFieldProxy(type, displayText) {
        this.type = type;
        this.displayText = displayText;
    }

    FormFieldProxy.prototype = {

        // Define a property to store the reference to the object instance of the original
        // "class" once instantiated
        formField: null,

        // Define a new 'initialize' method whose task it is to create the object instance of
        // FormField if it does not already exist and execute the constructor function from the
        // original "class"
        initialize: function() {
            if (!this.formField) {
                this.formField = new FormField(this.type, this.displayText);
            }
        },

        // Proxy the original methods with new ones that call the intialize() method to
        // instantiate the FormField "class" only when one of these methods are called
        getElement: function() {
            this.initialize();
            return this.formField.getElement();
        },

        isValid: function() {
            this.initialize();
            return this.formField.isValid();
        }
    };

    // Return the proxied "class" to replace the original with
    return FormFieldProxy;
}(FormField));
```

```
// Create two object instances, both of which will actually be calling the proxy rather than the
// original "class", meaning the DOM elements will not be created at this stage, saving memory
// and improving performance
var textField = new FormField("text", "Enter the first line of your address"),
    emailField = new FormField("email", "Enter your email address");

// Add the elements stored in these objects to the current page when loaded - at this point the
// getElement() method is called, which in turn calls initialize(), creating an instance of the
// original "class" and executing its constructor function which performs the actual DOM element
// creation. This ensures the memory used to store the DOM element is only taken up at the exact
// point it is required
window.addEventListener("load", function() {
    document.body.appendChild(textField.getElement());
    document.body.appendChild(emailField.getElement());
}, false);

// Execute another method from the proxy, this time the object instance of the original "class"
// won't be recreated and the stored instance will be used instead
alert(emailField.isValid()); // false
```

You could extend the proxy pattern further to improve performance and reduce memory by delaying or grouping together calls, such as Ajax requests, or other network-related calls, for objects that could potentially make multiple calls around the same time.

The proxy pattern is best used when you need to override the behavior of specific methods on an object or "class," or applied in a way to improve the performance of an existing "class" such that it is not actually instantiated until one of its methods are called. To read more about the proxy pattern online, look at the following resources:

- "Proxy Pattern In JavaScript" on Using jQuery (via http://bit.ly/proxy_pattern)

- "JavaScript Design Patterns: Proxy" by Joseph Zimmerman on Adobe Developer Connection (via http://bit.ly/proxy_js)

Summary

In this chapter, we have looked at structural design patterns that you can use where appropriate to help you structure large JavaScript applications and improve their performance. These are tools in your Swiss Army knife of JavaScript development but, like all tools, you need to know when and where to use them best. Remember the old adage: "When you have a hammer, everything looks like a nail." Familiarize yourself with the patterns in this chapter and their use cases, and ensure that you don't use a design pattern before you recognize the need for it in your code.

In the following chapter, we will look at a number of behavioral design patterns, which can be used to simplify the communication between different objects in your JavaScript application's code base.

CHAPTER 7

■ ■ ■

Design Patterns: Behavioral

In this chapter, we will continue our look at design patterns, focusing on *behavioral design patterns*. Where creational design patterns we looked at in Chapter 5 focus on object creation and the structural design pattern we looked at in the previous chapter focus on object structure, behavioral design patterns focus on aiding the communication between multiple objects in a code base. The point here is to make it easier to understand how your code functions together as a whole, rather than just focusing on the construction and structure of individual objects. Let's look together at eight behavioral design patterns you may find useful in your code, together with examples.

The Chain of Responsibility Pattern

The *chain of responsibility* pattern is used when any of a number of objects based on the same "class" could handle a request or method call. The request is sent to one object and, if it is not the most appropriate object to handle the request, it passes it on to another object to handle. So it continues until an object handles the request and passes back the result of the operation through the chain of objects back to the original request or method call. Each object in the chain knows about one other object, the next in the chain that could handle the request if it cannot fulfill the request itself. The pattern is best used for objects that together form some kind of hierarchy, as demonstrated in Listing 7-1, that you do not wish to expose the implementation of to other parts of your code.

Listing 7-1. The chain of responsibility pattern

```
// Define an object listing different levels of logging in a system - info, warn, and error -
// each indicating something more severe than the last
var LogLevel = {
        INFO: 'INFO',
        WARN: 'WARN',
        ERROR: 'ERROR'
    },
    log;

// Define a "class" to create appropriately formatted log messages for different logging levels
function LogFormatter(logLevel) {
    this.logLevel = logLevel;
}

LogFormatter.prototype = {

    // Define a property to store the successor to this object instance in the chain
    // of responsibility
    nextInChain: null,
```

163

```javascript
    // Define a method to set the successor in the chain of responsibility
    setNextInChain: function(next) {
        this.nextInChain = next;
    },

    // Define a method to create an appropriately formatted log message based on the current
    // logging level
    createLogMessage: function(message, logLevel) {
        var returnValue;

        // If the logging level assigned to the current object instance is the same as that
        // passed in, then format the log message
        if (this.logLevel === logLevel) {

            // Format the log message as appropriate according to the logging level
            if (logLevel === LogLevel.ERROR) {
                returnValue = logLevel + ": " + message.toUpperCase();
            } else if (logLevel === LogLevel.WARN) {
                returnValue = logLevel + ": " + message;
            } else {
                returnValue = message;
            }

        // If the logging level assigned to the current object instance does not match that
        // passed in, then pass the message onto the next object instance in the chain
        // of responsibility
        } else if (this.nextInChain) {
            returnValue = this.nextInChain.createLogMessage(message, logLevel);
        }

        return returnValue;
    }
};

// Define a singleton we can use for storing and outputting logs in a system
log = (function() {

    // Define a storage array for log messages
    var logs = [],

        // Create object instances representing the three levels of logging - info, warn,
        // and error
        infoLogger = new LogFormatter(LogLevel.INFO),
        warnLogger = new LogFormatter(LogLevel.WARN),
        errorLogger = new LogFormatter(LogLevel.ERROR),

        // Set the 'error' logging level to be the first and highest level in our chain of
        // responsibility, which we'll store in the 'logger' variable
        logger = errorLogger;
```

```
    // Set the chain of responsibility hierarchy using the setNextInChain() method on each
    // object instance - we're assuming that the 'error' logging level is the most important and
    // is first in the chain

    // The next in the logging hierarchy after 'error' should be 'warn' as this is
    // less important
    errorLogger.setNextInChain(warnLogger);

    // The next in the chain after the 'warn' logging level should be 'info' as this is the
    // least important level
    warnLogger.setNextInChain(infoLogger);

    return {

        // Define a method for reading out the stored log messages
        getLogs: function() {
            return logs.join("\n");
        },

        // Define a method for formatting a log message appropriately according to its
        // logging level
        message: function(message, logLevel) {

            // We call the createLogMessage() method on the first object instance in our
            // hierarchy only, which in turn calls those further down the chain if it does not
            // handle the specified logging level itself. The message passes further down the
            // chain of responsibility until it reaches an object instance who can handle the
            // specific logging level
            var logMessage = logger.createLogMessage(message, logLevel);

            // Add the formatted log message to the storage array
            logs.push(logMessage);
        }
    };
}());

// Execute the message() method of the 'log' singleton, passing in a message and the logging
// level. The first object in the chain of responsibility handles the 'error' logging level, so
// the message is not passed down the chain of responsibility and is returned by the
// errorLogger object
log.message("Something vary bad happened", LogLevel.ERROR);

// This message is passed through the errorLogger object to the warnLogger object through the
// chain of responsibility since the errorLogger object is only told to handle messages with the
// 'error' logging level
log.message("Something bad happened", LogLevel.WARN);

// This message is passed through the errorLogger object to the warnLogger object, and onto the
// infoLogger object which is the one handling 'info' type log messages
log.message("Something happened", LogLevel.INFO);
```

```
// Output the stored logs
alert(log.getLogs());

// Outputs the following:
/*
ERROR: SOMETHING VERY BAD HAPPENED
WARN: Something bad happened
Something happened
*/
```

The chain of responsibility pattern is best used when you have a hierarchy of objects that you want access to throughout your code without exposing this structure. To learn more about the chain of responsibility pattern, look at the following online resources:

- "JavaScript Design Patterns: Chain Of Responsibility" by Joseph Zimmerman (via http://bit.ly/chain_pattern)

- "Chain Of Responsibility Pattern" on Wikipedia (via http://bit.ly/chain_wiki)

The Command Pattern

The *command* pattern is used to provide a layer of abstraction between the calling code and the specific methods of an object by ensuring that all calls are made through a single, public method on that object, often named run() or execute(). Using this pattern provides the ability to change the underlying code and API without affecting the calling code. The example in Listing 7-2 shows a simple example of the command pattern in action, passing the method name to execute, along with the parameters, to a single execute() method.

Listing 7-2. The command pattern

```
var cookie = (function() {
    var allCookies = document.cookie.split(";"),
        cookies = {},
        cookiesIndex = 0,
        cookiesLength = allCookies.length,
        cookie;

    for (; cookiesIndex < cookiesLength; cookiesIndex++) {
        cookie = allCookies[cookiesIndex].split("=");

        cookies[unescape(cookie[0])] = unescape(cookie[1]);
    }

    return {
        get: function(name) {
            return cookies[name] || "";
        },

        set: function(name, value) {
            cookies[name] = value;
            document.cookie = escape(name) + "=" + escape(value);
        },
```

```
    remove: function(name) {

        // Remove the cookie by removing its entry from the cookies object and setting its
        // expiry date in the past
        delete cookies[name];
        document.cookie = escape(name) + "=; expires=Thu, 01 Jan 1970 00:00:01 GMT;";
    },

    // Supply an execute() method, which is used to abstract calls to other methods so that
    // other method names can be changed as needs be in future without affecting the API
    // available to the rest of the code - provided this execute() method continues to exist
    execute: function(command, params) {

        // The command parameter contains the method name to execute, so check that the
        // method exists and is a function
        if (this.hasOwnProperty(command) && typeof this[command] === "function") {

            // If the method exists and can be executed, then execute it, passing across the
            // supplied params
            return this[command].apply(this, params);
        }
    }
    };
}());

// Set a cookie using the execute() method to indirectly call the set() method of the cookie
// singleton and supplying parameters to pass onto that method
cookie.execute("set", ["name", "Den Odell"]);

// Check that the cookie was set correctly using execute() with the "get" method
alert(cookie.execute("get", ["name"])); // Den Odell
```

The command pattern can also be used within the context of an application that requires "undo" functionality, where executed statements might need to be reversed at some point in future, for example, within the context of a word processing web application. Commands, in this case, are passed through a command execution object that uses this abstraction to store the appropriate function to reverse the method call that is passed to it, as shown in Listing 7-3, which shows a simple command execution object and an example using cookies based on the code in Listing 7-2.

Listing 7-3. Command execution object to support multiple levels of undo in a web application

```
// Create a singleton for allowing execution of other methods and providing the ability to
// 'undo' the actions of those methods
var command = (function() {

    // Create an array to store the 'undo' commands in order, also known as a 'stack'
    var undoStack = [];

    return {

        // Define a method to execute a supplied function parameter, storing a second function
        // parameter for later execution to 'undo' the action of the first function
```

```
        execute: function(command, undoCommand) {
            if (command && typeof command === "function") {

                // If the first parameter is a function, execute it, and add the second
                // parameter to the stack in case the command needs to be reversed at some point
                // in future
                command();
                undoStack.push(undoCommand);
            }
        },

        // Define a method to reverse the execution of the last command executed, using the
        // stack of 'undo' commands
        undo: function() {

            // Remove and store the last command from the stack, which will be the one most
            // recently added to it. This will remove that command from the stack, reducing the
            // size of the array
            var undoCommand = undoStack.pop();
            if (undoCommand && typeof undoCommand === "function") {

                // Check the command is a valid function and then execute it to effectively
                // 'undo' the last command
                undoCommand();
            }
        }
    };
}());

// Wrap each piece of functionality that can be 'undone' in a call to the command.execute()
// method, passing the command to execute immediately as the first parameter, and the function
// to execute to reverse that command as the second parameter which will be stored until such
// point as it is needed
command.execute(function() {

    // Using the code from Listing 7-2, set a cookie - this will be executed immediately
    cookie.execute("set", ["name", "Den Odell"]);
}, function() {

    // The reverse operation of setting a cookie is removing that cookie - this operation will
    // be stored for later execution if the command.undo() method is called
    cookie.execute("remove", ["name"]);
});

// Execute a second piece of functionality, setting a second cookie
command.execute(function() {
    cookie.execute("set", ["company", "AKQA"]);
}, function() {
    cookie.execute("remove", ["company"]);
});
```

```
// Check the value of the two cookies
alert(cookie.get("name"));    // Den Odell
alert(cookie.get("company")); // AKQA

// Reverse the previous operation, removing the 'company' cookie
command.undo();

// Check the value of the two cookies
alert(cookie.get("name"));    // Den Odell
alert(cookie.get("company")); // "" (an empty string), since the cookie has now been removed

// Reverse the first operation, removing the 'name' cookie
command.undo();

// Check the value of the two cookies
alert(cookie.get("name"));    // "", since the cookie has now been removed
alert(cookie.get("company")); // ""
```

The command pattern is best used when you need to abstract specific method names away from the rest of your code. By referring to methods by their names, as stored in strings, the underlying code can change at any point without affecting the rest of the code. To read more about the command pattern online, check out the following resources:

- "JavaScript Design Patterns: Command" by Joseph Zimmerman on Adobe Developer Connection (via http://bit.ly/command_pattern)

- "The Command Pattern In JavaScript" by Peter Michaux (via http://bit.ly/command_js)

The Iterator Pattern

The *interator* pattern, as the name suggests, is one that allows the code in your application to iterate, or *loop*, over a collection of data without necessarily needing to be aware of how that data is stored or constructed internally. Iterators typically provide a set of standard methods for moving to the next item in the collection and for checking to see whether the current item is the first or last in the collection.

An example of a generic "class" that can iterate over both Array-type and Object-type data is shown in Listing 7-4. Instances of this iterator can be manipulated and queried manually using the supplied methods rewind(), current(), next(), hasNext(), and first(), or can provide automatic self-iteration using its each() method, where a function callback parameter is executed once for each item in the data set, providing a useful equivalent form to a for loop.

Listing 7-4. The iterator pattern

```
// Define a generic iterator "class" for iterating/looping over arrays or object-like data
// structures
function Iterator(data) {
    var key;

    // Store the supplied data in the 'data' property
    this.data = data || {};

    this.index = 0;
    this.keys = [];
```

```
    // Store an indicator to show whether the supplied data is an array or an object
    this.isArray = Object.prototype.toString.call(data) === "[object Array]";

    if (this.isArray) {

        // If the supplied data is an array, store its length for fast access
        this.length = data.length;
    } else {

        // If object data is supplied, store each property name in an array
        for (key in data) {
            if (data.hasOwnProperty(key)) {
                this.keys.push(key);
            }
        }

        // The length of the property name array is the length of the data to iterate over,
        // so store this
        this.length = this.keys.length;
    }
}

// Define a method to reset the index, effectively rewinding the iterator back to the start of
// the data
Iterator.prototype.rewind = function() {
    this.index = 0;
};

// Define a method to return the value stored at the current index position of the iterator
Iterator.prototype.current = function() {
    return this.isArray ? this.data[this.index] : this.data[this.keys[this.index]];
};

// Define a method to return the value stored at the current index position of the iterator,
// and then advance the index pointer to the next item of data
Iterator.prototype.next = function() {
    var value = this.current();
    this.index = this.index + 1;
    return value;
};

// Define a method to indicate whether the index position is at the end of the data
Iterator.prototype.hasNext = function() {
    return this.index < this.length;
};

// Define a method to reset the index of the iterator to the start of the data and return
// the first item of data
Iterator.prototype.first = function() {
    this.rewind();
    return this.current();
};
```

```
// Define a method to iterate, or loop, over each item of data, executing a callback
// function each time, passing in the current data item as the first parameter to
// that function
Iterator.prototype.each = function(callback) {
    callback = typeof callback === "function" ? callback : function() {};

    // Iterate using a for loop, starting at the beginning of the data (achieved using the
    // rewind() method) and looping until there is no more data to iterate over (indicated
    // by the hasNext() method)
    for (this.rewind(); this.hasNext();) {

        // Execute the callback function each time through the loop, passing in the current
        // data item value and incrementing the loop using the next() method
        callback(this.next());
    }
};
```

The code in Listing 7-4 can be used as shown in Listing 7-5, which demonstrates different ways of iterating and looping over data stored using the generic iterator "class."

Listing 7-5. The iterator pattern in use

```
// Define an object and an array which we can use to iterate over
var user = {
        name: "Den Odell",
        occupation: "Head of Web Development",
        company: "AKQA"
    },
    daysOfWeek = ["Monday", "Tuesday", "Wednesday", "Thursday", "Friday", "Saturday", "Sunday"],

    // Create instances of the Iterator "class" using these two different types of data
    userIterator = new Iterator(user),
    daysOfWeekIterator = new Iterator(daysOfWeek),

    // Create three arrays for storing outputs of interations to be displayed later
    output1 = [],
    output2 = [],
    output3 = [];

// The userIterator is ready for use, so let's use a for loop to iterate over the stored data -
// note how we don't need to supply the first argument to the for loop as the data is already
// reset and initialized in its start position, and we don't require the last argument since the
// next() method call within the for loop body performs the advancement of the index position
// for us
for (; userIterator.hasNext();) {
    output1.push(userIterator.next());
}

// Since we iterated over an object, the resulting data consists of the values stored in each of
// the object's properties
alert(output1.join(", ")); // Den Odell, Head of Web Development, AKQA
```

```
// Before iterating over the same data again, its index must be rewound to the start
userIterator.rewind();

// Iterate over the object properties using a while loop, which continues to execute until the
// iterator has no further data items
while (userIterator.hasNext()) {
    output2.push(userIterator.next());
}

alert(output2.join(", ")); // Den Odell, Head of Web Development, AKQA

// Iterate over the array data using the Iterator's built-in each() method - using this
// approach requires no manual work to manipulate the position of the index, simply pass a
// callback function
daysOfWeekIterator.each(function(item) {
    output3.push(item);
});

alert(output3.join(", ")); // Monday, Tuesday, Wednesday, Thursday, Friday, Saturday, Sunday
```

The iterator pattern is best used when you need to provide a standard way for the rest of your code to loop over your complex data structures, without exposing how that data is ultimately stored or represented. To learn more about the iterator pattern online, check out the following online resources:

- "JavaScript Iterator Design Pattern" on DoFactory (via http://bit.ly/iterator_pattern)
- "Iterator Pattern" on Wikipedia (via http://bit.ly/iterator_wiki)

The Observer Pattern

The *observer* pattern is used in larger code bases consisting of a number of individual code modules that depend on, or must communicate between, each other. In such a code base, hardcoded references from one module to other modules provides what is known as *tight coupling*, the need to know explicitly about every other module in the system for the whole code to function correctly together. Ideally, however, modules in a large code base should be *loosely coupled*. References aren't made explicitly to other modules; rather, systemwide events are triggered and listened for throughout the code base, like a custom version of the standard DOM event handling.

As an example, if one module were responsible for all client-server communication via Ajax, and another module were responsible for rendering and validating a form before transmission to the server, on successful submission and validation of the form by the user, the code base could trigger a global "form submitted" event together with the data from the form, which the communication module would be listening out for. The communication module would then perform its task of sending the data to the server and receiving its response before itself triggering a "response received" event, which the form module would be listening out for. On receipt of this event, the form module could render a message indicating that the form was successfully submitted, all without either module needing to know about each other—the only thing each module is aware of is a set of globally configured event names to which any module in the system could trigger or respond.

The system implementing the observer pattern must have three global methods avilable to the system code base: publish(), which triggers an event by name, passing along any optional data; subscribe(), which allows a module to assign a function to execute when a specific, named event is triggered; and unsubscribe(), which deassigns the function so that it will no longer be executed when the named event is triggered. The code in Listing 7-6 demonstrates a simple object that can be used globally in your applications to implement these methods in the observer pattern.

Listing 7-6. The observer pattern

```
// Define an object containing global publish(), subscribe(), and unsubscribe() methods to
// implement the observer pattern
var observer = (function() {

    // Create an object for storing registered events in by name along with the associatedw
    // callback functions for any part of the full code base that subscribes to those
    // event names
    var events = {};

    return {

        // Define the subscribe() method, which stores a function along with its associated
        // event name to be called at some later point when the specific event by that name
        // is triggered
        subscribe: function(eventName, callback) {

            // If an event by the supplied name has not already been subscribed to, create an
            // array property named after the event name within the events object to store
            // functions to be called at a later time when the event by that name is triggered
            if (!events.hasOwnProperty(eventName)) {
                events[eventName] = [];
            }

            // Add the supplied callback function to the list associated to the specific
            // event name
            events[eventName].push(callback);
        },

        // Define the unsubscribe() method, which removes a given function from the list of
        // functions to be executed when the event by the supplied name is triggered
        unsubscribe: function(eventName, callback) {
            var index = 0,
                length = 0;

            if (events.hasOwnProperty(eventName)) {
                length = events[eventName].length;

                // Cycle through the stored functions for the given event name and remove the
                // function matching that supplied from the list
                for (; index < length; index++) {
                    if (events[eventName][index] === callback) {
                        events[eventName].splice(index, 1);
                        break;
                    }
                }
            }
        },
```

```
        // Define the publish() method, which executes all functions associated with the given
        // event name in turn, passing to each the same optional data passed as arguments to
        // the method
        publish: function(eventName) {

            // Store all parameters but the first passed to this function as an array
            var data = Array.prototype.slice.call(arguments, 1),
                index = 0,
                length = 0;

            if (events.hasOwnProperty(eventName)) {
                length = events[eventName].length;

                // Cycle through all of the functions associated with the given event name and
                // execute them each in turn, passing along any supplied parameters
                for (; index < length; index++) {
                    events[eventName][index].apply(this, data);
                }
            }
        }
    };
}());
```

The code in Listing 7-7 demonstrates how to use the publish(), subscribe(), and unsubscribe() methods of the observer pattern given in Listing 7-6. It assumes it is running within the context of a HTML page containing a <form id="my-form"> tag with a valid action attribute, and containing several <input type="text"> tags representing form fields.

Listing 7-7. The observer pattern in use

```
// Define a module for Ajax communication, with a dependency on the observer object
// from Listing 7-6
(function(observer) {

    // Define a function for performing an Ajax POST based on a supplied URL, form-encoded data
    // string, and a callback function to execute once a response has been received from
    // the server
    function ajaxPost(url, data, callback) {
        var xhr = new XMLHttpRequest(),
            STATE_LOADED = 4,
            STATUS_OK = 200;

        xhr.onreadystatechange = function() {
            if (xhr.readyState !== STATE_LOADED) {
                return;
            }

            if (xhr.status === STATUS_OK) {
```

```
                    // Execute the supplied callback function once a successful response has been
                    // received from the server
                    callback(xhr.responseText);
                }
            };

            xhr.open("POST", url);

            // Inform the server that we will be sending form-encoded data, where names and values
            // are separated by the equals sign (=) character, and name/value pairs are separated by
            // the ampersand (&) character
            xhr.setRequestHeader("Content-type", "application/x-www-form-urlencoded");

            // POST the data to the server
            xhr.send(data);
        }

        // Subscribe to the global, custom "form-submit" event and, when this event is triggered by
        // another module in the code base, make a Ajax POST request to the server using the
        // supplied URL and data. Trigger the "ajax-response" event when complete, passing in the
        // server's response from the Ajax call
        observer.subscribe("form-submit", function(url, formData) {
            ajaxPost(url, formData, function(response) {

                // Trigger the global "ajax-response" event, passing along the data returned from
                // the server during the Ajax POST
                observer.publish("ajax-response", response);
            });
        });
    }(observer));

    // Define a module for handling submission of a simple form on the page containing text fields
    // only with an ID of "my-form". Note that neither of the modules in this code listing reference
    // each other, they only reference the observer object which handles all communication between
    // modules in the system. Each module is said to be "loosely-coupled" as it has no hardcoded
    // dependency on any other module
    (function(observer) {

        // Get a reference to a form on the current HTML page with ID "my-form"
        var form = document.getElementById("my-form"),

            // Get the "action" attribute value from the form, which will be the URL we perform an
            // Ajax POST to
            action = form.action,
            data = [],

            // Get a reference to all <input> fields within the form
            fields = form.getElementsByTagName("input"),
            index = 0,
            length = fields.length,
            field,
```

```
    // Create a HTML <p> tag for use as a thank you message after form submission has
    // taken place
    thankYouMessage = document.createElement("p");

// Define a function to execute on submission of the form which uses the observer pattern to
// submit the form field data over Ajax
function onFormSubmit(e) {

    // Prevent the default behavior of the submit event, meaning a normal in-page HTML form
    // submission will not occur
    e.preventDefault();

    // Loop through all <input> tags on the page, creating an array of name/value pairs of
    // the data entered into the form
    for (; index < length; index++) {
        field = fields[index];

        data.push(escape(field.name) + "=" + escape(field.value));
    }

    // Trigger the global "form-submit" event on the observer object, passing it the URL to
    // use for the Ajax POST and the form data to be sent. The Ajax communication module is
    // listening for this event and will handle everything pertaining to the submission of
    // that data to the server.
    observer.publish("form-submit", action, data.join("&"));
}

// Wire up the onFormSubmit() function to the "submit" event of the form
form.addEventListener("submit", onFormSubmit, false);

// Subscribe to the global, custom "ajax-response" event, and use the server's response data
// sent along with the event to populate a Thank You message to display on the page beside
// the form
observer.subscribe("ajax-response", function(response) {
    thankYouMessage.innerHTML = "Thank you for your form submission.<br>The server responded
    with: " + response;

    form.parentNode.appendChild(thankYouMessage);
});
}(observer));
```

The observer pattern allows you to remove hardcoded references between modules in your code in favor of a maintained list of custom, systemwide events. As your code base grows and the number of modules increases, consider the use of this pattern to simplify your code and to decouple modules from each other. Be aware that if an error occurs in one of your modules and an event is not triggered that should be, the source of that error might not be immediately obvious and may require extra debugging. I would recommend adding debug logging of your own into your observer object during development to allow you to more easily trace the events in your code.

The observer pattern is best used when you wish to loosely couple modules together to reduce spaghetti code. To read more about this popular pattern online, look at the following resources:

- "JavaScript Design Patterns: Observer" by Joseph Zimmerman on Adobe Developer Connection (via http://bit.ly/observer_pattern)

- "JavaScript Design Patterns: Observer" by Rob Dodson (via http://bit.ly/observer_js)

The Mediator Pattern

The *mediator* pattern is a variation of the observer pattern that differs in one crucial way. Whereas the observer pattern defines a global object for publishing and subscribing to events in the whole system, the mediator pattern defines localized objects for specific purposes, each with the same publish(), subscribe(), and unsubscribe() methods. As your code base grows ever larger and the observer pattern proves to yield an unwieldy number of events to manage, so the mediator pattern can be used to break down this larger list of events into smaller groupings. Whereas the observer pattern was realized through a global singleton object, the mediator pattern is realized through the use of a "class" so that as many object instances can be created as are needed to support features of the code. Listing 7-8 shows the "class" to use to implement the mediator pattern in your code. Note the similarities to the object created to implement the observer pattern in Listing 7-6.

Listing 7-8. The mediator pattern

```
// Define a "class" containing publish(), subscribe(), and unsubscribe() methods to implement
// the mediator pattern. Note the similarilty to the observer pattern, the only difference is
// that we are creating a "class" here for creating object instances from later, and that we
// initialize the events array afresh for each object instance to avoid all instances sharing
// the same array in memory.
function Mediator() {
    this.events = {};
}

Mediator.prototype.subscribe = function(eventName, callback) {
    if (!this.events.hasOwnProperty(eventName)) {
        this.events[eventName] = [];
    }

    this.events[eventName].push(callback);
};

Mediator.prototype.unsubscribe = function(eventName, callback) {
    var index = 0,
        length = 0;

    if (this.events.hasOwnProperty(eventName)) {
        length = this.events[eventName].length;

        for (; index < length; index++) {
            if (this.events[eventName][index] === callback) {
                this.events[eventName].splice(index, 1);
                break;
            }
        }
    }
};
```

```
Mediator.prototype.publish = function(eventName) {
    var data = Array.prototype.slice.call(arguments, 1),
        index = 0,
        length = 0;

    if (this.events.hasOwnProperty(eventName)) {
        length = this.events[eventName].length;

        for (; index < length; index++) {
            this.events[eventName][index].apply(this, data);
        }
    }
};
```

The mediator pattern in Listing 7-8 can be implemented as demonstrated in Listing 7-9, creating mediator objects to represent specific features within the code and allowing modules in the code base. It assumes it is running within the context of a HTML page containing a <form id="my-form"> tag containing several <input type="text"> tags representing form fields.

Listing 7-9. The mediator pattern in use

```
// Define two mediators for our code base, one pertaining to code for a forms feature, and
// another to enable a message logging feature.
// The formsMediator will feature two events: "form-submit", and "ajax-response", whereas
// the loggingMediator will feature three events, "log", "retrieve-log", and "log-retrieved".
// Note how we're able to separate events for different features in our code using the
// mediator pattern
var formsMediator = new Mediator(),
    loggingMediator = new Mediator();

// Define a module for Ajax communication which POSTs some supplied data to the server when a
// "form-submit" event is triggered within the formsMediator
(function(formsMediator) {
    function ajaxPost(url, data, callback) {
        var xhr = new XMLHttpRequest(),
            STATE_LOADED = 4,
            STATUS_OK = 200;

        xhr.onreadystatechange = function() {
            if (xhr.readyState !== STATE_LOADED) {
                return;
            }

            if (xhr.status === STATUS_OK) {
                callback(xhr.responseText);
            }
        };

        xhr.open("POST", url);
        xhr.setRequestHeader("Content-type", "application/x-www-form-urlencoded");
        xhr.send(data);
    }
```

```
        formsMediator.subscribe("form-submit", function(url, formData) {
            ajaxPost(url, formData, function(response) {
                formsMediator.publish("ajax-response", response);
            });
        });
    }(formsMediator));

    // Define a module for handling submission of a simple form on the page containing text fields
    // only with an ID of "my-form". When the form is submitted, the "form-submit" event is
    // triggered within the formsMediator
    (function(formsMediator) {
        var form = document.getElementById("my-form"),
            action = form.action,
            data = [],
            fields = form.getElementsByTagName("input"),
            index = 0,
            length = fields.length,
            field,

            thankYouMessage = document.createElement("p");

        function onFormSubmit(e) {
            e.preventDefault();

            for (; index < length; index++) {
                field = fields[index];
                data.push(escape(field.name) + "=" + escape(field.value));
            }

            formsMediator.publish("form-submit", action, data.join("&"));
        }

        form.addEventListener("submit", onFormSubmit, false);

        formsMediator.subscribe("ajax-response", function(response) {
            thankYouMessage.innerHTML = "Thank you for your form submission.<br>The server responded
            with: " + response;
            form.parentNode.appendChild(thankYouMessage);
        });
    }(formsMediator));

    // Define a module for logging messages within the system to aid with debugging of issues that
    // might occur. Uses the loggingMediator to separate the logging feature of the code base
    // separate from that handling the form submission with the formsMediator
    (function(loggingMediator) {

        // Create an array to store the logs
        var logs = [];
```

```
    // When the "log" event is triggered on the loggingMediator, add an object to the logs
    // containing a supplied message and the date / time that the message was received at
    loggingMediator.subscribe("log", function(message) {
        logs.push({
            message: message,
            date: new Date()
        });
    });

    // When the "retrieve-log" event is triggered on the loggingMediator, trigger the
    // "log-retrieved" event, passing along the current state of the stored logs
    loggingMediator.subscribe("retrieve-log", function() {
        loggingMediator.publish("log-retrieved", logs);
    });
}(loggingMediator));

// Define a module which allows the stored logs in the loggingMediator to be displayed on screen
(function(loggingMediator) {

    // Create a button which, when clicked, will display the current state of the log
    var button = document.createElement("button");

    button.innerHTML = "Show logs";

    button.addEventListener("click", function() {

        // Trigger the "retrieve-log" event within the loggingMediator. This triggers the
        // "log-retrieved" event, passing along the current state of the logs
        loggingMediator.publish("retrieve-log");
    }, false);

    // When the "log-retrieved" event occurs, display the logs on screen
    loggingMediator.subscribe("log-retrieved", function(logs) {
        var index = 0,
            length = logs.length,
            ulTag = document.createElement("ul"),
            liTag = document.createElement("li"),
            listItem;

        // Loop through each log in the list of logs, rendering the date / time and message
        // stored within a <li> tag
        for (; index < length; index++) {
            listItem = liTag.cloneNode(false);
            listItem.innerHTML = logs[index].date.toUTCString() + ": " + logs[index].message;
            ulTag.appendChild(listItem);
        }

        // Add the <ul> tag containing all the <li> tags representing the log data to the bottom
        // of the page
        document.body.appendChild(ulTag);
    });
```

```
    // Add the button to the bottom of the current page
    document.body.appendChild(button);
}(loggingMediator));

// Define a module which logs events that occur within the formsMediator. This is the only
// module in this example to use more than one mediator
(function(formsMediator, loggingMediator) {

    // Use the loggingMediator's "log" events to log the URL the form is submitted to when the
    // "form-submit" event is triggered within the formsMediator
    formsMediator.subscribe("form-submit", function(url) {
        loggingMediator.publish("log", "Form submitted to " + url);
    });

    // Log the response from the server that is supplied when the "ajax-response" event is
    // triggered within the formsMediator
    formsMediator.subscribe("ajax-response", function(response) {
        loggingMediator.publish("log", "The server responded to an Ajax call with: " + response);
    });
}(formsMediator, loggingMediator));
```

As your code base grows, you may find it makes sense to move from the observer pattern to the mediator pattern in order to group together your system's events into more manageable *features*.

The mediator pattern is best used when you wish to loosely couple modules together in a very large code base where the number of events to handle would be unweildly if using the observer pattern. To learn more about the mediator pattern, look at the following online resources:

- "JavaScript Design Patterns: Mediator" by HB Stone (via http://bit.ly/mediator_pattern)
- "Patterns For Large-Scale JavaScript Application Architecture: Mediator" by Addy Osmani (via http://bit.ly/mediator_js)

The Memento Pattern

The *memento* pattern defines the storage of object data in a static form in memory so that it can be restored at a later time in the course of the execution of the code; it's as if you could take a snapshot of an object at any time that you could later restore. Listing 7-10 shows a simple "class" that can be used to implement this pattern by storing snapshots of objects as JSON-format string representations, and providing methods to store and restore the original JavaScript objects.

Listing 7-10. The memento pattern

```
// Define a simple "class" to be used to implement the memento pattern. It can be used to
// provide the ability to save and restore a snapshot of an object in memory.
// Certain older browsers (e.g. Internet Explorer 7) do not support the JSON.stringify() and
// JSON.parse() methods natively. For these, you should include Doug Crockford's json2.js
// library found at https://github.com/douglascrockford/JSON-js
function Memento() {

    // Define an object in memory to store snapshots of other objects under a specified key
    this.storage = {};
}
```

```
// Define a method to save the state of any object under a specified key
Memento.prototype.saveState = function(key, obj) {

    // Convert the supplied object to a string representation in JSON format
    this.storage[key] = JSON.stringify(obj);
};

// Define a method to restore and return the state of any object stored under a specified key
Memento.prototype.restoreState = function(key) {
    var output = {};

    // If the supplied key exists, locate the object stored there
    if (this.storage.hasOwnProperty(key)) {
        output = this.storage[key];

        // Convert the stored value from a JSON string to a proper object
        output = JSON.parse(output);
    }

    return output;
};
```

Listing 7-11 demonstrates the application of the memento "class" from Listing 7-10.

Listing 7-11. The memento pattern in use

```
// Define an instance of a memento to allow us to save and restore the state of objects
var memento = new Memento(),

    // Define an object whose state we wish to be able to save and restore
    user = {
        name: "Den Odell",
        age: 35
    };

// Save the current state of the user object using the memento
memento.saveState("user", user);

// Prove that the state of the object is save in JSON format by reading from the storage object
// of the memento directly
alert(memento.storage["user"]); // {"name":"Den Odell","age":35}

// Now change the values in the user object as you wish
user.name = "John Smith";
user.age = 21;

// Output the current state of the user object
alert(JSON.stringify(user)); // {"name":"John Smith","age":21}
```

```
// Whenever you wish to restore the last saved state of the user object, simply call the
restoreState() method of the memento
user = memento.restoreState("user");

// Output the new value of the user object, which has been restored to its last saved state
alert(JSON.stringify(user)); // {"name":"Den Odell","age":35}
```

The memento pattern is best used when you need to store and restore snapshots of objects in your application at specific points in its execution. To read more about the memento pattern online, look at the following resources:

- "JavaScript Memento Design Pattern" on DoFactory (via http://bit.ly/memento_pattern)

- "Memento Pattern" on Wikipedia (via http://bit.ly/memento_wiki)

The Promises Pattern

When dealing with asynchronous functions, typically one would pass a callback function to such a function. That function, when it has completed its work, will execute the callback function on our behalf. This works as we would want it to; the only problem is that it can create code that becomes harder to read and rather more vague—you have to know that the function called is an asynchronous one, and that the function passed to it is used as a callback within it. If you wish to wait for the results of several asynchronous functions to complete before executing a callback, this makes the resulting code ever more vague and difficult to follow. Enter the *promises* pattern, a design pattern created in the 1970s but updated for JavaScript in work untaken by the CommonJS group (http://bit.ly/common_js). It defines a way of returning a promise from an asynchronous call that can then be chained with a call to another function that will only execute once the promise is complete, which occurs when the asynchronous call is complete. This has the benefit of ensuring that the callback is suffiently separated from the call to the asynchronous function as to improve the clarity of your code, making it more readable and therefore easier to understand and maintain.

A promise is manifest in JavaScript as an object instance containing a then() method, which is executed once the asynchronous function in question has completed execution. Consider a simple Ajax call that requires a callback function as its second parameter, executed as such:

```
ajaxGet("/my-url", function(response) {
    // Do something with response
}).
```

Using the promises pattern, the resulting JavaScript for the same Ajax call would look like the following:

```
ajaxGet("/my-url").then(function(response) {
    // Do something with response
});
```

You may think that there's very little difference between the two, but in fact the latter has more clarity: it distinctly tells us that the second function will execute once the first has completed, whereas that was merely implied to be the case in the former. Once used with multiple asynchronous calls, the promises pattern is shown to be even clearer than the equivalent code using callbacks. Consider the following code, for example, which makes an Ajax call to one URL before making a second Ajax call to a different URL:

```
ajaxGet("/my-url", function() {
    ajaxGet("/my-other-url", function() {
        // Do something
    });
});
```

Using the promises pattern, this code is reduced to something far more understandable, and avoids the levels of nested code, which would become ever more extreme the more asynchronous calls in the chain:

```
ajaxGet("/my-url").then(ajaxGet("/my-other-url")).then(function() {
    // Do something
});
```

Things become even more complicated when attempting to execute a single callback after a number of simultaneous, asynchronous calls have taken place in standard JavaScript. Using the promises pattern, you can simply pass an array of promises to its all() method and it will execute each simultaneously, returning a single promise that will be fulfilled when each method in the array has fulfilled its individual promise, as shown here:

```
Promise.all([ajaxGet("/my-url"), ajaxGet("/my-other-url")]).then(function() {
    // Do something with the data returned from both calls
});
```

A "class" to represent promises in JavaScript is shown in Listing 7-12. I manage a standalone verison of this code as a GitHub project at http://bit.ly/js_promises, which you may feel free to use within your projects.

Listing 7-12. The promises pattern

```
// Define a "class" representing a promise, allowing readable and understandable code to be
// written to support asynchronous methods and their callbacks. Instances created from this
// "class" adhere to the Promises/A+ specification detailed at http://promisesaplus.com and
// pass all the official unit tests found at https://github.com/promises-aplus/promises-tests
// which prove compliance of this specification.
var Promise = (function() {

    // Define the three possible states a promise can take - "pending" - the default value
    // meaning it has not resolved yet, "fulfilled" - meaning the promise has resolved
    // successfully, and "rejected" - meaning the promise has failed and an error has occurred
    var state = {
            PENDING: "pending",
            FULFILLED: "fulfilled",
            REJECTED: "rejected"
        };

    // Define the "class" to represent a promise. If an asynchronous function is passed in at
    // the point of instantiation, it will be executed immediately
    function Promise(asyncFunction) {
        var that = this;

        // Define a property to represent the current state of the promise, set to "pending" by
        // default
        this.state = state.PENDING;

        // Define a property to be used to store a list of callback functions to call once the
        // asynchronous method has completed execution
        this.callbacks = [];
```

```
    // Define a property to store the value returned by the asynchronous method represented
    // by this promise
    this.value = null;

    // Define a property to store the details of any error that occurs as a result of
    // executing the asynchronous method
    this.error = null;

    // Define two functions which will be passed to the asynchronous function
    // represented by this promise. The first will be executed if the asynchronous
    // function executed successfully, the second will be executed if the execution
    // failed in some way
    function success(value) {

        // Executes the resolve() method of this promise, which will ensure that any
        // functions linked to this promise to be executed once its asynchronous method
        // has executed successfully is executed at this point
        that.resolve(value);
    }

    function failure(reason) {

        // Executes the reject() method of this promise, which will execute any
        // linked callback functions for displaying or handling errors. Any further
        // associated promises chained to this one will not be executed.
        that.reject(reason);
    }

    // If an asynchronous function is passed to this promise at instantiation, it is
    // executed immediately, and the success() and failure() functions defined above
    // are passed in as function parameters. The asynchronous function must ensure it
    // executes the most appropriate of these two functions depending on the outcome
    // of the behaviour it is attempting to perform
    if (typeof asyncFunction === "function") {
        asyncFunction(success, failure);
    }
}

// Define a then() method, the crux of the Promises/A+ spec, which allows callbacks to
// be associated to the result of the asynchronous function's execution depending on
// whether that function completed its task successfully or not. It allows chaining of
// promises to each other to allow further asynchronous functions to be executed at
// the point at which the current one is completed successfully
Promise.prototype.then = function(onFulfilled, onRejected) {

    // Create a new promise (and return it at the end of this method) to allow for
    // chaining of calls to then()
    var promise = new Promise(),
```

```
            // Define a callback object to be stored in this promise and associate the new
            // promise instance to it to act as the context of any callback methods
            callback = {
                promise: promise
            };

        // If a function was provided to be executed on successful completion of the
        // asynchronous function's action, store that function in the callback object
        // together with its newly created promise as context
        if (typeof onFulfilled === "function") {
            callback.fulfill = onFulfilled;
        }

        // If a function was provided to be executed on unsuccessful completion of the
        // asynchronous function's action, store that function in the callback object
        // together with the new context promise
        if (typeof onRejected === "function") {
            callback.reject = onRejected;
        }

        // Add the callback object to the list of callbacks
        this.callbacks.push(callback);

        // Attempt to execute the stored callbacks (will only do this if the asynchronous
        // function has completed execution by this point - if not, it will be called at
        // such time as it has by other code in the "class")
        this.executeCallbacks();

        // Return the newly created promise, to allow for chaining of other asynchronous
        // functions through repeated calls to the then() method
        return promise;
    };

// Define a method to execute any callbacks associated with this promise if the
// associated asynchronous function has completed execution
Promise.prototype.executeCallbacks = function() {
    var that = this,
        value,
        callback;

    // Define two functions to use as defaults to execute if an equivalent function has
    // not been stored in the list of callbacks tied to this promise
    function fulfill(value) {
        return value;
    }

    function reject(reason) {
        throw reason;
    }
```

```
        // Only execute the callbacks if the promise is not in its pending state, i.e. that
        // the asynchronous function has completed execution
        if (this.state !== state.PENDING) {

            // Point 2.2.4 of the Promises/A+ spec dictates that callback functions should
            // be executed asynchronously, outside of the flow of any other calls to then()
            // which might take place. This ensures the whole chain of promises is in place
            // before calls to the callbacks take place. Using a setTimeout with a delay of
            // 0 milliseconds gives the JavaScript engine a split second to complete the
            // process of going through the promise chain before any callbacks are run.
            // Browsers have a minimum delay value possible for a setTimeout call so in
            // reality the callbacks will be executed after, typically, 4 milliseconds
            setTimeout(function() {

                // Loop through all the callbacks associated with this promise and execute
                // them each in turn, selecting the callback's fulfill method if the promise
                // was fulfilled (by the asynchronous function completing execution
                // successfully), or its reject method if the function returned an error
                // during execution
                while(that.callbacks.length) {
                    callback = that.callbacks.shift();

                    // Wrap the execution of the callback in a try/catch block, in case it
                    // throws an error. We don't want the promise chain to stop executing if
                    // an error is thrown, rather we want to reject the promise, allowing
                    // the calling code to handle the error itself
                    try {

                        // Execute the appropriate callback method based on the state of
                        // the promise. If no callback method has been associated, fall
                        // back to the default fulfill() and reject() functions defined at
                        // the top of the executeCallbacks() method, above
                        if (that.state === state.FULFILLED) {
                            value = (callback.fulfill || fulfill)(that.value);
                        } else {
                            value = (callback.reject || reject)(that.error);
                        }

                        // Pass the result of executing the callback function to the
                        // resolve() method, which will either mark the promise as fulfilled
                        // or continue to further execute chained calls to the then() method
                        callback.promise.resolve(value);
                    } catch (reason) {

                        // If an error is thrown by the callback
                        callback.promise.reject(reason);
                    }
                }
            }, 0);
        }
    };
```

```
// The fulfill() method will mark this promise as fulfilled provided it has not already
// been fulfilled or rejected before. Any associated callbacks will be executed at
// this point
Promise.prototype.fulfill = function(value) {

    // Only transition the promise to the fulfilled state if it is still in the pending
    // state, and a value is passed to this method when it is executed
    if (this.state === state.PENDING && arguments.length) {
        this.state = state.FULFILLED;
        this.value = value;

        this.executeCallbacks();
    }
};

// The reject() method will mark this promise as rejected provided it has not already
// been fulfilled or rejected before. Any associated callbacks will be executed at
// this point
Promise.prototype.reject = function(reason) {

    // Only transition the promise to the rejected state if it is still in the pending
    // state, and a value is passed to this method when it is executed
    if (this.state === state.PENDING && arguments.length) {
        this.state = state.REJECTED;
        this.error = reason;

        this.executeCallbacks();
    }
};

// The resolve() method takes the return value from a successfull call to a promise's
// fulfill() callback and uses it to fulfill the promise if it is the last promise in
// a chain of then() method calls. If it is not the last promise, it continues down
// the promise chain, recursively fulfilling and rejecting the linked promises as
// appropriate
Promise.prototype.resolve = function(value) {
    var promise = this,

        // Detect the type of the value returned from the fulfill() callback method. If
        // this is the last promise in a chain, this should be the result of executing
        // the asynchronous function itself. If this promise has other chained promises
        // then the value passed to this method will contain another promise which will
        // call the resolve() method again, recursively
        valueIsThisPromise = promise === value,
        valueIsAPromise = value && value.constructor === Promise,

        // The term "thenable" refers to an object that looks like a promise in that it
        // contains a then() method of its own, yet isn't an instance of this Promise
        // "class" - useful for connecting promises created by other implementations of
        // the Promises/A+ spec together
        valueIsThenable = value && (typeof value === "object" || typeof value === "function"),
```

```
    isExecuted = false,
    then;

// Reject this promise if the value passed to this method represents the same
// promise represented here - otherwise we could potentially get stuck in a loop
if (valueIsThisPromise) {

    // The Promises/A+ spec dictates that should this promise be the same as the
    // one passed to this method, then a TypeError should be passed to the reject()
    // method, effectively stopping execution of further promises in the chain
    promise.reject(new TypeError());

// If the value passed to the resolve() method is another instance of this Promise
// "class", then either fulfill or reject the current promise based on the state of
// the provided promise
} else if (valueIsAPromise) {

    // If the promise passed into this method has already been fulfilled or
    // rejected, pass on the value or error contained within it to this promise
    if (value.state === state.FULFILLED) {
        promise.fulfill(value.value);
    } else if (value.state === state.REJECTED) {
        promise.reject(value.error);

    // If the promise passed into this method hasn't yet been fulfilled or rejected,
    // execute its then() method to ensure the current promise will get resolved
    // or rejected along with that promise once it has completed execution of its
    // asynchronous function
    } else {
        value.then(function(value) {
            promise.resolve(value);
        }, function(reason) {
            promise.reject(reason);
        });
    }

// If the value passed to the resolve() method is not an instance of this Promise
// "class" but resembles a promise in that it is an object containing its own
// then() method, then execute its then() method, fulfilling or rejecting the
// current promise based on the state of this promise. This comes in useful when
// attempting to connect promises created with other implementations of the same
// spec together with this one
} else if (valueIsThenable) {

    // Wrap execution in a try/catch block in case an error is thrown in the
    // underlying code of the other promise implementation
    try {
        then = value.then;
```

```
            // If the object stored in the value variable contains a then() method,
            // execute it to ensure the current promise gets fulfilled or rejected when
            // that promise does
            if (typeof then === "function") {
                then.call(value, function(successValue) {
                    if (!isExecuted) {
                        isExecuted = true;
                        promise.resolve(successValue);
                    }
                }, function(reason) {
                    if (!isExecuted) {
                        isExecuted = true;
                        promise.reject(reason);
                    }
                });
            } else {
                promise.fulfill(value);
            }
        } catch (reason) {
            if (!isExecuted) {
                isExecuted = true;
                promise.reject(reason);
            }
        }

        // If the value passed to the resolve() method is not a promise, then fulfill the
        // current promise using its value. Any associated callbacks will then be executed
    } else {
        promise.fulfill(value);
    }
};

// Add a bonus method, Promise.all(), which isn't part of the Promises/A+ spec, but is part
// of the spec for ECMAScript 6 Promises, which bring the benefits of promises straight into
// the JavaScript language itself.
//
// The method accepts an array of promises, each representing an asynchronous function,
// which are executed simultaneously, and returns a single promise, allowing a single
// then() method to be executed at such point all the supplied promsies are fulfilled. The
// value passed on fulfillment contains an array of all the returned values of the
// individual promises, in the same order as the promises in the original array passed to
// this method
Promise.all = function(promises) {
    var index = 0,
        promiseCount = promises.length;

    // Return a single promise representing all the promises supplied to this method. It
    // will be fulfilled as soon as every one of the supplied promises have been fulfilled.
    return new Promise(function(fulfill, reject) {
        var promise,
            results = [],
            resultsCount = 0;
```

```
            // Execute an onSuccess() function each time one of the supplied promises is
            // fulfilled, adding its resulting value to an array in the same index position as
            // the promise was in the original array
            function onSuccess(result, index) {
                results[index] = result;
                resultsCount++;

                // If we have collected the results for all of the promises, then fulfill the
                // current single promise, passing across the array of fulfilled values from
                // the individual promises
                if (resultsCount === promiseCount) {
                    fulfill(results);
                }
            }

            // If any of the supplied promises are rejected, then reject the current promise
            function onError(error) {
                reject(error);
            }

            // Resolve a given promise, executing onSuccess() if fulfilled, or onError() if not
            function resolvePromise(index, promise) {
                promise.then(function(value) {
                    onSuccess(value, index);
                }, onError);
            }

            // Loop through all the promises supplied to this method, resolving each in turn
            for (; index < promiseCount; index++) {
                promise = promises[index];
                resolvePromise(index, promise);
            }
        });
    };

    return Promise;
}());
```

Take a look at Listing 7-13, which shows examples of how to create and use promises in your code by taking advantage of the Promise "class" from Listing 7-12.

Listing 7-13. The promises pattern in use

```
// Define a variable to use as a counter further down in this code
var millisecondCount = 0;

// Define a method to get the data returned by a GET request to a given URL. Returns a promise
// to which callback functions can be hooked into using its then() method.
function ajaxGet(url) {

    // Return a new promise, initializing it with the asynchronous function to perform the Ajax
    // request. When the promise executes the function, it will pass in two function parameters,
    // the first should be called by our code if and when the asynchronous request succeeds, and
```

```
    // the second should be called if and when an error occurs in the execution of the
    // asynchronous request.
    return new Promise(function(fulfill, reject) {
        var xhr = new XMLHttpRequest(),
            STATE_LOADED = 4,
            STATUS_OK = 200;

        xhr.onreadystatechange = function() {
            if (xhr.readyState !== STATE_LOADED) {
                return;
            }

            // If the Ajax GET request returns data successfully, execute the fulfill method
            if (xhr.status === STATUS_OK) {
                fulfill(xhr.responseText);

            // If the Ajax request does not return data successfully, execute the reject method
            } else {
                reject("For the URL '" + url + "', the server responded with: " + xhr.status);
            }
        };

        // Perform the Ajax GET request
        xhr.open("GET", url);
        xhr.send();
    });
}


// Define a method which waits a given number of milliseconds before continuing. Returns
// a promise.
function wait(milliseconds) {
    return new Promise(function(fulfill, reject) {

        // If the value provided for milliseconds is a number greater than 0, call the
        // setTimeout method to wait that number of milliseconds before executing the fulfill
        // method
        if (milliseconds && typeof milliseconds === "number" && milliseconds > 0) {
            setTimeout(function() {
                fulfill(milliseconds);
            }, milliseconds);

        // If the value provided for milliseconds is not a number or is less than or equal to
        // 0, then reject the promise immediately
        } else {
            reject("Not an acceptable value provided for milliseconds: " + milliseconds);
        }
    });
}

// Define two functions for use if a particular promise is fulfilled or rejected, respectively
function onSuccess(milliseconds) {
    alert(milliseconds + "ms passed");
}
```

```
function onError(error) {
    alert(error);
}


// EXAMPLE 1: Success
// Execute the wait() function with a value we know will cause it to succeed, and show that
// the first of the two supplied functions to the then() method is executed
wait(500).then(onSuccess, onError); // After 0.5 seconds, outputs: "500ms passed"

// EXAMPLE 2: Error
// Execute the wait() function with a value we know will cause it to error. Because this
// rejects immediately, this will alert the user before the result of example 1 is known
wait(0).then(onSuccess, onError); // "Not an acceptable value provided for milliseconds: 0"

// EXAMPLE 3: Chaining
// Multiple promises can be chained together using the then() method which allows operations to
// be executed in order once the result of the execution of the previous asynchronous function
// is known. This considerably simplifies the nesting of callbacks which would be necessary
// without the use of promises.
wait(1000)
    .then(function(milliseconds) {

        // After a delay of 1 second, increment the counter by the number of milliseconds
        // passed into the function parameter (in this case, 1000)
        millisecondCount += milliseconds;

        // Returning a promise in this function means that the operation indicated by that
        // promise will be executed once the previous operation is complete
        return wait(1600);
    })
    .then(function(milliseconds) {

        // By this point, 2600 milliseconds have passed, and this is stored in our counter
        // variable
        millisecondCount += milliseconds;

        // Return another promise, indicating that a delay of 400 milliseconds should now
        // take place before the function specified in the following then() statement is
        // executed
        return wait(400);
    })
    .then(function(milliseconds) {

        // Increment the counter by the 400 milliseconds just passed, making its total 3000
        millisecondCount += milliseconds;

        // Finally, output the combined value of the counter, which indicates the number of
        // milliseconds passed since the first operation in this chain began
        alert(millisecondCount + "ms passed"); // After 3 seconds, outputs: "3000ms passed"
    });
```

```
// EXAMPLE 4: Multiple Promises
// Different promises can be chained together, since as in this example, which gets a page by
// the URL /page1.html (assuming it exists on the server), then waits 3 seconds before getting
// another page by the URL /page2.html (again, assuming it exists).
ajaxGet("/page1.html")
    .then(function() {
        return wait(3000);
    })
    .then(function() {
        return ajaxGet("/page2.html");
    })
    .then(function() {
        // This alert will fire only if both /page1.html and /page2.html exist and can
        // be accessed
        alert("/page1.html and /page2.html received, with a 3s gap between requests");
    });

// EXAMPLE 5: Simultaneous Promises
// The Promise.all() method accepts an array of promises which will be resolved simultaneously,
// passing the results as an array to the success function passed to its then() method. Get
// both /page1.html and /page2.html simultaneously, and when they are both complete, execute
// the success callback function with the contents of both files in the array parameter passed
// into this function, in the same order as in the array of promises. If any of the supplied
// promises fails, the error callback function will be executed, with the detail of the first
// error that occurred passed into this function parameter.
Promise.all([ajaxGet("/page1.html"), ajaxGet("/page2.html")])
    .then(function(files) {
        alert("/page1.html = " + files[0].length + " bytes. /page2.html = " + files[1].length +
        " bytes.");
    }, function(error) {
        alert(error);
    });
```

The promises pattern is best used when you have many asynchronous operations occurring in your code, causing a mess of nested callback functions. It allows callback functions to be chained to asynchronous calls, making the code easier to follow and understand, and therefore easier to develop and maintain. To read more about the promises pattern online, look at the following resources:

- "Promises/A+ Specification" by the Promises/A+ Organization (via http://bit.ly/promises_aplus)

- "Promise Patterns" by Rhys Brett-Bowen (via http://bit.ly/promises_js)

The Strategy Pattern

The *strategy* pattern is of use in those cases in which you have a "class" containing a large conditional statement (if...else, or switch) where each option causes a specific behavior of that "class" to alter in a different way. Rather than manage a large conditional statement, each behavior can be split into separate objects, each of which is called a *strategy*. Only one of these is applied to the original object, known as the *client*, at any one time. Having multiple strategy objects helps improve the quality of your code, also, as the strategy objects can be unit tested independently of each other.

Listing 7-14 shows an example of a "class" ripe to which to apply the strategy pattern—it contains a number of conditional statements that alter a very specific behavior of the objects created from it.

Listing 7-14. Code ripe for applying a strategy pattern to

```javascript
// Define a "class" representing a form field in an HTML page
function FormField(type, displayText){
    this.type = type || "text";
    this.displayText = displayText || "";

    // Create a new <input> tag, setting its field type to the value supplied upon instantiation
    this.element = document.createElement("input");
    this.element.setAttribute("type", this.type);

    // Create a new <label> tag, setting its text to the value supplied upon instantiation
    this.label = document.createElement("label");
    this.label.innerHTML = this.displayText;

    // Add the <label> and <input> tags to the current page
    document.body.appendChild(this.label);
    document.body.appendChild(this.element);
}

// Give each form field object instance three methods
FormField.prototype = {

    // Return the current value stored in the form field
    getValue: function() {
        return this.element.value;
    },

    // Set a new value for the form field
    setValue: function(value) {
        this.element.value = value;
    },

    // Return a true / false value depending on whether the value in the form field is valid
    isValid: function() {
        var isValid = false,
            value;

        // If this is a <input type="text"> field, it is considered valid if its value is not
        // an empty string
        if (this.type === "text") {
            isValid = this.getValue() !== "";

        // If this is a <input type="email"> field, it is considered valid if its value is not
        // an empty string, contains the "@" character and contains the "." character after "@"
        } else if (this.type === "email") {
            value = this.getValue();
            isValid = value !== "" && value.indexOf("@") > 0 && value.indexOf(".",
            value.indexOf("@")) > 0;
```

```
    // If this is a <input type="number"> field, it is considered valid if its value is
    // a number
    } else if (this.type === "number") {
        value = this.getValue();
        isValid = !isNaN(parseInt(value, 10));

    // This could go on a while as there are 24 possible <input> types in HTML5. We need a
    // way to simplify this to make it easier to understand and extend in future - this is
    // where the strategy pattern comes into play, as shown in Listing 7-14
    } else {
        // etc.
    }

    return isValid;
    }
};
```

The code in Listing 7-15 shows how we can refactor the code in Listing 7-14 into a more efficient and easier-to-manage structure by applying the strategy pattern.

Listing 7-15. The Strategy Pattern

```
// Define a "class" representing a form field in an HTML page. Note a new object is passed into
// the third parameter at instantiation, containing a strategy object. This object contains a
// specific implementation of the isValid() method pertaining to the specific type of form field
// we are creating - for example, a "text" field would require an isValid() method that checks
// to see if the stored value is not an empty string, so we create an object containing this
// method and pass it in through the strategy object at instantiation time
function FormField(type, displayText, strategy){
    this.type = type || "text";
    this.displayText = displayText || "";

    this.element = document.createElement("input");
    this.element.setAttribute("type", this.type);

    this.label = document.createElement("label");
    this.label.innerHTML = this.displayText;

    // Check to see if the strategy object passed in contains the isValid() method to use and,
    // if so, store the stragety object for use when the isValid() method of this object is
    // executed. If no strategy object is supplied, use a default
    if (strategy && typeof strategy.isValid === "function") {
        this.strategy = strategy;
    } else {
        this.strategy = {
            isValid: function() {
                return false;
            }
        };
    }
```

```
        document.body.appendChild(this.label);
        document.body.appendChild(this.element);
}


FormField.prototype = {
    getValue: function() {
        return this.element.value;
    },

    setValue: function(value) {
        this.element.value = value;
    },

    // Replace the previous isValid() method with one that simply calls the isValid() method
    // provided by the stored strategy object - no more extensive if..else statements, making
    // the code for this "class" much smaller and easier to manage
    isValid: function() {
        return this.strategy.isValid.call(this);
    }
};

// Define three strategy objects for three different types of form field to be used with the
// FormField "class" when it is instantiated. Here we provide specific implementations for the
// isValid() method, but we could have extended these to include more methods and/or properties
// to meet our needs. In cases like this, we would have created a strategy "class" and created
// these objects as instances of that "class". Here we have simple objects so it is smarter to
// keep the code short and to the point
var textFieldStrategy = {

        // Specific functionality for validation of a <input type="text"> field
        isValid: function() {
            return this.getValue() !== "";
        }
    },
    emailFieldStrategy = {

        // Specific functionality for validation of a <input type="email"> field
        isValid: function() {
            var value = this.getValue();
            return value !== "" && value.indexOf("@") > 0 && value.indexOf(".",
            value.indexOf("@")) > 0;
        }
    },
    numberFieldStrategy = {

        // Specific functionality for validation of a <input type="number"> field
        isValid: function() {
            var value = this.getValue();
            return !isNaN(parseInt(value, 10));
        }
    };
```

The code in Listing 7-15 can then be used as shown in Listing 7-16.

Listing 7-16. The strategy pattern in use

```
// Create three form fields for our HTML page, each with different types. We pass in the type,
// the text for the associated <label> tag, and the strategy object associated with this field
// type to provide the required behavior for field value validation
var textField = new FormField("text", "First Name", textFieldStrategy),
    emailField = new FormField("email", "Email", emailFieldStrategy),
    numberField = new FormField("number", "Age", numberFieldStrategy);

// Set values for each form field we know will validate
textField.setValue("Den Odell");
emailField.setValue("denodell@me.com");
numberField.setValue(35);

// Check to see if the values in the fields validate correctly
alert(textField.isValid());    // true
alert(emailField.isValid());   // true
alert(numberField.isValid()); // true

// Change the values in the fields to ones we know will fail validation
textField.setValue("");
emailField.setValue("denodell");
numberField.setValue("Den Odell");

// Check to ensure the isValid() method is working correctly, reflecting the new field values
alert(textField.isValid());    // false
alert(emailField.isValid());   // false
alert(numberField.isValid()); // false
```

The strategy pattern is best used when you would otherwise need to manage a bulk of conditional logic to implement the behavior of the methods in your "class." To learn more about the strategy pattern, look at the following online resources:

- "Strategy Design Pattern In JavaScript" by Michael Sokol (via http://bit.ly/strategy_pattern)

- "The Strategy Pattern In JavaScript" by Mike Pennisi (via http://bit.ly/strategy_js)

Summary

In this chapter, we have looked at behavioral design patterns that you can use in your own JavaScript applications to simplify the communication between different objects. These are tools in your Swiss Army knife of JavaScript development but, like all tools, you need to know when and where to use them best. Familiarize yourself with the patterns in this chapter and their use cases, and ensure that you don't use a design pattern before you recognize the need for it in your code.

In the following chapter, we will look at architectural design patterns, which are in fact combinations of existing design patterns that we have already covered, to solve specific problems in larger JavaScript code bases.

■ ■ ■

## CHAPTER 8

Design Patterns: Architectural

A number of the creational, structural, and behavioral design patterns that we've looked at in the past three chapters can be combined together to form *architectural patterns* that can help solve specific problems in larger code bases. In this chapter, we'll look at three of the most common architectural patterns that apply to JavaScript applications, together with examples for each.

The Model-View-Controller (MVC) Pattern

The *Model-View-Controller* (MVC) pattern is one that allows the separation of code in a JavaScript applicaton into three distinct parts: the *Model*, which groups together code related to the underlying data structure in your code, including the storage and retrieval of that data; the *View*, which groups together code relating to the display of the data stored in the Model on screen—essentially dealing with DOM elements; and the *Controller*, which handles any business logic in the system and updates the Model and/or View when necessary—it ensures the Model and View don't need to directly talk to each other, making them loosely coupled from each other. This separation of concerns leads to code that is easier to understand and work with, easier to test, and allows multiple developers working on the same project the ability to divide tasks between the Model, View, and Controller layers in the application.

The MVC architectural pattern is actually the combination of three specific design patterns we've seen before in chapters 6 and 7 used together: *observer*, *composite*, and *strategy*. When data in the Model is changed, the observer pattern is used to trigger an event passing across the updated data for use in other parts of the system. Similarly, the View uses this same pattern to listen for changes to Model data and update the user interface with this new data. A View can only read data directly from a model, not set it; that's the role of the Controller. A View can also contain child views, to handle reusable sections of a larger UI, and the composite pattern is used to ensure that the Controller does not need to be aware of the number of views its logic needs to affect. Finally, the Controller utilizes the strategy pattern to apply a particular View to itself, allowing multiple Views in a larger system to share the same controller logic provided they all expose a similar method, which I choose to name render(), that is passed the data from the Model and places the View on the current page, connecting it up to the events broadcast by the rest of the system, ready for use. It's worth noting that in JavaScript applications the Model is often connected via Ajax to a back-end service acting as a database for stored data represented there.

Listing 8-1 shows how we might create a "class" to handle the representation of Model data in a simple system adopting the MVC pattern that allows the management of a list of email addresses on screen.

Listing 8-1. Model

```
// The Model represents the data in the system. In this system, we wish to manage a list of
// email addresses on screen, allowing them to be added and removed from the displayed list. The
// Model here, therefore, represents the stored email addresses themselves. When addresses are
// added or removed, the Model broadcasts this fact using the observer pattern methods from
// Listing 7-6
//
```

```javascript
// Define the Model as a "class" such that multiple object instances can be created if desired
function EmailModel(data) {

    // Create a storage array for email addresses, defaulting to an empty array if no addresses
    // are provided at instantiation
    this.emailAddresses = data || [];
}

EmailModel.prototype = {

    // Define a method which will add a new email address to the list of stored addresses
    add: function(email) {

        // Add the new email to the start of the array
        this.emailAddresses.unshift(email);

        // Broadcast an event to the system, indicating that a new email address has been
        // added, and passing across that new email address to any code module listening for
        // this event
        observer.publish("model.email-address.added", email);
    },

    // Define a method to remove an email address from the list of stored addresses
    remove: function(email) {
        var index = 0,
            length = this.emailAddresses.length;

        // Loop through the list of stored addresses, locating the provided email address
        for (; index < length; index++) {
            if (this.emailAddresses[index] === email) {

                // Once the email address is located, remove it from the list of stored email
                // addresses
                this.emailAddresses.splice(index, 1);

                // Broadcast an event to the system, indicating that an email address has been
                // removed from the list of stored addresses, passing across the email address
                // that was removed
                observer.publish("model.email-address.removed", email);

                // Break out of the for loop so as not to waste processor cycles now we've
                // found what we were looking for
                break;
            }
        }
    },

    // Define a method to return the entire list of stored email addresses
    getAll: function() {
        return this.emailAddresses;
    }
};
```

The code in Listing 8-2 shows how we might define the View code for our user interface. It will consist of a panel containing two child views, one containing a simple input form for adding new email addresses, and the other displaying a list of the stored email addresses, with a "Remove" button beside each to allow the user to remove individual email addresses from the list. The screenshot shown in Figure 8-1 shows an example of the View that we are constructing.

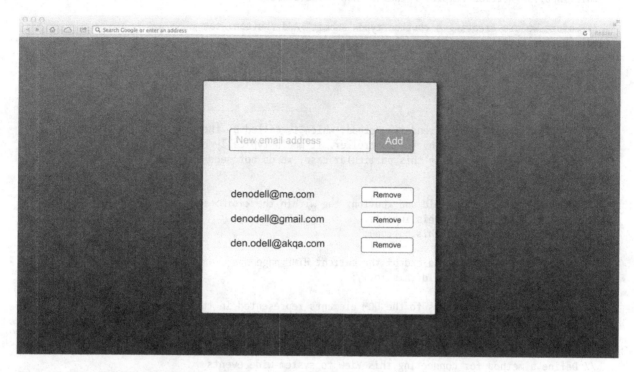

Figure 8-1. *A system for managing email addresses, built using the MVC architectural pattern*

Listing 8-2. View

```
// We will be building a page consisting of two parts: a text input field and associated
// button, for adding new email addresses to our list of stored addresses, and a list displaying
// the stored email addresses with a "Remove" button beside each to allow us to remove email
// addresses from the list of stored addresses. We will also define a generic View which acts
// as a holder for multiple child views, and we'll use this as a way of linking the two views
// together in Listing 8-3. As with the Model in Listing 8-1, we will be taking advantage of
// the observer pattern methods from Listing 7-6
//
// Define a View representing a simple form for adding new email addresses to the displayed
// list. We define this as a "class" so that we can create and display as many instances of
// this form as we wish within our user interface
function EmailFormView() {

    // Create new DOM elements to represent the form we are creating (you may wish to store
    // the HTML tags you need directly within your page rather than create them here)
    this.form = document.createElement("form");
```

```
    this.input = document.createElement("input");
    this.button = document.createElement("button");

    // Ensure we are creating a <input type="text"> field with appropriate placeholder text
    this.input.setAttribute("type", "text");
    this.input.setAttribute("placeholder", "New email address");

    // Ensure we are creating a <button type="submit">Add</button> tag
    this.button.setAttribute("type", "submit");
    this.button.innerHTML = "Add";
}

EmailFormView.prototype = {

    // All Views should have a render() method, which is called by the Controller at some point
    // after its instantiation by the Controller. It would typically be passed the data from
    // the Model also, though in this particular case, we do not need that data
    render: function() {

        // Nest the <input> field and <button> tag within the <form> tag
        this.form.appendChild(this.input);
        this.form.appendChild(this.button);

        // Add the <form> to the end of the current HTML page
        document.body.appendChild(this.form);

        // Connect up any events to the DOM elements represented in this View
        this.bindEvents();
    },

    // Define a method for connecting this View to system-wide events
    bindEvents: function() {
        var that = this;

        // When the form represented by this View is submitted, publish a system-wide event
        // indicating that a new email address has been added via the UI, passing across this
        // new email address value
        this.form.addEventListener("submit", function(evt) {

            // Prevent the default behavior of the submit action on the form (to prevent the
            // page refreshing)
            evt.preventDefault();

            // Broadcast a system-wide event indicating that a new email address has been
            // added via the form represented by this View. The Controller will be listening
            // for this event and will interact with the Model on behalf of the View to
            // add the data to the list of stored addresses
            observer.publish("view.email-view.add", that.input.value);
        }, false);
```

```javascript
            // Hook into the event triggered by the Model that tells us that a new email address
            // has been added in the system, clearing the text in the <input> field when this
            // occurs
            observer.subscribe("model.email-address.added", function() {
                that.clearInputField();
            });
        },

        // Define a method for emptying the text value in the <input> field, called whenever an
        // email address is added to the Model
        clearInputField: function() {
            this.input.value = "";
        }
    };


// Define a second View, representing a list of email addresses in the system. Each item in
// the list is displayed with a "Remove" button beside it to allow its associated address to
// be removed from the list of stored addresses
function EmailListView() {

    // Create DOM elements for <ul>, <li>, <span> and <button> tags
    this.list = document.createElement("ul");
    this.listItem = document.createElement("li");
    this.listItemText = document.createElement("span");
    this.listItemRemoveButton = document.createElement("button");

    // Give the <button> tag the display text "Remove"
    this.listItemRemoveButton.innerHTML = "Remove";
}

EmailListView.prototype = {

    // Define the render() method for this View, which takes the provided Model data and
    // renders a list, with a list item for each email address stored in the Model
    render: function(modelData) {
        var index = 0,
            length = modelData.length,
            email;

        // Loop through the array of Model data containing the list of stored email addresses
        // and create a list item for each, appending it to the list
        for (; index < length; index++) {
            email = modelData[index];

            this.list.appendChild(this.createListItem(email));
        }

        // Append the list to the end of the current HTML page
        document.body.appendChild(this.list);
```

```
        // Connect this View up to the system-wide events
        this.bindEvents();
    },

    // Define a method which, given an email address, creates and returns a populated list
    // item <li> tag representing that email
    createListItem: function(email) {

        // Cloning the existing, configured DOM elements is more efficient than creating new
        // ones from scratch each time
        var listItem = this.listItem.cloneNode(false),
            listItemText = this.listItemText.cloneNode(false),
            listItemRemoveButton = this.listItemRemoveButton.cloneNode(true);

        // Assign a "data-email" attribute to the <li> element, populated with the email
        // address it represents - this simplifies the attempt to locate the list item
        // associated with a particular email address in the removeEmail() method later
        listItem.setAttribute("data-email", email);
        listItemRemoveButton.setAttribute("data-email", email);

        // Display the email address within the <span> element, and append this, together with
        // the "Remove" button, to the list item element
        listItemText.innerHTML = email;
        listItem.appendChild(listItemText).appendChild(listItemRemoveButton);

        // Return the new list item to the calling function
        return listItem;
    },

    // Define a method for connecting this View to system-wide events
    bindEvents: function() {
        var that = this;

        // Create an event delegate on the list itself to handle clicks of the <button> within
        this.list.addEventListener("click", function(evt) {
            if (evt.target && evt.target.tagName === "BUTTON") {

                // When the <button> is clicked, broadcast a system-wide event which will be
                // picked up by the Controller. Pass the email address associated with the
                // <button> to the event
                observer.publish("view.email-view.remove", evt.target.getAttribute("data-email"));
            }
        }, false);

        // Listen for the event fired by the Model indicating that a new email address has
        // been added, and execute the addEmail() method
        observer.subscribe("model.email-address.added", function(email) {
            that.addEmail(email);
        });
```

```
    // Listen for the event fired by the Model indicating that an email address has been
    // removed, and execute the removeEmail() method
    observer.subscribe("model.email-address.removed", function(email) {
        that.removeEmail(email);
    });
},

// Define a method, called when an email address is added to the Model, which inserts a
// new list item to the top of the list represented by this View
addEmail: function(email) {
    this.list.insertBefore(this.createListItem(email), this.list.firstChild);
},

// Define a method, called when an email address is removed from the Model, which removes
// the associated list item from the list represented by this View
removeEmail: function(email) {
    var listItems = this.list.getElementsByTagName("li"),
        index = 0,
        length = listItems.length;

    // Loop through all the list items, locating the one representing the provided email
    // address, and removing it once found
    for (; index < length; index++) {
        if (listItems[index].getAttribute("data-email") === email) {
            this.list.removeChild(listItems[index]);

            // Once we've removed the email address, stop the for loop from executing
            break;
        }
    }
}
};

// Define a generic View which can contain child Views. When its render() method is called, it
// calls the render() methods of its child Views in turn, passing along any Model data
// provided upon instantiation
function EmailView(views) {
    this.views = views || [];
}

EmailView.prototype = {

    // All Views need to have a render() method - in the case of this generic View, it simply
    // executes the render() method of each of its child Views
    render: function(modelData) {
        var index = 0,
            length = this.views.length;
```

```
        // Loop through the child views, executing their render() methods, passing along any
        // Model data provided upon instantiation
        for (; index < length; index++) {
            this.views[index].render(modelData);
        }
    }
};
```

Changes made in the Model can be reflected immediately in the View through the use of the observer pattern. However, changes made in the View are not passed immediately to the Model; they will be handled by the Controller, which is shown in Listing 8-3.

Listing 8-3. Controller

```
// The Controller connects a Model to a View, defining the logic of the system. This allows
// alternative Models and Views to be provided whilst still enabling a similar system behavior,
// provided the Model provides add(), remove() and getAll() methods for accessing its data, and
// the View provides a render() method - this is the strategy pattern in action. We will also
// use the observer pattern methods from Listing 7-6.
//
// Define a "class" to represent the Controller for connecting the Model and Views in our email
// address system. The Controller is instantiated after the Model and View, and their object
// instances provided as inputs
function EmailController(model, view) {

    // Store the provided Model and View objects
    this.model = model;
    this.view = view;
}

EmailController.prototype = {

    // Define a method to use to initialize the system, which gets the data from the Model using
    // its getAll() method and passes it to the associated View by executing that View's
    // render() method
    initialize: function() {

        // Get the list of email addresses from the associated Model
        var modelData = this.model.getAll();

        // Pass that data to the render() method of the associated View
        this.view.render(modelData);

        // Connect Controller logic to system-wide events
        this.bindEvents();
    },

    // Define a method for connecting Controller logic to system-wide events
    bindEvents: function() {
        var that = this;
```

```
    // When the View indicates that a new email address has been added via the user
    // interface, call the addEmail() method
    observer.subscribe("view.email-view.add", function(email) {
        that.addEmail(email);
    });

    // When the View indicates that an email address has been remove via the user
    // interface, call the removeEmail() method
    observer.subscribe("view.email-view.remove", function(email) {
        that.removeEmail(email);
    });
},

// Define a method for adding an email address to the Model, called when an email address
// has been added via the View's user interface
addEmail: function(email) {

    // Call the add() method on the Model directly, passing the email address added via
    // the View. The Model will then broadcast an event indicating a new email address has
    // been added, and the View will respond to this event directly, updating the UI
    this.model.add(email);
},

// Define a method for removing an email address from the Model, called when an email
// address has been removed via the View's user interface
removeEmail: function(email) {

    // Call the remove() method on the Model directly, passing the email address added via
    // the View. The Model will then broadcast an event indicating an email address has
    // been removed, and the View will respond to this event directly, updating the UI
    this.model.remove(email);
    }
};
```

Listing 8-4 shows how we might use the "classes" created in Listings 8-1 through 8-3 to build the simple page shown in Figure 8-1, according to the MVC architectural pattern.

Listing 8-4. The Model-View-Controller pattern in use

```
// Create an instance of our email Model "class", populating it with a few email addresses to
// get started with
var emailModel = new EmailModel([
        "denodell@me.com",
        "denodell@gmail.com",
        "den.odell@akqa.com"
    ]),

    // Create instances of our form View and list View "classes"
    emailFormView = new EmailFormView(),
    emailListView = new EmailListView(),
```

```
// Combine together the form and list Views as children of a single View object
emailView = new EmailView([emailFormView, emailListView]),

// Create an instance of our email system Controller, passing it the Model instance and
// the View to use. Note that the Controller does not need to be aware whether the View
// contains a single View or multiple, combined Views, as it does here - this is an example
// of the composite pattern in action
emailController = new EmailController(emailModel, emailView);
```

```
// Finally, initialize the Controller which gets the data from the Model and passes it to the
// render() method of the View, which, in turn, connects up the user interface to the
// system-wide events, bringing the whole application together
emailController.initialize();
```

This MVC application example can be run within the context of any simple HTML page by combining the code listing from Listing 7-6 (the observer pattern) with those from Listings 8-1 through 8-4, in order. For example:

```html
<!DOCTYPE html>
<html>
<head>
    <title>MVC Example</title>
</head>
<body>
    <script src="Listing7-6.js"></script>
    <script src="Listing8-1.js"></script>
    <script src="Listing8-2.js"></script>
    <script src="Listing8-3.js"></script>
    <script src="Listing8-4.js"></script>
</body>
</html>
```

When the user enters a new email address using the `<input>` field and submits the form, the new email will appear at the top of the list beneath (the message is passed in the system from the View to the Controller to the Model, which then broadcasts an event, updating the View). When the user clicks the Remove button beside any email address, that email will be removed from the display and also from the underlying data store in the Model.

The MVC pattern is useful in larger applications containing a set of data that needs to be displayed, interacted with, and updated in a user interface without overcomplicating the code base. The code is divided into that responsible for storing and manipulating the data, that responsible for the display of the data, and that responsible for the business logic and connections between data and display. To learn more about the Model-View-Controller pattern, look at the following online resources:

- "Model-View-Controller (MVC) With JavaScript" by Alex Netkachov
  (via http://bit.ly/mvc_pattern)

- "Model-View-Controller" on Wikipedia (via http://bit.ly/mvc_wiki)

The Model-View-Presenter (MVP) Pattern

The *Model-View-Presenter* (MVP) architectural pattern is a derivative of the MVC pattern that attempts to clarify the boundaries between the Model, View, and the code that connects them (in MVC, this is the Controller, in MVP, this is known as the *Presenter*). It is based on the same underlying design patterns, but in the MVC pattern, a View can be updated based on changes made in the Model directly, whereas in MVP, all communication between the Model and View must go through the Presenter layer—a subtle but important difference. In addition, the View in the MVP pattern should not contain event handler code directly—this should be passed into the View from the Presenter, meaning that the View code renders the user interface only and the Presenter performs the handling of events instead.

Let's take the email address list example shown in Figure 8-1, which we previously built using the MVC pattern, and build it using the MVP pattern. We'll keep the Model the same as in Listing 8-1, but we'll need to build a new View and replace the Controller from before with a Presenter. The code in Listing 8-5 shows how the Presenter could be written; there are similarities to the Controller from Listing 8-3, but notice the difference in how all the communication between both Model and View is handled here rather than split between the Presenter and the View.

Listing 8-5. A Presenter for the email address list application

```
// The Presenter "class" is created in much the same was as the Controller in the MVC pattern.
// Uses the observer pattern methods from Listing 7-6.
function EmailPresenter(model, view) {
    this.model = model;
    this.view = view;
}

EmailPresenter.prototype = {

    // The initialize() method is the same as it was for the Controller in the MVC pattern
    initialize: function() {
        var modelData = this.model.getAll();

        this.view.render(modelData);
        this.bindEvents();
    },

    // The difference is in the bindEvents() method, where we connect the events triggered from
    // the Model through to the View, and vice versa - no longer can the Model directly update
    // the View without intervention. This clarifies the distinction between the Model and View,
    // making the separation clearer, and giving developers a better idea where to look should
    // problems occur connecting the data to the user interface
    bindEvents: function() {
        var that = this;

        // When the View triggers the "add" event, execute the add() method of the Model
        observer.subscribe("view.email-view.add", function(email) {
            that.model.add(email);
        });

        // When the View triggers the "remove" event, execute the remove() method of the Model
        observer.subscribe("view.email-view.remove", function(email) {
            that.model.remove(email);
        });
```

```
        // When the Model triggers the "added" event, execute the addEmail() method of the View
        observer.subscribe("model.email-address.added", function(email) {

            // Tell the View that the email address has changed. We will need to ensure this
            // method is available on any View passed to the Presenter on instantiation, which
            // includes generic Views that contain child Views
            that.view.addEmail(email);
        });

        // When the Model triggers the "removed" event, execute the removeEmail() method of
        // the View
        observer.subscribe("model.email-address.removed", function(email) {
            that.view.removeEmail(email);
        });
    }
};
```

The View will now be shorter than before since we've extracted some of its event handling code into the Presenter, as you can see in Listing 8-6. Note the addition of addEmail() and removeEmail() methods on each View, including the generic View, which will contain child Views.

Listing 8-6. Views for the MVP pattern

```
// Define the EmailFormView "class" constructor as before to initialize the View's DOM elements.
// Uses the observer pattern methods from Listing 7-6.
function EmailFormView() {
    this.form = document.createElement("form");
    this.input = document.createElement("input");
    this.button = document.createElement("button");

    this.input.setAttribute("type", "text");
    this.input.setAttribute("placeholder", "New email address");

    this.button.setAttribute("type", "submit");
    this.button.innerHTML = "Add";
}

EmailFormView.prototype = {

    // The render() method is the same as it was in the MVC pattern
    render: function() {
        this.form.appendChild(this.input);
        this.form.appendChild(this.button);

        document.body.appendChild(this.form);

        this.bindEvents();
    },

    // Note how the bindEvents() method differs from that in the MVC pattern - we no longer
    // subscribe to events broadcast from the Model, we only trigger View-based events and the
```

```javascript
    // Presenter handles the communication between Model and View
    bindEvents: function() {
        var that = this;

        this.form.addEventListener("submit", function(evt) {
            evt.preventDefault();

            observer.publish("view.email-view.add", that.input.value);
        }, false);
    },

    // We make an addEmail() method available to each View, which the Presenter calls when
    // the Model indicates that a new email address has been added
    addEmail: function() {
        this.input.value = "";
    },

    // We make an removeEmail() method available to each View, which the Presenter calls when
    // the Model indicates that an email address has been removed. Here we do not need to do
    // anything with that information so we leave the method empty
    removeEmail: function() {

    }
};

// Define the EmailListView "class" constructor as before to initialize the View's DOM elements.
function EmailListView() {
    this.list = document.createElement("ul");
    this.listItem = document.createElement("li");
    this.listItemText = document.createElement("span");
    this.listItemRemoveButton = document.createElement("button");

    this.listItemRemoveButton.innerHTML = "Remove";
}

EmailListView.prototype = {
    render: function(modelData) {
        var index = 0,
            length = modelData.length,
            email;

        for (; index < length; index++) {
            email = modelData[index];

            this.list.appendChild(this.createListItem(email));
        }

        document.body.appendChild(this.list);

        this.bindEvents();
    },
```

```javascript
    createListItem: function(email) {
        var listItem = this.listItem.cloneNode(false),
            listItemText = this.listItemText.cloneNode(false),
            listItemRemoveButton = this.listItemRemoveButton.cloneNode(true);

        listItem.setAttribute("data-email", email);
        listItemRemoveButton.setAttribute("data-email", email);

        listItemText.innerHTML = email;
        listItem.appendChild(listItemText).appendChild(listItemRemoveButton);

        return listItem;
    },

    // The bindEvents() method only publishes View events, it no longer subscribes to Model
    // events - these are handled in the Presenter
    bindEvents: function() {
        this.list.addEventListener("click", function(evt) {
            if (evt.target && evt.target.tagName === "BUTTON") {
                observer.publish("view.email-view.remove", evt.target.getAttribute("data-email"));
            }
        }, false);
    },

    // Create this View's addEmail() method, called by the Presenter when the Model indicates
    // that an email address has been added
    addEmail: function(email) {
        this.list.insertBefore(this.createListItem(email), this.list.firstChild);
    },

    // Create this View's removeEmail() method, called by the Presenter when the Model indicates
    // that an email address has been removed
    removeEmail: function(email) {
        var listItems = this.list.getElementsByTagName("li"),
            index = 0,
            length = listItems.length;

        for (; index < length; index++) {
            if (listItems[index].getAttribute("data-email") === email) {
                this.list.removeChild(listItems[index]);
                break;
            }
        }
    }
};

// Create the generic View which can contain child Views
function EmailView(views) {
    this.views = views || [];
}
```

```javascript
EmailView.prototype = {

    // The render() method is as it was in the MVC pattern
    render: function(modelData) {
        var index = 0,
            length = this.views.length;

        for (; index < length; index++) {
            this.views[index].render(modelData);
        }
    },

    // Even the generic View needs the addEmail() and removeEmail() methods. When these are
    // called, they must execute the methods of the same name on any child Views, passing
    // along the email address provided
    addEmail: function(email) {
        var index = 0,
            length = this.views.length;

        for (; index < length; index++) {
            this.views[index].addEmail(email);
        }
    },

    removeEmail: function(email) {
        var index = 0,
            length = this.views.length;

        for (; index < length; index++) {
            this.views[index].removeEmail(email);
        }
    }
};
```

Finally, Listing 8-7 shows how to bring the MVP system together almost identically to that of the MVC pattern that we looked at earlier in the chapter.

Listing 8-7. The Model-View-Presenter pattern in use

```javascript
// Use EmailModel from Listing 8-1
var emailModel = new EmailModel([
        "denodell@me.com",
        "denodell@gmail.com",
        "den.odell@akqa.com"
    ]),
    emailFormView = new EmailFormView(),
    emailListView = new EmailListView(),
    emailView = new EmailView([emailFormView, emailListView]),

    // Create the Presenter as you would the Controller in the MVC pattern
    emailPresenter = new EmailPresenter(emailModel, emailView);

emailPresenter.initialize();
```

213

This MVP application example can be run within the context of any simple HTML page by combining the code listing from Listing 7-6 (the observer pattern) with those from Listings 8-1 (the shared Model from our original MVC application), 8-5, 8-6, and 8-7, in order. For example:

```
<!DOCTYPE html>
<html>
<head>
    <title>MVP Example</title>
</head>
<body>
    <script src="Listing7-6.js"></script>
    <script src="Listing8-1.js"></script>
    <script src="Listing8-5.js"></script>
    <script src="Listing8-6.js"></script>
    <script src="Listing8-7.js"></script>
</body>
</html>
```

The Model-View-Presenter pattern provides a more defined separation between layers than the Model-View-Controller pattern, which can be useful as code bases grow to larger sizes. It is seen as a means of simplifying the MVC pattern as it becomes less easy to follow events in larger applications. To read more about the Model-View-Presenter pattern online, look at the following resources:

- "An MVP Guide To JavaScript" by Roy Peled (via `http://bit.ly/mvp_pattern`)
- "Model-View-Presenter" on Wikipedia (via `http://bit.ly/mvp_wiki`)

The Model-View-ViewModel (MVVM) Pattern

The *Model-View-ViewModel* (MVVM) pattern is a more recent derivative of the MVC pattern that, like the MVP pattern, aims to completely separate the Model and View from communicating directly with each other. Rather than a Presenter, however, the two are separated by a ViewModel, which fulfills a similar role but contains all the code otherwise present in the View. The View itself can therefore be replaced with something much simpler and connected (or *bound*) to the ViewModel via HTML5 data- attributes. In fact, the separation between ViewModel and View is so clear-cut that the View can actually be provided as a static HTML file that can be used as a template to build the user interface directly using bindings to the ViewModel contained in these data- attributes.

Let's return to the same email list application example shown in Figure 8-1 and apply the MVVM pattern to it. We can reuse the same Model code as in Listing 8-1, but we'll be creating a new View and replacing the Controller or Presenter from previously with a ViewModel instead. The code in Listing 8-8 shows a HTML page with specific HTML5 data-attributes on relevant tags that indicate to the ViewModel what it should do to this View based on its internal business logic.

Listing 8-8. A View defined as a simple HTML page

```
<!--
The View is now a simple HTML document - it could be created through DOM elements in JavaScript
but it does not need to be any more. The View is connected to the ViewModel via HTML5 data
attributes on certain HTML tags which are then bound to specific behaviors in the ViewModel as
required
-->
<!DOCTYPE html>
```

```html
<html>
<head>
    <meta charset="utf-8">
    <title>Model-View-ViewModel (MVVM) Example</title>
</head>
<body>
    <!--
    The <form> tag has a specific HTML5 data attribute indicating that when submitted it should
    be bound to an addEmail() method in the ViewModel
    -->
    <form data-submit="addEmail">
        <input type="text" placeholder="New email address">
        <button type="submit">Add</button>
    </form>

    <!--
    The <ul> list has a specific HTML5 data attribute indicating that the tags within should be
    looped through for each item in the stored Model data. So if the Model contained three email
    addresses, three <li> tags would be produced and rendered in place of the one templated <li>
    tag that currently exists
    -->
    <ul data-loop>
        <li>
            <!--
            We will use the data-text attribute to indicate that the ViewModel should replace
            the tag contents with the individual email address represented as we loop through
            the stored Model data
            -->
            <span data-text></span>

            <!--
            We use the data-click attribute as we used data-submit previously on the <form>
            tag, i.e. to execute a specific method exposed by the ViewModel when the button is
            clicked
            -->
            <button data-click="removeEmail">Remove</button>
        </li>
    </ul>

    <!--
    We will add <script> tags to the end of this page in future to load the observer pattern,
    the Model, the ViewModel, and the initialization code
    -->
</body>
</html>
```

I have chosen a data-loop attribute on the <ul> tag to indicate that the <li> tag shown beneath should be repeated for each email address stored in the Model. A data-text attribute on a specific tag within this loop indicates that its contents should be replaced by the email address itself. A data-submit attribute, together with a specific method name as its value, indicates that a submit event handler should be connected to that element, executing the given method name stored in the ViewModel when the event occurs. The value of a data-click attribute similarly represents a method name from the ViewModel to be executed when that element is clicked by the user. These attribute names were chosen arbitrarily; they have no specific meaning in HTML or JavaScript other than that which I have defined here. Note the comment at the end of the file indicating that we will be adding <script> tags to the end of this code listing to load and initialize the code, something that we will add after we've looked into the ViewModel and initialization code.

The code in Listing 8-9 shows the specific ViewModel for binding the relevant data and behavior to the View from Listing 8-8 to represent the application.

Listing 8-9. ViewModel

```
// Define a ViewModel for the email system which connects up a static View to the data stored in
// a Model. It parses the View for specific HTML5 data attributes and uses these as instructions
// to affect the behavior of the system. Provided the ViewModel is expecting the specific data
// attributes included in the View, the system will work as expected. The more generic the
// ViewModel, therefore, the more variation is possible in the View without needing to update
// thes code here. Uses the observer pattern methods from Listing 7-6.
function EmailViewModel(model, view) {
    var that = this;

    this.model = model;
    this.view = view;

    // Define the methods we wish to make available to the View for selection via HTML5 data
    // attributes
    this.methods = {

        // The addEmail() method will add a supplied email address to the Model, which in turn
        // will broadcast an event indicating that the Model has updated
        addEmail: function(email) {
            that.model.add(email);
        },

        // The removeEmail() method will remove a supplied email address from the Model, which
        // in turn will broadcast an event indicating that the Model has updated
        removeEmail: function(email) {
            that.model.remove(email);
        }
    };
}


// Define the method to initialize the connection between the Model and the View
EmailViewModel.prototype.initialize = function() {

    // Locate the <ul data-loop> element which will be used as the root element for looping
    // through the email addresses stored in the Model and displaying each using a copy of the
    // <li> tag located beneath it in the DOM tree
    this.listElement = this.view.querySelectorAll("[data-loop]")[0];

    // Store the <li> tag beneath the <ul data-loop> element
    this.listItemElement = this.listElement.getElementsByTagName("li")[0];
```

```javascript
    // Connect the <form data-submit> in the View to the Model
    this.bindForm();

    // Connect the <ul data-loop> in the View to the Model
    this.bindList();

    // Connect the events broadcast by the Model to the View
    this.bindEvents();
};

// Define a method to configure the <form data-submit> in the View
EmailViewModel.prototype.bindForm = function() {
    var that = this,

        // Locate the <form data-submit> tag
        form = this.view.querySelectorAll("[data-submit]")[0],

        // Get the method name stored in the "data-submit" HTML5 attribute value
        formSubmitMethod = form.getAttribute("data-submit");

    // Create an event listener to execute the method by the given name when the <form> is
    // submitted
    form.addEventListener("submit", function(evt) {

        // Ensure the default <form> tag behavior does not run and the page does not refresh
        evt.preventDefault();

        // Grab the email address entered in the <input> field within the <form>
        var email = form.getElementsByTagName("input")[0].value;

        // Locate the given method in the ViewModel's "methods" property and execute it,
        // passing in the email address entered in the <form>
        if (that.methods[formSubmitMethod] && typeof that.methods[formSubmitMethod] === "function")
{
            that.methods[formSubmitMethod](email);
        }
    });
};

// Define a method to construct the list of email addresses from the data stored in the Model.
// This method is later connected to the events triggered by the Model such that the list is
// recreated each time the data in the Model changes
EmailViewModel.prototype.bindList = function() {

    // Get the latest data from the Model
    var data = this.model.getAll(),
        index = 0,
        length = data.length,
        that = this;
```

```
    // Define a function to create an event handler function based on a given email address,
    // which executes the method name stored in the "data-click" HTML5 data attribute when the
    // <button> tag containing that attribute is clicked, passing across the email address
    function makeClickFunction(email) {
        return function(evt) {

            // Locate the method name stored in the HTML5 "data-click" attribute
            var methodName = evt.target.getAttribute("data-click");

            // Locate the given method in the ViewModel's "methods" property and execute it,
            // passing in the email address provided
            if (that.methods[methodName] && typeof that.methods[methodName] === "function") {
                that.methods[methodName](email);
            }
        };
    }

    // Empty the contents of the <ul data-loop> element, removing all previously created <li>
    // elements within it
    this.listElement.innerHTML = "";

    // Loop through the email addresses stored in the Model, creating <li> tags for each
    // based on the structure from the original state of the View which we stored previously
    for (; index < length; index++) {
        email = data[index];

        // Create a new <li> tag as a clone of the stored tag
        newListItem = this.listItemElement.cloneNode(true);

        // Locate the <span data-text> element and populate it with the email address
        newListItem.querySelectorAll("[data-text]")[0].innerHTML = email;

        // Locate the <button data-click> element and execute the makeClickFunction() function
        // to create an event handler specific to the email address in this turn of the loop
        newListItem.querySelectorAll("[data-click]")[0].addEventListener("click",
        makeClickFunction(email), false);

        // Append the populated <li> tag to the <ul data-loop> element in the View
        this.listElement.appendChild(newListItem);
    }
};

// Define a method to clear the email address entered in the <input> field
EmailViewModel.prototype.clearInputField = function() {
    var textField = this.view.querySelectorAll("input[type=text]")[0];

    textField.value = "";
};
```

```
// The bindEvents() method connects the events broadcast by the Model to the View
EmailViewModel.prototype.bindEvents = function() {
    var that = this;

    // Define a function to execute whenever the data in the Model is updated
    function updateView() {

        // Recreate the list of email addresses from scratch
        that.bindList();

        // Clear any text entered in the <input> field
        that.clearInputField();
    }

    // Connect the updateView() function to the two events triggered by the Model
    observer.subscribe("model.email-address.added", updateView);
    observer.subscribe("model.email-address.removed", updateView);
};
```

Finally, we can pull together the Model from Listing 8-1, the plain HTML View from Listing 8-8, and the ViewModel from Listing 8-9, using the code in Listing 8-10 to initialize the application. To run the code, add `<script>` tag references to the View in Listing 8-8 at the denoted place at the end of the file to load these code listings together with the observer pattern from Listing 7-6. For example:

```
<script src="Listing7-6.js"></script>
<script src="Listing8-1.js"></script>
<script src="Listing8-9.js"></script>
<script src="Listing8-10.js"></script>
```

Because we are adding these `<script>` references into the View HTML page, we are able to get a reference to the DOM representation of the page simply using the `document.body` property, as shown in Listing 8-10, which initializes the application.

Listing 8-10. The MVVM pattern in use

```
// Use EmailModel from Listing 8-1
var emailModel = new EmailModel([
        "denodell@me.com",
        "denodell@gmail.com",
        "den.odell@akqa.com"
    ]),

    // Now our View is a HTML document, we can get a reference to the whole page and use that
    emailView = document.body,

    // Create an instance of our ViewModel as we would do with either Controller or Presenter in
    // MVC and MVP patterns, respectively. Pass in the Model data and View (HTML document).
    emailViewModel = new EmailViewModel(emailModel, emailView);

emailViewModel.initialize();
```

It should be clear that the benefit of the Model-View-ViewModel pattern is the simpler form that Views can take compared with the Model-View-Presenter and Model-View-Controller patterns, which becomes more useful the more Views you have in your application. The more distinct separation of View from the code connecting it to the Model also means different developers in a team can work on the different layers independently from each other, merging their work together at appropriate stages with less risk of conflicting with each other's code. At the time of writing, MVVM is fast becoming the most used architectural pattern by professional JavaScript developers.

To learn more about the Model-View-ViewModel pattern, look at the following online resources:

- "Understanding MVVM—A Guide For JavaScript Developers" by Addy Osmani (via `http://bit.ly/mvvm_pattern`)

- "Model-View-ViewModel" on Wikipedia (via `http://bit.ly/mvvm_wiki`)

Architectural Pattern Frameworks

There are a number of prebuilt Model-View-Controller (MVC), Model-View-Presenter (MVP) and Model-View-ViewModel (MVVM) JavaScript libraries available in the wild for implementing the architectural patterns we've covered in this chapter within your own applications. These can simplify the development of larger code bases as they separate the data management code from the code to render the user interface. Be wary, though, as many of these frameworks are large and may slow down the loading of your application as a result. Apply a framework to your code once it reaches a certain size and you will realize that the use of one of these architectural patterns will solve a development problem you are experiencing. Remember that design patterns are tools in your development toolbox and must be used with care to meet specific needs you have in your code.

If you are looking for a framework to adopt an architectural pattern in your code, look at the following list of popular alternatives:

Framework	Pattern	Notes
Maria	MVC	Based on the original MVC framework from the 1970s, this is as authentic as MVC frameworks get. `http://bit.ly/maria_mvc`
SpineJS	MVC	Spine strives to have the most thorough documentation of any JavaScript MVC framework. `http://bit.ly/spinejs`
EmberJS	MVC	Ember relies on configuration to simplify development and get developers up to speed quickly with the framework. `http://bit.ly/ember_js`
Backbone	MVP	Backbone is a popular framework with a large API allowing virtually any type of application to flourish using the MVP pattern. `http://bit.ly/backbone_mvp`
AgilityJS	MVP	Agility prides itself in being the lightest MVP framework around, at 4KB minified and gzipped. `http://bit.ly/agilityjs`
KnockoutJS	MVVM	Knockout is built to support the MVVM pattern and its data bindings to HTML user interfaces. It has good, thorough documentation, supports older versions of Internet Explorer back to version 6, and has a large community behind it. `http://bit.ly/knockout_mvvm`
AngularJS	MVVM	Angular, by Google, is quickly becoming the most popular architectural framework, supporting the MVVM principle of data binding to connect user interface to underlying data models. Be aware that later versions only support version 9 and up of Internet Explorer. `http://bit.ly/angular_js`

Summary

In this chapter, we have looked at three major architectural patterns you can use to better structure and maintain your JavaScript applications, bringing the section on design patterns to a close. These are tools in your Swiss Army knife of JavaScript development but, like all tools, you need to know when and where to use them best. Familiarize yourself with the patterns in this chapter, and ensure that you don't use a pattern before you recognize the need for it in your code. This is particularly important advice as many make the mistake of building their small application on top of a large preexisting framework, for example, without realizing that they could have saved a lot of development time, and page load time, by writing the exact code they needed themselves. Don't fall into this trap—start with the exact code you need for your applications and then apply a design pattern if you realize you need it, not vice versa.

In the next chapter, we will look at a modern improvement to the module design pattern that we covered in Chapter 6, allowing modules to be loaded asynchronous at the exact point they are needed by your large JavaScript applications, together with any of their required dependencies.

■ ■ ■

## CHAPTER 9

Managing Code File Dependencies

As each year passes, we developers tread further into the brave new world of JavaScript-heavy websites and applications. Using code libraries such as jQuery, frameworks such as AngularJS (http://angularjs.org), Backbone (http://backbonejs.org) or Ember (http://emberjs.com), together with a number of other high quality, reusable plugins, it is possible to simplify the core aspects of JavaScript development to free us up to build richer user experiences that are both functional and a joy to use.

Each extra JavaScript file we add to our solutions introduces an extra level of complexity, notably how we manage that file's relationship with the rest of the JavaScript files in the code base. We may write some code in one file to interact with our page using a jQuery plugin from a separate file, which in turn relies on jQuery being present and loaded from another file. As the size of the solution grows, so do the number of possible connections between files. We say that any JavaScript file that requires another file to be present for it to function correctly has a dependency on that file.

Most often we manage our dependencies in a linear and manual way. At the end of our HTML file, before the closing </body> tag, we usually list our JavaScript files in order, starting with the most generic library and framework files and working through to the most application-specific files, ensuring that each file is listed after its dependencies so no errors occur trying to access variables defined in other script files that are not yet loaded. As the number of files in our solution grows, this method of dependency management becomes increasingly difficult to maintain, particularly if you wish to remove a file without affecting any other code relying on it.

Using RequireJS to Manage Code File Dependencies

We clearly need a more robust method than this for managing dependencies in larger websites and applications. In this chapter, I'll explain how better to manage your code file dependencies using RequireJS, a JavaScript module loader created to solve this exact problem, which has the added advantage of on-demand asynchronous script file loading, something we touched on in Chapter 4 as a means of improving website performance.

The RequireJS library is based on the Asynchronous Module Definition (AMD) API (http://bit.ly/amd_api), a cross-language unified way of defining code blocks together with their dependencies, and is gaining a lot of traction in the industry and implemented on sites such as BBC, Hallmark, Etsy, and Instagram, among others.

To demonstrate how to incorporate RequireJS in an application, let's start with the simple index HTML page as shown in Listing 9-1, which contains a very basic form that, when submitted, posts an e-mail address to a separate Thank You page, as shown in Listing 9-2. The code in Listing 9-3 shows the CSS styles applied to this demonstration page, which we'll store in a file named main.css. We're using the fonts Lobster and Abel from Google Fonts (http://bit.ly/g_fonts).

Listing 9-1. HTML code for the main demonstration page, containing a form for adding an e-mail to a mailing list

```
<!doctype html>
<html>
<head>
    <meta charset="utf-8">
    <title>Mailing list</title>
    <link href="http://fonts.googleapis.com/css?family=Lobster|Abel" rel="stylesheet"
type="text/css">
    <link rel="stylesheet" href="Listing9-3.css">
</head>
<body>
    <form action="Listing9-2.html" id="form" method="post">
        <h1>Join our mailing list</h1>
        <label for="email">Enter your email address</label>
        <input type="text" name="email" id="email" placeholder="e.g. me@mysite.com">
        <input type="submit" value="Sign up">
    </form>
</body>
</html>
```

Listing 9-2. HTML thank you page to direct users to once the e-mail address has been submitted

```
<!doctype html>
<html>
<head>
    <meta charset="utf-8">
    <title>Thank you</title>
    <link href="http://fonts.googleapis.com/css?family=Lobster|Abel" rel="stylesheet" type="text/css">
    <link rel="stylesheet" href="Listing9-3.css">
</head>
<body>
    <div class="card">
        <h1>Thank you</h1>
        <p>Thank you for joining our mailing list.</p>
    </div>
</body>
</html>
```

Listing 9-3. CSS style rules applied to the HTML pages in Listing 9-1 and Listing 9-2

```
html,
body {
    height: 100%;
}

body {
    font-size: 62.5%;
    margin: 0;
    background: #32534D;
    background-image: -webkit-gradient(linear, 0% 0%, 0% 100%, from(#1a82f7), to(#2F2727));
```

```css
    background-image: -webkit-linear-gradient(top, #1a82f7, #2F2727);
    background-image: -moz-linear-gradient(top, #1a82f7, #2F2727);
    background-image: -ms-linear-gradient(top, #1a82f7, #2F2727);
    background-image: -o-linear-gradient(top, #1a82f7, #2F2727);
}

body,
input {
    font-family: "Lobster", sans-serif;
}

h1 {
    font-size: 4.4em;
    letter-spacing: -1px;
    padding-bottom: 0.25em;
}

form,
.card {
    position: absolute;
    top: 100px;
    bottom: 100px;
    min-height: 250px;
    left: 50%;
    margin-left: -280px;
    width: 400px;
    padding: 20px 80px 80px;
    border: 2px solid #333;
    border-radius: 5px;
    box-shadow: 5px 5px 15px #000;
    background: #fff;
    background-image: -webkit-gradient(linear, 0% 0%, 0% 100%, from(#eee), to(#fff));
    background-image: -webkit-linear-gradient(top, #eee, #fff);
    background-image: -moz-linear-gradient(top, #eee, #fff);
    background-image: -ms-linear-gradient(top, #eee, #fff);
    background-image: -o-linear-gradient(top, #eee, #fff);
}

label,
input,
p {
    display: block;
    font-size: 1.8em;
    width: 100%;
}

label,
input[type=email],
p {
    font-family: "Abel", cursive;
}
```

```
input {
    margin-bottom: 1em;
    border: 1px solid #42261B;
    border-radius: 5px;
    padding: 0.25em;
}

input[type=submit] {
    background: #dda;
    color: #000;
    font-weight: bold;
    width: 103%;
    font-size: 3em;
    margin: 0;
    box-shadow: 1px 1px 2px #000;
}

.error {
    border: 1px solid #f99;
    background: #fff5f5;
}
```

Running the code we have so far produces the page with the layout shown in Figure 9-1.

Figure 9-1. *The final page we're building represents a newsletter sign-up form, which will only submit if the e-mail address provided is in a valid format*

Before we write any JavaScript code, we'll download a copy of RequireJS from the project homepage at http://bit.ly/require_dl. At the time of writing, the current version of this library is 2.1.9, and it's supported in all the major web browsers all the way back to Internet Explorer 6, Firefox 2, Safari 3.2, Chrome 3, and Opera 10.

Now, before we add RequireJS to our page, we need to review which JavaScript files we're going to need for our application and organize them into an appropriate folder structure. We'll start with our main application script file, which, using jQuery, will listen for the submit event on the HTML form and perform form validation when this occurs, only allowing the form to continue submitting if there are no errors. We will therefore have three JavaScript files in addition to the RequireJS library, as shown in Table 9-1.

Table 9-1. *The three JavaScript files used in our project, in addition to RequireJS*

File Name	Description
jquery-1.10.2.js	The latest version of the jQuery library at time of writing, for accessing and manipulating DOM elements on the page
validation-plugin.js	Form validation script as a jQuery plugin
main.js	The main application script file

Let's arrange these files together with RequireJS and the rest of the files for the project into a sensible folder structure, as shown in Figure 9-3, with third-party scripts and plugins grouped together in a subfolder named lib within a scripts folder.

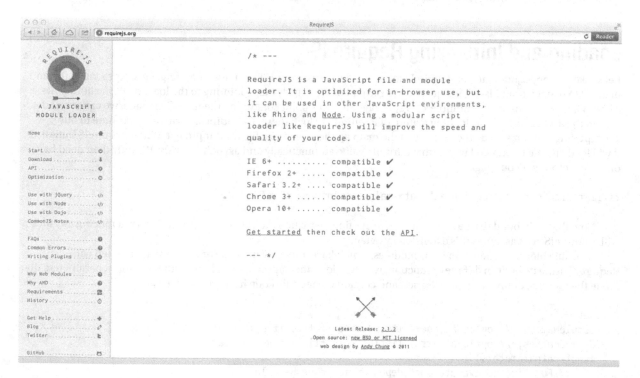

Figure 9-2. *The RequireJS homepage at requirejs.org contains the library files plus plenty of documentation*

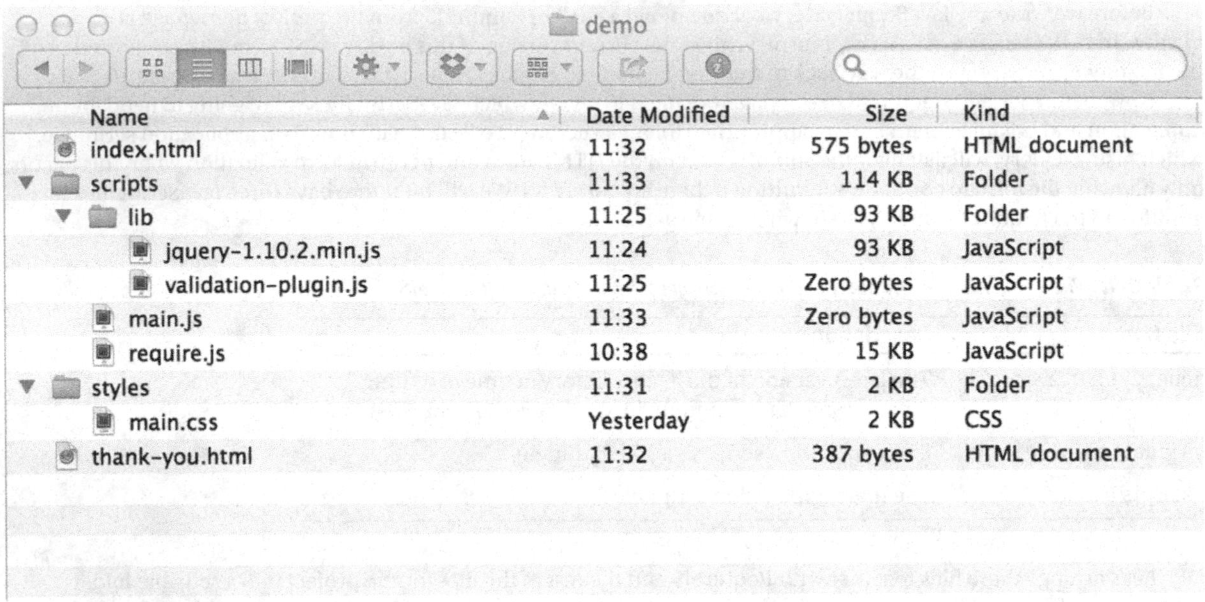

Name		Date Modified	Size	Kind
index.html		11:32	575 bytes	HTML document
▼ 📁 scripts		11:33	114 KB	Folder
▼ 📁 lib		11:25	93 KB	Folder
	jquery-1.10.2.min.js	11:24	93 KB	JavaScript
	validation-plugin.js	11:25	Zero bytes	JavaScript
main.js		11:33	Zero bytes	JavaScript
require.js		10:38	15 KB	JavaScript
▼ 📁 styles		11:31	2 KB	Folder
main.css		Yesterday	2 KB	CSS
thank-you.html		11:32	387 bytes	HTML document

Figure 9-3. Folder structure for our RequireJS-based project

Loading and Initializing RequireJS

Let's take this opportunity to get RequireJS loaded and set up on our HTML page by adding a `<script>` tag to the end of the HTML page from Listing 9-1, just before the end of the `</body>` tag, pointing to the location of the library file. Although we could then add multiple `<script>` tags after this point containing the rest of our code, we can instead rely on the asynchronous file-loading feature of RequireJS to load these. By adding a `data-main` attribute to our `<script>` tag, we can specify the location of the main application script file for our project. When RequireJS initializes, it will load any file referenced within that attribute value automatically and asynchronously. We only then need have one `<script>` tag on our page:

```
<script src="scripts/require.js" data-main="scripts/main"></script>
```

Note that as in our `data-main` attribute here, it's fine to exclude the `.js` file extension when referencing any files with RequireJS, as it assumes this extension by default.

Reusable blocks of code, known as modules, which have a specific purpose or behavior are defined with RequireJS using its built-in `define()` function, which follows the pattern shown here, with three input parameters that name the module, define its dependencies, and contain the module code itself, respectively:

```
define(
    moduleName,   // optional, defaults to name of file if parameter is not present
    dependencies, // optional array listing this file's dependencies
    function(parameters) {
        // Function to execute once dependencies have been loaded
        // parameters contain return values from the dependencies
    }
);
```

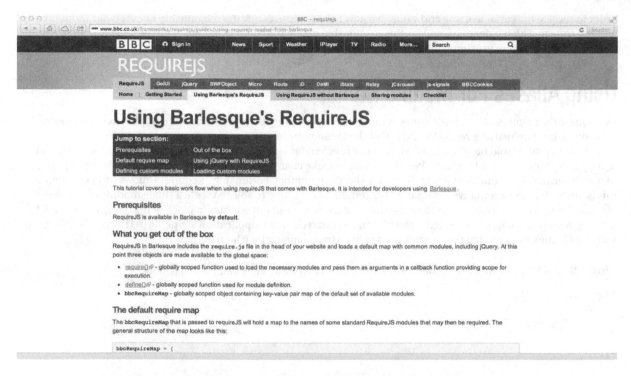

Figure 9-4. *The BBC is a proponent of RequireJS and has its own documentation site for their developers to refer to when building JavaScript modules*

All that's required to be present within a call to `define()` is a function containing the module code to execute. Typically, we would create a separate file for each module in our code base, and by default the module name would be identified in RequireJS by its file name. If your module relies on other code files to function correctly (e.g., a jQuery plugin requires jQuery), you should list these so-called dependencies in an array passed to `define()` before the function parameter containing the module code. The names to use in this array usually correspond to the file names of the dependencies relative to the location of the RequireJS library file itself. In the case of our project, if we wanted to list the jQuery library as a dependency of another module, we would include it in the dependencies array, as shown in Listing 9-4.

Listing 9-4. Defining a module with a dependency on jQuery

```
define(["lib/jquery-1.10.2"], function($) {
    // Module code to execute once jQuery is loaded goes here. The jQuery library
    // is manifest through the first parameter to this function, here named $
});
```

Recall that we do not need to specify the `.js` file extension, so we leave this off when listing our dependencies in the array parameter. Incidentally, recent versions of jQuery contain code to register themselves as modules using the `define()` function should this be present on the page, so we do not need to write any special code to get the jQuery library into the format we need for use with RequireJS. Other libraries might require some initial setup before they can be used with RequireJS. Read the documentation section regarding creating shims for use in this case via `http://bit.ly/require_shim`.

Any return values provided by dependent code files are passed through to the module's function through input parameters, as shown in Listing 9-4. Only these parameters passed through to this function should be used within this module so as to properly encapsulate the code with its dependencies. This also has a mild performance benefit as it is faster for JavaScript to access a local variable scoped to a function than it is for it to ascend to the surrounding scope in order to resolve the variable name and value. We now have a way to codify the relationship between our module code and the code to which it depends, and it's this relationship that tells RequireJS to load in all the code essential to our module function before executing that function.

Using Aliases For Module Names

The jQuery development team has a convention of naming its library file with the version number of the release it represents; here we're using version 1.10.2. If we had numerous references throughout multiple files to jQuery as a dependency, we would be creating a maintenance problem for ourselves should we wish to update the version of jQuery used in our site at a later date. We would have to make changes to all of these files with jQuery as a dependency to match the new file name containing the updated version number. Fortunately, RequireJS allows us to get around this issue by defining alternative alias names for certain modules; we're able to create a single module name alias mapped to our versioned file name so we can use that name throughout our files in place of the direct file name. This is set up within the RequireJS configuration object. Let's start our main application script file (main.js) with the code shown in Listing 9-5, creating this module alias to file name mapping for jQuery.

Listing 9-5. Beginning the main application script file by creating an alias mapping to jQuery

```
requirejs.config({
    paths: {
        "jquery": "lib/jquery-1.10.2"
    }
});
```

We can now use the module name jquery rather than its file name in our dependency arrays in our modules and this will map to the specified version of jQuery.

Content Delivery Networks and Fallbacks

Many developers prefer to reference a copy of jQuery or other popular libraries from one of the many global Content Delivery Networks (CDN) around the web. With the right conditions, this decreases the time taken to download the file and increases the likelihood that the file might be cached on the user's machine already, if they have previously visited another website that loads the same version of jQuery from the same CDN.

RequireJS allows you to link to modules hosted on other domains simply by using its URL in the dependencies array, but we can simplify the management of our external file dependencies using the same configuration setting we used to configure jQuery earlier. We will replace the last code snippet with a new one, to reference jQuery from Google's CDN while still allowing it to fall back to a local version of the file should the external file fail to load. We can chain a list of fallback scripts using an array in the configuration object, as shown in Listing 9-6.

Listing 9-6. A module with two possible locations, one to be used as a fallback in case the first does not load

```
requirejs.config({
    paths: {
        "jquery": [
            "https://ajax.googleapis.com/ajax/libs/jquery/1.10.2/jquery.min",
            // If the CDN fails, load from this local file instead
            "lib/jquery-1.10.2"
        ]
    }
});
```

Creating Modules

Now that we have our file structure in place and RequireJS loaded and configured on our page, it's time to think about how the files within our application depend on each other. We've established that our main application script is dependent on jQuery, in order to set up the form submit handler and the validation script to validate that form. Because the validation script will be built as a jQuery plugin, it, too, is dependent on jQuery. We might describe these dependencies with the table shown in Table 9-2.

Table 9-2. *The code file dependencies for each script in our project*

Script File	Dependencies
jQuery	No dependencies
Validation Plugin	jQuery only
Main Application Script	jQuery and Validation Plugin

We can now write the code for our validation jQuery plugin module within the `validation-plugin.js` file, specifying jQuery as its only dependency. The module checks the value of a given field is in the typical format of an e-mail address and returns true if it is a valid e-mail address, false if not, as shown in Listing 9-7.

Listing 9-7. A RequireJS module that acts as a validation plugin for jQuery

```
define(["jquery"], function($) {
    $.fn.isValidEmail = function() {
        var isValid = true,
            // Regular expression that matches if one or more non-whitespace characters are
            // followed by an @ symbol, followed by one or more non-whitespace characters,
            // followed by a dot (.) character, and finally followed by one or more non-
            // whitespace characters
            regEx = /\S+@\S+\.\S+/;

        this.each(function() {
            if (!regEx.test(this.value)) {
                isValid = false;
            }
        });

        return isValid;
    };
});
```

We omitted the optional module name parameter from our call to the `define()` function, so the module will be registered with the name of the file relative to the location of RequireJS. It can be referenced in other dependencies by the module name `lib/validation-plugin`.

Now we've established our dependencies, it's time to complete the code in our main application script file. We're not going to use the `define()` function here; instead, we're going to use the `require()` function of RequireJS and the AMD API. The two methods have identical patterns, but they differ in the way they are intended to be used. The former is used to declare modules for later use, whereas the latter is used to load dependencies for immediate execution without needing to create a reusable module from it. This latter case suits our main application script, which will be executed once only.

Below the configuration code in our `main.js` file, we need to declare our code for attaching to the submit event of our HTML form, as shown in Listing 9-8, performing validation using our new jQuery plugin script, and allowing the form to submit if the provided e-mail address is valid.

Listing 9-8. Additions to our project's main application script, to connect the page up to our modules

```
require(["jquery", "lib/validation-plugin"], function($) {
    var $form = $("#form"),
        $email = $("#email");

    $form.on("submit", function(e) {
        e.preventDefault();
        if ($email.isValidEmail()) {
            $form.get(0).submit();
        } else {
            $email.addClass("error").focus();
        }
    });

    $email.on("keyup", function() {
        $email.removeClass("error");
    });
});
```

When the code from Listing 9-8 is executed in the browser within the context of the landing page from Listing 9-1, the jQuery library will be loaded first, followed by our validation plugin module. You will recall that when we defined our validation module, we specified that it too had a dependency on jQuery. One of the great features of RequireJS is that if it comes across a dependency that has already been referenced, it will use the stored value from memory rather than downloading it again, allowing us to properly define our code file dependencies without affecting the amount of data downloaded.

Once the dependencies have loaded, the function is executed, with any return values from the dependencies passed through as parameters. Because we defined the validator module to be a jQuery plugin, we specified no return value; it will be added to the jQuery $ variable as is common with other plugins.

Loading Additional Scripts On Demand

We can extend our code to take advantage of the fact that RequireJS can load JavaScript dependencies on demand at the exact point in time they are needed within your application. Rather than load in our validation plugin immediately when the page loads (as we're doing now), we only really need that plugin loaded and available when the user is submitting the form. Offloading the load of this script would boost page load performance by reducing the amount of data downloaded and code executed when the page is initially requested, moving to a script-on-demand model that is more efficient.

RequireJS allows us to do this simply by calling the `require()` function at the point we wish to download extra dependencies. We can rewrite our main application script, removing the dependency on the validation plugin on initial page load, and adding it into the page at the point at which the user attempts to submit the form. If the user never submits the form, this file is never loaded. I've highlighted the extra call to the `require()` function in the updated code for the main application script shown in Listing 9-9.

Listing 9-9. Main application script updated to load the validation plugin on demand when it is needed

```
require(["jquery"], function($) {
    var $form = $("#form"),
        $email = $("#email");
```

```
$form.on("submit", function(e) {
    e.preventDefault();
    require(["lib/validation-plugin"], function() {
        if ($email.isValidEmail()) {
            $form.get(0).submit();
        } else {
            $email.addClass("error").focus();
        }
    });
});

$email.on("keyup", function() {
    $email.removeClass("error");
});
});
```

When the user attempts to submit the form using this updated script, the validator plugin is loaded and validation attempted. If the user attempts validation a second time, the validator plugin is already loaded so it will not be downloaded again. Figure 9-5 shows a waterfall timeline chart of the scripts loading on the page. The second vertical line indicates that the page has fully loaded, while the small dot on the far right indicates when the validation plugin script loaded, at the point the user interacted with the form, thus reducing the amount of data loaded before the page is ready to use.

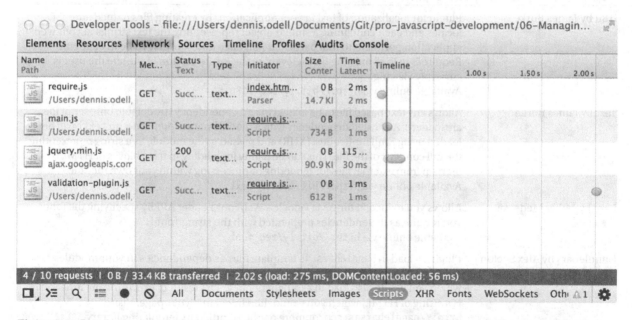

Figure 9-5. *RequireJS supports the loading of JavaScript files dynamically on demand as needed by your application, reducing the number of HTTP requests on page load*

Of course, form submission might not occur until the file has downloaded, so if the plugin script were a large file, this might have an impact on the perceived responsiveness of the page. Should you wish, you may counteract this effect by downloading the validator plugin at the point at which the user first focuses on the text field in the form. This should give the browser enough time to download the plugin file so that it is ready for the point at which the user attempts to submit the form.

The RequireJS Code Optimizer Tool

If you're running a build tool in your development setup, or are packaging your code for deployment after coding, you can take advantage of the RequireJS optimization tool available from `http://requirejs.org`. This combines related scripts and minifies them using UglifyJS or the Google Closure Compiler, which we covered in Chapter 3.

The optimizer was built to be run on Java or NodeJS (preferred, as it runs faster), so it can be run from the command line or via an automated tool. It studies the dependencies listed within your application and associated with each module in your JavaScript files and combines dependency files that are always used together into a single file, dynamically updating the dependency lists in your files to match. This results in fewer HTTP requests when your code executes, improving the experience for end users without altering your original code used in development.

If you'd like to know more about the RequireJS optimization tool, please see the documentation and examples via `http://bit.ly/require_opt`.

Additional Plugins for RequireJS

RequireJS supports the extension of its own functionality by means of plugin scripts that you place together with RequireJS in your scripts folder. Table 9-3 shows a set of standout plugins I have encountered that you may wish to consider using in your applications.

Table 9-3. *Plugins for RequireJS*

Plugin	Description
i18n by James Burke	Plugin for localization of text in your application. By creating files named after ISO locales and each containing a similar object representing the text strings in your web application pertinent to that particular language and country, you can configure RequireJS to load only the files relevant to the locale version of the site the user is currently viewing. Available online via `http://bit.ly/req_i18n`
Text by James Burke	Allows any text-based file to be loaded in as a dependency (by default, only script files are loaded). Any listed dependency with a module names prefixed with `text!` will be loaded using XmlHttpRequest (XHR) and passed to the module as a string representing the full contents of the file. This can be handy for loading in fixed blocks of HTML markup from external files for rendering or processing within your own module. Available online via `http://bit.ly/req_text`
Font by Miller Medeiros	Allows you to load in fonts via Google's WebFont Loader API by specifying the fonts you require as dependencies prepended with the string `font!`. Available online via `http://bit.ly/req_font`
Handlebars by Alex Secton	Plugin to load in `handlebars.js` template files as dependencies in your modules. The template parameter returned is a function into which you can pass your data, which you would also load in as a dependency. The result of executing the function is a string of HTML, which you would then inject into your page. Visit `http://handlebarsjs.com` for more on the Handlebars templating library. Available online via `http://bit.ly/req_handle`
Cache by Jens Arps	By default, RequireJS will store modules in memory once loaded and if a page refresh occurs, will download the modules again. With this plugin, any loaded modules will be stored in `localStorage` within the browser and loaded from there on subsequent page refreshes, to reduce the number of HTTP requests made on page refresh. Available online via `http://bit.ly/req_cache`

If you see functionality that you feel is missing or not up to scratch (or you're simply feeling adventurous), you can write your own plugin by using the RequireJS plugin API, detailed via `http://bit.ly/req_plugin`.

Alternatives To RequireJS

Although RequireJS is the most often used library for managing code dependencies within the browser, it is not the only available option. Because each is based on the AMD specification, each of the alternatives shown in Table 9-4 work in a similar way, so, with a little coaxing, they can be used in place of each other.

Table 9-4. *Browser-based module loaders*

Library	URL
BDLoad	`http://bdframework.org/bdLoad/`
Cajon	`https://github.com/requirejs/cajon`
CurlJS	`https://github.com/cujojs/curl`
LoaderJS	`https://github.com/pinf/loader-js`
RequireJS	`http://requirejs.org`
UMD	`https://github.com/umdjs/umd`
Yabble	`https://github.com/jbrantly/yabble`

Summary

In this chapter, I have taken you through how to build a simple page that uses RequireJS to simplify the management of code file dependencies and enable the delaying of script file loading until such point as it's needed. Not only does this approach make it easier to manage your code as it grows, it also allows you to improve the performance of your web applications by only loading the code needed at the exact moment it's required.

RequireJS is capable of even more than I've covered in this chapter. I encourage you to read through the documentation on the library homepage: to learn how to use the many useful configuration options, how to give modules alternative names, how to load and store data from JSONP web services directly, and how to load and manage multiple versions of the same module at the same time (among many other features).

This approach to code dependency management and script file loading is an emerging industry best practice in today's world of ever-growing JavaScript-heavy code bases for websites and applications. I wholeheartedly encourage you to learn more about this approach and to adopt it in your own websites and reap the benefits for yourself.

In the next chapter, we will cover JavaScript development as it pertains to mobile devices, with techniques for getting the most out of your code with the smallest memory footprint and for learning how to handle inputs from sensors present on many of the smartphone and tablet devices on the market today.

CHAPTER 10

■ ■ ■

Mobile JavaScript Development

Of all the technological advances in recent years, few have had the reach and effect that the mobile smartphone and tablet revolution has had. Industry trends indicate that desktop computer sales are on the decline, while mobile device adoption is growing at breakneck speed. For many, the web is accessed more frequently on small screen devices than on desktop machines. We need to ensure that we keep up with this change, adapting our websites and applications to the needs of our users, many of whom will soon be familiar with a World Wide Web that they access through their fingers.

In this chapter, we will learn the constraints of web development for mobile devices and how to overcome these, how to access data from the sensors on board these devices through JavaScript, how to deal with network problems and poor connections, and, finally, how to adapt our JavaScript to suit websites adopting the principle and techniques of Responsive Design.

The Constraints of Mobile Web Development

With a device so much smaller than a desktop computer, it's not hard to believe that some compromises are made in the design and construction of a mobile device. Some of these compromises are related to the technology within the device itself, and some are a knock-on effect of the networks used to transfer data between the device and its nearest cell tower or WiFi network. Understanding these constraints allows us to adapt our website and application development to minimize their effect and produce the best experience for our end users.

Battery Life

At the time of writing, most smartphone batteries give their owners a day or two of battery life under normal conditions. Performance-intensive apps and websites can drain battery levels over and above the standard power draw of running the device idle.

We need to construct the code in our websites and applications to have the least impact on battery life possible. This involves updating the display area of the page as infrequently as possible, and executing the least amount of JavaScript possible to deliver the desired user experience. Avoid using JavaScript to perform animations and transitions on the page; where these are essential, use CSS3 transitions (`http://bit.ly/css_trans`) and animations (`http://bit.ly/css_anims`) instead, which are far more CPU-efficient, sparing battery usage. If you intend to access data from the mobile device's sensors, such as geolocation or orientation, only access these values sporadically and only for the duration you actually need to, disconnecting any event listeners in your code at the point in which you no longer need access to the data. Use the principle of event framing discussed in Chapter 4 to execute less code when sensor data changes frequently.

Network Bandwidth Speeds And Latency

You might not be surprised to learn that the speeds advertised by mobile network providers don't always match up with reality. The truth is that connection speeds on mobile devices can become constrained by a number of factors including the distance to the cell tower mast you are connected to, the number of other people connected to that same mast, and environmental factors such as weather and the density of surrounding buildings. With modern 4G/LTE mobile networks, the problem of speed is becoming less acute because the potential data transfer rates are that much higher; however, another factor affecting the perceived network speed of the device is that of latency, the time it takes for a HTTP data packet to get from the device to the server and back again. Latency is low on WiFi and wired networks, meaning client-server communication is snappy and feels very responsive; however, on mobile networks latency is a bigger issue, largely because the distances between the device and the cell tower masts are that much greater.

Poor latency will affect each and every HTTP request made by your website or application. The more requests you have, therefore, the slower it will feel your application is responding, as it will take longer for the full page to render completely. With this in mind, minify and concatenate JavaScript files together wherever possible for page load, and offload nonessential scripts to load on demand at the point they're needed, using the techniques covered in Chapters 4 and 9. Minify and concatenate CSS files in the same way (try the CSS Minifier at `http://bit.ly/css_min`), and combine image files into sprites (the technique is explained in detail at `http://bit.ly/css_sprite`), where possible, or use base64 encoding to reference smaller icon-size image files as data URIs directly from within your CSS file (read more on base64 encoding and data URIs at `http://bit.ly/data_uris`). Browsers have limits as to number of files they are configured to download per domain name simultaneously, so by splitting assets across multiple domains, it's possible to download more files simultaneously—a process known as *parallelization*. However, this is a technique to be used with a lot of care, as each DNS lookup takes time and adds to the total latency of your page loading. By attempting to download a large number of files at the same time, the risk grows that none of the files will complete their download in a reasonable time since the network bandwidth available is spread across them all. Use this technique of parallelization wisely, if at all, because it is too easy to have the opposite effect of that intended. Ensure that your web server supports caching and gzipping of JavaScript and CSS files, as these will help reduce the amount of data loaded from the server each time. Later in this chapter we will look at using the HTML5 Application Cache as a means to store files to reduce the number of HTTP requests our page makes each time.

On-Board Memory Size

Web developers have not had to concern themselves with the amount of memory available on a device until the recent wave of smartphone adoption; desktop devices have housed reasonable amounts of memory for some time, plenty enough for rendering web pages with. Most entry-level desktop computers now come with 2GB of on-board memory at the time of writing, whereas the very top-end mobile devices come with only around 512MB. Not all the available memory is readily accessible to a web page either, as it must be shared between the operating system and other background applications and processes. Realistically, a 512MB device probably has less than half of that available to the actual foreground running application.

Consider images; once an image has downloaded from the server it is represented in the device's memory as pixel data in an uncompressed form. A web page with a large number of images will consume more of the device's available memory, and the larger the images, the more memory used. Be wary, therefore, of transmitting large images over the network to mobile devices and then resizing them smaller on the page as they consume the same amount of memory as a much larger image. The same applies to JavaScript, which may be compressed for more efficient data transmission, but once it arrives on the device, is uncompressed and stored in memory. Ensure that you do not transmit more, or larger, files than you need to in order to display your page, as each consumes memory. When the memory is filled, the operating system will attempt to free up memory by closing unused background tasks and applications, affecting the responsiveness and convenience of the user's mobile experience.

Many mobile devices sport graphical processors (GPUs) in addition to their standard processors, each having their own assigned memory. It is possible to offload images to the graphics memory, from where they are hardware accelerated, by applying the CSS transform shown in Listing 10-1 to the element containing the image.

Listing 10-1. CSS rules to offload visual page elements to graphics memory

```
.element {
    /* enforces hardware acceleration on the GPU */
    -webkit-transform: translateZ(0); /* Vendor-specific prefix for Safari 3.1+ / Chrome */
    -moz-transform: translateZ(0); /* Vendor-specific prefix for Firefox 3.5 - 15 */
    -ms-transform: translateZ(0); /* Vendor-specific prefix for Internet Explorer 9 */
    -o-transform: translateZ(0); /* Vendor-specific prefix for Opera 10.50–12.00 */
    transform: translateZ(0);  /* Standard rule (Firefox 16+, IE 10+, Opera 12.10+) */
}
```

Use this technique with caution and in limited amounts, however, as hardware composited images take up four times as much video memory as identical images would in standard memory, corresponding to the red, blue, green, and alpha channels within the image represented separately on the GPU.

Operating System Responsiveness

The users of our websites and applications expect a certain degree of responsiveness from their applications. Anecdotal evidence suggests that if the user does not receive feedback from an action within 300 milliseconds, they feel a distinct lag and form a negative impression of the application. For this reason, it is essential that any interaction they make with the page be shown to produce some visible reaction within this timeframe. If they click a button that triggers an Ajax call and, due to latency or connection speed, that call does not produce a response within 300ms, you should display an indicator on the page to show that an action is taking place in the background. This could take the form of a spinning wheel indicator, though many developers and designers are choosing to use a new generation of indicators such as those collected and curated by Tim Holman online at http://bit.ly/loaders_and_spinners.

Compounding this issue is the fact that the standard click event handler on most mobile devices is not triggered until 300ms after the user lifts their finger after a tap on the screen. This delay is intentional as the device needs to wait to see if the user intended to double-tap on the screen triggering a different action, such as page zoom; without the delay, every action would be interpreted as a single tap. To trigger an action at the very instant the user lifts their finger after a screen tap, connect your code up to the touchend event rather than the click event, although bear in mind the implication this will have for users who intend to double-tap on that element on the screen.

Accessing Mobile Device Sensors with JavaScript

Just as we humans call on our senses to provide us with data about our environment, so smartphones and tablet devices use their own digital senses—touchscreen, geolocation, orientation, direction and motion—to provide interaction and to tailor applications and games to the user and their real-world surroundings. Adding external accessories can give a mobile device even more senses—these include: add-ons for health, such as measuring blood sugar levels (http://bit.ly/bg_module) or tracking blood pressure (http://bit.ly/blood_pressure); add-ons for fitness, such as heart rate monitors (http://bit.ly/hr_monitor) and in-shoe sensors (http://bit.ly/nike_ipod); and add-ons for small businesses, such as credit card readers (http://bit.ly/cc_readers) for accepting payments.

There are three main ways that web developers can access the data reported by the in-built device sensors:

- Using native operating system application programming interfaces (APIs) for each platform (e.g. Google Android, Apple iOS, Microsoft Windows Phone) they wish to support.

- Using a framework such as PhoneGap (`http://phonegap.com`), which enables developers to write their code once in HTML5 and recompile it into native apps for each operating system and device, interacting using native APIs.

- Sensor data can be accessed using standardized web standard APIs (details of the API via `http://bit.ly/1aIQVOx`) that work with different devices using JavaScript within mobile browsers such as Mobile Safari for iOS, Chrome for Android, IE for Windows Phone, Opera Mobile, and Firefox, among others.

The advantage of the third, web standard-based, approach is that it sidesteps the requirement to go through app-store approval processes each time the app is updated, or a bug fix is released. Nor do users have to manually update their apps (it can be done automatically), and it still allows functional and beautiful apps to be built. This is the approach that appeals to me most, and that I will cover in detail in this section.

I will discuss each sensor in turn and describe how to access its data through JavaScript, giving examples of real-world usage and offer some of my personal experience for getting the best results. Refer to the Mobile HTML5 Compatibility Tables (`http://mobilehtml5.org`) for full details on which browsers and devices currently support accessing sensor data.

Accessing The Geolocation Sensor

The geolocation sensor is the power behind mobile mapping applications, locating the user's position on Earth to help them plot routes to different destinations. The sensor uses a combination of approaches, which may include WiFi positioning (read more via `http://bit.ly/wifi_positioning`), GSM cell tower triangulation (read more via `http://bit.ly/mobile_tracking`), and GPS satellite positioning (read more via `http://bit.ly/gps_triangulate`) to retrieve latitude and longitude coordinates representing the user's location. To protect the user's privacy, the website or application must request permission (as specified the W3C guidelines via `http://bit.ly/geo_api`) before accessing data from the geolocation sensor. The user is presented with a dialog asking them to permit access to their location, as shown in Figure 10-1 which shows that presented to users of Apple iOS 7.

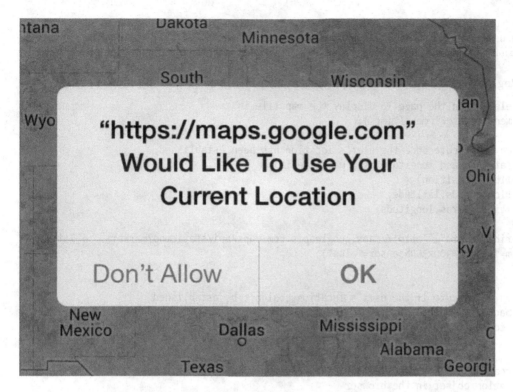

Figure 10-1. *Operating system dialog asking the user to permit access to their location from a website*

Using this geolocation data allows developers to improve user experience of their website or application by, for example, automatically pre-filling city and country fields in web forms, or by looking up what films are playing, at what time, at cinemas in the user's vicinity. Using this data in conjunction with the Google Maps API (usage instructions via http://bit.ly/maps_api) means we can build dedicated mapping and routing apps with maps that dynamically update the user interface as the user changes location. Knowing the location also enables a web app to show photos taken in the user's immediate area using the Panoramio API (usage instructions via http://bit.ly/panoramio_api) or a training assistant (follow the tutorial via http://bit.ly/exercise_app) to calculate how long it takes a runner to cover a certain distance, with the ability to compare performance with past and future runs.

The W3C Geolocation API (http://bit.ly/w3c_geo_api) allows us to access the user's location coordinates through JavaScript, providing a one-off position lock, or the ability to continuously track the user as they move. The browser's navigation.geolocation.getCurrentPosition() method executes a callback function passed to it one time only, which receives the user's location coordinates, whereas the navigation.geolocation.watchPosition() method executes a passed callback function every time the user's location changes allowing for geolocation monitoring. The API also allows us to establish the accuracy of the returned coordinates and specify whether we want the location to be returned normally or with high precision.

■ **Note**   Precision location will both take a little longer to pinpoint the user and potentially consume more device battery power in the process.

The example in Listing 10-2 shows how this API could be used to update a map on screen dynamically based on the user's location, using Google's Static Maps API (usage instructions via http://bit.ly/static_maps) for simplicity. It assumes it is running within the context of a HTML page that it will place the map tile image within.

Listing 10-2. Accessing the Geolocation sensor and displaying location on a map

```
// Create a <img> element on the page to display the map tile in
var mapElem = document.createElement("img");

// Define a function to execute once the user's location has been established,
// plotting their latitude and longitude as a map tile image
function successCallback(position) {
    var lat = position.coords.latitude,
        long = position.coords.longitude;

    mapElem.setAttribute("src", "http://maps.googleapis.com/maps/api/staticmap?markers=" + lat +
"," + long + "&zoom=15&size=300x300&sensor=false");
}

// Define a function to execute if the user's location couldn't be established
function errorCallback() {
    alert("Sorry - couldn't get your location.");
}

// Detect the Geolocation API before using it-'feature detection'-exposed in the
// navigator.geolocation object in the browser
if (navigator.geolocation) {

    // Start watching the user's location, updating once per second (1s = 1000ms)
    // and execute the appropriate callback function based on whether the user
    // was successfully located or not
    navigator.geolocation.watchPosition(successCallback, errorCallback, {
        maximumAge: 1000
    });

    // Size the map tile image element and add it to the current page
    mapElem.setAttribute("width", 300);
    mapElem.setAttribute("height", 300);
    document.body.appendChild(mapElem);
}
```

To prevent JavaScript errors, we use feature detection to ensure that access to the geolocation sensor is available before coding against its API, using a simple if statement around the code that may or may not be supported by the browser. It's possible to request access to the user's location on page load, but this is best avoided, as this forces them to choose to share their location before they know how it will be used, raising suspicion. Providing a button for the user to press to give permission to access their location gives them a greater sense of control over the site or application, which makes them much more likely to grant permission.

If the user denies access to their location, you may be able to locate their general position to city or country level using an IP-based fallback (such as FreeGeoIP at http://freegeoip.net). If this is not suitable, explain politely to the user that you are unable to provide them with some specific functionality until they grant you permission, thus letting them feel as if they're in control of their data and how it is used.

Further Reading On Geolocation

If you would like to read more on the W3C Geolocation API, the following links will help you dig deeper into this fascinating sensor.

- "Using Geolocation" on Mozilla Developer Network (via `http://bit.ly/using_geo`)

- "Exception Handling with the Geolocation API" by Jef Claes
  (via `http://bit.ly/geo_exception`)

- "A Simple Trip Meter Using the Geolocation API" by Michael Mahemoff on HTML5 Rocks
  (via `http://bit.ly/trip_meter`)

Accessing The Touch Sensor

Touchscreens allow users control of the interface of their mobile devices in a simple and natural manner. The touch sensors underneath the screen can detect contact by one or more fingers and track their movement across the screen. In JavaScript, this movement causes a `touchevent`, which you can read more about on the W3C website via `http://bit.ly/w3c_touch_event`.

The data from the touch sensor is accessed in JavaScript using the W3C Touch Events API (`http://bit.ly/w3c_touchevents`). This enables the enhancement of websites and apps with image carousels and slideshows, for example, which react to finger swipes. It also allows the development of advanced web apps that allow people to draw pictures using their fingers, such as one demonstrated by Artistic Abode via `http://bit.ly/abode_touch`, as shown in Figure 10-2, or to test their memory by flipping over cards with a finger to find the pairs, as in MemoryVitamins, found online at `http://bit.ly/mem_vitamins`.

Figure 10-2. *A picture being drawn using a finger on a touchscreen with Artistic Abode's web app*

Whenever the user touches, moves, or removes a finger from the screen, a touch event fires in the browser, first when a finger is placed onto the screen, the touchstart event, when that finger is moved, the touchmove event, and finally when that finger is removed from the screen, the touchend event. Event handler functions can be assigned to each of these events to create the desired behavior for our web applications. As well as giving us the location of the current touch point, the sensor can also tell us through our event handler which page element was touched and provide a list of all other finger touches currently on screen, those within a specific element, and those which have changed since the last touch event fired.

Certain touch actions trigger behavior within the operating system of the mobile device itself: holding down a finger over an image, for example, might trigger a context menu to appear or two fingers moving apart over a page might trigger a page zoom. If you are coding for the touch sensor, you can override this default OS behavior within your event-handler function using the preventDefault() method of the event object passed to the event handler when a touch event fires.

Listing 10-3 shows how the touchscreen API can be used to display the current number of touches on the screen at any one time, updating whenever a finger, or fingers, are added or removed from the screen. It assumes running in the context of an HTML page, to which it adds a <p> element for displaying the number of screen touches in.

Listing 10-3. Accessing data from the touch sensors

```
// Create a <p> element on the page to output the total number of current touches
// on the screen to
var touchCountElem = document.createElement("p");

// Define an event handler to execute when a touch event occurs on the screen
function handleTouchEvent(event) {

    // Get the list of all touches currently on the screen
    var allTouches = event.touches,
        allTouchesLength = allTouches.length;

    // Prevent the default browser action from occurring
    // when the user touches and holds their finger on the screen
    if (event.type === "touchstart") {
        event.preventDefault();
    }

    // Write the number of current touches onto the page
    touchCountElem.innerHTML = "There are currently " + allTouchesLength + " touches on the
screen.";
}

// Add the output <p> element to the current page
document.body.appendChild(touchCountElem);

// Assign the event handler to execute when a finger touches (touchstart) or is removed
// from (touchend) the screen
window.addEventListener("touchstart", handleTouchEvent, false);
window.addEventListener("touchend", handleTouchEvent, false);
```

Apple iOS devices support a more advanced set of JavaScript events relating to gestures. These events fire when the user pinches or rotates two or more fingers on the screen and reports back how far the figures moved. These are device-specific, however, so if you wish to replicate these events on different devices, you might find the JavaScript library Hammer.js (http://bit.ly/hammer_js) useful, which enables you to utilize touch gestures easily across multiple devices within your websites and applications.

Further Reading on Touch Sensors

You might find the following links handy if you wish to read more about the W3C touch events API:

- Developing for Multi-Touch Web Browsers by Boris Smus on HTML5 Rocks (http://bit.ly/multitouch_dev)

- Touch Events on the Mozilla Developer Network (http://bit.ly/touchevents)

- Handling Gesture Events on Apple Safari Web content guide (http://bit.ly/handling_events)

Accessing The Orientation and Direction Sensors

The orientation sensor establishes which way up the device is being held; it can also detect how the device is being positioned about three different rotational axes, as shown in Figure 10-3, assuming the device has an internal gyroscope. Some devices, such as Apple's iPhone and iPad, also include a magnetometer, which helps to establish the precise direction the device is pointing in. The rotation around the x-, y-, and z-axes may respectively be referred to as roll pitch, and yaw, or expressed in degrees of beta, gamma, and alpha rotation.

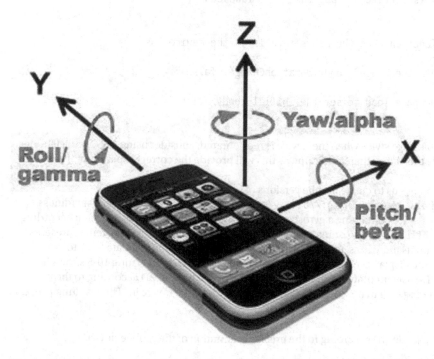

Figure 10-3. *Rotation around the x, y, z axes of a mobile device. Source:* http://hillcrestlabs.com

By knowing the mobile device's orientation, we can adjust features of our sites to suit, such as repositioning a navigation menu above or beside the main content area, as appropriate. The W3C Screen Orientation API (http://bit.ly/screen_orientation) in JavaScript informs us of the device's current orientation, whether portrait or landscape, as well as whether it is being held upside down or not. It fires an orientationchange event that we can hook code into, to execute at the very moment the device is reorientated. The example in Listing 10-4 shows how to use the Screen Orientation API to add a CSS class to your page's <body> tag to indicate whether the device is in portrait or landscape orientation and to allow appropriate styling changes to be made through that.

Listing 10-4. Changing a class name on a HTML page based on the orientation of the mobile device

```
// Define an event handler function to execute when the device orientation changes between
// portrait and landscape
function onOrientationChange() {

    // The device is in portrait orientation if the device is held at 0 or 180 degrees, and in
    // landscape orientation if the device is held at 90 or -90 degrees
    var isPortrait = window.orientation % 180 === 0;

    // Add a class to the <body> tag of the page according to the orientation of the device
    document.body.className += isPortrait ? " portrait" : " landscape";
}

// Execute the event handler function when the browser tells us the device has
// changed orientation
window.addEventListener("orientationchange", onOrientationChange, false);

// Execute the same function on page load to set the initial <body> class
onOrientationChange();
```

If you only wish to change visible page styles when the device is reorientated, consider using CSS Media Queries (http://bit.ly/css_mq) to achieve this rather than JavaScript, as this will provide the correct separation of concerns (http://bit.ly/concerns_web).

Access to a built-in gyroscope allows us to create mobile versions of games such as Jenga (http://bit.ly/jenga_game) or Marble Madness (http://bit.ly/marble_madness) to test the user's steadiness and nerves. When rotating a mobile device containing a gyroscope, the browser fires a reorientation event according to the W3C DeviceOrientation API (http://bit.ly/orientation_event). Data supplied with this event represents the amount the device rotated around its three axes, measured in degrees. Feeding this motion data back to our JavaScript code allows us to update the display according to our program logic. The code in Listing 10-5 shows how to use the built-in gyroscope with the DeviceOrientation API to rotate an image on a page in 3D according to the precise orientation of the device. It adds an <img> tag to the current HTML page to display the image in. The resulting pseudo-3D effect can be seen in Figure 10-4.

Listing 10-5. Rotating an image in pseudo-3D according to the precise orientation of the mobile device

```
// Create a <img> element on the page and point to an image of your choosing
var imageElem = document.createElement("img");
imageElem.setAttribute("src", "Listing10-5.jpg");

// Create an event handler function for processing the device orientation event
function handleOrientationEvent(event) {
```

```
// Get the orientation of the device in 3 axes, known as alpha, beta, and gamma, and
// represented in degrees from the initial orientation of the device on load
var alpha = event.alpha,
    beta = event.beta,
    gamma = event.gamma;

// Rotate the <img> element in 3 axes according to the device's orientation using CSS
    imageElem.style.webkitTransform = "rotateZ(" + alpha + "deg) rotateX(" + beta + "deg)
rotateY(" + gamma + "deg)";
}

// Add the <img> element to the page
document.body.appendChild(imageElem);

// Listen for changes to the device orientation using the gyroscope and fire the event
// handler accordingly
window.addEventListener("deviceorientation", handleOrientationEvent, false);
```

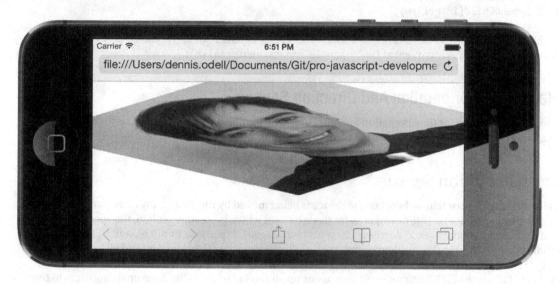

Figure 10-4. *Running Listing 10-5, creating a pseudo-3D effect on an image using device sensors*

We could combine data from a magnetometer with a CSS rotation transform to construct a virtual compass or to align an on-screen map to the direction in which the user is facing. An experimental Webkit-specific property is available in Apple's Mobile Safari browser, returning the current compass heading in degrees from due north whenever the device is moved, allowing us to update the display accordingly. There is no standardized API for accessing the magnetometer at present, although this is envisioned as an extension to the DeviceOrientation API already mentioned.

The code in Listing 10-6 shows how to rotate an <img> tag on a HTML page representing a compass (with due north represented by the image pointing directly upward on the page) according to the current heading to which the device is pointing.

Listing 10-6. Rotating an image according to the compass heading of the mobile device

```
// Create a <img> element on the page and point to an image of a compass
var imageElem = document.createElement("img");
imageElem.setAttribute("src", "Listing10-6.jpg");

// Create a function to execute when the compass heading of the device changes
function handleCompassEvent(event) {

    // Get the current compass heading of the iPhone or iPad, in degrees from due north
    var compassHeading = event.webkitCompassHeading;

    // Rotate an image according to the compass heading value. The arrow pointing to due north
    // in the image will continue to point north as the device moves
    imageElem.style.webkitTransform = "rotate(" + (-compassHeading) + "deg)";
}

// Add the <img> element to the page
document.body.appendChild(imageElem);

// Observe the orientation of the device and call the event handler when it changes
window.addEventListener("deviceorientation", handleCompassEvent, false);
```

Further Reading On Orientation And Direction Sensors

To discover more about coding for the orientation and direction sensors, check out "Detecting Device Orientation" on the Mozilla Developer Network website via http://bit.ly/detect_orientation.

Accessing The Motion Sensor

A mobile device's motion sensor tells us how fast the device is being moved by the user in any of its three linear axes, x (side-to-side), y (forward/back), z (up/down) and, for those devices with a gyroscope built in, the speed at which it moves around its three rotational axes, x (degrees of beta rotation, or roll), y (gamma, or pitch), and z (alpha, or yaw).

The motion sensor is used in flip-to-silence apps, such as Flip4Silence (available for Android via Google Play via http://bit.ly/flip4silence) and games such as Sega's Super Monkey Ball 2 (available for Apple iOS on the App Store via http://bit.ly/smball2). The motion sensor opens up all sorts of possibilities from enabling users to reset a form or undo an action with a shake of their device to advanced web apps, such as the virtual seismograph found online via http://bit.ly/is_quake.

The W3C DeviceMotionEvent API (http://bit.ly/device_motion) dictates that the mobile device fires a JavaScript event whenever a it is moved or rotated, this passes on sensor data giving device acceleration (in meters per second squared—m/s^2) and rotation speed (in degrees per second—deg/s). Acceleration data is given in two forms: one taking into account the effect of gravity and one ignoring it. In the latter case, the device will report a downward acceleration of 9.81 meters per second squared even while sitting perfectly still. The code in Listing 10-7 shows how to report the current acceleration of the device to the user using the DeviceMotionEvent API. It assumes to be running within the context of a HTML page, and adds two <p> tags to display the values returned by the motion sensor, without the effects of gravity, and with it, respectively.

Listing 10-7. Accessing the motion sensor to display the device's maximum acceleration in any direction

```
// Create <p> elements for displaying current device acceleration values in
var accElem = document.createElement("p"),
    accGravityElem = document.createElement("p");

// Define an event handler function for processing the device's acceleration values
function handleDeviceMotionEvent(event) {

    // Get the current acceleration values in 3 axes and find the greatest of these
    var acc = event.acceleration,
        maxAcc = Math.max(acc.x, acc.y, acc.z),

        // Get the acceleration values including gravity and find the greatest of these
        accGravity = event.accelerationIncludingGravity,
        maxAccGravity = Math.max(accGravity.x, accGravity.y, accGravity.z);

    // Output to the user the greatest current acceleration value in any axis, as well as the
    // greatest value in any axis including the effect of gravity
    accElem.innerHTML = "Current acceleration: " + maxAcc + "m/s^2";
    accGravityElem.innerHTML = "Including gravity: " + maxAccGravity + "m/s^2";
}

// Add the <p> elements to the page
document.body.appendChild(accElem);
document.body.appendChild(accGravityElem);

// Assign the event handler function to execute when the device is moving
window.addEventListener("devicemotion", handleDeviceMotionEvent, false);
```

Further Reading On The Motion Sensor

To discover more about accessing the motion sensor on mobile devices, take a look at the following material online.

- "Device Motion Event Class Reference" at Apple Safari Developer Library (http://bit.ly/devicemotion)

- "Orientation and Motion Data Explained" at Mozilla Developer Network (http://bit.ly/orientaton_motion)

The Missing Sensors

At the time of writing, neither camera nor microphone sensors are accessible through JavaScript within a mobile browser. If we were able to access these sensors, we could, for example, potentially capture an image of the user's face to assign to an online account or allowed the user to record audio notes for themselves.

Disagreements between different browser vendors are in part to blame for the lack of a standardized API for access to this data. The recent W3C Media Capture and Streams API (http://bit.ly/media_capture) is gaining traction, however, and in time should enable developers to capture a still image or video stream from the camera or an audio stream from the microphone (with the user's permission) for use within our JavaScript code. At present, this API is only available in Google's Chrome browser and Mozilla's Firefox browser on the desktop, but support looks to be added soon. See the latest browser support for this feature by visiting http://bit.ly/caniuse_stream in your browser.

Event Framing For Sensor Data

In Chapter 4, I described the process of event framing for handling events that trigger very frequently, to improve performance by reducing the amount of code executed each time such an event fired. This technique should be used in earnest when it comes to mobile devices, which aren't capable of processing JavaScript as quickly as desktop browsers can. Without framing, event handler functions will consume additional extra memory on the device and cause the website or application to feel unresponsive. Listing 10-8 shows how we might adjust the code from Listing 10-5 apply the technique of event framing to the DeviceOrientation API.

Listing 10-8. Rotating an image according to the precise orientation of the mobile device using event framing

```
// Create variables to store the data returned by the device orientation event
var alpha = 0,
    beta = 0,
    gamma = 0,
    imageElem = document.createElement("img");

imageElem.setAttribute("src", "Listing10-5.jpg");

// Update the event handler to do nothing more than store the values from the event
function handleOrientationEvent(event) {
    alpha = event.alpha;
    beta = event.beta;
    gamma = event.gamma;
}

// Add a new function to perform just the image rotation using the stored variables
function rotateImage() {
    imageElem.style.webkitTransform = "rotateZ(" + alpha + "deg) rotateX(" + beta + "deg)
rotateY(" + gamma + "deg)";
}

document.body.appendChild(imageElem);

// Connect the event to the handler function as normal
window.addEventListener("deviceorientation", handleOrientationEvent, false);

// Execute the new image rotation function once every 500 milliseconds, instead of every time
// the event fires, effectively improving application performance
window.setInterval(rotateImage, 500);
```

Taking Sensor Data Further

The possibilities and opportunities for enhancing sites and creating web apps based on sensor data using JavaScript are huge. I have considered a few examples here—and with a little creativity, I'm sure you can come up with many more. Try combining data from different sensors (such as geolocation and direction or motion and orientation) to help you build enhanced sites and web apps that respond to the user and their environment in new and exciting ways. Experiment and have fun with it!

Network Connection Failures And Offline States

A well-known problem of browsing the web on mobile devices is the issue of drops in network connection, particularly if the user is in motion, for example onboard a train or in the back of a car. When following a link to open a new page, it is clear to the user that the network has dropped as they will see a familiar screen for those on mobile devices. Figure 10-5 shows how such a screen looks on Apple iOS 7.

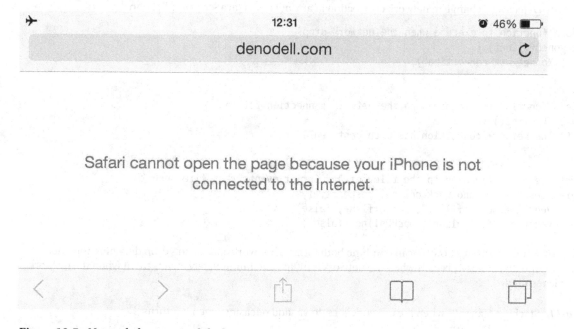

Figure 10-5. *Network drops on mobile devices cause inconvenient experiences for those browsing the web*

If we're building a web application driven by JavaScript, in which hard page transitions are removed in favor of a single-page experience, the user won't be presented with a such a screen if the network connection drops, and it's therefore up to us as developers to handle this in our applications ourselves, to indicate to the user that the network connection has dropped on screen, for example, or to store HTTP calls in a buffer until such time as the network connection returns.

Detecting Online and Offline States

The code in Listing 10-9 shows how to detect, at any point in your JavaScript code's execution, if the network connection has dropped, using the browser's `navigator.onLine` property.

Listing 10-9. Detecting a drop in network connection at a specific point during JavaScript code execution

```
var isOnline = navigator.onLine;

if (isOnline) {
    // Run code dependent on network access, for example, execute an Ajax call to the server
} else {
    alert("The network has gone offline. Please try again later.");
}
```

The code in Listing 10-9 is useful for wrapping around any network connection code, such as an Ajax call using XmlHttpRequest, or creating a `<script>`, `<img>`, or `<link>` DOM element dynamically which refers to an external file resource. You may wish, however, to present the user with an indication on screen if the network is connected or not. Rather than poll the value of `navigator.onLine` continuously, we can take advantage of two JavaScript events that fire when the network drops and when it is restored, named `offline` and `online`, respectively. You can then hook code to execute onto these events to update the page when the network state changes, as shown in Listing 10-10.

Listing 10-10. Detecting a change in network connection at any point in a JavaScript application

```
// Define a function to execute when the network drops
function goneOffline() {
    alert("No network connection");
}

// Define a function to execute when the network connection returns
function backOnline() {
    alert("The network connection has been restored");
}

// Connect these functions up to the relevant JavaScript events that fire when the
// network goes offline and back online, respectively
window.addEventListener("offline", goneOffline, false);
window.addEventListener("online", backOnline, false);
```

Listing 10-11 demonstrates how we can combine both forms of network connection drop detection together into a code routine that stores Ajax calls when the network is offline and immediately enacts them when the network connection is restored.

Listing 10-11. Stacking Ajax calls when the network goes down, and releasing when it returns

```
// Define a variable to store our stack of Ajax calls in if they can't be made immediately
// because of a dropped network connection
var stack = [];

// Define the function that makes Ajax calls
function ajax(url, callback) {

    // The XMLHttpRequest class enables Ajax requests to be made in the browser
    var xhr = new XMLHttpRequest(),
        LOADED_STATE = 4,
        OK_STATUS = 200;

    // If the browser has gone offline, add the function arguments (the url and callback) to the
    // stack for sending later
    if (!navigator.onLine) {
        stack.push(arguments);
    } else {

        // If the browser is online, make the Ajaz call
        xhr.onreadystatechange = function() {
```

```
        // A readyState of 4 indicates that the server response is complete
        if (xhr.readyState !== LOADED_STATE) {
            return;
        }

        // Execute the callback function if the server responded with a HTTP 200
        // status message ("OK")
        if (xhr.status === OK_STATUS) {
            callback(xhr.responseText);
        }
    };

    // Trigger the Ajax HTTP GET operation
    xhr.open("GET", url);
    xhr.send();
  }
}

// Define a function that loops through the stack of unsent Ajax calls, sending each in turn
function clearStack() {

    // Loop through the items in the stack until the stack length is 0 (a falsy value)
    while (stack.length) {

        // Make the Ajax call, using the data from the stack. The shift() method pulls the first
        // item off the array and returns it, altering the original array
        ajax.apply(ajax, stack.shift());
    }
}

// Ensure the clearStack function executes as soon as the network connection is restored

window.addEventListener("online", clearStack, false);
```

You would then make Ajax calls in your code using the ajax() method, as shown here. The code in Listing 10-11 will then handle whether to make the network call immediately or wait until the network connection returns.

```
ajax("/my-service-url", function(data) {
    alert("Received the following data: " + JSON.stringify(data));
});
```

You could adapt this example further to allow your website or application to deal with occasional network drops without affecting the user's experience at any point in their interaction with your code.

Persisting Data With The Web Storage API

When your web application goes offline, we saw in Listing 10-11 how to stack up the calls that would have been so that they can continue once the network connection returns. The user, however, isn't aware in this case that this is going on, that the calls they made to, for example, save personal data, didn't go through to the server and are only being stored in memory. If they chose to close the tab down in their browser, these memory contents are wiped, meaning those calls will never be made to the server. We need a way to persist this stack in memory, even if the browser gets closed down, so that when the user returns to the application in future, the calls can then be made from the stack, provided the network is connected.

Persistent variable storage used to be handled through the creation of cookies, small files that get dropped on the user's machine and get sent with each HTTP request to the server. This is inefficient—a large cookie file that gets sent with every request could result in a much less performant application. Today, we have access to the HTML5 Web Storage API (http://bit.ly/webstorage_api) and specifically the window.sessionStorage and window.localStorage objects defined within that specification. The former, sessionStorage, allows data to be stored only for the duration of the user's browser session. Typically, once they close down the browser any stored values are deleted. The localStorage object, on the other hand, allows data to persist across sessions until deleted by the user or your application. There are three methods available on the object to get, set, and remove items by name from the local storage memory block: getItem, setItem, and removeItem, respectively. Listing 10-12 shows how to use these methods to persist variable data in memory, even after the browser is closed down.

Listing 10-12. Using the Web Storage API to persist data values after the browser is closed down

```
// Check to see if we have stored a value for the "favoriteBrowser" key before
var favoriteBrowser = window.localStorage.getItem("favoriteBrowser");

// If not, prompt the user to tell us their favorite web browser
if (!favoriteBrowser || favoriteBrowser === "") {
    favoriteBrowser = prompt("Which is your favorite web browser?", "Google Chrome");

    // Store their favorite browser in localStorage for next time they visit
    window.localStorage.setItem("favoriteBrowser", favoriteBrowser);
}

// Show the user that we know what their favorite browser is, even if they told us some time ago
alert("Your favorite browser is " + favoriteBrowser);

// Ask if the user would like us to remove their favorite browser value from persistent storage
if (confirm("Would you like us to forget your favorite browser?")) {

    // Remove the value from localStorage
    window.localStorage.removeItem("favoriteBrowser");
}
```

The getItem, setItem and removeItem methods can be replaced in favor of a simplified, more familiar syntax, treating the localStorage object as a standard object in JavaScript, creating, accessing, and deleting properties from that object to persist their data, as shown in Listing 10-13 which performs the exact same function as Listing 10-12. Note also how the localStorage object can be accessed directly without needing to go through the window object to get a reference to it.

Listing 10-13. An alternative method for accessing the Web Storage API

```
// Data within localStorage can be accessed as if they were properties on a standard object
var favoriteBrowser = localStorage["favoriteBrowser"];

if (!favoriteBrowser || favoriteBrowser === "") {
    localStorage["favoriteBrowser"] = prompt("Which is your favorite web browser?", "Google
Chrome");
}

alert("Your favorite browser is " + favoriteBrowser);
```

```
if (confirm("Would you like us to forget your favorite browser?")) {

    // The delete keyword allows the removal of a property from localStorage
    delete localStorage["favoriteBrowser"];
}
```

We can apply the Web Storage API to the code we wrote in Listing 10-11 to stack Ajax calls when the network is disconnected, persisting that stack if the user closes the browser down, and making those calls when the user reopens the browser and the network connection is restored, as shown in Listing 10-14.

Listing 10-14. Stacking Ajax calls when the network drops, and persisting them after the browser is closed down

```
localStorage["stack"] = localStorage["stack"] || [];

function ajax(url, callback) {
    var xhr = new XMLHttpRequest(),
        LOADED_STATE = 4,
        OK_STATUS = 200;

    if (!navigator.onLine) {

        // Data in localStorage is stored as strings, so to store complex data structures such
        // as arrays or objects, we need to convert those into a JSON-formatted string first
        localStorage["stack"].push(JSON.stringify(arguments));
    } else {
        xhr.onreadystatechange = function() {
            if (xhr.readyState !== LOADED_STATE) {
                return;
            }

            if (xhr.status === OK_STATUS) {
                callback(xhr.responseText);
            }
        };

        xhr.open("GET", url);
        xhr.send();
    }
}

function clearStack() {
    if (navigator.onLine) {
        while (localStorage["stack"].length) {

            // After reading the JSON-formatted string data out of localStorage, it needs to be
            // converted back into a complex data form for use with the ajax() function
            ajax.apply(ajax, JSON.parse(localStorage["stack"].shift()));
        }
    }
}

// Check on page load if there are any previously stacked Ajax calls that could now be sent
window.addEventListener("load", clearStack, false);
window.addEventListener("online", clearStack, false);
```

Before you go ahead and start adding megabytes worth of data locally using this API, it's worth considering the limitations enforced by the browser on the amount of data that can be stored this way. Each domain name gets to store a maximum of 5MB of data locally. Although this is a setting that can be changed in many browsers, this is the default amount and there is no way to change that via JavaScript. If you attempt to write more than 5MB of data using localStorage, JavaScript will throw an error and will not allow you to save your extra data until you delete previously stored data. If you wish to clear the entire contents stored locally in this way, you can call the localStorage.clear() method, which will free up all the space available to your application, restoring you to the 5MB default data storage amount.

For a thorough look into the Web Storage API, have a read of "The DOM Storage Guide" on Mozilla's Developer Network online via http://bit.ly/dom_storage.

The HTML5 Application Cache

The final technology we have at our disposal for handling the offline state is the HTML5 Application Cache. Using a specially formatted file, known as a cache manifest, you are able to list specific files in your application to download and store in a cache on the local device, allowing those files to be loaded from there instead of directly from the network each time. This means that once you've visited a website or application once, you should be able to access that same site again even if your network connection is offline. This is not only beneficial to those on mobile devices or with poor network connections, the benefits can be experienced on desktop devices too, meaning sites, once cached in this way, will load virtually instantaneously.

The cache manifest file is a simple text file which convention dictates should have an .appcache file extension, although really this is not essential or part of any specification. More important, the cache manifest file must be served with a MIME type of text/cache-manifest, which for most web servers will mean a specific rule will need to be added to the server configuration for that specific file extension.

A manifest file must be referenced from your HTML file by referencing it using the manifest attribute on the <html> tag:

```
<html manifest="manifest.appcache">
```

The manifest file itself looks like a standard text file, the first line of which must read CACHE MANIFEST in order to be properly identified. In its simplest use, there should then follow a list of files, one per line, which will then be cached for future requests of the same page. If any file listed in the manifest file does not exist, or returns a HTTP error status (for example, 404, or 500) when requested, the whole manifest file will be considered invalid and no files will be cached using this mechanism. The next time the page is loaded, the browser treats the manifest file as if it has never seen it before, attempting to download all referenced assets again.

If the browser detects that the manifest file has been updated since files were last cached, it will go back to the web server to download any of the referenced files that have changed—it sends an If-Modified-Since HTTP header for each file request when it does this, meaning that only files that have been updated since the last round of caching are actually replaced in the cache. A good tip is to include a commented line, indicated by a hash (#) character at the start of the line, in the manifest file, which references a version number for the file, and/or an optional date of the change. When you update the referenced files, update the version number in the file so that the browser detects the change and begins to check for updated files. Without a change in the manifest file, the browser will continue to serve the cached version of the files until such time as the user deletes the cache manually. When requesting a page that has been cached in this way in the past, the browser will first load the cached version of the page before downloading the updated files in the background. Only when the page is next refreshed will the updated assets load. This is in contrast to how many expect the browser behavior to be, expecting the page to redownload and render the whole page based on the new assets immediately if a change in the manifest file is detected.

Listing 10-15 shows a simple cache manifest file, listing file assets that should be loaded and cached for the next time the page is loaded, whether that is online or offline. Note that you do not need to list the HTML page referencing the manifest file itself, as this will be cached by default.

Listing 10-15. A simple cache manifest file

```
CACHE MANIFEST
# Version 1.0.1 - 2013-01-02
/library/styles/main.css
/library/scripts/lib/jquery.min.js
/library/scripts/main.js
/images/background.jpg
/images/logo.png
```

A cache manifest file may contain three optional sections, each denoted by the headings: CACHE:, NETWORK:, and FALLBACK:. The CACHE: section is the same as if there were no sections listed, that is to say that it contains the files listed that should be stored in the offline cache.

The NETWORK: section lists URLs that require the user to be online to access them, for example form action URLs, web services, and other network-essential files. Any resource listed in this section will be accessed directly via the network, bypassing the cache altogether. This section requires only partial URLs, so if a set of web services are exposed via the same foundation URL, for example, https://api.twitter.com/1.1/, then this is all that need be listed. Wildcard values are permitted by using the asterisk (*) character.

The FALLBACK: section lists locally cached files to be used in place of network-essential URLs when the network is offline. It consists of a file name, URL or pattern, followed by the local cached file to be used in place if the network connection is down. In its simplest incarnation, with a static HTML site, you could use a wildcard to reference all .html files and have them fallback to a single offline HTML file, explaining to the user that the site is currently offline on that single page, for a more pleasing user experience. In more advanced cases, you can provide fallbacks to any server-side script, image, stylesheet, JavaScript file, or more, to provide a good experience for your users when the network drops.

Listing 10-16 shows a more advanced cache manifest file using the optional CACHE:, NETWORK:, and FALLBACK: sections.

Listing 10-16. A cache manifest file containing three sections

```
CACHE MANIFEST
# Version 1.0.1 - 2013-10-02

CACHE:
/library/styles/main.css
/library/scripts/lib/jquery.min.js
/library/scripts/main.js
/images/background.jpg
/images/logo.png

# Always go straight to the network for API calls from a base /api/ URL
NETWORK:
/api/

# Replace a 'network online' image with a 'network offline' image when the network is down
FALLBACK:
/images/network-status-online.png /images/network-status-offline.png
```

If you would like to read more about the HTML5 Application Cache, visit the "Using The Application Cache" article on Mozilla's Developer Network site (http://bit.ly/app_cache).

JavaScript For Responsive Design

Responsive Web Design is an emerging technique of designing and constructing websites and apps by allowing the interface to adapt to the characteristics of the device it is being viewed upon. Devices with a small screen, such as a smartphone, will display an appropriately sized and scaled user interface, as will those users on larger devices. CSS3 Media Queries allow the application of different style rules to page elements based on the current characteristics of the device.

In many cases, a visual change to a website using this technique might warrant a change in the behavior of the interface. A navigation menu that might be fully displayed on a larger device, might be hidden offscreen on a smaller device, with a toggle button used to trigger the display of the menu; the toggle button's behavior would only apply to the small-screen view.

Different JavaScript code can be executed based on which CSS3 Media Query rule is currently active by using the window.matchMedia() method of the browser, passing the Media Query or partial query to be compared with the current display. This returns a MediaQueryList object containing a matches property, which will be set to true if the Media Query it represents is active at that time.

If the applied Media Query changes, you will need to recheck the state of the matches properties of each of your MediaQueryList objects. Fortunately, in the vast majority of cases, this should be a simple case of hooking into the browser window's resize event, as shown in Listing 10-17.

Listing 10-17. Executing specific JavaScript based on CSS3 Media Queries

```
// Create MediaQueryList objects for different CSS3 Media Query rules
var landscapeMQL = window.matchMedia("(orientation: landscape)"),
    smallScreenMQL = window.matchMedia("(max-width: 480px)");

function checkMediaQueries() {

    // Execute specific code if the browser is now in landscape orientation
    if (landscapeMQL.matches) {
        alert("The browser is now in landscape orientation");
    }

    // Execute specific code if the browser window is 480px or narrower in width
    if (smallScreenMQL.matches) {
        alert("Your browser window is 480px or narrower in width");
    }
}

// Execute the function on page load and when the screen is resized or its orientation changes
window.addEventListener("load", checkMediaQueries, false);
window.addEventListener("resize", checkMediaQueries, false);
```

Read more about the matchMedia method on Mozilla's Developer Network via http://bit.ly/matchmedia.

Summary

In this chapter, we've considered the web, and specifically JavaScript, as it applies to a user browsing on a mobile, smartphone, or tablet device. We've seen the restrictions we need to consider in terms of memory, bandwidth, latency, and speed, and how best to work around these. We've looked at how to access data directly from the sensors onboard such devices, allowing our applications to react to location, motion, direction, and more. We've also looked at what happens when the network connection drops and how to provide a smooth user experience despite this, dealing with network operations as soon as the network is restored. Finally, we've learned how to execute specific JavaScript based on CSS3 Media Queries applied in the browser on responsive websites.

Mobile-focused development is a growing area, and with the release of new devices and operating system updates each year, we have access to more and more features of the device directly through JavaScript using open, standard W3C APIs. Ensure you keep abreast of the latest developments on a regular basis so as not to be left behind in this fast-moving world of technological progress.

In the next chapter, we will look at how to use the HTML5 Canvas drawing API to build online games for desktop and mobile, without relying on any third-party plugins, such as Adobe Flash.

■ ■ ■

## CHAPTER 11

Building Games with Canvas API

One of the web browser's most exciting new capabilities in recent years has been the adoption of the `<canvas>` tag in HTML5 and its associated JavaScript API. Alone in an HTML document, it does nothing. However, combine it with the power of JavaScript and you have a blank drawing surface in your page to which you can add shapes, images and text to your heart's content. The contents of a canvas element are represented by pixel data on a flat drawing surface rather than individual DOM elements in a document, so if you draw over an existing shape with another, there's no record in the document that the original shape ever existed. By repeatedly clearing and redrawing on the same canvas over a period of time with small variations, we can give the impression of animation and movement within the element. By connecting up this animation to a controller on a touchscreen, mouse or keyboard, we allow the user the ability to manipulate what happens on screen. Combine this with some behavioral logic and we can use the `<canvas>` element to build games that run in the browser. In this chapter, we'll look at the basic drawing operations in the Canvas JavaScript API before delving into detail on how to build games using it, including building a working version of the classic arcade game, Frogger.

Basic Drawing Operations in Canvas

All drawing on a canvas surface occurs through JavaScript alone, and all canvases are blank by default. Before drawing, we need to get a reference to the *two-dimensional drawing context* of the canvas element, which returns a reference to the surface we wish to draw on—future development of the canvas specification is possible by creating additional *contexts* for different needs, such as three-dimensional graphics which are now possible in canvas through the WebGL specification (`http://webgl.org`). Getting the drawing context reference is as simple as executing the `getContext()` method of the canvas DOM element, and from there a number of methods can be executed to draw shapes and add text onto the canvas, as shown in Listing 11-1.

Listing 11-1. Basic drawing operations in Canvas

```
// Create a new <canvas> element
var canvas = document.createElement("canvas"),

    // Get a reference to the drawing context of the canvas
    context = canvas.getContext("2d");

// Set the dimensions of the canvas
canvas.width = 200;
canvas.height = 200;
```

```
// By default, a canvas is drawn empty, however if we needed to empty its contents after
// drawing to it, we could execute this function
function emptyCanvas() {

    // Erase the contents of the canvas from the top-left of the canvas to the position at
    // 200px x 200px from the top-left corner
    context.clearRect(0, 0, 200, 200);
}

// With the drawing context established, we can now execute any of the drawing commands we
// would like on our blank canvas. For example, if we want to draw a circle in the top-left
// corner of our canvas, we could execute the following function
function drawCircle() {

    // First, we tell the drawing context that we're creating a path—essentially a line
    // between one point and another that could take any course between the two points

    context.beginPath();

    // The context's arc() method tells the path to take an arc shape. The method's first
    // two parameters indicate its starting position of the arc in pixels along the x- and
    // y-axes, respecitvely. The third parameter indicates the size of the arc, in pixels,
    // and the final two parameters indicate the arc's start and end angle, in radians,
    // respsecitvely. To draw a circle, the start angle will always be 0, and the end angle
    // will always be twice the value of PI, which indicates a full 360 degrees in radians.
    context.arc(100, 100, 100, 0, 2 * Math.PI);

    // By default, this line's path would be invisible, however the stroke() method ensures
    // that a visible line is drawn along the path making its outline visible. We could also
    // have used the fill() method to fill the circle with a fixed color.
    context.stroke();
}

// Drawing a straight line works in a similar way to drawing a circle in that we must define
// our line before calling the stroke() method to actually apply the graphical "ink" to the
// canvas
function drawLine() {

    // Move the drawing context location to position 50px (from the left edge of the canvas) x 40px
    // (from the top edge of the canvas)
    context.moveTo(50, 40);

    // Mark out a staright line from the context's current position to position 150px x 160px,
    // without actually drawing a line onto the canvas
    context.lineTo(150, 160);

    // Apply the "ink" to the canvas to fill in the marked-out line
    context.stroke();
}
```

```
// Define a function to draw a red square onto the canvas using the drawing context's
// fillRect() method, setting the draw color to use first before performing the action
function drawSquare() {

    // Set the fill style of the next draw operation. #FF000 is the hex value representing red.
    context.fillStyle = "#FF0000";

    // Draw a 100px red square starting at position 20px x 20px
    context.fillRect(20, 20, 100, 100);
}

// We could even add text onto our canvas using the fillText() and strokeText() drawing
// context methods as shown in this function
function writeText() {

    // First set the font style to use for the text to draw onto the canvas
    context.font = "30px Arial";

    // Write some text onto the canvas at position 0px x 0px
    context.fillStyle = "#000";
    context.fillText("Filled Text", 0, 30);

    // Write some outlined text onto the canvas beneath the existing text at position 0px x 40px
    context.strokeText("Outlined Text", 0, 70);
}

// Execute the defined drawing functions, adding their shapes and text to the canvas
emptyCanvas();
drawCircle();
drawLine();
drawSquare();
writeText();

// Add the new <canvas> DOM element to the end of the current HTML page once loaded
window.addEventListener("load", function() {
    document.body.appendChild(canvas);
}, false);
```

Executing the code in Listing 11-1 within the context of a web page results in the image shown in Figure 11-1 being added to the page within a <canvas> element.

Figure 11-1. *Basic drawing operations in Canvas*

For a more detailed overview of the drawing methods available in the Canvas API, check out the "Canvas Tutorial" hosted on Mozilla's Developer Network via `http://bit.ly/canvas_tutorial`.

High-Definition Canvas Elements

Recent advances in screen technology for mobile and desktop devices have brought the advent of high-definition graphics to such devices, sometimes called *retina* graphics as the individual pixel boundaries should be indistinguishable to the retina within the naked eye. By default, canvas elements do not appear to create higher-definition graphics for such screen types and standard canvas-based graphics typically look pixelated or blurred on these screens. Fortunately there are techniques to help us work around this to create high-resolution canvas elements.

To ensure that your canvas is only rendering the correct number of pixels for the device screen it is displayed upon, we can take advantage of the `devicePixelRatio` property on the browser's `window` object. The value stored in this property indicates the resolution factor over the standard display resolution the current screen supports, for example, 1 for a standard screen, and 2 for a retina display. We use this value to scale up the width and height of our `<canvas>` element if appropriate for the screen type, using CSS as before to scale it down to the correct size again for display. The dimensions and sizes of all drawing operations must also be scaled by this factor as appropriate, therefore, to render in the correct size on the device. Paul Lewis has written some thorough documentation on how to achieve this on the HTML5 Rocks blog via `http://bit.ly/hidpi_canvas`, which is worth reading thoroughly, however if you are confident the graphics you are drawing are not particularly intensive operations to perform, you could simply create your canvas at double the size you intend to display it at, rendering everything assuming this larger size (i.e., without using a scale factor), then simply use CSS to set the width and height of the canvas element back to the desired display size within the HTML page. This results in higher resolution graphics being visible on the canvas by simply rendering more pixels in the smaller space. If your end user does not have a high-definition screen, we are rendering extra pixels which aren't displayed, which is why this technique should only be used for less-intensive graphics operations so as not to affect browser performance.

Building Games Using Canvas

One common use of the Canvas API is for building games that run in the browser, once only the domain of proprietary code written for Adobe's Flash player. Because the API is supported on a wide range of devices, both desktop and mobile, games written using the Canvas API can also be played on the move from within the browser.

Many games consist of similar procedures and structures, including:

- The presence of a game board, or world, which defines the constraints of action within the game

- Drawing and animating the player the user controls, and any enemies or obstacles present on the game board and keeping track of the position of each on the game board

- Controlling the player's movement over the game board using input mechanisms such as keypresses, clicks, taps, movement, and other relevant input devices

- Keeping an updated score, high score, and keeping track of the number of lives the player has remaining and/or how much time the player has remaining to complete the level

- Detecting when one or more players or obstacles collide with each other on the game board as well as the handling of the player losing a life or completing the level or game

Let's look in some detail now at how to code each of these structures in a way that can work together to form a working game using the Canvas API.

Drawing Images onto a Canvas

Most games involve the movement of images on a screen—the player's character is rarely a simple shape such as a circle or square, it can be easiest to design game graphics as images for use within the game. The involves needing to draw images from files straight onto a canvas, which can be done using the `drawImage()` method of the canvas' drawing context, passing it a reference to an `<img>` element and the position on the canvas to draw the image, as shown in Listing 11-2.

Listing 11-2. Drawing an image onto a canvas

```
// Create a new <canvas> element to draw the image to
var canvas = document.createElement("canvas"),

    // Get the drawing context of the <canvas> element
    context = canvas.getContext("2d"),

    // Create a new <img> element to reference the image to draw onto the <canvas>
    img = document.createElement("img");

// Assign a function to execute once the assigned image has loaded—the image will not begin to
// load until its "src" attribute has been set
img.addEventListener("load", function() {

    // Draw the image onto the <canvas> element at position 0px x 0px—the top-left corner of
    // the element
    context.drawImage(img, 0, 0);
}, false);
```

```
// Assign the "src" attribute of the <img> element to point to the location of the image we wish
// to display within the <canvas> element. The image will then load and the event handler
// assigned previously will be executed
img.src = "filename.png";

 // Append the new <canvas> element to the end of the current HTML page once loaded
window.addEventListener("load", function() {
    document.body.appendChild(canvas);
}, false);
```

Avoiding Multiple Image Files by Using Sprite Map Images

A common technique for avoiding loading multiple small image files that are used together on a web page is to combine those images together into a *sprite map*, a larger image containing each individual image within it. This helps improve performance by reducing the number of HTTP requests generated that the browser and server need to fulfill. In a standard webpage, the individual images can then be extracted from the larger image for display by using the CSS background-position property in conjunction with the width and height properties. In the case of displaying images on a canvas, a variation of the parameters used in the drawImage() method allow us to extract a smaller portion of an image from a larger sprite map image file, as shown in Listing 11-3.

Listing 11-3. Drawing an individual image from a sprite map onto a canvas

```
var canvas = document.createElement("canvas"),
    context = canvas.getContext("2d"),
    img = document.createElement("img");

img.addEventListener("load", function() {
    var individualImagePositionTop = 200,
        individualImagePositionLeft = 150,
        individualImageWidth = 300,
        individualImageHeight = 40,
        displayPositionTop = 100,
        displayPositionLeft = 100,
        displayWidth = 150,
        displayHeight = 40;

    // Draw the individual image located at position 200px x 150px and with dimensions 300px x
    // 40px onto the <canvas> element at position 100px x 100px, rendering at half the size of
    // the original, at 150px x 40px
    context.drawImage(img, individualImagePositionTop, individualImagePositionLeft,
individualImageWidth, individualImageHeight, displayPositionTop, displayPositionLeft,
displayWidth, displayHeight);
}, false);

img.src = "sprite-map.png";

window.addEventListener("load", function() {
    document.body.appendChild(canvas);
}, false);
```

Animation in Canvas

Animation is a fundamental aspect of any game and for the Canvas API to be a good platform for building games on, it needs to support the ability to update the position and appearance of pixels drawn within it. Because the contents of a canvas are represented as nothing other than pixels in a fixed space, we've no way of locating an individual image, shape, or other part of the canvas and updating that without affecting the rest of the contents of the canvas.

To create the illusion of animation, we therefore need to re-render the contents of the canvas frequently enough for the human eye not to detect the changes as anything other than smooth animation. We draw each constituent part of the canvas then clear the canvas and redraw it after a fixed time, with elements moved to new positions if necessary. By redrawing several times per second, we create the illusion of animation.

Listing 11-4 shows a simple animation of a circle moving across a <canvas> element, created by redrawing the canvas once every 50 milliseconds with the circle's new position updated each time.

Listing 11-4. Simple animation in Canvas

```
var canvas = document.createElement("canvas"),
    context = canvas.getContext("2d"),

    // Define the position, size and properties of the circle to be drawn onto the canvas
    leftPosition = 0,
    topPosition = 100,
    radius = 100,
    startDegree = 0,
    endDegree = 2 * Math.PI; // = 360 degrees in radians

// Define a function to be executed periodically to update the position of the circle and redraw
// it in its new position
function animate() {

    // Update the position on the screen where the circle should be drawn
    leftPosition++;

    // Empty the contents of the canvas
    context.clearRect(0, 0, canvas.width, canvas.height);

    // Draw the circle onto the canvas at the new position
    context.beginPath();
    context.arc(leftPosition, topPosition, radius, startDegree, endDegree);
    context.stroke();
}

// Execute the animate() function once every 50 milliseconds, redrawing the circle in its
// updated position each time
setInterval(animate, 50);

// Add the <canvas> element to the current page once loaded
window.addEventListener("load", function() {
    document.body.appendChild(canvas);
}, false);
```

Game Control

All games react to some form of input from the device they're being played on—they'd be pretty boring otherwise. Most often, this involves controlling a main character, attempting to use some form of dexterity to ensure that character reaches a certain goal, avoiding enemies and obstacles on the way. On desktop computers, pressing specific keys on the keyboard or by moving or clicking the mouse typically controls the character's position. On mobile devices, character control is possible by tapping on the touch-sensitive screen, or by rotating or moving the device in a certain way. Because canvas-based games can be played on both types of device, you should ensure that any game you create could be controlled by input types present on any type of device.

Listing 11-5 shows how to capture specific keypresses or taps on a screen in order to control a player in a canvas-based game.

Listing 11-5. Capturing inputs to control a character in a game

```
var canvas = document.createElement("canvas");

// Define a function call to move the player's character in the <canvas>
function move(direction) {
    // Insert code here to update the position of the character on the canvas
}

// When the player presses the arrow keys on the keyboard, move the player's
// character in the appropriate direction
window.addEventListener("keydown", function(event) {

    // Define the key codes for the arrow keys
    var LEFT_ARROW = 37,
        UP_ARROW = 38,
        RIGHT_ARROW = 39,
        DOWN_ARROW = 40;

    // Execute the move() function, passing along the correct direction based on the
    // arrow key pressed. Ignore any other key presses.
    if (event.keyCode === LEFT_ARROW) {
        move("left");
    } else if (event.keyCode === RIGHT_ARROW) {
        move("right");
    } else if (event.keyCode === UP_ARROW) {
        move("up");
    } else if (event.keyCode === DOWN_ARROW) {
        move("down");
    }
}, false);

// When the player taps in certain places on the <cavnas> on their touch-sensitive
// screen, move the player's character in the appropriate direction according to where the
// screen has been tapped
canvas.addEventListener("touchstart", function(event) {

    // Get a reference to the position of the touch on the screen in pixels from the
    // top-left position of the <canvas>
    var touchLeft = event.targetTouches[0].clientX,
        touchTop = event.targetTouches[0].clientY;
```

```
    // Execute the move() function, passing along the correct direction based on the
    // position tapped on the <canvas> element
    if (touchLeft < (canvas.width / 8)) {
        move("left");
    } else if (touchLeft > (3 * canvas.width / 8)) {
        move("right");
    } else if (touchTop < (canvas.height / 8)) {
        move("up");
    } else if (touchTop > (3 * canvas.height / 8)) {
        move("down");
    }
}, false);

// Add the <canvas> element to the current HTML page once loaded
window.addEventListener("load", function() {
    document.body.appendChild(canvas);
}, false);
```

Collision Detection

So far we've seen how to draw, animate, and control the graphical elements of a game on a <canvas> element, the next thing to handle is what happens when the player's character comes into contact with an obstacle or enemy—in game development parlance, this is known as a *collision*. In a number of games, the player's character would sustain some damage or potentially lose a life when it collides with an enemy character. Because the <canvas> element contains only pixel data, we have no way of distinguishing between one character and another simply by using JavaScript to scan the visual content of the element. What we need to do in our game is to maintain the position of our main character and all obstacles and enemies, as we would have to do anyway to calculate their next movement in their animation sequence. We can get the position of each element and compare them using a function to determine whether the bounds surrounding the player's character intersects with the bounds surrounding an obstacle or enemy character. The code in Listing 11-6 shows an example function that could be used to determine if a collision has occurred between the player and another element within the <canvas>.

Listing 11-6. Simple collision detection

```
// Define a function to establish if the bounds of the player's character intersects with those
// of an obstacle or enemy, causing a collision
function intersects(characterLeft, characterWidth, characterTop, characterHeight, obstacleLeft,
obstacleWidth, obstacleTop, obstacleHeight) {

    // Define Boolean variables to indicate whether a collision occurs on the y-axis and whether
    // it occurs on the x-axis
    var doesIntersectVertically = false,
        doesIntersectHorizontally = false,

        // Establish the bounds of the character and obstacle based on the supplied parameters
        characterRight = characterLeft + characterWidth,
        characterBottom = characterTop + characterHeight,
        obstacleRight = obstacleLeft + obstacleWidth,
        obstacleBottom = obstacleTop + obstacleHeight;

    // A collision occurs on the y-axis if the top position of the character sits between the
    // top and bottom positions of the obstacle or if the bottom position of the character sits
```

```
        // between the same positions of the obstacle
        if ((characterTop > obstacleTop && characterTop < obstacleBottom) ||
            (characterBottom > obstacleTop && characterTop < obstacleBottom)) {
            doesIntersectVertically = true;
        }

        // A collision occurs on the x-axis if the left position of the character sits between the
        // left and right positions of the obstacle or if the right position of the character sits
        // between the same positions of the obstacle
        if ((characterLeft > obstacleLeft && characterLeft < obstacleRight) ||
            (characterRight > obstacleLeft && characterLeft < obstacleRight)) {
            doesIntersectHorizontally = true;
        }

        // A collision occurs if the character intersects the obstacle on both the x- and y-axes.
        return doesIntersectVertically && doesIntersectHorizontally;
}
```

The Game Loop

The game loop is a function that is called repeatedly according to a fixed duration and is, in essence, the core of the game—it updates the position of any characters within the game board, checks for collisions, and renders the characters within the <canvas> element in their updated positions. Although the player's input may occur at any time to attempt to update the character's position on screen, it is only when the next call of the game loop function takes place that the character is drawn in its new position based on that input.

One technique for ensuring that the game loop runs on a specific interval to keep animation smooth at a fixed frame rate is to use the browser's setInterval() function, as shown in Listing 11-7.

Listing 11-7. Running a game loop at a fixed frame rate using the setInterval() function

```
// Define a function to act as the game loop
function gameLoop() {
    // Update character positions, check for collisions and draw characters in new positions
}

// Execute the gameLoop() function once every 50 milliseconds, resulting in a frame rate of 20
// frames per second (=1000/50)
setInterval(gameLoop, 50);
```

The trouble with using the setInterval() function to run the game loop is that if the browser does not complete executing the game loop function's code in time before it gets initiated again, a backlog of code gathers and causes the browser to appear to lock up, or cause stuttering in any animation—not good. Fortunately, browser manufacturers have worked on a way around this particular issue so that, instead of you demanding your code to run regardless of its effect on the browser, the browser can tell you when it is available and able to process more commands. This is surfaced through a call to the requestAnimationFrame() method on the window object, to which a function is passed and is executed at the next available opportunity by the browser. By combining the use of this method with a timer to ensure commands are executed according to a fixed frame rate, we give more control to the browser, allowing for smoother animations as shown in Listing 11-8. Due to some cross-browser differences in naming until the spec is settled upon, we need a simple polyfill to ensure cross-browser operation, as shown at the start of Listing 11-8, which shows an example game loop.

Listing 11-8. Running a game loop using requestAnimationFrame

```
// Create a simple cross-browser polyfill for modern browsers' requestAnimationFrame()
// method to enable smooth, power-efficient animations. Credit to Paul Irish via
// http://bit.ly/req_anim_frame
window.requestAnimationFrame = (function(){
    return window.requestAnimationFrame || window.webkitRequestAnimationFrame ||
window.mozRequestAnimationFrame || function (callback){
        window.setTimeout(callback, 1000 / 60);
    };
})();

// Store a reference to the last time the game loop began in a local variable—initialize it
// to the current time
var lastTimeGameLoopRan = (new Date()).getTime(),

    // Define the refresh rate we desire for our game loop to re-render our canvas within.
    // A 20 millisecond refresh rate gives a frame rate of 50 frames per second (=1000 / 20)
    refreshRate = 20;

// Define a function to act as the game loop
function gameLoop() {

    // Get the current time and infer from there the difference between it and the last time
    // the game loop ran
    var currentTime = (new Date()).getTime(),
        timeDifference = currentTime - lastTimeGameLoopRan;

    // Execute this function again when the next animation frame is ready for use by
    // the browser - keeps the game loop looping but within the confines of the browser's
    // performance and constraints, which is ultimately best for the player
    window.requestAnimationFrame(gameLoop);

    // the time difference between the current execution of the gameLoop() function and
    // its previous execution is greater than or equal to the defined refresh rate, then
    // run the typical game loop operations
    if (timeDifference >=refreshRate) {

        // Update character positions, check for collisions and draw characters in
        // new positions

        // Update the last time the game loop ran so its next execution will occur at the
        // correct time
        lastTimeGameLoopRan = currentTime;
    }
}

// Start the first run of the game loop
gameLoop();
```

Layering Canvases for Better Performance

Each draw operation to a `<canvas>` element takes a certain amount of time to execute. Multiply this numerous times if you have a complex game with lots of characters and you start to realize that every drawing operation counts in terms of performance, therefore any opportunity to avoid redrawing static parts of the game should be avoided where possible. For some games with static backgrounds, for example, it makes more sense to create two `<canvas>` elements, one to draw the background onto, and the other for all the regularly updating character movement and animation. CSS can then be used to position the two elements above each other, with the element containing all the movement positioned above the element containing the background, which need only be drawn once and never updated.

Building a "Frogger" Game in Canvas

Let's use the Canvas API to put what we've learned into practice. We're going to build a simple game based on the 1981 arcade classic, *Frogger* (`http://bit.ly/frogger_game`), showing how best to draw and animate characters, handle input from game controllers, handle collision detection between two or more characters in the game and how to regulate frame rates to keep performance optimal for the player.

The purpose of the game, if you're not familiar, is to guide a frog across the screen from bottom to top, first by leading the character across a busy road without hitting any traffic, and then over a river using floating logs and the backs of occasionally-surfacing turtles while avoiding dangers lurking in the water, before finally delivering our hero character to one of five goal stations at the top of the screen, at which point a new frog is created at the bottom of the screen again. Once the character has entered each goal station once, the game is won. As the one controlling the game, the user must ensure that the frog does not get hit by a vehicle, get transported off the side of the screen, touch the water, including stand on top of a turtle when it dives underwater, and that the character reaches one of the goal stations within the allotted time. If an accident befalls the character, one of its five lives are lost until none remain and the game is deemed over.

A typical level in Frogger looks like that shown in Figure 11-2.

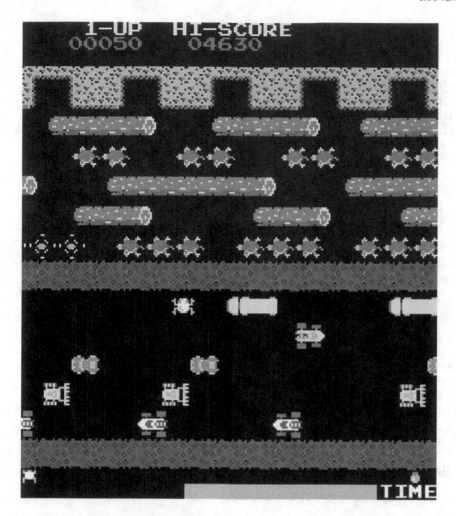

Figure 11-2. *Frogger—the arcade classic*

Let's start by creating the basic HTML page to house our game, as shown in Listing 11-9. We fix the width of the viewport for mobile devices using a specially formatted `<meta>` tag in the `<head>`. We also require a custom font, named "Arcade Classic" and available for download for free from `http://bit.ly/arcade_font`, to display the scores and other text within the canvas, so we also load this in here. We then create two `<canvas>` elements, one to house the background and one the animating foreground, and define the CSS to layer the two canvases above each other, ensuring that they display at half the size of the actual canvas dimensions so as to support high-definition displays.

Listing 11-9. HTML page to host a Frogger game in Canvas

```
<!DOCTYPE html>
<html>
<head>
    <title>Frogger In Canvas</title>
    <meta charset="utf-8">
    <meta name="viewport" content="width=480, initial-scale=1.0">
```

```html
<style>
@font-face {
    font-family: "Arcade Classic";
    src: url("arcadeclassic.eot");
    src: url("arcadeclassic.eot?#iefix") format("embedded-opentype"),
        url("arcadeclassic.woff") format("woff"),
        url("arcadeclassic.ttf") format("truetype"),
        url("arcadeclassic.svg#arcadeclassic") format("svg");
    font-weight: normal;
    font-style: normal;
}

.canvas {
    position: absolute;
    top: 0;
    left: 0;
    border: 2px solid #000;
    width: 480px;
    height: 640px;
}
</style>
</head>
<body>
    <canvas id="background-canvas" class="canvas" width="960" height="1280"></canvas>
    <canvas id="canvas" class="canvas" width="960" height="1280"></canvas>

    <!-- Load in scripts here once defined -->
</body>
</html>
```

With our HTML in place, we start on the JavaScript. Listing 11-10 shows how we might start off our game code by creating a namespace to house our code and defining some key properties and methods for use throughout the rest of the code, including the *observer* design pattern methods which we will use to communicate between code modules throughout our game code.

Listing 11-10. Defining a namespace and key properties and methods for use throughout our game

```javascript
// Define a namespace to contain the code for our game within a single global variable
var Frogger = (function() {

    // Locate the main <canvas> element on the page
    var canvas = document.getElementById("canvas"),

        // Get a reference to the <canvas> element's 2-D drawing surface context
        drawingSurface = canvas.getContext("2d"),

        // Locate the background <canvas> element on the page
        backgroundCanvas = document.getElementById("background-canvas"),

        // Get a reference to the background <canvas> element's 2-D drawing surface context
        backgroundDrawingSurface = backgroundCanvas.getContext("2d"),
```

```
    // Get a reference to the <canvas> element's width and height, in pixels
    drawingSurfaceWidth = canvas.width,
    drawingSurfaceHeight = canvas.height;

return {

    // Expose the <canvas> element, its 2-D drawing surface context, its width and
    // its height for use in other code modules
    canvas: canvas,
    drawingSurface: drawingSurface,
    drawingSurfaceWidth: drawingSurfaceWidth,
    drawingSurfaceHeight: drawingSurfaceHeight,

    // Expose the background <canvas> element's 2-D drawing surface context
    backgroundDrawingSurface: backgroundDrawingSurface,

    // Define an object containing references to directions the characters in our game can
    // move in. We define it here globally for use across our whole code base
    direction: {
        UP: "up",
        DOWN: "down",
        LEFT: "left",
        RIGHT: "right"
    },

    // Define the observer design pattern methods subscribe() and publish() to allow
    // application-wide communication without the need for tightly-coupled modules. See
    // Chapter 7 for more information on this design pattern.
    observer: (function() {
        var events = {};

        return {
            subscribe: function(eventName, callback) {

                if (!events.hasOwnProperty(eventName)) {
                    events[eventName] = [];
                }

                events[eventName].push(callback);
            },

            publish: function(eventName) {
                var data = Array.prototype.slice.call(arguments, 1),
                    index = 0,
                    length = 0;

                if (events.hasOwnProperty(eventName)) {
                    length = events[eventName].length;

                    for (; index < length; index++) {
                        events[eventName][index].apply(this, data);
                    }
                }
```

```
            }
        }
    };
}()),

    // Define a method to determine whether two obstacles on the game board intersect
    // each other on the horizontal axis. By passing in two objects, each with a 'left'
    // and 'right' property indicating the left-most and right-most position of each
    // obstacle in pixels on the game board, we establish whether the two intersect
    // each other - if they do, and they are both on the same row as each other on the
    // game board, this can be considered a collision between these two obstacles
    intersects: function(position1, position2) {
        var doesIntersect = false;

        if ((position1.left > position2.left && position1.left < position2.right) ||
            (position1.right > position2.left && position1.left < position2.right)) {
            doesIntersect = true;
        }

        return doesIntersect;
    }
};
}());
```

Each code listing that follows needs to be referenced in order within <script> tags from the HTML page in Listing 11-9 to see the finished result.

Now let's create our core game logic, including the game state, the game loop, score handling, and establishing the player's remaining lives and time remaining to complete the level, as shown in Listing 11-11.

Listing 11-11. The core game logic for Frogger

```
// Create a simple cross-browser polyfill for modern browsers' requestAnimationFrame()
// method to enable smooth, power-efficient animations. Credit to Paul Irish via
// http://bit.ly/req_anim_frame
window.requestAnimationFrame = (function(){
    return window.requestAnimationFrame || window.webkitRequestAnimationFrame || window.
mozRequestAnimationFrame || function (callback){
        window.setTimeout(callback, 1000 / 60);
    };
})();

// Define the game logic module which keeps track of the game state, the players's score,
// the number of lives remaining, handles collisions between the player's character and
// other obstacles and ensures the game graphics are drawn onto the <canvas> at the
// right moment. This module contains the brains behind the game play and instructs other
// code modules to do the heavy lifting through the use of the observer design pattern.
(function(Frogger) {

    // Define a variable to hold the current player's score
    var _score = 0,
```

```
    // Define and initialize a variable to hold the high score achieved in the game
    _highScore = 1000,

    // Define the number of lives the player has remaining before the game is over
    _lives = 5,

    // Define the number of milliseconds the player has to get their character to
    // the goal (60 seconds). If they take too long, they will lose a life
    _timeTotal = 60000,

    // Define a variable to store the current time remaining for the player to reach
    // the goal
    _timeRemaining = _timeTotal,

    // Define the refresh rate of the graphics on the <canvas> element (one draw every
    // 33 1/3 milliseconds = 30 frames per second). Attempting to redraw too frequently
    // can cause the browser to slow down so choose this value carefully to maintain a
    // good balance between fluid animation and smooth playability
    _refreshRate = 33.333,

    // Define a variable to store the number of times the player's character has
    // reached the goal
    _timesAtGoal = 0,

    // Define a variable to indicate the number of times the player's character needs
    // to reach the goal for the game to be won
    _maxTimesAtGoal = 5,

    // Define a Boolean variable to indicate whether the player's movement is currently
    // frozen in place
    _isPlayerFrozen = false,

    // Define a variable to store the last time the game loop ran - this helps keep
    // the animation running smoothly at the defined refresh rate
    _lastTimeGameLoopRan = (new Date()).getTime();

// Define a function to be called to count down the time remaining for the player to
// reach the goal without forfeiting a life
function countDown() {
    if (_timeRemaining > 0) {

        // This function will be called as frequently as the _refreshRate variable
        // dictates so we reduce the number of milliseconds remaining by the
        // _refreshRate value for accurate timing
        _timeRemaining -= _refreshRate;

        // Publish the fact that the remaining time has changed, passing along the
        // new time remaining as a percentage - which will help when we come to display
        // the remaining time on the game board itself
        Frogger.observer.publish("time-remaining-change", _timeRemaining / _timeTotal);
    } else {
```

```
            // If the remaining time reaches zero, we take one of the player's remaining
            // lives
            loseLife();
        }
    }

    // Define a function to be called when all the player's lives have gone and the game
    // is declared over
    function gameOver() {

        // Pause the player's movements as they are no longer in the game
        freezePlayer();

        // Inform other code modules in this application that the game is over
        Frogger.observer.publish("game-over");
    }

    // Define a function to be called when the player has reached the goal
    function gameWon() {

        // Inform other code modules that the game has been won
        Frogger.observer.publish("game-won");
    }

    // Define a function to be called when the player loses a life
    function loseLife() {

        // Decrease the number of lives the player has remaining
        _lives--;

        // Pause the player's movements
        freezePlayer();

        // Inform other code modules that the player has lost a life
        Frogger.observer.publish("player-lost-life");

        if (_lives === 0) {

            // Declare the game to be over if the player has no lives remaining
            gameOver();
        } else {

            // If there are lives remaining, wait 2000 milliseconds (2 seconds) before
            // resetting the player's character and other obstacles to their initial
            // positions on the game board
            setTimeout(reset, 2000);
        }
    }

    // Define a function to be called when the player's character is required to be frozen
    // in place, such as when the game is over or when the player has lost a life
    function freezePlayer() {
```

```
    // Set the local variable to indicate the frozen state
    _isPlayerFrozen = true;

    // Inform other code modules - including that which controls the player's
    // character - that the player is now be frozen
    Frogger.observer.publish("player-freeze");
}

// Define a function to be called when the player's character is free to move after
// being previously frozen in place
function unfreezePlayer() {

    // Set the local variable to indicate the new state
    _isPlayerFrozen = false;

    // Inform other code modules that the player's character is now free to move around
    // the game board
    Frogger.observer.publish("player-unfreeze");
}

// Define a function to increase the player's score by a specific amount and update
// the high score accordingly
function increaseScore(increaseBy) {

    // Increase the score by the supplied amount (or by 0 if no value is provided)
    _score += increaseBy || 0;

    // Inform other code modules that the player's score has changed, passing along
    // the new score
    Frogger.observer.publish("score-change", _score);

    // If the player's new score beats the current high score then update the high
    // score to reflect the player's new score and inform other code modules of a
    // change to the high score, passing along the new high score value
    if (_score > _highScore) {
        _highScore = _score;
        Frogger.observer.publish("high-score-change", _highScore);
    }
}

// Define a function to execute once the player reaches the designated goal
function playerAtGoal() {

    // When the player reaches the goal, increase their score by 1000 points
    increaseScore(1000);

    // Increment the value indicating the total number of times the player's character
    // has reached the goal
    _timesAtGoal++;

    // Freeze the player's character movement temporarily to acknowledge they have
    // reached the goal
    freezePlayer();
```

```
        if (_timesAtGoal < _maxTimesAtGoal) {

            // The player must enter the goal a total of 5 times, as indicated by the
            // _maxTimesAtGoal value. If the player has not reached the goal this many
            // times yet, then reset the player's character position and obstacles on the
            // game board after a delay of 2000 milliseconds (2 seconds)
            setTimeout(reset, 2000);
        } else {

            // If the player has reached the goal 5 times, the game has been won!
            gameWon();
        }
}

// Define a function to execute when the player moves their character on the game
// board, increasing their score by 20 points when they do
function playerMoved() {
    increaseScore(20);
}

// Define a function to be called when the game board needs to be reset, such as when
// the player loses a life
function reset() {

    // Reset the variable storing the current time remaining to its initial value
    _timeRemaining = _timeTotal;

    // Release the player's character if it has been frozen in place
    unfreezePlayer();

    // Inform other code modules to reset themselves to their initial conditions
    Frogger.observer.publish("reset");
}

// The game loop executes on an interval at a rate dictated by value of the
// _refreshRate variable (once every 50 milliseconds), in which the game board is
// redrawn with the character and obstacles drawn at their relevant positions on
// the board and any collisions between the player's character and any obstacles
// are detected
function gameLoop() {

    // Calculate how many milliseconds have passed since the last time the game loop
    // was called
    var currentTime = (new Date()).getTime(),
        timeDifference = currentTime - _lastTimeGameLoopRan;

    // Execute this function again when the next animation frame is ready for use by
    // the browser - keeps the game loop looping
    window.requestAnimationFrame(gameLoop);

    // If the number of milliseconds passed exceeds the defined refresh rate, draw
    // the obstacles in the updated position on the game board and check for collisions
    if (timeDifference >= _refreshRate) {
```

```
    // Clear the <canvas> element's drawing surface - erases everything on the
    // game board so we can redraw the player's character and obstacles in their
    // new positions
    Frogger.drawingSurface.clearRect(0, 0, Frogger.drawingSurfaceWidth, Frogger.
    drawingSurfaceHeight);

    if (!_isPlayerFrozen) {

        // As long as the player's character is not frozen in place, ensure the
        // timer is counting down, putting pressure on the player to reach the
        // goal in time
        countDown();

        // Inform other code modules to check the player has not collided with an
        // obstacle on the game board
        Frogger.observer.publish("check-collisions");
    }

    // Now on our empty canvas we draw our game board and the obstacles upon it in
    // their respective positions
    Frogger.observer.publish("render-base-layer");

    // After the game board and obstacles, we draw the player's character so that
    // it is always on top of anything else on the <canvas> drawing surface
    Frogger.observer.publish("render-character");

    // Store the current time for later comparisons to keep the frame rate smooth
    _lastTimeGameLoopRan = currentTime;
    }
}

// Define a function to kick-start the application and run the game loop, which renders
// each frame of the game graphics and checks for collisions between the player's
// character and any obstacles on the game board
function start() {

    // Inform other code modules of the initial state of the game's high score
    Frogger.observer.publish("high-score-change", _highScore);

    // Start the game loop running
    gameLoop();
}

// Execute the start() function to kick off the game loop once the "game-load" event
// is fired. We'll trigger this event after we've configured the rest of our code
// modules for the game
Frogger.observer.subscribe("game-load", start);

// Execute the playerAtGoal() function when another code module informs us that the
// player has reached the goal
Frogger.observer.subscribe("player-at-goal", playerAtGoal);
```

```
        // Execute the playerMoved() function when we have been informed that the player has
        // moved their character
        Frogger.observer.subscribe("player-moved", playerMoved);

        // Execute the loseLife() function when we are informed by another code base that the
        // player's character has collided with an obstacle on the game board
        Frogger.observer.subscribe("collision", loseLife);
// Pass the global Frogger variable into the module so it can be accessed locally,
// improving performance and making its dependency clear
}(Frogger));
```

Now let's create some reusable base code for creating images and animations of our main character as well as the obstacles on the game board from a large sprite image, which is shown in Figure 11-3. You should be able to see where the boundaries of each individual image lie within the larger sprite.

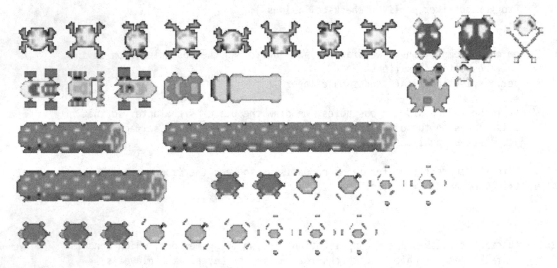

Figure 11-3. *The sprite map containing all the images required to support our game in a single file*

You may download this sprite image for use with the code listings in this chapter via http://bit.ly/frogger_image. The code to allow us to create individual images and animations from this sprite image is shown in Listing 11-12.

Listing 11-12. Base code for creating images and animations from a sprite image

```
// Define a "class" for creating images to place on the game board. All the individual
// images are stored together in a single large image file called a Sprite Map. By knowing
// the position within this sprite file of the image to display, together with its width
// and height, we can pull out the individual images for display. By only loading in a
// single image file we improve the loading performance of the game
Frogger.ImageSprite = function(startPositionLeft, startPositionTop) {

    // Each instance stores its starting position on the game board so it can later be
    // reset to its initial position if necessary
    this.startLeft = startPositionLeft || 0;
    this.startTop = startPositionTop || 0;
```

```javascript
    // Initialize an object property to later store any animations for this image
    this.animations = {};

    // Set this image to its initial state for display
    this.reset();
};

// Define a "class" for assigning animations to an ImageSprite instance to allow any image
// on the game board to appear to animate. An animation is a sequence of images which will
// be displayed in order over a fixed time period to give the impression of movement
Frogger.Animation = function(options) {
    options = options || {};

    // Store the rate to move between the images in the animation sequence, in milliseconds
    // - defaults to a rate of 150 milliseconds
    this.rate = options.rate || 150;

    // Store a Boolean value to indicate whether this animation is to loop or play once
    this.loop = options.loop || false;

    // Store the supplied position in pixels from the left-hand side of the spite map image
    // where the first image in this animation sequence is located
    this.spriteLeft = options.spriteLeft || 0;

    // Store the animation sequence which indicates a multiple of the image with as an
    // offset from the spriteLeft value. A sequence value of [0, 1, 2] would indicate there
    // are three images in this animation sequence located at the position stored in the
    // spriteLeft property, that position + the width of the sprite image, and that
    // position + double the width of the sprite image, respectively. It is therefore
    // expected that an animation sequence of images are stored horizontally beside each
    // other in order within the sprite map image file
    this.sequence = options.sequence || [];
};

// Define and initialize properties and methods to be inherited by each instance of the
// Frogger.Animation "class"
Frogger.Animation.prototype = {

    // Define a value to indicate the current frame shown from the animation sequence.
    // As the sequence property is an Array, this is effectively an index within that Array
    frame: 0,

    // Define a property to indicate whether the animation is currently playing - that is
    // that the frame index of the animation sequence is being actively incremented at the
    // rate supplied at initiation time
    playing: false,

    // Define a property to store a timer indicator to start and stop the incrementing of
    // the frame index on demand
    timer: null,
```

```
    // Define a function to start playing the animation - essentially incrementing the
    // frame index on a timer at the rate supplied upon instantiation
    play: function() {
        var that = this;

        // If the animation is not currently playing, then reset it to its initial state
        if (!this.playing) {
            this.reset();
            this.playing = true;
        }

        // Increment the current frame index of the animation on a timer at a rate given
        // by the supplied value upon instantiation, storing a reference to the timer in
        // the timer property so that it can be stopped at a later time
        this.timer = setInterval(function() {
            that.incrementFrame();
        }, this.rate);
    },

    // Define a function to rewind the current frame index of the animation sequence back
    // to the start
    reset: function() {
        this.frame = 0;
    },

    // Define a function to increment the current frame index of the animation sequence
    incrementFrame: function() {

        // Only increment the current frame if the animation should be playing
        if (this.playing) {

            // Increment the current frame index of the animation sequence
            this.frame++;

            // If we have reached the end of the animation sequence, stop the animation if
            // it was not intended to loop, otherwise reset the current frame index of the
            // animation back to the start
            if (this.frame === this.sequence.length - 1) {
                if (!this.loop) {
                    this.stop();
                } else {
                    this.reset();
                }
            }
        }
    },

    // Define a function to return the value stored in the animation sequence at the
    // current frame index. This value will be used later on to correctly identify which
    // individual image from the large sprite map to display within the <canvas> element
    getSequenceValue: function() {
        return this.sequence[this.frame];
    },
```

```
    // Define a function to return the number of pixels from the left-hand edge of the
    // sprite map of the first frame of this animation. This is used in conjunction with
    // the current value of the animation sequence and the image width to decide which
    // image to display within the <canvas> element
    getSpriteLeft: function() {
        return this.spriteLeft;
    },

    // Define a function to stop the timer from incrementing the current frame index, and

    // hence stop the animation from playing
    stop: function() {

        // Terminate the timer
        clearInterval(this.timer);

        // Indicate that the animation is no longer playing
        this.playing = false;
    }
};

// Define and initialize properties and methods to be inherited by each instance of the
// Frogger.ImageSprite "class" to enable individual images from a larger sprite map to be
// drawn onto the <canvas> element
Frogger.ImageSprite.prototype = {

    // Define properties to store the current position in pixels of the image on the
    // game board from the top and left-hand edges
    top: 0,
    left: 0,

    // Define properties to store the initial position in pixels of the images on the game
    // board from the top and left-hand edges so that the image can be returned to its
    // initial position at a later stage if needed
    startLeft: 0,
    startTop: 0,

    // Define a property containing a reference to a new <img> tag holding the single
    // large sprite map image. Because this is an object, it will be shared across all
    // instances of the Frogger.ImageSprite "class", saving on memory usage
    sprite: (function() {
        var img = document.createElement("img");
        img.src = "spritemap.png";
        return img;
    }()),

    // Define properties to define the default width and height, in pixels, of an
    // individual image within the large sprite map image file
    width: 80,
    height: 80,

    // Define properties denoting the location of the top and left positions, in pixels,
    // of the individual image within the large sprite map image. Together with the width
    // and height properties, we are able to pull out an individual image from the sprite
```

```
    // map to display within the <canvas> element
    spriteTop: 0,
    spriteLeft: 0,

    // Declare no animations by default
    animations: null,

    // Define a property indicating the name of the currently playing animation, if any
    currentAnimation: "",

    // Define a property to indicate whether the individual image represented by this
    // object instance is currently hidden from display
    isHidden: false,

    // Define a function to reset this image back to its initial position and to reset any
    // associated animation of that image
    reset: function() {

        // Reset the top and left position of the image on the game board back to its
        // initial position defined upon instantiation
        this.left = this.startLeft;
        this.top = this.startTop;

        // Reset any associated animations to their initial state
        this.resetAnimation();

        // Declare this image no longer to be hidden
        this.isHidden = false;
    },

    // Define a function to associate one or more animation with this image - data is
    // passed in as an object literal with each key representing the name of the animation
    registerAnimation: function(animations) {
        var key,
            animation;

        // Loop through the supplied object literal data indicating the animations to
        // register
        for (key in animations) {
            animation = animations[key];

            // Create instances of the Frogger.Animation "class" for each item in the
            // supplied data object. Each item's data is passed to the "class" upon
            // instantiation to define its animation sequence, animation rate, and other
            // initial properties
            this.animations[key] = new Frogger.Animation(animation);
        }
    },

    // Define a function to reset any currently playing animation back to its initial state
    resetAnimation: function() {
        if (this.animations[this.currentAnimation]) {
```

```
        // If an animation is currently playing, then call its reset() method to
        // restore it to its initial state
        this.animations[this.currentAnimation].reset();
    }

    // Once reset, there should be no currently playing animation
    this.currentAnimation = "";
},

// Define a function to play a specific animation sequence by name. The name must
// correspond with one provided to the registerAnimation() method previously
playAnimation: function(name) {

    // Set the current animation to the provided name
    this.currentAnimation = name;

    if (this.animations[this.currentAnimation]) {

        // If an animation is found by the supplied name, then call its play() method
        // to begin incrementing its current frame index using its internal timer
        this.animations[this.currentAnimation].play();
    }
},

// Define a function to draw the individual image onto the <canvas> element at the
// supplied left and top positions, in pixels. If an animation is currently playing,
// ensure the correct image is displayed based on that animation's current sequence
// value
renderAt: function(left, top) {

    // Locate the animation that is currently playing, if any
    var animation = this.animations[this.currentAnimation],

        // If an animation is playing, get its current sequence value based on its
        // internal frame index. If no animation is playing, assume a sequence value
        // of 0. This value will be multiplied by the width of the individual image
        // within the sprite map to identify the exact image to show based on the
        // animation's current frame index
        sequenceValue = animation ? animation.getSequenceValue() : 0,

        // If an animation is playing, get the location of the animation's initial
        // frame as an offset in pixels from the left-hand edge of the sprite map image.
        // We make an assumption that the top offset of the animation images is the
        // same as the main image itself represented in this object instance - meaning
        // that all frames of the animation should be positioned together with the main
        // non-animating image on the same row of the sprite map image
        animationSpriteLeft = animation ? animation.getSpriteLeft() : 0,

        // Calculate the offset in pixels from the left-hand edge of the sprite map
        // image where the individual image to display is to be found, based on whether
        // an animation is currently playing or not. If no animation is playing, the
```

```
                // offset will be the same as that stored in the spriteLeft property of this
                // object instance
                spriteLeft = this.spriteLeft + animationSpriteLeft + (this.width * sequenceValue);

            // If the image is not currently to be considered hidden, then extract the individual
            // image from the sprite map and draw it onto the <canvas> drawing surface at the
            // top and left positions, in pixels, as provided to this method, when called
            if (!this.isHidden) {
                Frogger.drawingSurface.drawImage(this.sprite, spriteLeft, this.spriteTop, this.width,
                    this.height, left, top, this.width, this.height);
            }
        },

    // Define a function to set the stored left and top offset positions, in pixels,
    // indicating where on the game board the image should be displayed. These values are
    // then used in the renderAt() method to draw the image at this position
    moveTo: function(left, top) {
        this.left = left || 0;

            // Since most images are moved left and right in this game, rather than up and down,
            // we let the top offset value be optional
            if (typeof top !== "undefined") {
                this.top = top || 0;
            }
        },

    // Define a function return the width of the individual image we are extracting from
    // the large sprite map image
    getWidth: function() {
        return this.width;
    },

    // Define a function to return the left and right positions, in pixels, of the image
    // which we can use later to perform collision detection with other obstacles on the
    // game board
    getPosition: function() {
        return {
            left: this.left,

            // The right position is derived as the left position plus the width of the
            // individual image
            right: this.left + this.width
        };
    },

    // Define a function to hide this image from the game board by effectively stopping
    // the drawing of the image to the <canvas> within the renderAt() method
    hide: function() {
        this.isHidden = true;
    }
};
```

Now let's create a code module to define the limits and parameters of the game board, including the bounds within which the character is allowed to move, as shown in Listing 11-13. The game board itself is essentially a grid within which obstacles are fixed to a certain vertical grid position and move only horizontally—the player's character is the one exception to this rule as this is able to jump up and down the game board, moving one grid position at a time.

Listing 11-13. Coding the game board parameters

```
// Define a code module to define the parameters of the game board itself, the number of
// rows and columns within the grid, along with their relative positions in pixels, and
// the bounds within which the player's character may move
(function(Frogger) {

    // Define the width and height of each square on the game board grid, in pixels. The
    // game board is divided into rows with different obstacles on each, and columns within
    // which the player's character can move
    var _grid = {
            width: 80,
            height: 80
    },

    // Define the number of rows on the game board. The top two rows contain the score,
    // the next two contain the home base the player is attempting to reach. There then
    // follow five rows of water-based obstacles before reaching a 'safe' row where the
    // player's character may take refuge without obstacles. There then follow five rows
    // of road-based obstacles before another 'safe' row, which is where the player's
    // character starts its game from. The final row holds the remaining time and number
    // of lives remaining. There are 17 rows, therefore, though since we start counting
    // rows at position 0, the total number of rows is said to be 16 using the grid
    // square defined previously
    _numRows = 16,

    // Define the number of columns on the game board, from left to right, based on the
    // game board grid defined previously. The total number of columns is 12 but since
    // we count position 0 as a column, we represent the number as 11 instead
    _numColumns = 11,

    // Define the limits of movement of the player's character on the game board in
    // pixels, returning the left-, right-, top- and bottom-most positions the
    // character can be placed. This is to ensure the player is not able to move
    // their character onto the parts of the game board that show the score, the time
    // remaining, etc.
    _characterBounds = {
        left: 0,
        right: _numColumns * _grid.width,
        top: 2 * _grid.height,
        bottom: (_numRows - 2) * _grid.height
    },
```

```
    // Define an array containing the pixel positions of each of the 17 rows as
    // measured from the left-most edge of the game board - each is essentially a
    // multiple of the grid width. This allows easy access to pixel positions by
    // row number.
    _rows = (function() {
        var output = [],
            index = 0,
            length = _numRows;

        for (; index < length; index++) {
            output.push(index * _grid.width);
        }

        return output;
    }()),

    // Define an array containing the pixel positions of each of the 12 columns as
    // measured from the top-most edge of the game board - each is essentially a
    // multiple of the grid height. This allows easy access to pixel positions by
    // column number.
    _columns = (function() {
        var output = [],
            index = 0,
            length = _numColumns;

        for (; index < length; index++) {
            output.push(index * _grid.height);
        }

        return output;
    }());
// Listen for the "game-load" event, which will be fired once all our code modules
// are configured
Frogger.observer.subscribe("game-load", function() {

    // Publish the "game-board-initialize" event, passing along relevant information
    // about the game board for other code modules to use to ensure they draw their
    // images to the correct place on the board, and allow the character to only
    // move between certain limits as defined in this code module
    Frogger.observer.publish("game-board-initialize", {

        // Pass across the number of rows and columns the board consists of
        numRows: _numRows,
        numColumns: _numColumns,

        // Pass across arrays representing the pixel positions of each of the rows
        // and columns on the board to simplify the drawing of images onto the <canvas>
        // element in the correct place
        rows: _rows,
        columns: _columns,
```

```
            // Pass across the width and height of each grid square on the game board
            grid: {
                width: _grid.width,
                height: _grid.height
            },

            // Pass across the object containing the left, right, top and bottom positions
            // in pixels which the player's character is allowed to move within on the
            // game board
            characterBounds: _characterBounds
        });
    });
}(Frogger));
```

Listing 11-14 shows how we might add current and high scores as well as other text to the <canvas> element using the custom *Arcade Classic* font. By storing all of the code together in a module that handles the rendering of text and game status messages, such as "Game Over" and "You Win!" to the game board, we know exactly where to look if a problem occurs with text rendering to the canvas.

Listing 11-14. Adding text to the game board, including score and messages such as "Game Over"

```
// Define a code module to add text-based visuals to the game board, e.g. the score, high
// score, and any informative text for the player about the game state, such as "Game Over"
// or "You Win!"
(function(Frogger) {

    // Define the text size and font name to use for the text. You can find the Arcade
    // Classic font for download for free online at http://bit.ly/arcade_font
    var _font = "67px Arcade Classic",

        // Define variables to store the current game state locally in this module
        _score = 0,
        _highScore = 0,
        _gameWon = false,
        _gameOver = false,

        // Define a variable to store the initialized data from the game board module
        // defined previously - this will be populated later with data from that module
        _gameBoard = {};

    // Define a function to render the player's score and high score to the <canvas> element
    function renderScore() {

        // Select the font face and size
        Frogger.drawingSurface.font = _font;

        // Right-align text at the position we define to draw the text at
        Frogger.drawingSurface.textAlign = "end";

        // Write the text "1-UP", right-aligned to the 4th column position and ending half
        // a row down from the top of the game board in white (hex color value #FFF)
        Frogger.drawingSurface.fillStyle = "#FFF";
        Frogger.drawingSurface.fillText("1-UP", _gameBoard.columns[3], _gameBoard.grid.height / 2);
```

```
    // Write out the current score in red (hex color value #F00) right-aligned beneath
    // the "1-UP" text previously drawn to the <canvas>
    Frogger.drawingSurface.fillStyle = "#F00";
    Frogger.drawingSurface.fillText(_score, _gameBoard.columns[3], _gameBoard.grid.height);

    // Write the text "HI-SCORE", right-aligned to the 8th column position and ending
    // half a row down from the top of the game board in white (hex color value #FFF)
    Frogger.drawingSurface.fillStyle = "#FFF";
    Frogger.drawingSurface.fillText("HI-SCORE", _gameBoard.columns[8],
    _gameBoard.grid.height / 2);

    // Write out the current high score in red (hex color value #F00) right-aligned
    // beneath the "HI-SCORE" text previously drawn to the <canvas>
    Frogger.drawingSurface.fillStyle = "#F00";
    Frogger.drawingSurface.fillText(_highScore, _gameBoard.columns[8], _gameBoard.grid.height);
}

// Define a function to render the text "GAME OVER" to the <canvas>. This will only be
// called when the game is over
function renderGameOver() {

    // Use the Arcade Classic font as previously defined, and write the text centered
    // around the given drawing position in white
    Frogger.drawingSurface.font = _font;
    Frogger.drawingSurface.textAlign = "center";
    Frogger.drawingSurface.fillStyle = "#FFF";

    // Write the text center aligned within the <canvas> and at the 9th row position
    // from the top of the game board
    Frogger.drawingSurface.fillText("GAME OVER", Frogger.drawingSurfaceWidth / 2,
    _gameBoard.rows[9]);
}

// Define a function to render the text "YOU WIN!" to the <canvas> which will be called
// when the player has won the game by reaching the home base position five times
function renderGameWon() {

    // Use the Arcade Classic font as previously defined, and write the text centered
    // around the given drawing position in yellow (hex value #FF0)
    Frogger.drawingSurface.font = _font;
    Frogger.drawingSurface.textAlign = "center";
    Frogger.drawingSurface.fillStyle = "#FF0";

    // Write the text center aligned within the <canvas> and at the 9th row position
    // from the top of the game board
    Frogger.drawingSurface.fillText("YOU WIN!", Frogger.drawingSurfaceWidth / 2,
    _gameBoard.rows[9]);
}

// Define a function to render the "TIME" label in the bottom-right corner of the
// game board
function renderTimeLabel() {
```

```
        // Use the Arcade Classic font as previously defined, and write the text centered
        // around the given drawing position in yellow (hex value #FF0)
        Frogger.drawingSurface.font = _font;
        Frogger.drawingSurface.textAlign = "end";
        Frogger.drawingSurface.fillStyle = "#FF0";

        // Write the text right aligned within the <canvas> and in the bottom right corner
        // of the game board
        Frogger.drawingSurface.fillText("TIME", Frogger.drawingSurfaceWidth, Frogger.
        drawingSurfaceHeight);
    }

    // Define a function to render the text-based visuals to the game board as appropriate
    // depending on the current game state - we'll connect this up later to be called
    // once on every cycle of the game loop
    function render() {
        renderScore();
        renderTimeLabel();

        // Only render the "GAME OVER" text if the game is actually over
        if (_gameOver) {
            renderGameOver();
        }

        // Only render the "YOU WIN!" text if the players has won the game
        if (_gameWon) {
            renderGameWon();
        }
    }

    // When the game logic publishes a message declaring that the player has won the game,
    // set the local variable to indicate this also so that the "YOU WIN!" text will be
    // drawn onto the <canvas> during any following execution of the game loop
    Frogger.observer.subscribe("game-won", function() {
        _gameWon = true;
    });

    // When the game logic module publishes a message indicating that the game has been
    // lost, set the local variable to reflect this fact so that the "GAME OVER" text gets
    // written to the <canvas> element on the next cycle around the game loop
    Frogger.observer.subscribe("game-over", function() {
        _gameOver = true;
    });

    // Reset the local variables indicating the game state if the game logic has forced
    // a game state reset to occur
    Frogger.observer.subscribe("reset", function() {
        _gameOver = false;
        _gameWon = false;
    });

    // Update the local score variable when the player's score changes throughout the
    // course of the game. The updated score will then be written onto the <canvas> on
```

```
    // the next cycle of the game loop
    Frogger.observer.subscribe("score-change", function(newScore) {
        _score = newScore;
    });

    // Update the local high score variable when the game's high score changes throughout
    // the course of the game. The updated high score will then be drawn to the <canvas>
    // on the next cycle of the game loop
    Frogger.observer.subscribe("high-score-change", function(newHighScore) {
        _highScore = newHighScore;
    });

    // Subscribe to the "game-board-initialize" event fired by the previous code module,
    // storing the game board properties and settings in a local variable
    Frogger.observer.subscribe("game-board-initialize", function(gameBoard) {
        _gameBoard = gameBoard;

        // Start listening to the "render-base-layer" event, fired from within the game
        // loop, and execute the render() function when it occurs, drawing the text onto
        // the game board in the appropriate position for each cycle of the game loop
        Frogger.observer.subscribe("render-base-layer", render);
    });
}(Frogger));
```

It's time we added our background image to the background canvas, and this is what we'll do in Listing 11-15, as well as rendering the number of player lives remaining and the time remaining for the player's character to reach the goal. Because the background is static, we will only draw it once at the start of the game and won't need to touch or amend it again after that. The image we'll use for the game board is shown in Figure 11-4, and can be downloaded for use with the code listings in this chapter via http://bit.ly/frogger_gameboard.

Listing 11-15. Draw the game background, the number of lives remaining, and the time remaining

```
// Define a code module to draw the game board background image to the background <canvas>
// element. We will draw the image once only since it is static and will not change - all
// graphical elements that could change are drawn to the main <canvas> element instead.
(function(Frogger) {

    // To draw an image file onto the <canvas> we need to create a new <img> element to
    // contain the image first
    var _background = document.createElement("img");

    // Once the image has loaded, draw the image onto the background <canvas> element's
    // drawing surface, starting at the top-left corner and covering the full width and
    // height of the drawing surface
    _background.addEventListener("load", function() {
        Frogger.backgroundDrawingSurface.drawImage(_background, 0, 0, Frogger.drawingSurfaceWidth,
            Frogger.drawingSurfaceHeight);
    }, false);

    // Setting the "src" attribute of the <img> causes the file to load immediately, which
    // is why it was essential to configure our "load" event handler first. We load the
    // file named "gameboard.gif" which contains the background of the game board. This
```

```
        // will only be drawn once since we are not within the game loop at this point. By
        // splitting the background out into a separate element, we avoid needing to redraw
        // the background each time the game loop executes since it is static.
        _background.src = "gameboard.gif";
}(Frogger));

// Define a code module to show the number of lives the player has remaining, and how much
// time remains before automatically losing a life, within the <canvas> element
(function(Frogger) {

    // Define an array, to be populated later, which will represent the number of lives the
    // player has remaining
    var _lives = [],

        // Define a variable indicating the time remaining on the countdown before the
        // player automatically loses a life, represented as a percentage, starting at
        // 100% and counting down to 0
        _timeRemainingAsPercentage = 100,

        // Define a variable for storing the game board properties and settings
        _gameBoard;

    // Define a subclass of Frogger.ImageSprite to represent the individual image found
    // at position 720px from the left and 80px from the top of the sprite map image which
    // is 40px wide by 40px tall and depicts a small frog to be used to denote a remaining
    // life
    function Life(left, top) {

        // The left and top parameters indicate the starting position of this instance of
        // the Life "class". We pass those parameters directly onto the parent
        // Frogger.ImageSprite() constructor function
        Frogger.ImageSprite.call(this, left, top);
    }

    // Inherit properties and methods from the Frogger.ImageSprite "class"
    Life.prototype = new Frogger.ImageSprite();
    Life.prototype.constructor = Life;

    // Set the dimensions and location of the remaining life image from within the larger
    // sprite map image file
    Life.prototype.spriteLeft = 720;
    Life.prototype.spriteTop = 80;
    Life.prototype.width = 40;
    Life.prototype.height = 40;

    // Define a function to be executed when the game board has initialized, passing along
    // the properties and settings from the game board code module
    function initialize(gameBoard) {

        // Define a variable representing the position from the top of the game board
        // to display the remaining lives
        var lifePositionTop;
```

295

```
        // Store the game board properties and settings in a local variable within this
        // code module
        _gameBoard = gameBoard;

        // Set the lifePositionTop variable to the appropriate position in the bottom-left
        // corner of the game board
        lifePositionTop = (_gameBoard.numRows - 1) * _gameBoard.grid.height;

        // Define five lives for the player by populating the _lives array with five
        // instances of the Life "class", each one initialized with its starting position
        // from left to right along the bottom-left corner of the game board
        _lives = [

            // Each life is displayed at the same position from the top of the game board
            // and each spaced horizontally according to the width of the individual
            // image so they sit right beside each other
            new Life(0, lifePositionTop),
            new Life(1 * Life.prototype.width, lifePositionTop),
            new Life(2 * Life.prototype.width, lifePositionTop),
            new Life(3 * Life.prototype.width, lifePositionTop),
            new Life(4 * Life.prototype.width, lifePositionTop)
        ];

        // Listen for the "render-base-layer" event fired from within the game loop and
        // execute the render() function, defined further down, when it is called
        Frogger.observer.subscribe("render-base-layer", render);
    }

    // Define a function to render the number of lives remaining on the game board
    function renderLives() {
        var index = 0,
            length = _lives.length,
            life;

        // Loop through the number of remaining lives stored in the _lives array, and
        // call the renderAt() method of each of the Life "class" instances contained
        // within, drawing the life on the game board at the appropriate position
        for (; index < length; index++) {
            life = _lives[index];

            life.renderAt(life.left, life.top);
        }
    }

    // Define a function to render the time remaining as a green rectangular bar along the
    // bottom edge of the game board
    function renderTimeRemaining() {

        // Define the width of the rectangle. When full, this will be the width of 10
        // columns on the game board. As the time remaining decreases, the width will
        // decrease accordingly
        var rectangleWidth = _timeRemainingAsPercentage * _gameBoard.rows[10],
```

```
        // Define the height of the rectangle, which will always be half of one grid
        // square on the game board
        rectangleHeight = _gameBoard.grid.height / 2,

        // Define the left-hand edge, in pixels, where the rectangle should be drawn
        // from on the <canvas>. Since the countdown should appear to be decreasing
        // from the left to the right, this will be the inverse of the time remaining
        // percentage, multiplied by the full width of the rectangle
        rectangleLeft = (1 - _timeRemainingAsPercentage) * _gameBoard.rows[10],

        // Define the top edge, in pixels, where the rectangle should be drawn from
        // on the <canvas> element. This will be the bottom edge of the game board so
        // we need to subtract the desired height of the rectangle from the height
        // of the game board itself
        rectangleTop = Frogger.drawingSurfaceHeight - rectangleHeight;

    // Set the drawing context to draw in green (hex color #0F0)
    Frogger.drawingSurface.fillStyle = "#0F0";

    // Draw the rectangle on the game board at the given positions
    Frogger.drawingSurface.fillRect(rectangleLeft, rectangleTop, rectangleWidth,
    rectangleHeight);
}

// Define a function to draw the remaining lives and time remaining on the game board,
// executed when the "render-base-layer" event is fired from within the game loop
function render() {
    renderLives();
    renderTimeRemaining();
}

// When the game logic module informs us that the player has lost a life, we remove
// the last entry from the _lives array, which removes the right-most life image from
// the bottom-left corner of the canvas, indicating the correct number of lives
// remaining
Frogger.observer.subscribe("player-lost-life", function() {
    _lives.pop();
});

// When the game logic module informs us that the time remaining for the player to
// reach the goal has changed, we store the new value returned as a percentage
Frogger.observer.subscribe("time-remaining-change", function(newTimeRemainingPercentage) {
    _timeRemainingAsPercentage = newTimeRemainingPercentage;
});

// When the game board initializes its properties and settings, execute the
// initialize() function
Frogger.observer.subscribe("game-board-initialize", initialize);
}(Frogger));
```

Figure 11-4. *The game board background image, containing all the static elements in one image file*

With the background visible and our base code in place to extract individual images from the sprite map, it's time to define the obstacles for our game board, including vehicles, logs, turtles, and the goals the player is trying to reach, along with the images and animations to display for each. This is shown together in Listing 11-16.

Listing 11-16. Creating images and animations for obstacles and goals on the game board

```
// Define a namespace to store the individual obstacles and images to place on the game
// board as "classes" representing the individual images from the sprite map for each
Frogger.Image = (function(Frogger) {

    // Define a race car obstacle whose starting position on the x-axis can be set when
    // instantiated
    function RaceCar(left) {
        Frogger.ImageSprite.call(this, left);
    }
```

```
// The race car is defined as the image found in the sprite map at position 0px x 80px
// respectively from the left and top edges of the sprite map image file
RaceCar.prototype = new Frogger.ImageSprite();
RaceCar.prototype.constructor = RaceCar;
RaceCar.prototype.spriteLeft = 0;
RaceCar.prototype.spriteTop = 80;

// Define a bulldozer obstacle
function Bulldozer(left) {
    Frogger.ImageSprite.call(this, left);
}

// The bulldozer is the image found at position 80px x 80px within the sprite map
Bulldozer.prototype = new Frogger.ImageSprite();
Bulldozer.prototype.constructor = Bulldozer;
Bulldozer.prototype.spriteLeft = 80;
Bulldozer.prototype.spriteTop = 80;

// Define a turbo race car obstacle
function TurboRaceCar(left) {
    Frogger.ImageSprite.call(this, left);
}

// The turbo race car is the image found at position 160px x 80px within the sprite map
TurboRaceCar.prototype = new Frogger.ImageSprite();
TurboRaceCar.prototype.constructor = TurboRaceCar;
TurboRaceCar.prototype.spriteLeft = 160;
TurboRaceCar.prototype.spriteTop = 80;

// Define a road car obstacle
function RoadCar(left) {
    Frogger.ImageSprite.call(this, left);
}

// The road car is the image found at position 240px x 80px within the sprite map
RoadCar.prototype = new Frogger.ImageSprite();
RoadCar.prototype.constructor = RoadCar;
RoadCar.prototype.spriteLeft = 240;
RoadCar.prototype.spriteTop = 80;

// Define a truck obstacle
function Truck(left) {
    Frogger.ImageSprite.call(this, left);
}

// The truck is the image found at position 320px x 80px within the sprite map, with a
// width of 122px as opposed to the standard 80px width of the other individual images
Truck.prototype = new Frogger.ImageSprite();
Truck.prototype.constructor = Truck;
Truck.prototype.spriteLeft = 320;
Truck.prototype.spriteTop = 80;
Truck.prototype.width = 122;
```

```
// Define a short log obstacle
function ShortLog(left) {
    Frogger.ImageSprite.call(this, left);
}

// The short log is the image found at position 0px x 160px within the sprite map, with
// a width of 190px
ShortLog.prototype = new Frogger.ImageSprite();
ShortLog.prototype.constructor = ShortLog;
ShortLog.prototype.spriteLeft = 0;
ShortLog.prototype.spriteTop = 160;
ShortLog.prototype.width = 190;

// Define a medium log obstacle
function MediumLog(left) {
    Frogger.ImageSprite.call(this, left);
}

// The medium log is the image found at position 0px x 240px within the sprite map,
// with a width of 254px
MediumLog.prototype = new Frogger.ImageSprite();
MediumLog.prototype.constructor = MediumLog;
MediumLog.prototype.spriteLeft = 0;
MediumLog.prototype.spriteTop = 240;
MediumLog.prototype.width = 254;

// Define a long log obstacle
function LongLog(left) {
    Frogger.ImageSprite.call(this, left);
}

// The long log is the image found at position 240px x 160px within the sprite map,
// with a width of 392px
LongLog.prototype = new Frogger.ImageSprite();
LongLog.prototype.constructor = LongLog;
LongLog.prototype.spriteLeft = 240;
LongLog.prototype.spriteTop = 160;
LongLog.prototype.width = 392;

// Define a turtle obstacle. There are two types of turtle obstacle on the game board,
// one representing a group of two turtles and one representing a group of three
// turtles. Both types of turtle obstacle have some shared behavior which is defined
// in this "class" which acts as a base for both obstacles to inherit from.
function Turtle(left) {
    Frogger.ImageSprite.call(this, left);
}

Turtle.prototype = new Frogger.ImageSprite();
Turtle.prototype.constructor = Turtle;

// The turtles will animate and appear to dip underwater on occasion. We need to
// know when the turtle is underwater so that if the player's character is positioned
// above the turtle at that point, they will lose a life. This will be handled by the
```

```
// collision detection code later, but for now we just need to create a method to
// tell us when the turtle in underwater
Turtle.prototype.isUnderwater = function() {
    var isUnderwater = false,

        // Get a reference to the current animation of the turtle diving underwater
        // and resurfacing
        animation = this.animations[this.currentAnimation];

    // The turtle is deemed to be underwater when it is showing the furthestmost image
    // from the sprite map in the animation sequence. This is represented by the
    // largest number in the animation frame sequence which we can get using the
    // Math.max() method in JavaScript. If the current animation sequence value matches
    // this furthestmost image in the sprite map, the turtle is underwater.
    if (animation.getSequenceValue() === Math.max.apply(Math, animation.sequence)) {
        isUnderwater = true;
    }

    return isUnderwater;
};

// Define an obstacle representing a group of two turtles together
function TwoTurtles(left) {
    Turtle.call(this, left);
}

// Inherit from the Turtle base "class" defined previously
TwoTurtles.prototype = new Turtle();
TwoTurtles.prototype.constructor = TwoTurtles;

// The group of two turtles is the image found at position 320px x 240px within the
// sprite map, with a width of 130px
TwoTurtles.prototype.spriteLeft = 320;
TwoTurtles.prototype.spriteTop = 240;
TwoTurtles.prototype.width = 130;

// Override the reset() method to define and auto-play the animation of the turtle
// diving and surfacing
TwoTurtles.prototype.reset = function() {
    Turtle.prototype.reset.call(this);

    // Register the dive and surface animation which plays each frame in the sequence
    // at a frame rate of 200 milliseconds, and loops once it reaches the end of the
    // sequence. The numbers in the sequence represent the multiples of offset of the
    // width of the individual image to grab the animating image from - essentially
    // switching between a number of side-by-side images from the sprite map file to
    // give the illusion of movement
    this.registerAnimation({
        "diveAndSurface": {
            sequence: [0, 1, 2, 3, 3, 2, 1, 0, 0, 0, 0, 0, 0, 0, 0, 0, 0, 0, 0, 0, 0],
            loop: true,
            rate: 200
        }
    });
```

```
        // Play the animation straight away
        this.playAnimation("diveAndSurface");
};

// Define an obstacle representing a group of three turtles together
function ThreeTurtles(left) {
    Turtle.call(this, left);
}

// Inherit from the Turtle base "class" defined previously
ThreeTurtles.prototype = new Turtle();
ThreeTurtles.prototype.constructor = ThreeTurtles;

// The group of three turtles is the image found at position 0px x 320px within the
// sprite map, with a width of 200px
ThreeTurtles.prototype.spriteLeft = 0;
ThreeTurtles.prototype.spriteTop = 320;
ThreeTurtles.prototype.width = 200;

// Register the dive and surface animation as before, but animating over a greater
// number of frames and at a slower animation rate than with the group of two turtles
ThreeTurtles.prototype.reset = function() {
    Turtle.prototype.reset.call(this);

    this.registerAnimation({
        "diveAndSurface": {
            sequence: [0, 1, 2, 3, 3, 3, 2, 1, 0, 0, 0, 0, 0, 0, 0, 0, 0, 0, 0, 0, 0],
            loop: true,
            rate: 300
        }
    });

    this.playAnimation("diveAndSurface");
};

// Define a "class" representing the frog image displayed when the player's character
// reaches the goal
function GoalFrog(left) {
    Frogger.ImageSprite.call(this, left);
}

// The goal frog is the image found at position 640px x 80px within the sprite map
GoalFrog.prototype = new Frogger.ImageSprite();
GoalFrog.prototype.constructor = GoalFrog;
GoalFrog.prototype.spriteLeft = 640;
GoalFrog.prototype.spriteTop = 80;

// Override the moveTo() method so that this image cannot be moved from its place
// on the game board once it has been placed down
GoalFrog.prototype.moveTo = function() {};
```

```
// Define a "class" representing the goal the player will be aiming to meet with at
// the far end of the game board from their start position
function Goal(left) {
    Frogger.ImageSprite.call(this, left);
}

// Since the goal is drawn onto the game board as part of the background <canvas>
// we do not need to draw it again here, so we specify the image position as being
// a transparent block from the sprite map image so effectively nothing is actually
// drawn to the canvas. We can still take advantage of the other features of the
// ImageSprite "class", however, to simplify collision checking later on, which
// will tell us when the player's character has reached a goal
Goal.prototype = new Frogger.ImageSprite();
Goal.prototype.constructor = Goal;
Goal.prototype.spriteLeft = 800;
Goal.prototype.spriteTop = 320;

// Override the moveTo() method so that the goal cannot be moved from its place
// on the game board once it has been placed down
Goal.prototype.moveTo = function() {};

// Add a custom property to this "class" to denote whether the goal instance has been
// met by the player's character
Goal.prototype.isMet = false;

// Expose the "classes" defined in this module to the wider code base within the
// Frogger.Image namespace
return {
    RaceCar: RaceCar,
    Bulldozer: Bulldozer,
    RoadCar: RoadCar,
    TurboRaceCar: TurboRaceCar,
    Truck: Truck,
    ShortLog: ShortLog,
    MediumLog: MediumLog,
    LongLog: LongLog,
    TwoTurtles: TwoTurtles,
    ThreeTurtles: ThreeTurtles,
    GoalFrog: GoalFrog,
    Goal: Goal
};
}(Frogger));
```

With the obstacles defined, it's time to define the code, images, and animations to represent the player's character and its froglike movement around the game board, which is shown in Listing 11-17.

Listing 11-17. The player's character

```
// Define a code module to represent the player's character on the game board and to
// handle its movement and behavior according to the current game state
Frogger.Character = (function(Frogger) {

    // Define a variable to store the image representing the player's character
    var _character,

        // Define a variable to store the game board properties and settings
        _gameBoard = {},

        // Define a variable to denote the starting row of the player's character on the
        // game board
        _startRow = 14,

        // Define a variable to denote the starting columns of the player's character on
        // the game board - essentially centered
        _startColumn = 6,

        // Define a variable to store the current row the player's character has reached
        _currentRow = _startRow,

        // Define a Boolean variable to indicate whether the player's character is
        // currently frozen in place, as happens temporarily when the player loses a life
        // or reaches the goal
        _isFrozen = false;

    // Define a "class" to represent the player's frog character, inheriting from the
    // Frogger.ImageSprite "class". The left and top values passed in on instantiation
    // reflect the starting position in pixels of the player's character from the top-left
    // hand corner of the game board
    function Character(left, top) {
        Frogger.ImageSprite.call(this, left, top);

        // Register five animations to play when the player loses a life or when the
        // character is moved in any of four different directions - up, down, left or right
        this.registerAnimation({

            // When the player loses a life, switch between the three images found starting
            // at 640px from the left of the sprite map image at a rate of 350 milliseconds,
            // stopping on the last image
            "lose-life": {
                spriteLeft: 640,
                sequence: [0, 1, 2],
                rate: 350
            },

            // When the player's character moves up a row on the game board, switch between
            // the two images found starting at the left-hand edge of the sprite map
            "move-up": {
                spriteLeft: 0,
                sequence: [1, 0]
            },
```

```
    // When the player's character moves right on the game board, switch between
    // the two images found starting at 160px from left-hand edge of the sprite map
    "move-right": {
        spriteLeft: 160,
        sequence: [1, 0]
    },

    // When the player's character moves down on the game board, switch between
    // the two images found starting at 320px from left-hand edge of the sprite map
    "move-down": {
        spriteLeft: 320,
        sequence: [1, 0]
    },

    // When the player's character moves left on the game board, switch between
    // the two images found starting at 480px from left-hand edge of the sprite map
    "move-left": {
        spriteLeft: 480,
        sequence: [1, 0]
    }
    });
}

// Inherit from the Frogger.ImageSprite "class"
Character.prototype = new Frogger.ImageSprite();
Character.prototype.constructor = Character;

// Define the individual images for the player's character sprite as being found at
// position 0px x 0px within the sprite map image file
Character.prototype.spriteLeft = 0;
Character.prototype.spriteTop = 0;

// Define a method to move the character up one row on the game board
Character.prototype.moveUp = function() {

    // Move the top position of the character up by the height of one grid square
    // on the game board
    this.top -= _gameBoard.grid.height;

    // Ensure the character does not move outside of the bounds restricting its
    // movement around the game board - we don't want it appearing on top of the
    // score at the top of the screen
    if (this.top < _gameBoard.characterBounds.top) {
        this.top = _gameBoard.characterBounds.top;
    }

    // Play the animation named "move-up", making it look like the character is moving
    this.playAnimation("move-up");

    // Keep track of the current row the character sits upon
    _currentRow--;
};
```

```javascript
// Define a method to move the character down one row on the game board
Character.prototype.moveDown = function() {

    // Move the top position of the character down by the height of one grid square
    // on the game board
    this.top += _gameBoard.grid.height;

    // Ensure the character does not move outside of the bounds restricting its
    // movement around the game board - we don't want it appearing on top of the
    // countdown timer at the base of the screen
    if (this.top > _gameBoard.characterBounds.bottom) {
        this.top = _gameBoard.characterBounds.bottom;
    }

    // Play the animation named "move-down", making it look like the character is moving
    this.playAnimation("move-down");

    // Keep track of the current row the character sits upon
    _currentRow++;
};

// Define a method to move the character one column to the left on the game board
Character.prototype.moveLeft = function() {

    // Move the position of the character on the game board left by the width of one
    // grid square on the game board
    this.left -= _gameBoard.grid.width;

    // Ensure the character does not move outside of the bounds restricting its
    // movement around the game board - we don't want it disappearing off the side
    if (this.left < _gameBoard.characterBounds.left) {
        this.left = _gameBoard.characterBounds.left;
    }

    // Play the animation named "move-left", making it look like the character is moving
    this.playAnimation("move-left");
};

// Define a method to move the character one column to the right on the game board
Character.prototype.moveRight = function() {

    // Move the position of the character on the game board right by the width of one
    // grid square on the game board
    this.left += _gameBoard.grid.width;

    // Ensure the character does not move outside of the bounds restricting its
    // movement around the game board - we don't want it disappearing off the side
    if (this.left > _gameBoard.characterBounds.right) {
        this.left = _gameBoard.characterBounds.right;
    }
```

```
    // Play the animation named "move-right", making it look like the character is moving
    this.playAnimation("move-right");
};

// Define a function which returns the current position of the player's character in
// pixels from the top of the game board
function getTop() {

    // Look up the top position in pixels from the game board properties by the current
    // row the character is sitting upon
    return _gameBoard.rows[_currentRow];
}

// Define a function which hides the player's character from display
function hide() {

    // Call the hide() method on the instance of the Character "class" that will
    // represent the player's character
    _character.hide();
}

// Define a function which moves the player's character in one of four possible
// directions - up, down, left, or right
function move(characterDirection) {

    // Only move the player's character if it is not deemed to be frozen in place
    if (!_isFrozen) {

        // Call the appropriate method on the Character instance based on the
        // direction the character is to move in
        if (characterDirection === Frogger.direction.LEFT) {
            _character.moveLeft();
        } else if (characterDirection === Frogger.direction.RIGHT) {
            _character.moveRight();
        } else if (characterDirection === Frogger.direction.UP) {
            _character.moveUp();
        } else if (characterDirection === Frogger.direction.DOWN) {
            _character.moveDown();
        }

        // Publish an event to the rest of the code modules, indicating that the
        // player's position has been moved by the player
        Frogger.observer.publish("player-moved");
    }
}

// Define a function to render the player's character on screen
function render() {

    // Call the Character instance's renderAt() method, passing along its current
    // left and top position
    _character.renderAt(_character.left, _character.top);
}
```

```
// Define a function, to be executed when the player loses a life, which plays the
// appropriate animation
function loseLife() {
    _character.playAnimation("lose-life");
}

// Define a function to move the player's character to the given position in pixels
// from the left-hand edge of the game board - this will be used when the character
// is sitting on a moving object to keep the character aligned with that object
function setPosition(left) {

    // Ensure the character does not move outside of its defined bounds on the game
    // board
    if (left > _gameBoard.characterBounds.right) {
        left = _gameBoard.characterBounds.right;
    } else if (left < _gameBoard.characterBounds.left) {
        left = _gameBoard.characterBounds.left;
    }

    // Move the character's position from the left-hand edge of the game board to match
    // the given position
    _character.moveTo(left);
}

// Define a function to reset the player's character's position on the game board
function reset() {
    _character.reset();

    // Reset the local variable indicating the current row the character sits upon
    _currentRow = _startRow;
}

// Define a function to return the current position of the character on the game board
function getPosition() {
    return _character.getPosition();
}

// Define a function to set the local _isFrozen variable to true, indicating that the
// player's character's position on the game board should be frozen in place
function freeze() {
    _isFrozen = true;
}

// Define a function to set the local _isFrozen variable to false, indicating that the
// player's character is free to move around the game board
function unfreeze() {
    _isFrozen = false;
}
```

```
// Define a function to be executed when the game board has initialized, passing along
// the properties and settings from the game board code module
function initialize(gameBoard) {
    _gameBoard = gameBoard;

    // Initialize an instance of the Character "class" to represent the player's
    // character, setting its start position on the game board
    _character = new Character(_gameBoard.columns[_startColumn], _gameBoard.rows[_startRow]);

    // Ensure the local render() function is executed when the "render-character"
    // event is fired from within the game loop to draw the player's character on
    // the screen
    Frogger.observer.subscribe("render-character", render);
}

// When the game logic module informs us that the player has lost a life, execute the
// loseLife() function to play the appropriate animation
Frogger.observer.subscribe("player-lost-life", loseLife);

// When the game logic informs us the player's position needs to be reset, execute the
// reset() function
Frogger.observer.subscribe("reset", reset);

// When the player has reached the goal, hide the player from the screen temporarily
Frogger.observer.subscribe("player-at-goal", hide);

// When the game logic tells us the player's character must stay in place on the
// game board, we set the appropriate local variable to reflect this
Frogger.observer.subscribe("player-freeze", freeze);

// When the game logic tells us the player's character is free to move around the
// game board again, we set the appropriate local variable to reflect this
Frogger.observer.subscribe("player-unfreeze", unfreeze);

// When the game board module initializes its properties and settings, execute the
// initialize() function
Frogger.observer.subscribe("game-board-initialize", initialize);

// When the player presses the arrow keys on the keyboard, move the player's
// character in the appropriate direction on the game board
window.addEventListener("keydown", function(event) {

    // Define the key codes for the arrow keys
    var LEFT_ARROW = 37,
        UP_ARROW = 38,
        RIGHT_ARROW = 39,
        DOWN_ARROW = 40;

    // Execute the move() function, passing along the correct direction based on the
    // arrow key pressed. Ignore any other key presses
```

```
        if (event.keyCode === LEFT_ARROW) {
            move(Frogger.direction.LEFT);
        } else if (event.keyCode === RIGHT_ARROW) {
            move(Frogger.direction.RIGHT);
        } else if (event.keyCode === UP_ARROW) {
            move(Frogger.direction.UP);
        } else if (event.keyCode === DOWN_ARROW) {
            move(Frogger.direction.DOWN);
        }
    }, false);

    // When the player taps in certain places on the game board on their touch-sensitive
    // screen, move the player's character in the appropriate direction on the game board
    // according to where the screen has been tapped. This is useful since users with
    // touch screens are typically on mobile devices that do not have access to
    // physical keyboards to press the arrow keys to move the character.
    Frogger.canvas.addEventListener("touchstart", function(event) {

        // Get a reference to the position of the touch on the screen in pixels from the
        // top-left position of the touched element, in this case the game board
        var touchLeft = event.targetTouches[0].clientX,
            touchTop = event.targetTouches[0].clientY;

        // Execute the move() function, passing along the correct direction based on the
        // position tapped on the game board
        if (touchLeft < (Frogger.drawingSurfaceWidth / 8)) {
            move(Frogger.direction.LEFT);
        } else if (touchLeft > (3 * Frogger.drawingSurfaceWidth / 8)) {
            move(Frogger.direction.RIGHT);
        } else if (touchTop < (Frogger.drawingSurfaceHeight / 8)) {
            move(Frogger.direction.UP);
        } else if (touchTop > (3 * Frogger.drawingSurfaceHeight / 8)) {
            move(Frogger.direction.DOWN);
        }
    }, false);

    // Expose the local getTop(), getPosition() and setPosition() methods so they are
    // available to other code modules
    return {
        getTop: getTop,
        getPosition: getPosition,
        setPosition: setPosition
    };
}(Frogger));
```

A look at the game board in Figure 11-2 reveals that all similar obstacles are contained together on the same row on the game board, all similar vehicles together, all turtles together, all logs together, and all goals together. We can therefore define the behavior of a "row" on the game board, as shown in Listing 11-18, which will contain references to the obstacle objects in that raw, along with the speed and direction of motion, which all obstacles on that row will follow.

Listing 11-18. Create a "row" for obstacles that can move together in a certain direction at the same speed

```
// Define a code module to define the types of obstacle rows that exist on the game board,
// representing a road-type row which will house vehicles, a water row containing log
// obstacles, a water row containing turtle obstacles, and a goal row containing the
// locations the player's character aims to reach to win the game
Frogger.Row = (function() {

    // Define a base row "class" containing the shared code required for each different
    // type of specialist row on the game board
    function Row(options) {
        options = options || {};

        // Define the direction of obstacles moving on this row, defaults to moving left
        this.direction = options.direction || Frogger.direction.LEFT;

        // Define the set of obstacles to place on this row and move
        this.obstacles = options.obstacles || [];

        // Define the top position, in pixels, of where this row sits on the game board
        this.top = options.top || 0;

        // Define the speed with which obstacles on this row move in the given direction
        // as a factor of the render rate set in game loop
        this.speed = options.speed || 1;
    }

    Row.prototype = {

        // Define a method to render each of the obstacles in the correct place on the
        // current row
        render: function() {
            var index = 0,
                length = this.obstacles.length,
                left,
                obstaclesItem;

            // Loop through each of the obstacles within this row
            for (; index < length; index++) {
                obstaclesItem = this.obstacles[index];

                // Update the left position, in pixels, of this obstacle based on its
                // current position along with the direction and speed of movement
                left = obstaclesItem.getPosition().left + ((this.direction === Frogger.direction.
                RIGHT ? 1 : -1) * this.speed);

                // Adjust the left position such that if the obstacle falls off one edge of
                // the game board, it then appears to return from the other edge
                if (left < -obstaclesItem.getWidth()) {
                    left = Frogger.drawingSurfaceWidth;
```

```
                } else if (left >=Frogger.drawingSurfaceWidth) {
                    left = -obstaclesItem.getWidth();
                }

                // Move the obstacle and draw it on the game board in the updated position
                obstaclesItem.moveTo(left);
                obstaclesItem.renderAt(left, this.top);
            }
        },

        // Define a method to return the top position, in pixels, of this row
        getTop: function() {
            return this.top;
        },

        // Define a method to detect whether the player's character is currently colliding
        // with an obstacle on this row
        isCollision: function(characterPosition) {
            var index = 0,
                length = this.obstacles.length,
                obstaclesItem,
                isCollision = false;

            // Loop through each of the obstacles on this row
            for (; index < length; index++) {
                obstaclesItem = this.obstacles[index];

                // If the player's character touches the current obstacle, a collision
                // has taken place and we return this fact to the calling code
                if (Frogger.intersects(obstaclesItem.getPosition(), characterPosition)) {
                    isCollision = true;
                }
            }

            return isCollision;
        },

        // Define a method to reset the obstacles on this row to their default state and
        // position on the game board
        reset: function() {
            var index = 0,
                length = this.obstacles.length;

            // Loop through each of the obstacles within this row, and call their reset()
            // methods in turn
            for (; index < length; index++) {
                this.obstacles[index].reset();
            }
        }
    };
```

```
// Define a new "class" representing a road-type row, containing vehicle obstacles which
// inherits from our base Row "class"
function Road(options) {
    Row.call(this, options);
}

Road.prototype = new Row();
Road.prototype.constructor = Road;

// Define a new "class" representing a row containing logs floating on water which
// inherits from our base Row "class"
function Log(options) {
    Row.call(this, options);
}

Log.prototype = new Row();
Log.prototype.constructor = Log;

// Override the isCollision() method, reversing its behavior. If the player's character
// touches a log it is safe, however it should be considered a collision if it touches
// the water beneath rather than the obstacle itself
Log.prototype.isCollision = function(characterPosition) {

    // Return the opposite Boolean state returned by a normal call to the isCollision()
    // method
    return !Row.prototype.isCollision.call(this, characterPosition);
};

// Override the render() method so that when the player's character lands on a log,
// it gets transported along the water with the log
Log.prototype.render = function() {

    // If the player's character is on this row, update its position based on the
    // direction and speed of motion of the log the player has landed on
    if (Frogger.Character.getTop() === this.getTop()) {
        Frogger.Character.setPosition(Frogger.Character.getPosition().left +
        ((this.direction === Frogger.direction.RIGHT ? 1 : -1) * this.speed));
    }

    // Call the inherited render() method to draw the log in its new position
    Row.prototype.render.call(this);

};

// Define a new "class" representing a row containing turtles swimming in the water
// which inherits from our Log "class" as it shares similarities
function Turtle(options) {
    Log.call(this, options);
}

Turtle.prototype = new Log();
Turtle.prototype.constructor = Turtle;
```

```
// Override the isCollision() method such that it behaves like the same method on
// the Log "class" apart from when the turtle obstacle has dipped underwater, in which
// case there will always be a collision if the player's character is on this row
Turtle.prototype.isCollision = function(characterPosition) {
    var isCollision = Log.prototype.isCollision.call(this, characterPosition);
    return this.obstacles[0].isUnderwater() || isCollision;
};

// Define a new "class" representing the goal row the player's character is aiming for
// in order to win the game, which inherits from our base Row "class"
function Goal(options) {

    // The goals placed within this row never move so we always force the speed
    // property to be 0
    options.speed = 0;

    Row.call(this, options);
}

Goal.prototype = new Row();
Goal.prototype.constructor = Goal;

// Override the isCollision() method to detect if the player's character has reached
// one of the available goals stored in this row
Goal.prototype.isCollision = function(characterPosition) {
    var index = 0,
        length = this.obstacles.length,
        obstaclesItem,
        isCollision = true;

    // Loop through the goals in this row to find out if the player has reached one
    // of them
    for (; index < length; index++) {
        obstaclesItem = this.obstacles[index];

        // If this goal has not been reached before and the player's character is
        // positioned above the goal, fire the "player-at-goal" event so the game logic
        // module registers that the goal has been reached
        if (!obstaclesItem.isMet && Frogger.intersects(obstaclesItem.getPosition(),
        characterPosition)) {
            this.obstacles[index].isMet = true;
            Frogger.observer.publish("player-at-goal");
            isCollision = false;

            // Add the image of the goal-reached frog to the row within the goal
            // reached so the user can see that they have reached this goal before
            this.obstacles.push(new Frogger.Image.GoalFrog(obstaclesItem.getPosition().left));
        }
    }

    return isCollision;
};
```

```
    // Return the "classes" defined in this code module for use in the rest of our code
    return {
        Road: Road,
        Log: Log,
        Turtle: Turtle,
        Goal: Goal
    };
}(Frogger));
```

With our base "row" and obstacle types defined, it's time to create the actual instances of rows and obstacles and place them on the game board, which we do in Listing 11-19.

Listing 11-19. Defining rows and obstacles, and placing them on the game board

```
// Define a code module to add rows containing obstacles to the game board for the player
// to avoid or make contact with in order to progress from the bottom to the top of the
// game board in order to win the game by reaching each of the five goals without losing
// all their lives or the allocated time running out
(function(Frogger) {

    // Define variables to store the populated rows on the game board, and the properties
    // and settings of the game board itself
    var _rows = [],
        _gameBoard = {};

    // Define a function to be called when the game board has initialized onto which we
    // place our rows and obstacles
    function initialize(gameBoard) {
        _gameBoard = gameBoard;

        // Add elevent rows of obstacles to the game board
        _rows = [

            // Add a goal row to the 3rd row on the game board (the rows start from index
            // 0), containing five goals positioned in the respective places according to
            // the designation on the game board background image
            new Frogger.Row.Goal({
                top: _gameBoard.rows[2],
                obstacles: [new Frogger.Image.Goal(33, 111), new Frogger.Image.Goal(237, 315), new
                Frogger.Image.Goal(441, 519), new Frogger.Image.Goal(645, 723), new Frogger.Image.
                Goal(849, 927)]
            }),

            // Add a row of medium-length logs to the 4th row on the game board, moving
            // right at a rate of 5 pixels per each time the game loop is called to
            // render this row within the <canvas>
            new Frogger.Row.Log({
                top: _gameBoard.rows[3],
                direction: Frogger.direction.RIGHT,
                speed: 5,
```

```
        // Add three medium-sized log obstacles to the game board, spaced out evenly
        obstacles: [new Frogger.Image.MediumLog(_gameBoard.columns[1]), new Frogger.Image.
        MediumLog(_gameBoard.columns[6]), new Frogger.Image.MediumLog(_gameBoard.
        columns[10])]
    }),

    // Add a row of turtles, grouped in twos, on the 5th row of the game board,
    // moving left (the default direction) at a rate of 6 pixels on each turn of the
    // game loop
    new Frogger.Row.Turtle({
        top: _gameBoard.rows[4],
        speed: 6,

        // Add four obstacles spaced out across the width of the game board
        obstacles: [new Frogger.Image.TwoTurtles(_gameBoard.columns[0]), new Frogger.Image.
        TwoTurtles(_gameBoard.columns[3]), new Frogger.Image.TwoTurtles(_gameBoard.
        columns[6]), new Frogger.Image.TwoTurtles(_gameBoard.columns[9])]
    }),

    // Add a row of long-length logs to the 6th row on the game board, moving right
    // at a rate of 7 pixels on each turn of the game loop
    new Frogger.Row.Log({
        top: _gameBoard.rows[5],
        direction: Frogger.direction.RIGHT,
        speed: 7,

        // Add two long-length log obstacles to this row
        obstacles: [new Frogger.Image.LongLog(_gameBoard.columns[1]), new Frogger.Image.
        LongLog(_gameBoard.columns[10])]
    }),

    // Add a row of short-length logs to the 7th row of the game board, moving right
    // at a rate of 3 pixels each time the game loop is called
    new Frogger.Row.Log({
        top: _gameBoard.rows[6],
        direction: Frogger.direction.RIGHT,
        speed: 3,

        // Add three short-length logs to this row
        obstacles: [new Frogger.Image.ShortLog(_gameBoard.columns[1]), new Frogger.Image.
        ShortLog(_gameBoard.columns[6]), new Frogger.Image.ShortLog(_gameBoard.columns[10])]
    }),

    // Add a row of turtles, grouped in threes, on the 8th row of the game board,
    // moving left at a rate of 5 pixels each time the game loop is called
    new Frogger.Row.Turtle({
        top: _gameBoard.rows[7],
        speed: 5,
        obstacles: [new Frogger.Image.ThreeTurtles(_gameBoard.columns[0]), new Frogger.
        Image.ThreeTurtles(_gameBoard.columns[3]), new Frogger.Image.ThreeTurtles
        (_gameBoard.columns[7]), new Frogger.Image.ThreeTurtles(_gameBoard.columns[10])]
    }),
```

```
        // Add a set of truck-style vehicle obstacles to the 10th row of the game
        // board (the 9th row is considered a "safe" row that contains no obstacles)
        new Frogger.Row.Road({
            top: _gameBoard.rows[9],
            speed: 3,
            obstacles: [new Frogger.Image.Truck(_gameBoard.columns[1]), new Frogger.Image.
            Truck(_gameBoard.columns[7])]
        }),

        // Add a set of turbo race car obstacles to the 11th row of the game board,
        // moving right at a fast rate
        new Frogger.Row.Road({
            top: _gameBoard.rows[10],
            direction: Frogger.direction.RIGHT,
            speed: 12,
            obstacles: [new Frogger.Image.TurboRaceCar(_gameBoard.columns[1]), new Frogger.
            Image.TurboRaceCar(_gameBoard.columns[7])]
        }),

        // Add a set of simple road car obstacles to the 12th row of the game board
        new Frogger.Row.Road({
            top: _gameBoard.rows[11],
            speed: 4,
            obstacles: [new Frogger.Image.RoadCar(_gameBoard.columns[1]), new Frogger.Image.
            RoadCar(_gameBoard.columns[7])]
        }),

        // Add a set of bulldozer-style obstacles to the 13th row of the game board
        new Frogger.Row.Road({
            top: _gameBoard.rows[12],
            direction: Frogger.direction.RIGHT,
            speed: 3,
            obstacles: [new Frogger.Image.Bulldozer(_gameBoard.columns[1]), new Frogger.Image.
            Bulldozer(_gameBoard.columns[7])]
        }),

        // Add a set of race car obstacles to the 14th row of the game board, which is
        // one row above where the player's character's starting position is
        new Frogger.Row.Road({
            top: _gameBoard.rows[13],
            speed: 4,
            obstacles: [new Frogger.Image.RaceCar(_gameBoard.columns[2]), new Frogger.Image.
            RaceCar(_gameBoard.columns[6])]
        })
    ];

    // With the rows and obstacles initialized, connect the local render() function to
    // the "render-base-layer" event fired from within the game loop to draw those
    // obstacles onto the game board
    Frogger.observer.subscribe("render-base-layer", render);
}
```

```
// Define a function to render each of the defined rows of obstacles onto the game board
function render() {
    var row,
        index = 0,
        length = _rows.length;

    // Loop through each row calling its render() method, which in turn calls the
    // render() method of each of the obstacles stored within it
    for (; index < length; index++) {
        row = _rows[index];
        row.render();
    }
}

// Define a function to detect whether a collision has occured between the player's
// character and the obstacles within each row
function isCollision() {
    var collided = false,
        row,
        index = 0,
        length = _rows.length;

    // Loop through each row calling its isCollision() method, which determines
    // whether the obstacles on that row come into contact with the player's
    // character on the game board
    for (; index < length; index++) {
        row = _rows[index];

        if (Frogger.Character.getTop() === row.getTop()) {
            collided = row.isCollision(Frogger.Character.getPosition());
            if (collided) {
                break;
            }
        }
    }

    // If a collision has occured, trigger the "collision" event which the game logic
    // module uses to cause the player to lose a life
    if (collided) {
        Frogger.observer.publish("collision");
    }

    return collided;
}

// Define a function to reset each of the rows to reset to their initial state
function reset() {
    var row;
```

```
        // Loop through each row calling its reset() method, which in turn calls the
        // reset() method of each of the obstacles within that row
        for (var index = 0, length = _rows.length; index < length; index++) {
            row = _rows[index];
            row.reset();
        }
    }

    // When the game logic wishes the game board to reset, call the local reset() function
    Frogger.observer.subscribe("reset", reset);

    // When the game loop wishes to check for collisions, call the local isCollision()
    // function, which will fire a "collision" event if a collision occurs
    Frogger.observer.subscribe("check-collisions", isCollision);
    // When the game board has initialized its properties and settings, call the local
    // initialize() function to place the rows and obstacles onto the game board
    Frogger.observer.subscribe("game-board-initialize", initialize);
}(Frogger));
```

All of the pieces of our game are now in place and we can simply start the game by triggering the game-load event, which starts the game loop running, drawing everything to the screen and checking for collisions between the player's character and the obstacles, as shown in Listing 11-20. Use the arrow keys on your keyboard, or tap on your touchscreen, to move the player character up, down, left, or right within the game board to reach the goals at the top of the screen and to win the game.

Listing 11-20. Starting the game

```
// Now the code modules have been registered, kick off the game logic and start the game
Frogger.observer.publish("game-load");
```

I have uploaded the completed code for this game, together with the fonts and images required to support it, to my GitHub account here for you to view in place: https://github.com/denodell/frogger. You can run the game directly from GitHub via the URL http://denodell.github.io/frogger.

I hope that by following the code for creating this game, you will have the inspiration and knowledge to build your own using some of the same techniques garnered here, including spriting, the game loop, and collision detection. For further reading on the wide area of game development with the Canvas API, I suggest you look at the following online resources:

- "The Complete Guide To Building HTML5 Games with Canvas and SVG" by David Rousset at SitePoint, via http://bit.ly/complete_games

- "HTML5 Game Development" via http://bit.ly/html5_game_dev

- "Canvas Demos" via http://www.canvasdemos.com

Summary

In this chapter, we've covered the basics of drawing shapes, text, and images onto the HTML5 <canvas> element through JavaScript. We've seen a series of techniques and steps that constitute the bulk of code in game development and we've seen how to build a real, working game using these techniques.

In the next chapter, we'll look at another native JavaScript API that we can use to build a video chat client connecting two remote users together, all within the browser.

CHAPTER 12

■ ■ ■

Using WebRTC for Video Chat

Recent years have seen browser manufacturers push the boundaries of what was previously considered possible in native JavaScript code, adding APIs to support a number of new features, including pixel-based drawing, as we saw in the previous chapter, and now, finally, a way to stream multimedia data (video and audio) from one browser to another across the Internet using an API known as the *Web Real Time Communication* (WebRTC) API, all without using plugins. Although support is, at the time of writing, only currently present in desktop versions of Chrome, Firefox, and Opera, making up just over 50 percent of the worldwide web usage (source: http://bit.ly/caniuse_webrtc), I feel this technology is so important to the future of Internet communication that, as developers, we need to know and understand this API while it is still in its adoption phase.

In this chapter, we will cover the basics of the WebRTC specification, including how to transmit and receive data from a webcam and microphone attached to a device using peer-to-peer networking, to build a simple video chat client within the browser using JavaScript.

The WebRTC Specification

The WebRTC specifiation was started by Google initially for inclusion in their Chrome browser and promises an API that allows developers to:

- Detect device capabilities, including support for video and/or audio based on the presence of a camera and/or microphone attached to the device

- Capture media data from the device's attached hardware

- Encode and stream that media across a network

- Establish direction peer-to-peer connections between browsers, handling any complications with firewalls or Network Address Translation (NAT) automatically

- Decode the media stream, presenting it to the end user with both audio and video synchronized and any audio echos cancelled out

The WebRTC project page can be found online via http://www.webrtc.org and includes the current status of the specification, and contains notes on cross-browser interoperability as well as demos and links to other sites covering the subject.

Accessing the Webcam and Microphone

If we want to use the WebRTC specification to create a video chat application, we need to establish how to access data from the webcam and microphone attached to the device running the application. The JavaScript API method navigator.getUserMedia() is the key to this. We call it by passing three parameters: an object detailing which type of media we wish to access (video and audio are the only property options available at present), a callback function to execute when the connection to the webcam and/or microphone is successfully established, and a callback function to execute if the connection to the webcam and/or microphone is not successfully established. When executing this method, the user is prompted in the browser that the current web page is attempting to access their webcam and/or microphone and they are offered whether to allow or deny access, as shown in Figure 12-1. If they deny access, or the user had no webcam or microphone to connect to, then the second callback function is executed, indicating that the multimedia data could not be accessed; otherwise, the first callback function is executed.

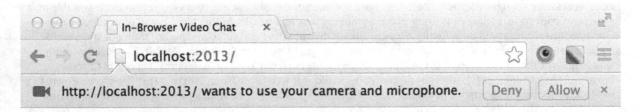

Figure 12-1. *The user must allow or deny access to their webcam and microphone before we can access them*

The getUserMedia() method is, at the time of writing, accessed via a prefixed method name in certain browsers, yet has the same input parameter sequence in all browsers. We can therefore write a small polyfill to enable access to this API in all supported browsers so that we can access it via the getUserMedia() method name throughout our code. The code in Listing 12-1 shows a simple polyfill for allowing access to the webcam and microphone through the same method calls in all supported web browsers.

Listing 12-1. A simple polyfill for the getUserMedia() API

```
// Expose the browser-specific versions of the getUserMedia() method through the standard
// method name. If the standard name is already supported in the browser (as it is in Opera),
// use that, otherwise fall back to Mozilla's, Google's or Microsoft's implementations as
// appropriate for the current browser
navigator.getUserMedia = navigator.getUserMedia || navigator.mozGetUserMedia ||
    navigator.webkitGetUserMedia || navigator.msGetUserMedia;
```

For security reasons, WebRTC only works when files trying to use it are accessed using a web server, rather than running the code directly from local files loaded in the browser. There are numerous ways that you can spin up a web server locally to run the code listings in this chapter, although the simplest is probably to download and run Apache web server software on your machine from http://httpd.apache.org. If you're feeling more adventurous, jump ahead to Chapter 14, where I explain how to create and run a local web server using the Node.js application platform.

We can use the polyfill from Listing 12-1 to call the getUserMedia() method to attempt to get access to the user's webcam and microphone as shown in Listing 12-2.

Listing 12-2. Accessing the webcam and microphone

```
// Define a function to execute if we are successfully able to access the user's webcam and
// microphone
function onSuccess() {
    alert("Successful connection made to access webcam and microphone");
}

// Define a function to execute if we are unable to access the user's webcam and microphone -
// either because the user denied access or because of a technical error
function onError() {
    throw new Error("There has been a problem accessing the webcam and microphone");
}

// Using the polyfill from Listing 12-1, we know the getUserMedia() method is supported in the
// browser if the method exists
if (navigator.getUserMedia) {

    // We can now execute the getUserMedia() method, passing in an object telling the browser
    // which form of media we wish to access ("video" for the webcam, "audio" for the
    // microphone). We pass in a reference to the onSuccess() and onError() functions which
    // will be executed based on whether the user grants us access to the requested media types
    navigator.getUserMedia({
        video: true,
        audio: true
    }, onSuccess, onError);
} else {
    // Throw an error if the getUserMedia() method is unsupported by the user's browser
    throw new Error("Sorry, getUserMedia() is not supported in your browser");
}
```

When running the code in Listing 12-2, if you find that you are not prompted to allow access to the webcam and microphone, check to ensure that you are running your code within the context of a HTML page hosted on a web server, whether local to your computer or over a network connection. If your browser shows that you are browsing a URL using the file:/// protocol, then you will need to run it instead using a web server over http:// instead. The browser will visually indicate that it is currently recording your audio and/or video through the use of a red circle icon next to the page name displayed in the browser tab in both Chrome and Opera, whereas Firefox shows a green camera icon in the address bar to indicate this fact.

Now that we're able to access the user's webcam and microphone, we need to be able to do something with the data returned by them. The onSuccess() callback method fired by the getUserMedia() method is passed a parameter representing the raw stream of data provided by the devices for use within your application. We could take this stream and pass it straight into the input of a HTML5 <video> element on the page, allowing the user to have the data from their own webcam and microphone relayed back to them. The code in Listing 12-3 shows how this can be done using the browser's window.URL.createObjectURL() method, which creates a specific local URL that can be used to access data provided by a multimedia stream in this way.

Listing 12-3. Relaying the webcam and microphone back to the user

```
// Use the getUserMedia() polyfill from Listing 12-1 for best cross-browser support

// Define a function to execute if we are successfully able to access the user's webcam and
// microphone, taking the stream of data provided and passing it as the "src" attribute of a
// new <video> element, which is then placed onto the current HTML page, relaying back to the
// user the output from theirwebcam and microphone
function onSuccess(stream) {

    // Create a new <video> element
    var video = document.createElement("video"),

        // Get the browser to create a unique URL to reference the binary data directly from
        // the provided stream, as it is not a file with a fixed URL
        videoSource = window.URL.createObjectURL(stream);

    // Ensure the <video> element start playing the video immediately
    video.autoplay = true;

    // Point the "src" attribute of the <video> element to the generated stream URL, to relay
    // the data from the webcam and microphone back to the user
    video.src = videoSource;

    // Add the <video> element to the end of the current page
    document.body.appendChild(video);
}

function onError() {
    throw new Error("There has been a problem accessing the webcam and microphone");
}

if (navigator.getUserMedia) {
    navigator.getUserMedia({
        video: true,
        audio: true
    }, onSuccess, onError);
} else {
    throw new Error("Sorry, getUserMedia() is not supported in your browser");
}
```

Now that we've the ability to access the user's webcam and microphone and relay their inputs back to the user, we have the beginnings of what will become a simple two-way video chat application running entirely within the browser.

Creating a Simple Video Chat Web Application

Let's learn the important parts of the WebRTC specifiation by creating an in-browser video chat web application.

The essentials of a video chat application are that we capture the video and audio from two users' devices that are browsing the same web server and that we transmit the captured video and audio streams from one to the other, and vice versa. We've already covered how to capture the streams from the users' devices using the getUserMedia() API method, so let's investigate how to set up a call and how to transmit and receive the data streams in order to build our video chat application.

Connection and Signalling

We need a means of connecting one device directly to another and maintaining an open data connection between the two. We want a direct, or *peer-to-peer*, connection between the two devices without the need for an intermediary server relaying data so as to keep the connection speed, and therefore video and audio quality, to its best possible level. That connection must also be possible regardless of whether either device is directly connected to the Internet with a public IP address, is behind a firewall, or is behind a router device that adopts Network Address Translation (NAT) to share a limited set of public IP addresses with a larger number of devices on a local network.

WebRTC relies on the Interactive Connectivity Establishment (*ICE*) framework, which is a specification that allows two devices to establish a peer-to-peer connection directly to each other regardless of whether one or both devices are connected directly to a public IP address, behind a firewall, or on a network adopting NAT. It simplifies the whole connection process so we that don't have to concern ourselves with that, and it's available for use in supported browsers using the RTCPeerConnection "class" interface.

The process of setting up a peer-to-peer connection involves creating an instance of this RTCPeerConnection "class," passing in an object that containing details of one or more servers capable of helping establish the connection between devices. There are two server protocols these servers can adopt that help in different ways to establish this connection: Session Traversal Utilities for NAT (*STUN*) and Traversal Using Relays around NAT (*TURN*).

A STUN server maps a device's internal IP address together with an unused local port number to its externally visible IP address and unused external-facing port number (outside of the local network) so that traffic can be routed directly to the local device using that port. This is a fast and effective system as the server is only required for the initial connection and can move onto other tasks once established, yet only works on fairly simple NAT configurations where only one device, the client, is actually behind a NAT. Any setup that supports multiple NAT devices or other large enterprise systems won't be able to establish a peer-to-peer connection using this type of server. That is where the alternative, TURN, steps in.

A TURN server uses a relay IP address on the public Internet, most usually the IP address of the public TURN server itself, to connect one device to another where both are behind NATs. Because it acts as a relay, it must relay all data between the two parties involved in the communication as direct connection is not possible. This means that data bandwidth is effectively reduced and the server must be active throughout the video call to relay the data, making it a less attractive solution, albeit one that still allows a video call to take place even within such complicated NAT setups.

The ICE framework establishes the connection between both parties in the video chat, using a STUN or TURN server as appropriate for the devices being connected. ICE is configured by passing a list of servers, known as *candidates*, which it then prioritizes and orders. It uses a *Session Description Protocol* (SDP) to inform the remote user of the connection details of the local user, which is known as an *offer*, and the remote user does the same when it identifies an offer, known as an *answer*. Once both parties have the other party's details, the peer-to-peer connection between them is established and the call can begin. Though it may seem like a lot of steps, it all happens very quickly.

There are many public STUN servers available for use from within your applications, including a number run and operated by Google, of which you can find a list online at http://bit.ly/stun_list. Public TURN servers are less common as they relay data and hence require a great deal of available bandwidth, which can be costly; however, a service is available via http://numb.viagenie.ca, which will allow you to set up a free account to run your own STUN/TURN server via their servers.

An example configuration object containing the ICE server details for establishing peer-to-connection with the RTCPeerConnection "class" might look like the following:

```
{
    iceServers: [{

        // Mozilla's public STUN server
        url: "stun:23.21.150.121"
    }, {

        // Google's public STUN server
        url: "stun:stun.l.google.com:19302"
    }, {

        // Create your own TURN server at http://numb.viagenie.ca - don't forget to
        // escape any extended characters in the username, e.g. the @ character becomes %40
        url: "turn:numb.viagenie.ca",
        username: "denodell%40gmail.com",
        credential: "password"
    }]
}
```

Now if you were reading carefully, you might have noticed a confusing situation regarding the setup of our peer-to-peer connection, namely: how can we set up a connection between two peers through an intermediary if we don't yet know who we're connecting to? The answer, of course, is we can't, and that leads us onto the next part of understanding how to set up our video call – the signaling channel.

What we need to do is provide a mechanism to send messages between the connected parties before and during call setup. Each party needs to be listening for messages sent from the other party and to send messages as and when required. This messaging could be handled using Ajax, although that would be inefficient as both parties would have to frequently ask an intermediary server whether the other party has sent any messages—and most of the time the answer will be "no." A better solution would be the newer EventSource API (read more at http://bit.ly/eventsource_basics) or WebSockets technologies (read more at http://bit.ly/websockets_basics), both of which allow a server to "push" a message to a connected client as and when a message is there to transmit, resulting in a much more efficient realtime data signalling system. The benefit of the latter approach is that it is supported in all the same browsers that WebRTC is supported in, so there's no need for polyfills or workarounds to use this approach.

Using the Firebase Service for Simple Signalling

Rather than build our own server to support WebSocket connections, we can take advantage of preexisting cloud-based solutions to store and transmit data between connected parties on our behalf. One such solution is Firebase (available at http://firebase.com, shown in Figure 12-2) that provides a simple online database and a small JavaScript API for accessing data over the web using WebSockets (it actually falls back to other solutions if WebSockets is not supported by the browser it is running in). Its free, basic solution is enough for our needs as a signaling service to connect and configure our video chat clients.

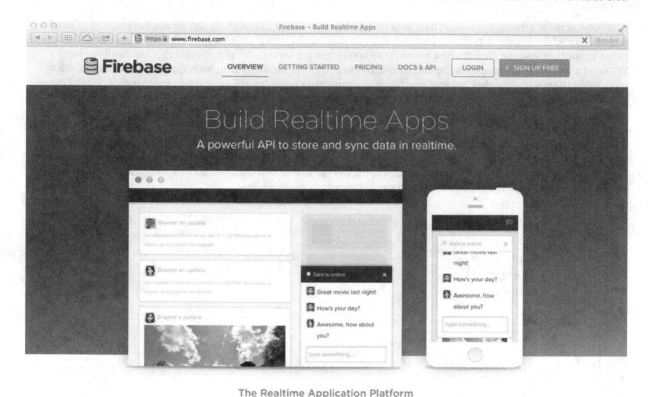

Figure 12-2. *Firebase provides a data-access API perfect for realtime communication between devices*

Visit the Firebase website and sign up for a free account. You will then be emailed access details for your newly created online database. Each has its own unique URL and details of the `<script>` tag to use on your page to load the Firebase API for use within your code. The `<script>` tag will always be the same regardless of the URL created:

```
<script src="https://cdn.firebase.com/v0/firebase.js"></script>
```

For a URL created with the given name `https://glaring-fire-9593.firebaseio.com/`, the following JavaScript code can then be used to set up the connection in your code and to save data in the database:

```
var dataRef = new Firebase("https://glaring-fire-9593.firebaseio.com");
dataRef.set("I am now writing data into Firebase!");
```

Data within Firebase is stored as nested objects in a similar way to a JavaScript object. In fact, when you visit your unique URL, you are able to view your data in a pseudo-JSON format that should look very familiar to you. Data can be added to the database using the Firebase API's `set()` method, and we are able to detect when data has been added by any connected client using the API's `on()` method. This means that in our video chat, both parties can inform each other once their connection has been made using the ICE framework, and when both parties have received the required information from the other, the video call can begin.

Now, if we're hosting our video chat client on a public web server that anyone can access, we're going to need a way to limit which people can chat to each other, otherwise we risk complete strangers establishing a call with each other simply because they are the first two users to connect to the server—we're not building Chat Roulette here! We need a way for specific users to be able to connect to each other, and one simple technique to do this is to allow connected users to create chat "rooms" and to allow connected clients the ability to either create or join one of these chat rooms. When two users have joined a room, we can limit our signaling to occur only between the users in that room so that only the designated parties can communicate with each other. We will allow the first party in the video chat, the *initiator*, to name their chat room. They can then inform their calling partner of this room name that they will then specify when they visit the chat client web page. We will then associate the *offer* and *answer* messages sent and received between parties to the chat room name, along with the ICE candidate details to connect the two parties directly, so that we can connect multiple parties to each other in this way. This results in a database structure within Firebase that can be represented in JSON in a similar format to the following:

```
{
    "chatRooms": {
        "room-001": {
            "offer": "...",
            "answer": "...",
            "candidate": "..."
        },
        "room-002": {
            ...
        }
    }
}
```

The simplicity of Firebase for use in applications that require client and server to push messages to each other is its advantage for use with a video chat client, providing the signaling channel required to connect both parties together in the same chat.

Building the Video Chat Client

We've reached the point at which we can bring together everything we've learned and build a video chat client, which we'll build to look like the example shown in Figure 12-3. We can access the local user's webcam and microphone, we can set up a signaling channel, locked to a known chat room name, to share information about how to connect both parties in the chat to each other, and we can then establish a peer-to-peer connection between the two parties using the ICE framework, streaming the video and audio data across this connection to be shown within the remote party's browser window.

In-Browser Video Chat

Created call with room name: room-231

Figure 12-3. *Example video call using our simple chat client*

We will divide our code into three files, the first an HTML page containing two HTML5 <video> tags, one to display the local video back to the user and the other to display the remote party's video—the audio is output through this tag also. This page also contains *Start Call* and *Join Call* buttons—the former will generate a chat room name at random, which can then be passed onto the remote party, and the latter will allow the user to enter a chat room name to join, connecting both parties through the use of the same room name. The second and third files are JavaScript files, the former to configure a reusable "class" for creating the code necessary to support a video chat and the latter the specific usage example, configured according to the needs of the current application itself displayed within the HTML web page.

We first need to set up a web server as the getUserMedia() API will only work within the context of a HTML page running over the http or http protocol. There are numerous products to use; however, the simplest way is probably to download, install, and configure Apache from http://httpd.apache.org.

Once you have a web server up and running, either locally or using a hosted solution online, you will create a HTML page into which the video and audio from the remote user will be presented, using the HTML5 <video> tag. An example of such a HTML page is shown in Listing 12-4.

Listing 12-4. A simple HTML page to present the captured video and audio from the remote party

```html
<!DOCTYPE html>
<html>
<head>
    <title>In-Browser Video Chat</title>
    <meta charset="utf-8">

    <style>
    body {
        font-family: Helvetica, Arial, sans-serif;
    }

    .videos {
        position: relative;
    }

    .video {
        display: block;
        position: absolute;
        top: 0;
        left: 0;
    }

    .local-video {
        z-index: 1;
        border: 1px solid black;
    }
    </style>

</head>

<body>
    <h1>In-Browser Video Chat</h1>

    <!-- Display the video chat room name at the top of the page -->
    <p id="room-name"></p>

    <!-- Create buttons which start a new video call or join an existing video call -->
    <button id="start-call">Start Call</button>
    <button id="join-call">Join Call</button>

    <!-- Display the local and remote video streams, with the former displayed smaller
    and layered above to the top left corner of the other -->
    <div class="videos">
        <video class="video local-video" id="local-video" width="200" autoplay muted></video>
        <video class="video" id="remote-video" width="600" autoplay></video>
    </div>

    <!-- Load the script to enable Firebase support within this application -->
    <script src="https://cdn.firebase.com/v0/firebase.js"></script>
```

```html
<!-- Load the VideoChat "class" definition -->
<script src="Listing12-5.js"></script>

<!-- Load the code to instantiate the VideoChat "class" and connect it to this page -->
<script src="Listing12-6.js"></script>
</body>
</html>
```

The code in Listing 12-5 shows how to create the VideoChat "class," which creates the necessary code to handle the communications between the local browser and the remote, streaming the video and audio between the two.

Listing 12-5. A VideoChat "class" to support in-browser video chat

```javascript
// Define a "class" that can be used to create a peer-to-peer video chat in the browser. We
// have a dependency on Firebase, whose client API script should be loaded in the browser
// before this script executes
var VideoChat = (function(Firebase) {

    // Polyfill the required browser features to support video chat as some are still using
    // prefixed method and "class" names

    // The PeerConnection "class" allows the configuration of a peer to peer connection
    // between the current web page running on this device and the same running on another,
    // allowing the addition of data streams to be passed from one to another, allowing for
    // video chat-style appliations to be built
    var PeerConnection = window.mozRTCPeerConnection || window.webkitRTCPeerConnection,

        // The RTCSessionDescription "class" works together with the RTCPeerConnection to
        // initialize the peer to peer data stream using the Session Description Protocol (SDP)
        SessionDescription = window.mozRTCSessionDescription || window.RTCSessionDescription,

        // The IceCandidate "class" allows instances of peer to peer "candidates" to be created
        //  - a candidate provides the details of the connection directly to our calling
        // partner, allowing the two browsers to chat
        IceCandidate = window.mozRTCIceCandidate || window.RTCIceCandidate,

        // Define the two types of participant in a call, the person who initiated it and the
        // person who responded
        _participantType = {
            INITIATOR: "initiator",
            RESPONDER: "responder"
        },

        // Define an object containing the settings we will use to create our PeerConnection
        // object, allowing the two participants in the chat to locate each other's IP
        // addresses over the internet
        _peerConnectionSettings = {

            // Define the set of ICE servers to use to attempt to locate the IP addresses
            // of each of the devices participating in the chat. For best chances of
            // success, we include at least one server supporting the two different
            // protocols, STUN and TURN, which provide this IP lookup mechanism
            server: {
                iceServers: [{
```

```javascript
                // Mozilla's public STUN server
                url: "stun:23.21.150.121"
        }, {

                // Google's public STUN server
                url: "stun:stun.l.google.com:19302"
        }, {

                // Create your own TURN server at http://numb.viagenie.ca
                url: "turn:numb.viagenie.ca",
                username: "denodell%40gmail.com",
                credential: "password"
        }]
    },

    // For interoperability between different browser manufacturers' code, we set
    // this DTLS/SRTP property to "true" as it is "true" by default in Firefox
    options: {
        optional: [{
            DtlsSrtpKeyAgreement: true
        }]
    }
};

// Polyfill the getUserMedia() method, which allows us to access a stream of data provided
// by the user's webcam and/or microphone
navigator.getUserMedia = navigator.getUserMedia || navigator.mozGetUserMedia ||
navigator.webkitGetUserMedia || navigator.msGetUserMedia;

// If the current browser does not support the "classes" and methods required for video
// chat, throw an error - at the time of writing, Google Chrome, Mozilla Firefox and
// Opera are the only browsers supporting the features required to support video chat
if (!navigator.getUserMedia && !window.RTCPeerConnection) {
    throw new Error("Your browser does not support video chat");
}

// Define a generic error handler function which will throw an error in the browser
function onError(error) {
    throw new Error(error);
}

// Define the VideoChat "class" to use to create a new video chat on a web page
function VideoChat(options) {
    options = options || {};

    // Allow two callback functions, onLocalStream() and onRemoteStream() to be passed in.
    // The former is executed once a connection has been made to the local webcam and
    // microphone, and the latter is executed once a connection has been made to the remote
    // user's webcam and microphone. Both pass along a stream URL which can be used to
    // display the contents of the stream inside a <video> tag within the HTML page
    if (typeof options.onLocalStream === "function") {
        this.onLocalStream = options.onLocalStream;
    }
```

```javascript
        if (typeof options.onRemoteStream === "function") {
            this.onRemoteStream = options.onRemoteStream;
        }

        // Initialize Firebase data storage using the provided URL
        this.initializeDatabase(options.firebaseUrl || "");

        // Set up the peer-to-peer connection for streaming video and audio between two devices
        this.setupPeerConnection();
}
VideoChat.prototype = {

        // Define the participant type for the current user in this chat - the "initiator", the
        // one starting the call
        participantType: _participantType.INITIATOR,

        // Define the participant type for the remote user in this chat - the "responder", the
        // one responding to a request for a call
        remoteParticipantType: _participantType.RESPONDER,

        // Create a property to store the name for the chat room in which the video call will
        // take place - defined later
        chatRoomName: "",

        // Define a property to allow loading and saving of data to the Firebase database
        database: null,

        // Define a method to be called when a local data stream has been initiated
        onLocalStream: function() {},

        // Define a method to be called when a remote data stream has been connected
        onRemoteStream: function() {},

        // Define a method to initialize the Firebase database
        initializeDatabase: function(firebaseUrl) {

            // Connect to our Firebase database using the provided URL
            var firebase = new Firebase(firebaseUrl);

            // Define and store the data object to hold all the details of our chat room
            // connections
            this.database = firebase.child("chatRooms");
        },

        // Define a method to save a given name-value pair to Firebase, stored against the
        // chat room name given for this call
        saveData: function(chatRoomName, name, value) {
            if (this.database) {
                this.database.child(chatRoomName).child(name).set(value);
            }
        },
```

```
    // Define a method to load stored data from Firebase by its name and chat room name,
    // executing a callback function when that data is found - the connection will wait
    // until that data is found, even if it is generated at a later time
    loadData: function(chatRoomName, name, callback) {
        if (this.database) {

            // Make a request for the data asynchronously and execute a callback function once
            // the data has been located
            this.database.child(chatRoomName).child(name).on("value", function(data) {

                // Extract the value we're after from the response
                var value = data.val();

                // If a callback function was provided to this method, execute it, passing
                // along the located value
                if (value && typeof callback === "function") {
                    callback(value);
                }
            });
        }
    },

    // Define a method to set up a peer-to-peer connection between two devices and stream
    // data between the two
    setupPeerConnection: function() {
        var that = this;

        // Create a PeerConnection instance using the STUN and TURN servers defined
        // earlier to establish a peer-to-peer connection even across firewalls and NAT
        this.peerConnection = new PeerConnection(_peerConnectionSettings.server,
    _peerConnectionSettings.options);

        // When a remote stream has been added to the peer-to-peer connection, get the
        // URL of the stream and pass this to the onRemoteStream() method to allow the
        // remote video and audio to be presented within the page inside a <video> tag
        this.peerConnection.onaddstream = function(event) {

            // Get a URL that represents the stream object
            var streamURL = window.URL.createObjectURL(event.stream);

            // Pass this URL to the onRemoteStream() method, passed in on instantiation
            // of this VideoChat instance
            that.onRemoteStream(streamURL);
        };

        // Define a function to execute when the ICE framework finds a suitable candidate
        // for allowing a peer-to-peer data connection
        this.peerConnection.onicecandidate = function(event) {
            if (event.candidate) {
```

```
                    // Google Chrome often finds multiple candidates, so let's ensure we only
                    // ever get the first it supplies by removing the event handler once a
                    // candidate has been found
                    that.peerConnection.onicecandidate = null;

                    // Read out the remote party's ICE candidate connection details
                    that.loadData(that.chatRoomName, "candidate:" + that.remoteParticipantType,
function(candidate) {

                        // Connect the remote party's ICE candidate to this connection forming
                        // the peer-to-peer connection
                        that.peerConnection.addIceCandidate(new
IceCandidate(JSON.parse(candidate)));
                    });

                    // Save our ICE candidate connection details for connection by the remote
                    // party
                    that.saveData(that.chatRoomName, "candidate:" + that.participantType, JSON.
                    stringify(event.candidate));
                }
            };
        },

        // Define a method to get the local device's webcam and microphone stream and handle
        // the handshake between the local device and the remote party's device to set up the
        // video chat call
        call: function() {
            var that = this,

                // Set the constraints on our peer-to-peer chat connection. We want to be
                // able to support both audio and video so we set the appropriate properties
                _constraints = {
                    mandatory: {
                        OfferToReceiveAudio: true,
                        OfferToReceiveVideo: true
                    }
                };

            // Get the local device's webcam and microphone stream - prompts the user to
            // authorize the use of these
            navigator.getUserMedia({
                video: true,
                audio: true
            }, function(stream) {

                // Add the local video and audio data stream to the peer connection, making
                // it available to the remote party connected to that same peer-to-peer
                // connection
                that.peerConnection.addStream(stream);
```

```
// Execute the onLocalStream() method, passing the URL of the local stream,
// allowing the webcam and microphone data to be presented to the local
// user within a <video> tag on the current HTML page
that.onLocalStream(window.URL.createObjectURL(stream));

// If we are the initiator of the call, we create an offer to any connected
// peer to join our video chat
if (that.participantType === _participantType.INITIATOR) {

    // Create an offer of a video call in this chat room and wait for an
    // answer from any connected peers
    that.peerConnection.createOffer(function(offer) {

        // Store the generated local offer in the peer connection object
        that.peerConnection.setLocalDescription(offer);

        // Save the offer details for connected peers to access
        that.saveData(that.chatRoomName, "offer", JSON.stringify(offer));

        // If a connected peer responds with an "answer" to our offer, store
        // their details in the peer connection object, opening the channels
        // of communication between the two
        that.loadData(that.chatRoomName, "answer", function(answer) {
            that.peerConnection.setRemoteDescription(
                new SessionDescription(JSON.parse(answer))
            );
        });
    }, onError, _constraints);

// If we are the one joining an existing call, we answer an offer to set up
// a peer-to-peer connection
} else {

    // Load an offer provided by the other party - waits until an offer is
    // provided if one is not immediately present
    that.loadData(that.chatRoomName, "offer", function(offer) {

        // Store the offer details of the remote party, using the supplied
        // data
        that.peerConnection.setRemoteDescription(
            new SessionDescription(JSON.parse(offer))
        );

        // Generate an "answer" in response to the offer, enabling the
        // two-way peer-to-peer connection we need for the video chat call
        that.peerConnection.createAnswer(function(answer) {

            // Store the generated answer as the local connection details
            that.peerConnection.setLocalDescription(answer);

            // Save the answer details, making them available to the initiating
            // party, opening the channels of communication between the two
            that.saveData(that.chatRoomName, "answer", JSON.stringify(answer));
```

```
                }, onError, _constraints);
            });
        }
    }, onError);
},

// Define a method which initiates a video chat call, returning the generated chat
// room name which can then be given to the remote user to use to connect to
startCall: function() {

    // Generate a random 3-digit number with padded zeros
    var randomNumber = Math.round(Math.random() * 999);

    if (randomNumber < 10) {
        randomNumber = "00" + randomNumber;
    } else if (randomNumber < 100) {
        randomNumber = "0" + randomNumber;
    }

    // Create a simple chat room name based on the generated random number
    this.chatRoomName = "room-" + randomNumber;

    // Execute the call() method to start transmitting and receiving video and audio
    // using this chat room name
    this.call();

    // Return the generated chat room name so it can be provided to the remote party
    // for connection
    return this.chatRoomName;
},

// Define a method to join an existing video chat call using a specific room name
joinCall: function(chatRoomName) {

    // Store the provided chat room name
    this.chatRoomName = chatRoomName;

    // If we are joining an existing call, we must be the responder, rather than
    // initiator, so update the properties accordingly to reflect this
    this.participantType = _participantType.RESPONDER;
    this.remoteParticipantType = _participantType.INITIATOR;

    // Execute the call() method to start transmitting and receiving video and audio
    // using the provided chat room name
    this.call();
}
};

// Return the VideoChat "class" for use throughout the rest of the code
return VideoChat;
}(Firebase));
```

The code from Listing 12-5 could then be used as shown in Listing 12-6 to create a simple video chat application within the browser, working together with the HTML page created in Listing 12-4.

Listing 12-6. Using the VideoChat "class" to create an in-browser video chat

```
// Get a reference to the <video id="local-video"> element on the page
var localVideoElement = document.getElementById("local-video"),

    // Get a reference to the <video id="remote-video"> element on the page
    remoteVideoElement = document.getElementById("remote-video"),

    // Get a reference to the <button id="start-call"> element on the page
    startCallButton = document.getElementById("start-call"),

    // Get a reference to the <button id="join-call"> element on the page
    joinCallButton = document.getElementById("join-call"),

    // Get a reference to the <p id="room-name"> element on the page
    roomNameElement = document.getElementById("room-name"),

    // Create an instance of the Video Chat "class"
    videoChat = new VideoChat({

        // The Firebase database URL for use when loading and saving data to the cloud - create
        // your own personal URL at http://firebase.com
        firebaseUrl: "https://glaring-fire-9593.firebaseio.com/",

        // When the local webcam and microphone stream is running, set the "src" attribute
        // of the <div id="local-video"> element to display the stream on the page
        onLocalStream: function(streamSrc) {
            localVideoElement.src = streamSrc;
        },

        // When the remote webcam and microphone stream is running, set the "src" attribute
        // of the <div id="remote-video"> element to display the stream on the page
        onRemoteStream: function(streamSrc) {
            remoteVideoElement.src = streamSrc;
        }
    });

// When the <button id="start-call"> button is clicked, start a new video call and
// display the generated room name on the page for providing to the remote user
startCallButton.addEventListener("click", function() {

    // Start the call and get the chat room name
    var roomName = videoChat.startCall();

    // Display the chat room name on the page
    roomNameElement.innerHTML = "Created call with room name: " + roomName;
}, false);

// When the <button id="join-call"> button is clicked, join an existing call by
// entering the room name to join at the prompt
joinCallButton.addEventListener("click", function() {
```

```
    // Ask the user for the chat room name to join
    var roomName = prompt("What is the name of the chat room you would like to join?");

    // Join the chat by the provided room name - as long as this room name matches the
    // other, the two will be connected over a peer-to-peer connection and video streaming
    // will take place between the two
    videoChat.joinCall(roomName);

    // Display the room name on the page
    roomNameElement.innerHTML = "Joined call with room name: " + roomName;
}, false);
```

And so we have created a simple but functional in-browser video chat client. You can extend the idea further by replacing the concept of chat room names with specific logged-in user IDs, connected users to each other through an interface that lists your "friends," such as that offered by Skype and the like, but with the added benefit of running within the browser rather than needing to download any special applications or plugins to support this.

As browser support improves for the APIs covered in this chapter, so will the possibilities of the applications that can be built. Keep up to date with the current level of browser support for WebRTC via http://bit.ly/caniuse_webrtc and experiment with your own ideas for peer-to-peer chat in the browser.

Summary

During this tutorial, I have explained what WebRTC is and demonstrated how to access the webcam and microphone from your user's machine via this API. I have then explained the basics of streams, peer-to-peer connections, and the signaling channel that, when used together, help to support the build of a simple video chat client in the browser.

In the next chapter, I will look at HTML templating within JavaScript and its potential to simplify the amount of data returned by the server within a web-based application.

CHAPTER 13

■ ■ ■

Using Client-Side Templates

JavaScript-based single page web applications, in which parts of the page update dynamically in place in response to server-side data updates or user actions, provide the user with an experience that closely matches that once reserved solely for native desktop and mobile apps, avoiding the need for full page refreshes to update individual parts of a page or append new user interface components to the current page. In this chapter, we will look into options for updating the current page while maintaining a distinct separation between the data to be displayed and the DOM structure within which to present it.

Dynamically Updating Page Content

We know that to update or create HTML content on our page through JavaScript, we use the Document Object Model (DOM) to alter attributes and the element tree in order to affect the desired content change. This works fine for simple and small page updates but does not scale well, as it requires a fair amount of JavaScript code per element and can require complicated and time-consuming lookups to locate the exact elements to be updated. Should the HTML page structure update without the JavaScript code being aware, we also run the risk of failing to find the required element to update.

Rather than manipulating the DOM tree node-by-node, we can manipulate larger chunks of HTML using an element's innerHTML property to dynamically access and update the HTML within that element as if it were a normal text string. The only issue with this is that the code to insert dynamic strings and other data within a complex HTML structure when it is represented as a string can be difficult to understand, making maintenance and development more difficult, something that the professional JavaScript developer seeks to avoid at all costs. An example of this, where text is inserted within a long string of HTML before being added to the page, is shown in Listing 13-1.

Listing 13-1. Combining JavaScript data with a string of HTML

```
var firstName = "Den",
    lastName = "Odell",
    company = "AKQA",
    city = "London",
    email = "denodell@me.com",
    divElem = document.createElement("div");

// Applying data and strings to HTML structures results in a complicated mess of difficult to
// maintain code
divElem.innerHTML = "<p>Name: <a href=\"mailto:" + email + "\">" + firstName + " " + lastName +
    "</a><br>Company: " + company + "</p><p>City: " + city + "</p>";
```

```
// Add the new <div> DOM element to the end of the current HTML page once loaded
window.addEventListener("load", function() {
    document.body.appendChild(divElem);
}, false);
```

Despite the complications with this approach, there is a definite need to combine JavaScript data, which may or may not be loaded via Ajax, with a string of HTML text to be dynamically displayed on a page. In this chapter, we will cover the acceptable solutions available to us to solve this problem, focusing largely on client-side HTML templating solutions that allow a page to be updated dynamically while keeping the data we wish to present separate from the HTML used to mark it up appropriately. As professional JavaScript developers, this separation of concerns is important to us, as it is scalable as our application grows and results in the least confusion for ourselves and other project team members.

Loading HTML Dynamically Via Ajax

The simplest solution to dynamically updating page content is to perform the combination of data with HTML code on the server-side, returning the combined HTML code as a string via a simple Ajax call that we can simply place on the page, perhaps replacing the contents of an existing element. This, of course, does not solve the problem, per se; we're just moving the problem from the client-side to the server-side where an appropriate solution is then required to exist. There are many such server-side templating solutions, such as Smarty (for PHP, http://bit.ly/smarty_template), Liquid (for Ruby, http://bit.ly/liquid_template), Apache Velocity (for Java, http://bit.ly/velocity_template), and Spark (for ASP.NET, http://bit.ly/spark_template). We merely need to hit a specific web service URL provided by the server and be returned a string of HTML to drop directly into an element on our page using that element's innerHTML property.

The clear advantage with this technique is that it requires very little code running in JavaScript within the browser. We simply need a function to load the required HTML from the server and place it within a designated element on the page. An example of one such function to request a string of HTML and append it to the current page is shown in Listing 13-2.

Listing 13-2. Loading HTML dynamically via Ajax and populating the current page with the response

```
// Define a method to load a string of HTML from a specific URL and place this within a given
// element on the current page
function loadHTMLAndReplace(url, element) {

    // Perform an Ajax request to the given URL and populate the given element with the response
    var xhr = new XMLHttpRequest(),
        LOADED_STATE = 4,
        OK_STATUS = 200;

    xhr.onreadystatechange = function() {
        if (xhr.readyState !== LOADED_STATE) {
            return;
        }

        if (xhr.status === OK_STATUS) {
            // Populate the given element with the returned HTML
            element.innerHTML = xhr.responseText;
        }
    };
```

```
        xhr.open("GET", url);
        xhr.send();
}

// Load the HTML from two specific URLs and populate the given elements with the returned markup
loadHTMLAndReplace("/ajax/ticket-form.html", document.getElementById("ticket-form"));
loadHTMLAndReplace("/ajax/business-card.html", document.getElementById("business-card"));
```

The disadvantage with this technique is that applications requiring frequent visual updates in response to changing data would end up downloading a lot of superfluous information from the server, as it reflects the updated data *and* the markup surrounding it, whereas all we really want to display is the data that has changed. Clearly, if the markup surrounding the data remains the same each time, there is redundant data being downloaded, which will result in a larger download each time and is likely to therefore be slower. Depending on your application, this may or may not be a large issue for you, but always consider your users and particularly those on traditionally slower mobile connections who may pay by the megabyte of data downloaded and may suffer as a result of such a decision.

It would be much more efficient to have a single block of HTML to act as a template, with the Ajax request to the server providing just the raw data, perhaps in JSON format, to populate that template with in the relevant places to produce the resulting page structure to update the display. This is where the idea of client-side templating comes into play and finds its prime use case.

Client-Side Templating

A template is simply a text string containing specific placeholder text markers within it that should be replaced with appropriate data before the results are outputted to the current page. Consider the following simple template, which uses a double braces marker pattern {{ and }}, uncommonly used in any other type of text string, to denote both the position of the text to be replaced, and the name of the data variable whose value should be used to replace the marker:

```
Template:
    <p>
        Name: <a href="mailto:{{email}}">{{firstName}} {{lastName}}</a><br>
        Company: {{company}}
    </p>
    <p>City: {{city}}</p>
```

By combining this template with values stored in a JavaScript data object resembling the following:

```
Data:
    {
        "firstName": "Den",
        "lastName": "Odell",
        "email": "denodell@me.com",
        "company": "AKQA",
        "city": "London"
    }
```

we will produce a string that we can then output to our page, containing the text we wish to display. By storing the template locally in our page and only needing to update the data via Ajax, we reduce the need to download superfluous, or repeated, data:

```
Output:
    <p>
        Name: <a href="mailto:denodell@me.com">Den Odell</a><br>
        Company: AKQA
    </p>
    <p>City: London</p>
```

Different templating solutions use different marker text patterns to denote the points at which the data should be provided. Although any marker could be used in theory, it's important to ensure that your markers are sufficiently distinct such that they wouldn't normally be present in any other text within your template that you wish to display, otherwise these will be accidentally replaced.

In the remainder of this chapter, we will look at a selection of solutions for client-side templating within your web applications, including some popular third-party open templating libraries used by other professional JavaScript developers.

Client-Side Templating without a Library

Because client-side templating is achieved through string replacement, we can write a very basic implementation in just a few lines of JavaScript built around a regular expression used to perform the replacement, appending the resulting HTML or text string to our page using a DOM element's innerHTML property. Listing 13-3 shows an example of such a templating solution that replaces specially formatted markers in a template string with property values from a JavaScript object to produce a string of HTML that is then added to the current page.

Listing 13-3. Basic client-side templating through string replacement

```
// Define the HTML template to apply data to, using {{ ... }} to denote the data property name
// to be replaced with real data
var template = "<p>Name: <a href=\"mailto:{{email}}\">{{firstName}} {{lastName}}</a><br>Company:
{{company}}</p><p>City: {{city}}</p>",

    // Define two data objects containing properties to be inserted into the HTML template using
    // the property name as key
    me = {
        firstName: "Den",
        lastName: "Odell",
        email: "denodell@me.com",
        company: "AKQA",
        city: "London"
    },
    bill = {
        firstName: "Bill",
        lastName: "Gates",
        email: "bill@microsoft.com",
        company: "Microsoft",
        city: "Seattle"
    };
```

```
// Define a simple function to apply data from a JavaScript object into a HTML template,
// represented as a string
function applyDataToTemplate(templateString, dataObject) {
    var key,
        value,
        regex;

    // Loop through each property name in the supplied data object, replacing all instances of
    // that name surrounded by {{ and }} with the value from the data object
    for (key in dataObject) {
        regex = new RegExp("{{" + key + "}}", "g");
        value = dataObject[key];

        // Perform the replace
        templateString = templateString.replace(regex, value);
    }

    // Return the new, replaced HTML string
    return templateString;
}

// Outputs:
// <p>Name: <a href="mailto:denodell@me.com">Den Odell</a><br>Company: AKQA</p>
//     <p>City: London</p>
alert(applyDataToTemplate(template, me));

// Outputs:
// <p>Name: <a href="mailto:bill@microsoft.com">Bill Gates</a><br>Company: Microsoft</p>
//     <p>City: Seattle</p>
alert(applyDataToTemplate(template, bill));
```

This solution works fine for simple templates and JavaScript data; however, if there is a need to iterate over arrays or objects of data, or add logic to show or hide different sections based on the value of certain data properties, this solution falls short and would need to be extended considerably to support this. In this case, it's best to hand over to prewritten and well-established third-party open source JavaScript client-side templating libraries to do the job.

Client-Side Templating with Mustache.js

Mustache is a logic-less templating language developed by Chris Wanstrath in 2009 and features implementations in most popular programming languages; *Mustache.js* is its JavaScript implementation. It was originally derived from *Google Templates* (later known as *cTemplates*), which was used as the templating system for generating Google's search results page. The term *logic-less* refers to the fact that the defined templating structure contains no if, then, else, or for loop statements; it does, however, contain a generic structure called *tags*, which allow the ability to perform this kind of behavior dependent on the value type stored in the referenced JavaScript data, referred to as the *data hash*. Each tag is denoted by double braces {{ and }} that, when viewed at right angles, look rather like mustaches, hence the name. You can download Mustache.js from its Github project page via http://bit.ly/mustache_github. The library weighs in at just 1.8KB once minified and served with gzip compression enabled.

Let us begin looking into Mustache.js by using it to perform the templating of our initial example to render the same HTML output as in Listing 13-3. We will split this into two code listings: one HTML page, shown in Listing 13-4, containing the template itself written out within a specially configured <script> tag and referencing the Mustache.js library, and one JavaScript file, the contents of which are shown in Listing 13-5, containing the data to apply to the template and making the call to Mustache.js to perform the rendering of the resulting HTML from this template.

Listing 13-4. HTML page containing a client-side template for use with Mustache.js

```html
<!doctype html>
<html>
<head>
    <meta charset="utf-8">
    <title>Mustache.js Example</title>
</head>
<body>
    <h1>Mustache.js Example</h1>

    <!-- Define the template we wish to apply our data to. The "type" attribute
         needs to be any non-standard MIME type in order for the element's contents
         to be interpreted as plain text rather than executed -->
    <script id="template" type="x-tmpl-mustache">
        <p>
            Name: <a href="mailto:{{email}}">{{firstName}} {{lastName}}</a><br>
            Company: {{company}}
        </p>
        <p>
            City: {{city}}
        </p>
    </script>

    <!-- Load the Mustache.js library -->
    <script src="lib/mustache.min.js"></script>

    <!-- Execute our script to combine the template with our data -->
    <script src="Listing13-5.js"></script>
</body>
</html>
```

The `<script>` tag containing the template in Listing 13-4 is given a type attribute that will be unrecognized by the browser as a standard MIME type. This will cause the browser to treat its contents as plain text rather than something to be executed, yet without writing the tag's contents visibly out to the page. The tag's contents can then be referenced through JavaScript by locating the element by its id attribute value and grabbing the contents of its innerHTML property. The HTML page represented in Listing 13-4 references the JavaScript code in Listing 13-5, shown below, producing the result shown in Figure 13-1 when run in a browser. Note the use of the `Mustache.render()` method used to produce the output string based on two input parameters: the template string and the JavaScript data hash object.

Listing 13-5. Combine data with a HTML template using Mustache.js

```javascript
// Locate and store a reference to the <script id="template"> element from our HTML page
var templateElement = document.getElementById("template"),

    // Extract the template as a string from within the template element
    template = templateElement.innerHTML,

    // Create two elements to store our resulting HTML in once our template is
    // combined with our data
    meElement = document.createElement("div"),
    billElement = document.createElement("div"),
```

```
    // Define two objects containing data to apply to the stored template
    meData = {
        firstName: "Den",
        lastName: "Odell",
        email: "denodell@me.com",
        company: "AKQA",
        city: "London"
    },
    billData = {
        firstName: "Bill",
        lastName: "Gates",
        email: "bill@microsoft.com",
        company: "Microsoft",
        city: "Seattle"
    };

// Use Mustache.js to apply the data to the template and store the result within the
// newly created elements
meElement.innerHTML = Mustache.render(template, meData);
billElement.innerHTML = Mustache.render(template, billData);

// Add the new elements, populated with HTML, to the current page once loaded
window.addEventListener("load", function() {
    document.body.appendChild(meElement);
    document.body.appendChild(billElement);
}, false);
```

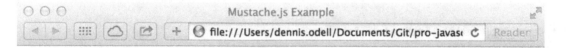

Mustache.js Example

Name: Den Odell
Company: AKQA

City: London

Name: Bill Gates
Company: Microsoft

City: Seattle

Figure 13-1. An example HTML page with data populated into templates with Mustache.js

The full detailed documentation of the Mustache templating format can be viewed online via http://bit.ly/mustache_docs. The format breaks down into four distinct types of data representation: *variables*, *sections, comments,* and *partials*.

Variables

The Mustache templating format allows for the substitution of any text token surrounded by double braces {{ and }} with an associated data property of the same name, as we've seen in the template we created within the HTML page in Listing 13-4. In Mustache's parlance, the name within the double braces is known as a variable, or *key*.

All variables are replaced as HTML-escaped strings, meaning that any HTML within the data string being placed into the variable will be written out as text rather than interpreted as HTML elements. Should you wish the text to be interpreted as HTML, you should surround your key name with the triple brackets marker {{{ and }}}, as shown here. Should you need to render the value of a JavaScript object property, you can use the standard dot notation to navigate object hierarchies.

```
Template:
    {{name}}
    {{{name}}}
    From {{address.country}}

Data Hash:
    {
        name: "Den <strong>Odell</strong>",
        address: {
            country: "UK"
        }
    }

Output:
    Den &lt;strong&gt;Odell&lt;&#x2F;strong&gt;
    Den <strong>Odell</strong>
    From UK
```

In the case in which the key name denoted in the template tag does not exist in the provided data hash object, an empty string will replace the tag in the output. This differs from our original semantic templating example from Listing 13-3, which would leave the tag intact in the resulting output if the associated data value did not exist.

Sections

A section in a Mustache template has start and end tags surrounding a block of the template. The contents of the template block between these tags is then repeated one or more times in the resulting output depending on the type of data stored in the associated data key value for that tag. The key name used in the tag is preceeded by a hash (#) character to denote the start tag of the section, and is preceeded by a slash (/) character to denote the end tag of a section, for example, {{#section}}{{/section}}. There are four types of section – *conditional, iterator, functional,* and *inverted* – that are declared similarly but perform different functionality based on the type of data passed to them.

Conditional Sections

If the data value of the referenced tag key is of Boolean type true, the contents of the section block are displayed; if false, the section is not displayed. The same applies for falsy values, such as empty strings or empty arrays – the section will not be displayed in these cases. This behavior provides us the ability to perform the equivalent of conditional if statements, as demonstrated here. The string YES will only be included in the output if the value of the isAvailable data property is truthy.

Template:
```
    Available:
    {{#isAvailable}}
        YES
    {{/isAvailable}}
```

Data Hash:
```
    {
        isAvailable: true
    }
```

Output:
```
    Available: YES
```

Iterator Sections

If the format of the data property referenced by a section tag is an array list containing one or more items, the contents of the section between the start and end tags will be repeated once for each item in the list, with each individual item's data passed into the section for each interation. This provides us the ability to perform the equivalent of iterative data loops, equivalent to JavaScript for loops, as demonstrated here:

Template:
```
    <h1>People</h1>
    {{#people}}
        <p>Name: {{name}}</p>
    {{/people}}
```

Data Hash:
```
    {
        people: [
            {name: "Den Odell"},
            {name: "Bill Gates"}
        ]
    }
```

Output:
```
    <h1>People</h1>
    <p>Name: Den Odell</p>
    <p>Name: Bill Gates</p>
```

Functional Sections

If the data format referenced by the section tag is a `function`, then things start to get really interesting. The function will be executed immediately by Mustache.js and should return a function that will then be executed each time the function's name is referenced by a section tag, with two parameters passed in: the literal text contents of the template section block as a string (before any template replacement has taken place), and a function that is a direct reference to Mustache.js's internal `render()` method to allow the value in the first parameter to be manipulated in some way before then outputting its contents together with the applied data. This makes it possible to create filters, apply caching, or perform other string-based template manipulation based on the input data. An example of this behavior is demonstrated here:

```
Template:
    {{#strongLastWord}}
        My name is {{name}}
    {{/strongLastWord}}

Data Hash:
    {
        name: "Den Odell",
        strongLastWord: function() {
            return function(text, render) {

                // Use the supplied Mustache.js render() function to apply the data to the
                // supplied template text
                var renderedText = render(text),

                    // Split the resulting text into an array of words
                    wordArray = renderedText.split(" "),
                    wordArrayLength = wordArray.length,

                    // Extract the final word from the array
                    finalWord = wordArray[wordArrayLength - 1];

                // Replace the last entry in the array of words with the final word wrapped
                // in a HTML <strong> tag
                wordArray[wordArrayLength - 1] = "<strong>" + finalWord + "</strong>";

                // Join together the word array into a single string and return this
                return wordArray.join(" ");
            }
        }
    }

Output:
    My name is Den <strong>Odell</strong>
```

Inverted Sections

When you start using Mustache templates in earnest, you will discover the need to display text or blocks of HTML based on inverted conditions. If a data value represents a `truthy` value or contains items to iterate over, you wish to display one section block. If the value is `falsy` or contains no items to iterate over, you wish to display another block.

Inverted sections allow this behavior and are denoted by the use of the caret (^) character in place of the hash (#) character preceeding the tag key name, as demonstrated here:

```
Template:
    Available:
    {{#isAvailable}}
        YES
    {{/isAvailable}}
    {{^isAvailable}}
        NO
    {{/isAvailable}}

    {{#people}}
        <p>Name: {{name}}</p>
    {{/people}}
    {{^people}}
        <p>No names found</p>
    {{/people}}

Data Hash:
    {
        isAvailable: false,
        people: []
    }

Output:
    Available: NO
    <p>No names found</p>
```

Comments

Should you wish to include development notes or comments within your Mustache template that you do not wish to be output to the resulting string, simply create a tag beginning with double braces and an exclamation point (!) character, and ending with double closing braces, as shown here:

```
Template:
    <h1>People</h1>
    {{! This section will contain a list of names}}

    {{^people}}
        <p>No names found</p>
    {{/people}}

Data Hash:
    {
        people: []
    }

Output:
    <h1>People</h1>
    <p>No names found</p>
```

Partial Templates

Mustache supports the ability to separate templates across multiple <script> tags or even separate files that can be combined together at runtime to produce the final result. This allows reusable snippets to be created and stored separately for use across several templates. Such a file that contains a snippet of code for use in a larger template is known as a *partial template* or, simply, a *partial*.

Partials are referenced by a given name within a standard tag, with the name preceeded by the greater-than (>) character to indicate it as a partial template. Imagine a HTML page containing the following two templates contained within <script> tags labeled with id attribute values of template and people, respectively:

```
<script id="template" type="x-tmpl-mustache">
    <h1>People</h1>
    {{>people}}
</script>

<script id="people" type="x-tmpl-mustache">
    {{#people}}
        <p>Name: {{name}}</p>
    {{/people}}
</script>
```

Note the reference in the first template to a partial named people. Although this name matches the id attribute given to the second template, the reference is not made automatically between the two, this needs to be configured within Mustache.js. To do this, you must pass any partials you wish to use in a JavaScript object to the third parameter of the Mustache.render() method, as shown in Listing 13-6. The first parameter is the master template and the second is the data to apply to the template. The property names in the partials JavaScript object (the third parameter) correlate to the tag names used in the template to reference any partials. Note that the data is made available to the combined template as if both templates were combined into a single file before the data is applied to it.

Listing 13-6. Referencing partial templates with Mustache.js

```
// Locate and store a reference to the <script id="template"> element from our HTML page
var templateElement = document.getElementById("template"),

    // Locate and store a reference to the <script id="people"> element
    peopleTemplateElement = document.getElementById("people"),

    // Extract the template as a string from within the template element
    template = templateElement.innerHTML,

    // Extract the "people" template as a string from within the <script> element
    peopleTemplate = peopleTemplateElement.innerHTML,

    // Create an element to store our resulting HTML in once our template is
    // combined with the partial and our data
    outputElement = document.createElement("div"),
```

```
    // Define an object containing data to apply to the stored template
    data = {
        people: [{
            name: "Den Odell"
        }, {
            name: "Bill Gates"
        }]
    };

// Use Mustache.js to apply the data to the template, and allow access to the named partial
// templates and store the result within the newly created element
outputElement.innerHTML = Mustache.render(template, data, {
    people: peopleTemplate
});

// Add the new element, populated with HTML, to the current page once loaded
window.addEventListener("load", function() {
    document.body.appendChild(outputElement);
}, false);

// The resulting HTML will be:
/*
People</h1>
<p>Name: Den Odell</p>
<p>Name: Bill Gates</p>
 */
```

Using partials in this way allows for larger applications to be created with shared components, navigation, headers and footers, and reusable code snippets, as partial files can inherit code from other partials. This reduces duplication of code and allows efficient templates to be produced and maintained. The only thing to remember is that all your partial templates must be ready to use by the time the main template that references them is rendered. This means that should you choose to load in your template files via Ajax rather than store them locally within the current HTML page, all must be loaded by the point of rendering so that they can be passed to the single `Mustache.render()` method against the main template.

Mustache.js is a small and incredibly useful library for taking client-side templating beyond simple variable replacement, allowing for conditional and iterative sections, and supporting external partial templates.

Client-Side Templating with Handlebars.js

Handlebars a client-side templating format designed to extend the abilities of the Mustache format. Handlebars is backwards compatible with Mustache templates but supports extra features including *block helpers*, an extension to the principle of Mustache *sections* to clarify and improve the behavior of each template block's display logic.

The Handlebars.js library that supports these templates can be downloaded directly from its homepage at `http://handlebarsjs.com`, shown in Figure 13-2, and the library weighs in at 13KB when minified and served with gzip compression, so compared to Mustache.js, a fair amount larger. As we'll see later on in this section, however, there is a technique for precompiling templates such that they can be used with a cutdown version of the Handlebars library, resulting in more comparable file sizes.

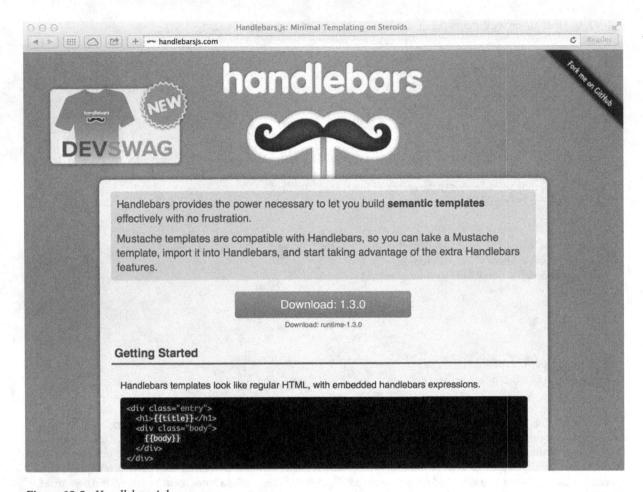

Figure 13-2. *Handlebars.js home page*

Handlebars is used very much like Mustache, the library is referenced from within your HTML page and templates are combined with a JavaScript data hash object to produce the desired output string to insert into the current page. Templates can be stored within `<script>` tags on the page itself, as we saw with Mustache, or loaded in via separate files using Ajax. The data object, likewise, can be stored directly within the JavaScript file, or loaded in dynamically via Ajax.

The library's global `Handlebars` object contains methods to assist in the rendering of templates; the `Handlebars.compile()` method takes a template string as an argument and returns a function. That function can then be executed, passing it the data hash object to use to render the template with, and it will return the resulting string combining the two for use within your page. A simple example of the `compile()` method used with a basic in-page template and local JavaScript data is shown in Listing 13-7.

Listing 13-7. HTML page containing a simple Handlebars template

```
<!doctype html>
<html>
<head>
    <meta charset="utf-8">
    <title>Handlebars.js Example</title>
</head>
<body>
    <h1>Handlebars.js Example</h1>

    <div id="result"></div>

    <!-- Define the template we wish to apply our data to. The "type" attribute
        needs to be any non-standard MIME type in order for the element's contents
        to be interpreted as plain text rather than executed -->
    <script id="template" type="x-tmpl-handlebars">
        <p>
            Name: <a href="mailto:{{email}}">{{firstName}} {{lastName}}</a><br>
            Company: {{company}}
        </p>
        <p>
            City: {{city}}
        </p>
    </script>

    <!-- Load the Handlebars.js library -->
    <script src="lib/handlebars.min.js"></script>

    <!-- Execute our script to combine the template with our data. Included
        here for brevity, move to an external JavaScript file for production -->
    <script>
        // Get a reference to the template element and result element on the page
        var templateElem = document.getElementById("template"),
            resultElem = document.getElementById("result"),

            // Get the string representation of the Handlebars template from the template
            // element
            template = templateElem.innerHTML,

            // Define the data object to apply to the template
            data = {
                firstName: "Den",
                lastName: "Odell",
                email: "denodell@me.com",
                company: "AKQA",
                city: "London"
            },

            // The compile() method returns a function which the data object can be passed to
            // in order to produce the desired output string
            compiledTemplate = Handlebars.compile(template);
```

```
            // Combine the data with the compiled template function and add the result to the page
            resultElem.innerHTML = compiledTemplate(data);
        </script>
    </body>
</html>
```

Let's look through some of the features of Handlebars templates and the Handlebars.js library together now, including partials, helpers, and template precompilation for improved performance.

Partials

A partial template in a Handlebars template looks identical to that in a Mustache template, but the two differ in the way the details of the partial template is provided to the library for rendering. The `Handlebars.registerPartial()` method allows a partial to be *registered* with Handlebars using two parameters: the name of the partial and the string representation of that partial template. This must be called before the partial is referenced from the template being rendered. Multiple partials can be registered by calling the `registerPartial()` method multiple times. Just as with Mustache.js, all partials must be loaded and registered before the main template can be rendered.

Helpers

Handlebars extends the concept of Mustache's *sections* with its own feature-filled handlers, known as *helpers*. These enable you to iterate over lists of data, or execute conditional expressions, using helpers with clear names that make the templates easier to read and understand—important, particularly as your templates become more complex, and a marked difference from Mustache. With Mustache, without knowing the type of data being passed to the template, you can't be sure whether a section is to be used as a conditional block, an iteration, or something else; here, the difference is made clear by the helper's name. There are a few built-in helpers, and Handlebars offers you the ability to create your own with ease, which can be reused simply across all your templates. The helper's name is preceded by a hash (#) character within its tag and followed by the name of the data key to apply to the helper. In this section, we will look at some common helpers and I will explain how you can easily create your own for your specific template's needs.

The `with` Helper

The `with` helper allows you to apply a different data context to the template block it surrounds. This provides an alternative to repetitive use of dot notation to navigate the specific data property hierarchy passed to the helper. To navigate back to the parent context from within a section, the `../` token can be used before the variable name. A simple example of the `with` helper that should make everything clear is shown here.

```
Template:
    <h1>{{name}}</h1>
    {{#with address}}
        <p>{{../name}} lives at: {{street}}, {{city}}, {{region}}, {{country}}</p>
    {{/with}}

Data Hash:
    {
        name: "Den Odell",
        address: {
            street: "1 Main Street",
            city: "Hometown",
```

```
            region: "Homeshire",
            country: "United Kingdom"
        }
    }
```

Output:
```
    <h1>Den Odell</h1>
    <p>Den Odell lives at: 1 Main Street, Hometown, Homeshire, United Kingdom</p>
```

The each Helper

The each helper allows you to iterate over a data list, such as an array or object. The value of the array item, if not an object or array itself, can be accessed by using the reserved variable name {{this}}. When looping over an array, the index of the current item in the original array is provided by the reserved variable name {{@index}}. When iterating over an object, the name of the key for the current property is provided by the reserved variable name {{@key}}. An optional {{else}} section can be added to allow you to provide a section block to be rendered if the provided data list is empty, as you can see demonstrated in this example:

Template:
```
    <h1>People</h1>
    {{#each people}}
        <p>Item {{@index}}: {{this}}</p>
    {{else}}
        <p>No names found</p>
    {{/each}}
```

Data Hash:
```
    {
        people: [
            "Den Odell",
            "Bill Gates"
        ]
    }
```

Output:
```
    <h1>People</h1>
    <p>Item 0: Den Odell</p>
    <p>Item 1: Bill Gates</p>
```

The if And unless Helpers

Template section blocks can be displayed conditionally based on the value of certain data properties using the if and unless Handlebars helpers. The if helper will display the associated section block provided the value passed to it is a truthy value (any value except false, undefined, null, an empty string or an empty array), whereas the unless helper will display the associated block only if the data value is falsy. In either case, an optional {{else}} section can be added to capture the inverted case, as demonstrated in the example here:

Template:
```
    <h1>People</h1>
    {{#if people}}
        <p>Item {{@index}}: {{this}}</p>
```

```
{{else}}
    <p>No names found</p>
{{/if}}

{{#unless isAvailable}}
    <p>Not available</p>
{{/unless}}
```

Data Hash:
```
{
    isAvailable: false,
    people: []
}
```

Output:
```
<h1>People</h1>
<p>No names found</p>
<p>Not available</p>
```

The log Helper

If you're providing a large, multilevel data object to your template, it can occasionally become confusing, when using multiple helpers throughout your template, to know where in the data hierarchy you are, or what data you have available to you, at any specific point. Thankfully, Handlebars provides a log debug helper that allows you to view the state of the data available to you at any point in your template. Simply pass the name of the data object variable you wish to view, or use {{log this}} to show the data available in the current context. Rather than being written out to the generated page itself, the data is then written out to the command line if final page generation is handled via a command line tool, or into the browser's developer console window if the generation occurs live within the browser.

Custom Helpers

Along with the built-in helpers, Handlebars offers the ability to create your own custom helpers to allow you to provide the exact functionality you require in your templates. These can work at a block level, to perform an operation on a section of a template, or at an individual data item level, such as to format a specific piece of data for display.

A custom helper can be created by using the Handlebars.registerHelper() method, passing it two parameters: a unique name for the helper, and a function to execute when the helper is encountered in the template upon rendering, which performs the desired behavior to the data passed to it in the template. Listing 13-8 shows a selection of simple custom helpers that you may find useful for your own templates.

Listing 13-8. Example custom Handlebars helpers

```
// The registerHelper() method accepts two arguments - the name of the helper, as it will
// be used within the template, and a function which will be executed whenever the
// helper is encountered within the template. The function is always passed at least one
// parameter, an object containing, amongst others, a fn() method which performs the same
// operation as Handlebars' own render ability. This method takes a data object and
// returns a string combining the template within the block helper with the data in
// this object

// Define a block helper which does nothing other than pass through the data in the
// current context and combine it with the template section within the block
Handlebars.registerHelper("doNothing", function(options) {
```

```
        // To use the current data context with the template within the block, simply use
        // the 'this' keyword
        return options.fn(this);
});


// The helper can be passed parameters, if required, listed one by one after the helper
// name within double braces. These are then made available within the function as
// separate input parameters. The final parameter is always the options object, as before
Handlebars.registerHelper("ifTruthy", function(conditional, options) {
    return conditional ? options.fn(this) : options.inverse(this);
});


// If more than one or two parameters need to be passed into the helper, named parameters
// can be used. These are listed as name/value pairs in the template when the helper is
// called, and are made available within the options.hash property as a standard
// JavaScript object ready to pass to the options.fn() method and used to render the
// data within
Handlebars.registerHelper("data", function(options) {

    // The options.hash property contains a JavaScript object representing the name/value
    // pairs supplied to the helper within the template. Rather than pass through the
    // data context value 'this', here we pass through the supplied data object to the
    // template section within the helper instead
    return options.fn(options.hash);
});


// Create a simple inline helper for converting simple URLs into HTML links. Inline helpers
// can be used without being preceded by a hash (#) character in the template.
Handlebars.registerHelper("link", function(url) {

    // The SafeString() method keeps HTML content intact when rendered in a template
    return new Handlebars.SafeString("<a href=\"" + url + "\">" + url + "</a>");
});
```

The custom helpers given in Listing 13-8 can be used as demonstrated in the following example template:

```
Base Template:
    {{#doNothing}}
        <h1>Dictionary</h1>
    {{/doNothing}}

    {{#ifTruthy isApiAvailable}}
        <p>An API is available</p>
    {{/ifTruthy}}

    {{#ifTruthy words}}
        <p>We have preloaded words</p>
    {{else}}
        <p>We have no preloaded words</p>
    {{/ifTruthy}}
```

```
<dl>
{{#data term="vastitude" definition="vastness; immensity"
url=" http://dictionary.com/browse/vastitude"}}
    {{>definition}}
{{/data}}

{{#data term="achromic" definition="colorless; without coloring matter"
url="http://dictionary.com/browse/achromic"}}
    {{>definition}}
{{/data}}
</dl>
```

```
Partial "definition" Template
    <dt>{{term}} {{link url}}</dt>
    <dd>{{definition}}</dd>
```

```
Data hash:
    {
        isApiAvailable: true,
        words: []
    }
```

```
Output:
    <h1>Dictionary</h1>

    <p>An API is available</p>

    <p>We have no preloaded words</p>

    <dl>
        <dt>vastitude <a href="http://dictionary.com/browse/vastitude">
http://dictionary.com/browse/vastitude</a></dt>
        <dd>vastness; immensity</dd>
        <dt>achromic <a href="http://dictionary.com/browse/achromic">
http://dictionary.com/browse/achromic</a></dt>
        <dd>colorless; without coloring matter</dd>
    </dl>
```

Precompiling Templates for Best Performance

As we've seen, the Handlebars.js compile() method takes a template string and converts it into a function, which can then be executed, passing in the data to apply to the template. The result is the final markup string for displaying on the page. If you know your template won't change during the runtime of your application, you can take advantage of Handlebars.js' *precompilation* feature, which allows you to perform this template-to-function conversion in advance, delivering a smaller JavaScript file to your application containing just the template function to which to apply your data. The file sizes are much smaller, as they can take advantage of a number of optimizations that otherwise wouldn't be possible at runtime, and they require only a cutdown *runtime version* of Handlebars.js running within your HTML page. This special version of the library removes functions made redundant through the precompilation process. The runtime version of Handlebars can be downloaded from the homepage at http://handlebarsjs.com and weighs in at a more svelte 2.3 KB after minification and when served using gzip compression. This is comparable in size to the Mustache library yet contains the extra benefits and simplicity of Handlebars, so it is a great solution to using templates in your code without sacrificing on file size and, therefore, download time. If you are looking for a solution for serving gzip compressed versions of the libraries mentioned in this chapter, visit http://cdnjs.com to locate a reference to a Content Delivery Network-hosted version of the desired file.

The precompilation step needs to happen in advance, before the template is used on the page, and we can take advantage of the command line tool provided by Handlebars.js to perform this step. The tool runs on the Node.js application framework, which we will cover in detail in the following chapter. For now, you can install the framework on your machine by downloading it from http://bit.ly/node_js and following the instructions. The Node Package Manager (NPM) tool is installed at the same time and allows the ability to easily install applications to run within the framework, including the Handlebars.js precompiler application. Enter the following command on the command line to install version 1.3.0 of the Handlebars.js precompiler (Mac and Linux users may need to precede the command with sudo to grant the necessary permissions to install the tool for access across any folder on their machine):

```
npm install -g handlebars@1.3.0
```

We explicitly state the version number of the tool that matches the version of the library available for download on the Handlebars.js homepage. Without the two versions matching, we cannot guarantee any precompiled template will function correctly.

Navigate on the command line to the directory containing your template file(s) and execute the following command to precompile the template, replacing templatefile.handlebars with the name of the template file to precompile:

```
handlebars templatefile.handlebars
```

You will notice that the generated precompiled template function is written straight out to the command line rather than saved to a file, which is not exactly what we need. To save the generated template to a new file, add the --output option on the command line and specify a file name with a .js extension (since we are returning a JavaScript function for use in our page). If we also add the --min option, the generated JavaScript file will be produced minified, saving us an optimization task later. The final command will therefore be as follows, with templatefile. handlebars replaced with the name of the template to be precompiled, and templatefile.js replaced with the name of the precompiled output JavaScript template file:

```
handlebars templatefile.handlebars --output templatefile.js --min
```

Let's create a real example to show how to use a precompiled template. Consider the template file shown in Listing 13-9.

Listing 13-9. A Handlebars template to be precompiled

```
<dl>
    {{#each words}}
        <dt>{{term}} <a href="{{url}}">{{url}}</a></dt>
        <dd>{{definition}}</dd>
    {{else}}
        <p>No words supplied</p>
    {{/each}}
</dl>
```

Let's take the template in Listing 13-9 and precompile it using the handlebars command line tool. We'll use the following command, which generates the minified JavaScript code shown in Listing 13-10, representing our precompiled template:

```
handlebars Listing13-9.handlebars --output Listing13-10.js --min
```

Listing 13-10. The precompiled version of the template in Listing 13-9

```
!function(){var a=Handlebars.template,t=Handlebars.templates=Handlebars.templates||{};t[
"Listing13-9"]=a(function(a,t,e,l,n){function r(a,t){var l,n,r="";return r+="\n          <dt>",(n=e.
term)?l=n.call(a,{hash:{},data:t}):(n=a&&a.term,l=typeof n===i?n.call(a,{hash:{},data:t}):n),r+=o(
l)+' <a href="',(n=e.url)?l=n.call(a,{hash:{},data:t}):(n=a&&a.url,l=typeof n===i?n.call(a,{hash:{},
data:t}):n),r+=o(l)+'">',(n=e.url)?l=n.call(a,{hash:{},data:t}):(n=a&&a.url,l=typeof n===i?n.call(a,
{hash:{},data:t}):n),r+=o(l)+"</a></dt>\n          <dd>",(n=e.definition)?l=n.call(a,{hash:{},data:t})
:(n=a&&a.definition,l=typeof n===i?n.call(a,{hash:{},data:t}):n),r+=o(l)+"</dd>\n      "}function s()
{return"\n          <p>No words supplied</p>\n      "}this.compilerInfo=[4,">=1.0.0"],e=this.merge
(e,a.helpers),n=n||{};var d,h="",i="function",o=this.escapeExpression,c=this;return h+="<dl>\n
",d=e.each.call(t,t&&t.words,{hash:{},inverse:c.program(3,s,n),fn:c.program(1,r,n),data:n}),(d||0===d)
&&(h+=d),h+="\n</dl>"})}();
```

Once precompiled, the template can be referenced for use within our HTML page. Because the compilation stage no longer needs to occur directly in the browser, we get a performance improvement over in-browser compilation. Combine this with the smaller download sizes required for this solution and you can see how useful this technique can be for ensuring good performance within larger web applications.

The code in Listing 13-11 shows an example HTML page we could use to plug our JavaScript data object into the precompiled template, and write the resulting HTML string out to the current page.

Listing 13-11. HTML page referencing a precompiled template and the runtime version of the Handlebars.js library

```
<!doctype html>
<html>
<head>
    <meta charset="utf-8">
    <title>Handlebars.js Example</title>
</head>
<body>
    <h1>Handlebars.js Example</h1>

    <!-- Create an element to store the result of applying the template to the data -->
    <div id="result"></div>

    <!-- Load the Handlebars.js runtime library, which should be used with
        precompliled templates only -->
    <script src="lib/handlebars.runtime.min.js"></script>

    <!-- Load our precompiled template -->
    <script src="Listing13-10.js"></script>

    <!-- Plug the data into the template and render onto the page -->
    <script>
        // Precompiled templates are added as properties to the Handlebars.templates object
        // using their original template name as the key (this name was set by the command line
        // tool and stored in the Listing13-10.js file)
        var template = Handlebars.templates["Listing13-9"],
```

```
            // The template is a function, which should be passed the data to render within the
            // template. The result is the combination of the two, as a String.
            result = template({
                words: [{
                    term: "vastitude",
                    url: "http://dictionary.com/browse/vastitude",
                    definition: "vastness; immensity"
                }, {
                    term: "achromic",
                    url: "http://dictionary.com/browse/achromic",
                    definition: "colorless; without coloring matter"
                }]
            });

        // Write the resulting string onto the current page within the <div id="result">
        // element. Produces the following result:
        /*
        <dl>
            <dt>vastitude
                <a href="http://dictionary.com/browse/vastitude">
http://dictionary.com/browse/vastitude</a>
            </dt>
            <dd>vastness; immensity</dd>

            <dt>achromic
                <a href="http://dictionary.com/browse/achromic">
http://dictionary.com/browse/achromic</a>
            </dt>
            <dd>colorless; without coloring matter</dd>
        </dl>
        */
        document.getElementById("result").innerHTML = result;
    </script>
</body>
</html>
```

Running the code from Listing 13-11 produces the result shown in Figure 13-3.

Handlebars.js Example

vastitude http://dictionary.com/browse/vastitude
vastness; immensity
achromic http://dictionary.com/browse/achromic
colorless; without coloring matter

Figure 13-3. *The resulting page from running the code in Listing 13-9 to combine data with a precompiled template*

Handlebars offers a more descriptive templating language over Mustache, and allows for extensibility through its custom helpers functionality. To overcome the extra size of the library required to process such a template, it offers the ability to precompile templates for use with a cutdown version of the library to offer improved performance and a similar data footprint size to the tiny Mustache.js library. It is for these reasons that Handlebars is so widely used in large web applications.

Alternative Client-Side Templating Libraries

We've looked in some detail at Mustache and Handlebars templating, which many, including myself, accept to be the most popular and well-supported JavaScript templating solutions available. These aren't the only options available to you, however, and libraries including Embedded JavaScript (EJS) and Underscore.js, also offer similar templating functionality, as I will explain in this section.

Client-Side Templating with Embedded JavaScript (EJS)

Embedded JavaScript (EJS) is an open source JavaScript templating language designed for those who are most comfortable with the JavaScript language and prefer to encode their template logic in a familiar code-friendly way. It allows the use of simple JavaScript-format `if` statements, `for` loops, and array indices to output a desired text string from a set of input data. The EJS library can be downloaded from the homepage via `http://bit.ly/ejs-template` and weighs in at just 2.4 KB when minified and served with gzip compression. The library has broad browser support reaching back all the way to Firefox 1.5 and Internet Explorer 6.

Within an EJS template, code to execute is contained within a section starting with <% and ending with %>, a style used by Ruby language developers for templating, and variables to output are wrapped in <%= and %> - note the additional equals (=) sign.

EJS supports the ability to add view helpers that simplify the creation of common types of output, such as HTML links, which can be created using the command `<%= link_to("link text", "/url") %>` to create the following output: `<a href="/url">link text</a>`. The full list of available helpers can be found on the EJS Wiki site at http://bit.ly/ejs_wiki.

A simple EJS example template is shown here:

```
Template:
    <h1><%= title %></h1>
    <dl>
        <% for (var index = 0; index < words.length; index++) { %>
            <dt><%= link_to(words[index].term, words[index].url) %></dt>
            <dd><%= words[index].definition %></dd>
        <% }

        if (!words) { %>
            <p>No words supplied</p>
        <% } %>
    </dl>
```

```
Data Hash:
    {
        title: "EJS Example",
        words: [{
            term: "vastitude",
            url: "http://dictionary.com/browse/vastitude",
            definition: "vastness; immensity"
        }, {
            term: "achromic",
            url: "http://dictionary.com/browse/achromic",
            definition: "colorless; without coloring matter"
        }]
    }
```

```
Output:
    <h1>EJS Example</h1>
    <dl>
        <dt><a href="http://dictionary.com/browse/vastitude">vastitude</a></dt>
        <dd>vastness; immensity</dd>

        <dt><a href="http://dictionary.com/browse/achromic">achromic</a></dt>
        <dd>colorless; without coloring matter</dd>
    </dl>
```

One advantage of EJS over Mustache.js and Handlebars.js is that out of the box it requires no special code to apply JavaScript data from a remote JSON file to a template stored in another remote file, something that requires additional Ajax code with Mustache.js and Handlebars.js.

The EJS "class" is typically instantiated by passing it a URL to an external template file to load asynchronously, and then executing either its render() or update() method, depending on whether the data to apply to the template is already present and loaded within JavaScript, in which case the render() method is passed the data object and returns the output string. The update() method is passed two parameters, the id of a HTML page element to render the resulting template within and the URL of the JSON data file to load asynchronously before applying its data to the template.

```
new EJS({url: "/templatefile.ejs"}).render(dataObject);
new EJS({url: "/templatefile.ejs"}).update("pageElementId", "/datafile.json");
```

If you prefer to work with templates whose logic closely resembles that you're familiar with in JavaScript files, then EJS may be the best templating solution for your needs.

Underscore.js

Underscore.js is a JavaScript library containing over eighty useful helper functions for working with data collections, arrays, objects, and functions in your code, and a selection of utility functions, one of which is specifically targeted toward basic templating. The library can be downloaded from its homepage via http://bit.ly/u-js and weighs in at 5 KB minified and served with gzip encoding. When included on your page, it offers access to its methods through the underscore (_) global variable. You may recognize Underscore.js if you've used the Backbone.js MVC library (http://bit.ly/backbone_mvp) in your code as it has a dependency on this library.

Templating is achieved through the Underscore.js _.template() method, which is passed a template string and returns a function that can then be executed, passing in the data to use to render the template with as a JavaScript object, much the way templating is achieved through Handlebars.js. In a similar way to EJS, the <% and %> delimiters denote code to be executed and the <%= and %> delimiters denote variables to be written out to the resulting string. As well as JavaScript commands such as if and for, you can also set variables and access the entire Underscore.js library to utilize its other utility methods within your templates.

A simple Underscore template might look like the following, using the Underscore.js _.each() method for iterating over a data list rather than using a for loop:

```
Template:
    <h1><%= title %></h1>
    <dl>
        <% _.each(words, function(word) { %>
            <dt><a href="<%= word.url %>"><%= word.term %></a></dt>
            <dd><%= word.definition %></dd>
        <% }

        if (!words) { %>
            <p>No words supplied</p>
        <% } %>
    </dl>

Data Hash:
    {
        title: "Underscore.js Example",
        words: [{
            term: "vastitude",
            url: "http://dictionary.com/browse/vastitude",
            definition: "vastness; immensity"
        }, {
```

```
            term: "achromic",
            url: "http://dictionary.com/browse/achromic",
            definition: "colorless; without coloring matter"
        }]
    }
```

Output:
```
    <h1>Underscore.js Example</h1>
    <dl>
        <dt><a href="http://dictionary.com/browse/vastitude">vastitude</a></dt>
        <dd>vastness; immensity</dd>

        <dt><a href="http://dictionary.com/browse/achromic">achromic</a></dt>
        <dd>colorless; without coloring matter</dd>
    </dl>
```

To use Underscore templates on your HTML page, reference the library and your template, which you will have to load manually via Ajax or reference directly from your HTML page or a JavaScript variable. Then execute the _.template() method to compile a template string to a function, which can then be called with data.

```
var template = _.template(templateString),
    output = template(data);
```

If you require additional familiar-looking helper methods in your templates, or you are already using the Backbone.js MVC library in your application, you may find Underscore.js the best templating solution for your needs.

Consider Progressive Enhancement

In this chapter, we've looked at client-side templating solutions that allow you to dynamically load in specially formatted templates, combine them with JavaScript data, and then append the resulting output to the current HTML page. This allows for a web application user experience devoid of page refreshes to fetch and display new content, much like that of desktop applications. With dynamic content loading comes a warning, however: building a web application whose display renders and updates entirely via JavaScript means an accidental page refresh could reset the entire application back to its initial view state, and that search engines may struggle to crawl the content represented through the application as not all can process JavaScript. It also goes somewhat against the principle of URLs on the web: a URL represents an object or piece of content rather than a full application.

Build your web application using the principle of progressive enhancement, where HTML links and forms go to separate and distinct URLs when followed, with JavaScript used to prevent those links and forms from causing page refreshes and layering on an improved user experience instead. Execute Ajax calls and load templates and data dynamically, using the HTML5 History API (http://bit.ly/historyapi) to update the URL in the address bar to match the URL representing the new data loaded or page section displayed. If the user then accidentally refreshes the page in their browser, they'll be taken to the content represented by the updated URL in their address bar, keeping them in the same place in the application they had previously reached. When JavaScript is disabled, as it is for most search engine crawlers, the links still work, allowing content and site data to be spidered as you would want them to, creating links directly into your application at key points.

Summary

In this chapter, I have covered client-side templating as a solution for building large web applications with dynamically updating page content, combining specially marked-up templates with JavaScript data to generate HTML for inclusion on the current page. I have covered the popular Mustache and Handlebars templating languages, and their associated JavaScript libraries, as well as some alternatives such as Embedded JavaScript (EJS) and Underscore.js.

In the next chapter, I will introduce Node.js, an application framework built for the JavaScript language that allows professional JavaScript developers the opportunity to write server-side code and server software to support their web applications, bringing the full development stack within the realm of the JavaScript developer.

CHAPTER 14

███

The Node.js Application Platform

In this chapter, we're going to take a deliberate step away from client-side JavaScript code that runs in the browser and move toward the server-side realm instead, taking a close look at an application platform called Node.js, designed by and for JavaScript developers.

█ **Note** JavaScript has a history on the server side. The first use of JavaScript in a product was not in fact within a web browser at all; it was within a server product released in 1994 called Netscape Enterprise Server, in which it served as a language for coding server-side behavior for HTTP applications.

Node.js was first released by its creator Ryan Dahl in 2011, a culmination of his vision to build an application platform allowing developers to build lightweight, scalable command-line or network applications. It is built upon the Google V8 JavaScript engine (http://bit.ly/google-v8), a virtual machine also used within Google's Chrome browser to parse and execute JavaScript. Like JavaScript in the browser, applications are built around an asynchronous event-based model meaning code should run efficiently and look familiar to the professional JavaScript developer. A large part of the appeal of Node.js for developers is that it was built to run on Microsoft Windows, Mac OS X, Linux, and SunOS operating systems, making it a useful platform for delivering command-line applications that run cross-platform without requiring any extra development steps. Because one of the original goals of the Node.js project was to allow developers to easily build applications that support server-push capabilities, a lot of attention under the hood is on its asynchronous event-driven I/O (input/output) system that, unlike some other application platforms, does not cause the main application process to pause while waiting for data to be written or read. This makes it a perfect candidate for running a scalable web server capable of handling a large number of simultaneous connections, and for running server-side code to support an application or website running in a connected web browser. To learn more about the technical reasons behind what makes Node.js what it is, check out the following page on the project's website: http://bit.ly/about-node.

Installing Node.js

Node.js can be installed by downloading the install package from the project homepage at http://nodejs.org, shown in Figure 14-1. Follow the instructions to install both the node system itself (at the time of writing the current version is v0.10.29) and the Node Package Manager tool (npm), which we will look in more detail at later in this chapter.

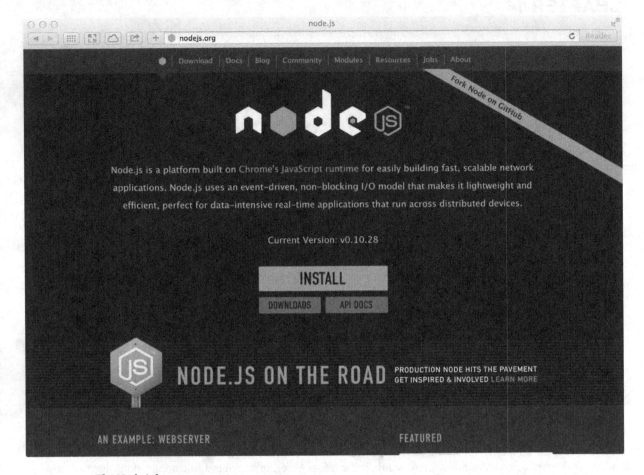

Figure 14-1. *The Node.js homepage*

With the node command line tool now installed globally on your machine, you can navigate to any folder containing a suitable JavaScript application file written for Node.js and run it by executing the following command, replacing `filename.js` with the name of the JavaScript file to run:

```
node filename.js
```

Writing Node.js Applications

Let's get familiar with writing Node.js applications by creating a basic example to demonstrate the platform's functionality and features. First, let's write the world's simplest Node.js application, one that displays `Hello, World` into the command line window. The code is one solitary line long and is shown in Listing 14-1.

Listing 14-1. Hello World Node.js application

```
console.log("Hello, World");
```

Save this into a file named Listing14-1.js and execute it on the command line with the following command:

```
node Listing14-1.js
```

Running this new application from the command line produces the output shown in Figure 14-2. The application stops running once complete and returns control to the command line cursor for the next command you wish to execute.

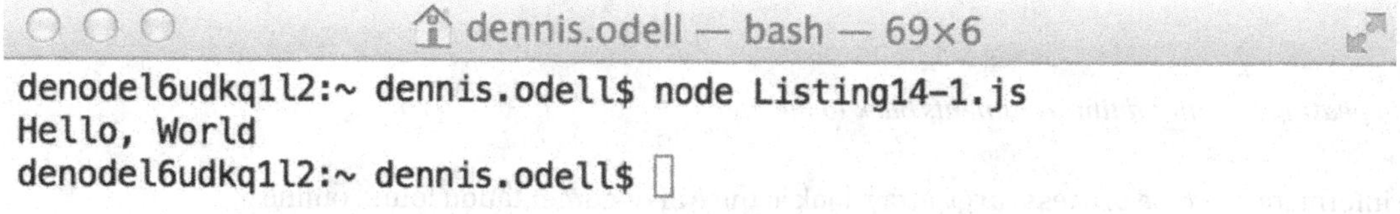

```
denode16udkq1l2:~ dennis.odell$ node Listing14-1.js
Hello, World
denode16udkq1l2:~ dennis.odell$ []
```

Figure 14-2. Running the Hello World application

The Console

The Node.js native console object contains methods for writing different types of message out to the command line, the log() method is the most basic of these—any string, number, array, or basic object passed to it will be written out to the command line when run in this way. Read more about the console methods in the API documentation via http://bit.ly/nodejs_console_api.

Should you wish to write a command line application to which you can pass arguments on the command line, you can use the process.argv array, which contains each argument used on the command line beginning with the call to node itself and the filename to execute. The code in Listing 14-2 shows a simple application that repeats each argument passed to it back onto the command line. Save this code into a file named Listing14-2.js.

Listing 14-2. Accessing command line arguments

```
var index = 2,
    length = process.argv.length;

// We start from index 2 as the first two arguments are node itself and the filename
// we are executing
for (; index < length; index++) {
    console.log(process.argv[index]);
}
```

Executing the following command on the command line to run the code in Listing 14-2, passing in arguments to the application. This produces the result shown in Figure 14-3.

```
node Listing14-2.js one 2 three
```

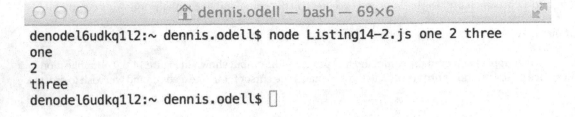

```
denode16udkq1l2:~ dennis.odell$ node Listing14-2.js one 2 three
one
2
three
denode16udkq1l2:~ dennis.odell$ []
```

Figure 14-3. *Repeating command line arguments back to the user*

For more information on the process.argv array, look at the API documentation found online at
http://bit.ly/nodejs_argv.

Loading Modules

In Chapter 9, we covered the Asynchronous Module Definition (AMD) and JavaScript libraries that allow file
dependencies to be loaded in a clear and descriptive way using a global method named require(). Node.js supports
AMD and the require() method out of the box, and it is the preferred way of dealing with the loading of file
dependencies.

In order for Node.js to remain a lean environment, many nonessential packages of behavior are not loaded
by default and must be specifically listed as dependencies in order to be loaded. Provided that you only list the
dependencies you need in your application code, this ensures that the only code loaded is the code you actually
require, keeping performance optimal.

The http Module

Node.js is commonly used as a networking environment, and more specifically as a web server for which its lean,
simple approach is well suited. You explicitly include the behavior you require reducing the bloat often found in other
server products. Node.js' http module dependency contains the methods required to spin up a simple web server.
Listing 14-3 shows this in action, creating a local web server on a given port number that, when accessed through a
web browser, writes Hello, World out to that requesting browser's window as HTML.

Listing 14-3. A simple Node.js web server

```
// Define a dependency on the Node.js "http" module which contains methods to allow the
// creation of a simple HTTP web server
var http = require("http"),

    // Define a variable to represent our HTTP server
    server,

    // Define a constant to represent the HTTP status code for an OK response
    HTTP_OK = 200,

    // Define a port number to listen for requests on
    PORT = 8000;

// Call the http.createServer() method to spin up a web server, defining the response to send
// to the calling HTTP application (usually a web browser) based on the request received. Here
```

```
// we ignore the request received (which would contain the URL requested and any data sent
// with the request, for example cookie or POST data) and simply respond with a single chunk
// of HTML to read "Hello, World" for any request received (try different URLs to prove this).
// The callback function passed to the method will be executed once for each request received
// at the time it is received, asynchronously.
    server = http.createServer(function(request, response) {

        // Send a HTTP header to the requesting browser to indicate a successful HTTP response
        // and defining the response body data will be sent as HTML text
        response.writeHead(HTTP_OK, {
            "Content-Type": "text/html"
        });

        // Send the HTML response
        response.write("<h1>Hello, World</h1>\n");

        // Close the connection - without this, the HTTP server will expect to continue to send
        // more data to the browser, the connection to the server would be kept open unnecessarily,
        // wasting server resources and potentially preventing others from connecting to that same
        // server, depending on demand. The end() method tells the connection that we're done
        // sending our response data. If we knew we were only going to send one string of data and
        // then close the connection, we could actually pass that string to the response.end()
        // method, which would call the write() method for us internally in that case
        response.end();
});

// The final step is to tell our new web server to start listening for requests on a specific
// socket port number. The host name by default will be http://localhost or http://127.0.0.1
// since we are running the application locally on our development machine. The listen() method
// is different to many others in that it keeps the Node.js application running - if it didn't
// we would no longer be able to listen for requests. You can manually stop the application on
// the command line by typing Ctrl+X (Microsoft Windows) or Command-X (Mac OS X) which will
// stop the web server from listening on this port
    server.listen(PORT);

// Output a message to the command line to instruct the user that the web server is running
// and what address they need to browse in order to view the defined response
    console.log("Now try browsing http://127.0.0.1: " + PORT);
```

Save the listing to a file named Listing14-3.js and execute the following command on the command line to spin up the simple web server.

```
node Listing14-3.js
```

When executed, the code in Listing 14-3 will produce the response on the command line shown in Figure 14-4. When visiting the URL http://127.0.0.1:8000 in a web browser, it will output the response shown in Figure 14-5. Note that you can add any extra path or query string value onto the end of that host name and the server responds with exactly the same HTML data each time. Later in this chapter, we will look at web server frameworks that allow us an easier route to creating web servers that respond appropriately to different path and query string values.

To read more about the http module, visit the specific Node.js API documentation via http://bit.ly/nodejs_http.

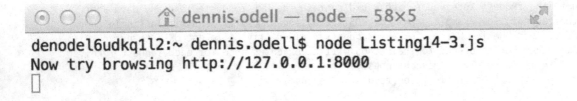

Figure 14-4. *Starting up a simple Node.js web server*

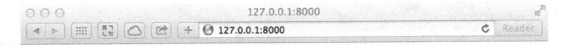

Hello, World

Figure 14-5. *Visiting the simple web server's URL in a browser outputs "Hello, World" in HTML*

We've now seen how to create a simple application that runs on the command line, and another that opens up the channels of communication over HTTP to a connected web browser, the basis of any web server and the foundation for any server-side code we wish to write. To learn more about the other low-level modules available to you, visit the full API documentation site via `http://bit.ly/nodejs_apidocs`.

Node.js Packages

Node.js comes bundled with the Node Package Manager (`npm`), a separate command line application that allows for third-party modules, known as *packages*, to be loaded and used either directly on the command line as applications in their own right, or for use as code dependencies within your Node.js applications to add extra functionality. A directory of available packages can be found online at `http://npmjs.org`, as shown in Figure 14-6, where you can search for the package or type of package in which you are interested.

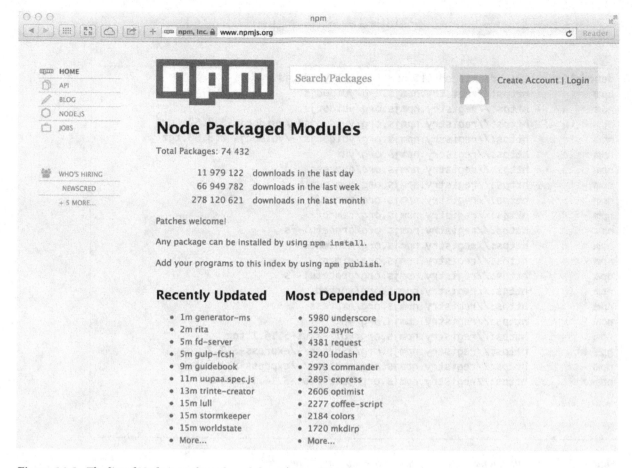

Figure 14-6. *The list of Node.js packaged modules at* http://npmjs.org

Installing applications from this list is as simple as running the command npm install on the command line, followed by the package name as it is listed in the directory; for example, to install the YUIDoc command line tool (which we looked at back in Chapter 2) for use in the current directory, execute the following command:

```
npm install yuidocjs
```

While this command is running, you will see a response written to the command line, shown in Figure 14-7, as the tool uses HTTP to download the requested package and its dependencies. Once installation is complete, we can use the installed yuidoc application within the current folder. You will notice a node_modules folder has appeared within the current folder, this is the default location that npm stores the requested application's files and dependencies so ensure that you do not delete it.

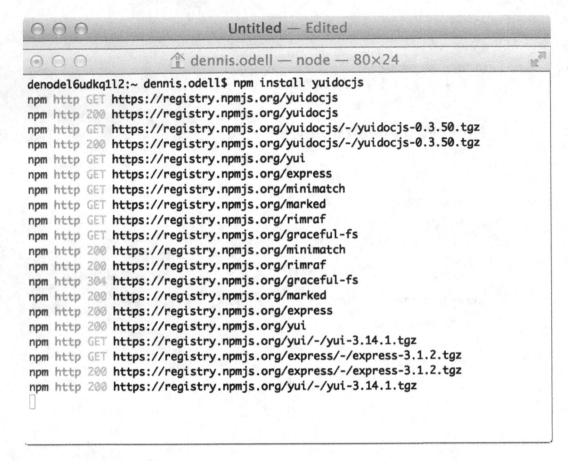

Figure 14-7. Installing a package from npm on the command line

We would like to be able to access certain applications from any folder on our machine and npm allows you to do this using the -g global option when installing a package. Mac and Linux users may find they need to precede the command with sudo to grant administrator user access to install packages globally in this way:

```
npm install -g yuidocjs
```

Once installed globally, the yuidoc application can then be run from within any folder on your machine.

Every Node.js package contains a package.json data file in its root folder, which contains structured metadata describing the package. This file lists the project's internal package name, which must not be the same as another name used within the NPM directory, and must be URL-friendly (e.g., contain no spaces), and a version number in the semantic versioning format, described online at http://semver.org, for example, 1.0.1. It is this file that also lists the project's dependencies such that these can be installed along with the package.

The command line tool npm contains the ability to create a package.json file on your behalf in response to a few questions. To create the file in the current directory, simple execute the following command on the command line:

```
npm init
```

An example package.json file is shown in Listing 14-4, which includes a selection of common properties. Please note that comments should be removed from any JSON format file before using in any application.

Listing 14-4. An example package.json file for use with npm

```
{
    // The "name" value is mandatory and must be URL-friendly so cannot contain any spaces
    // and should be in lower case
    "name": "my-test-project",

    // The "version" value is mandatory and must adhere to the semantic versioning format
    "version": "0.0.1",

    // An optional friendly description of the project to assist users when searching the npm
    // directory
    "description": "This is my test project",

    // A pointer to the project's homepage online - many use this field to point to the
    // GitHub (or equivalent hosting service) code repository page
    "homepage": "https://github.com/denodell/my-test-project",

    // Details of the code repository which other developers may find useful if they wish
    // to contribute to the project
    "repository": {

        // The type of repository, e.g. "git" (for Git) or "svn" (for Subversion)
        "type": "git",

        // The URL of the repository itself, designed for direct use with software and should
        // not be a link to the project home page
        "url": "https://github.com/denodell/my-test-project.git"
    },

    // Details of the project author, if there is only one. For multiple authors, this key
    // name should be changed to "contributors" and its value will be an array of names and
    // email addresses of those who have worked on the project
    "author": {
        "name": "Den Odell",
        "email": "denodell@me.com"
    },

    // List of package dependencies needed to run the project described by this file. Each is
    // listed by its package name as it is in the npm directory and the version number of the
    // dependency needed. By specifying the version, we can ensure that future breaking updates
    // to dependent packages won't impact our package
    "dependencies": {

        // Specify the exact version number of the dependency required by using its full
        // version number
        "async": "0.9.0",

        // Versions greater than or equal to specific releases can be specified using >=
        "request": ">=2.36.0",
```

```
        // Versions reasonably close to a given release can be specific using tilde (~).
        // Here, this means any version between 1.6.0 and any future release up to but not
        // including the next major release (i.e. 1.7.0 in this case)
        "underscore": "~1.6.0",

        // Git URLs can be used in place of version numbers to reference dependencies that
        // are stored in places outside of the npm directory. The latest contents of the repo
        // will be downloaded when this package is installed
        "promise-the-earth": "git+ssh://github.com/denodell/promise-the-earth.git"
    },

    // List of additional package dependencies required for developers who wish to contribute
    // to this project. Often this list includes development build tools, code quality checks
    // and unit test runners
    "devDependencies": {
        "yuidocjs": "~0.3.50"
    }
}
```

For more on the package.json file and to read about the different settings for the dependencies and devDependencies sections, read the documentation online at http://bit.ly/package_json.

If you have a local project on your machine that contains a package.json file, you can install that project and all of its required dependencies by navigating on the command line to that folder and executing the following command:

```
npm install
```

This has the same behavior as the use of the command that we have seen earlier except that, by leaving out the package name, the npm tool will instead look to the local folder it is run within to discover the project's settings and dependencies.

If you want to add dependencies to your project and automatically add the reference to it within your package.json file, you can do this by adding the --save option to the usual install command, which will add the reference to the dependencies section of the package file as well as download the package, for example:

```
npm install yuidocjs --save
```

To save the dependency to the devDependencies section instead, use the --save-dev option instead:

```
npm install jshint --save-dev
```

If you have written a project that you wish to publish yourself to npm for others to use as dependencies for their projects, you simply run the following command in the project directory that contains your package.json file to push it to the directory, making it available to any other developer:

```
npm publish
```

Once you have your package.json file and have run npm install to download all the project's dependencies before the project can be run, you can access the dependencies from within your Node.js application using the require() method. Let's imagine that you have a package.json file containing the following dependencies section that references the request and picture-tube packages from the npm directory:

```
"dependencies": {
    "request": "~2.36.0",
    "picture-tube": "~0.0.4"
}
```

These packages can then be referenced as dependencies within your application JavaScript file by using require(), as shown in Listing 14-5.

Listing 14-5. Referencing dependent packages within a Node.js application

```
// Reference a dependency on the "request" package, a simple HTTP request client
var request = require("request"),

    // Reference a dependency on the "picture-tube" package, allowing 256 color images to be
    // rendered out to the command line
    pictureTube = require("picture-tube"),

    // Reference an online image URL (PNG format only) to render to the command line
    imageUrl = "http://upload.wikimedia.org/wikipedia/commons/8/87/Google_Chrome_icon_(2011).png";

// Make a request to download the image URL, then use the Node.js Stream API to "pipe" the
// data through the "picture-tube" package to create command line codes representing the image.
// Finally pipe the output of that process out to the command line, represented by the
// process.stdout stream
request(imageUrl).pipe(pictureTube()).pipe(process.stdout);
```

Installing the depdendencies and then executing the code from Listing 14-5 on the command line produces the result shown in Figure 14-8. As you can see, the use of dependencies allows for advanced applications to be written with relatively little code. The npm directory contains over eighty-five thousand packages at the time of writing, and growing daily, so I encourage you to look here first when assembling your own applications to save rewriting code that someone else has already written.

```
○ ○ ○                    ⬆ dennis.odell — bash — 108×42
Den—Odell—LONM6UDKQ1L—2:~ dennis.odell$ node Listing14-5.js
```

```
Den—Odell—LONM6UDKQ1L—2:~ dennis.odell$ ▯
```

Figure 14-8. *Referencing dependencies allows us to draw simple images to the command line with very little code*

Splitting a Node.js Application across Multiple Files

So far in this chapter, the type of applications that we've covered have been simple and, other than their dependencies, self-contained within a single file. Node.js does, however, support the ability to split a larger application up into multiple files, which can then be referenced from each other using the `require()` method. Let's imagine we have a main application file, named `app.js`, and a second file, named `utility.js`, located within the same folder, in which we wish to store a number of utility methods for use within our application. We can reference the utility file from the main application file with the following use of the `require()` method. Note that to indicate this as a file rather than an external dependency loaded via `npm`, we specify the folder name along with the file name (a folder name of `./` indicates the same folder as the current file). We can exclude the `.js` file extension, as this is assumed:

```
var utlity = require("./utility");
```

Before we can use the utility methods, however, we need to specify which methods within our `utility.js` file are to be publicly accessible, and therefore available for use outside of that file. To do this, we use the Node.js `module.exports` property, which is local to each file, and set the methods and properties that we wish to make available externally from the file to this property. We can see a simple implementation of this for the `utility.js` file in Listing 14-6.

Listing 14-6. Exporting properties and methods for use in other files in a Node.js application

```
// Define a function which converts a text string to camel case, with an uppercase letter at
// the start of each word
function toCamelCase(inputString) {
    return inputString.replace(/\s+[a-z]/g, function(firstLetter) {
        return firstLetter.toUpperCase();
    });
}


// Define a function which converts a text string from camel case to hyphens, where all letters
// become lowercase, and spaces replaced with hyphens
function toHyphens(inputString) {
    return inputString.replace(/\s+([A-Z])/g, '-$1').toLowerCase();
}


// Export two public methods to any referenced file, toCamelCase(), which internally references
// the function of the same name, and toHyphens() which does the same
module.exports = {
    toCamelCase: toCamelCase,
    toHyphens: toHyphens
};
```

The methods exported from Listing 14-6, representing our utility.js file, can be used in our main application file as shown in Listing 14-7. Observe how data from JSON format files can be imported as a JavaScript object straight into a Node.js application by passing the JSON filename to require().

Listing 14-7. Using exported methods from a separate file in a Node.js application

```
// Reference our exported utility methods the utility.js file
var utility = require("./utility"),

    // Load the data from our comment-free package.json file (see Listing 14-4)
    pkg = require("./package.json"),

    // Use the exported utility method toCamelCase() to convert the description text from the
    // package.json file into camel case
    camelCaseDescription = utility.toCamelCase(pkg.description),

    // Use the utility method toHyphens() to convert the camel case description into a
    // lower case hyphenated form
    hyphensDescription = utility.toHyphens(camelCaseDescription);

// Write out the description of the package to the command line in its different forms
console.log(camelCaseDescription); // outputs: "This Is My Test Project"
console.log(hyphensDescription); // outputs: "this-is-my-test-project"
```

We can export any type of standard JavaScript data using module.exports, including functions, objects, strings, numbers, dates, and arrays, which can then be used directly in their referenced files. To read more about Modules in Node.js, check out the API documentation online via http://bit.ly/nodejs_modules.

Node.js Frameworks for Web Applications

Now that we've seen the basics of writing Node.js applications in JavaScript, let's take a look at a selection of frameworks designed to help write the server side of web applications that can scale. Be sure to read the documentation for each to ensure that you use the correct framework for your own project needs.

Express

One of the most popular Node.js web frameworks is *Express*, which simplifies the process of setting up a web server capable of responding to requests to different URLs using whichever type of HTTP method, for example, GET or POST, is required. The desired behavior for each URL can then be coded in JavaScript, which may be to simply respond with a HTML page, or to process submitted form data, for example. The code in Listing 14-8 shows a simple web server configured using the Express framework showing how to respond to HTTP GET and POST methods to various URLs. It takes advantage of Sencha Labs' *Connect* middleware, designed for use with web server frameworks in Node.js to add support for common actions such as accessing cookie data, decoding HTTP POST data, and Gzip compression. To read more about the Connect middleware library, check out the online documentation at http://bit.ly/nodejs_connect.

Listing 14-8. A simple Node.js web server using the Express framework

```
// Reference the Express framework through the "express" npm package dependency. Ensure
// you have a package.json file referencing this dependency
var express = require("express"),

    // Reference the "connect" package which provides a set of middleware for use with other
    // web server Node.js packages, including Express
    connect = require("connect"),

    // Initialize the framework, making its methods available through the app variable
    app = express(),

    // Define the port number we will host our web server on
    PORT = 3000;

// The Express use() method allows a piece of middleware to be connected up to the current
// server. Here we connect up the HTTP POST body data parser from the "connect" package
app.use(connect.bodyParser());

// The express.static() middleware allows the contents of a particular directory on the file
// system to be made available beneath a particular path name. Here we define a "/assets" path
// on our web server which maps to the contents of a "/dist/assets" folder found within the
// current directory this application file finds itself in (the __dirname is a Node.js global
// variable available to any file. A request to any file within the "/dist/assets" folder can
// now be requested, e.g. "/assets/css/styles.css" would return the contents of the file found
// at location "/dist/assets/css/styles.css" within the current folder. This is perfect for
// serving static files, such as JavaScript CSS, images, and flat HTML required as part of a
// web site or application
app.use('/assets', express.static(__dirname + "/dist/assets"));

// The get() method allows us to respond to a HTTP GET request at a specific URL, in this
// case we specify the server root, "/", which will give us our homepage. The callback will
// be executed when the given URL is requested using the GET method, passing in the details
```

```javascript
// of the request in the "request" object, including referer, user agent, and other useful
// information. The "response" object contains properties that can be set, and methods that
// can be called to alter the output data and headers sent to the requesting browser
app.get("/", function(request, response) {

    // The send() method of the response object allows us the send data to the requesting
    // browser. This method is smart enough to detect the data type being sent and to adjust
    // the HTTP response headers accordingly. Here we pass in a string, which is interpreted
    // as being in HTML format, but if we'd passed in a JavaScript object, this would be
    // sent as a JSON string to the browser, with the appropriate headers sent. This method
    // also sets the Content-Length HTTP header according to the length of the data sent,
    // which informs the browser that there is no more data to be sent back to the browser
    // besides that passed to the method
    response.send("<h1>Hello, World</h1>");
});

// Send a HTML form as a response to a GET request to the URL "/email"
app.get("/email", function(request, response) {

    // Send a HTML form whose action points to the URL "/email" and whose HTTP method is POST.
    // When the form is submitted, rather than hitting this callback, the callback below will
    // be called, which is associated specifically with the POST HTTP method. The form here has
    // one named field, "email", which will be set as the POST data when the form is submitted.
    response.send("<form method=\"post\" action=\"/email\">\
        <label for=\"email\">Email address</label>\
        <input type=\"email\" id=\"email\" name=\"email\" value=\"\">\
        <input type=\"submit\">\
    </form>");
});

// Respond to a HTTP POST of data to the URL "/email", writing out the
app.post("/email", function(request, response) {

    // When the "connect" package is used, and the current Express app is associated with the
    // bodyParser() middleware method from this package, the request.body property is an object
    // containing properties that directly correspond to the names of POSTed data values. Since
    // we posted a form field with the name "email", the request.body.email property contains
    // the value entered into the form field by that name
    var email = request.body.email || "";

    // Show the POSTed email address value within a HTML <h1> tag on the page
    response.send("<h1>Posted email: " + email + "</h1>");
});

// Just like the listen() method with the "http" package we saw in Listing 14-3, this starts
// the process of accepting requests to the web server from a browser on the given port. This
// keeps the Node.js application running continuously. If the application is stopped, the
// server will no longer be running and won't be able to accept any browser requests
app.listen(PORT);

// Output a message to the command line to instruct the user that the web server is running
console.log("Now try browsing http://127.0.0.1: " + PORT);
```

The code in Listing 14-8 shows how a web server capable of serving static files, responding to HTTP GET and POST requests to different URLs can be written in less than 20 lines of code using the Express framework for Node.js. Before we run the code as a Node.js application, we need to create our package.json file and install our dependencies. Run npm init on the command line in the folder containing this code listing to create a basic package.json file. Next install the dependencies with the following commands, which will also save the dependency version references within the package.json file:

```
npm install express --save
npm install connect --save
```

Now we can run our application on the command line with the following command (assuming that you saved the code listing to a file named Listing14-8.js):

```
npm Listing14-8.js
```

To learn more about all the advanced features of the Express framework, check out the API documentation online at http://bit.ly/nodejs_express_api.

Socket.IO

Although the Express framework is great for writing powerful, scalable web server applications that use standard HTTP methods, such as GET and POST, sometimes you find yourself wanting to write a real-time application, where data that is updating on the server or within the browser needs to be immediately sent and responded to from the other location, such as in a chat messaging application, an online whiteboard, or a collaborative game experience. Whereas Ajax is a fair enough solution for some of these types of application, it is only suitable for polling a server for data periodically, the server is not able to inform the browser that there is new data at the exact moment the new data is available. *Socket.IO* is a web server framework that uses a number of solutions behind the scenes, including the W3C WebSocket API (http://bit.ly/websocket-api), supported in the latest releases of all major web browsers, including Internet Explorer 10 and up, to provide bidirectional real-time communication between browser and server.

Let's build a simple application to demonstrate the Socket.IO framework. We'll create a HTML page with a single text form field for inputting messages that, when submitted, will send the given message to the server and add the message for display on the page, together with the current time. The server will then instantly respond with a new message, wrapping the received message in an object and sending it back to the browser. The browser will then display the message received together with the current time, which should show the speed of the real-time response from the server using Socket.IO to be less than a second. The resulting application is shown in Figure 14-9, which shows the response to a Hello, World message submitted via the form. Note the time next to each message, which shows that the message was sent to the server and the response received back again in less than one second.

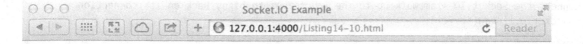

Socket.IO Example

 Send message

Messages Sent From Browser

Thu, 29 May 2014 07:40:44 GMT - {"sent":"Hello, world"}

Messages Received From Server

Thu, 29 May 2014 07:40:39 GMT - "Ready and waiting for messages"

Thu, 29 May 2014 07:40:44 GMT - {"received":{"sent":"Hello, world"}}

Figure 14-9. *A simple Socket.IO application for communicating simple messages in real time with a server*

The code in Listing 14-9 shows the Node.js server application that will initialize the web socket connection, listen for messages sent from the browser client, and respond to them immediately with a new message.

Listing 14-9. Socket.IO application for communicating simple messages in real-time with a browser

```
// Reference the Express framework through the "express" npm package dependency. Ensure
// you have a package.json file referencing this dependency
var express = require("express"),

    // Initialize the framework, making its methods available through the app variable
    app = express(),

    // Define a dependency on the Node.js "http" module - required for use with the
    // Socket.IO framework
    http = require("http"),

    // Create a simple web server, ensuring the Express framework handles all the requests by
    // passing the app variable to the http.createServer() method
    server = http.createServer(app),

    // Reference the Socket.IO framework through its "socket.io" npm package dependency.
    // Ensure this dependency is listed in your package.json file
    socketIo = require("socket.io"),
```

```
    // Connect the Socket.IO framework up to the web server to piggy back on its connection
    io = socketIo.listen(server),

    // Define a port number to listen for requests on
    PORT = 4000;

// Make the contents of the current directory available through our web server so we can
// serve up a HTML file
app.use("/", express.static(__dirname));

// Wait for the Socket.IO connection to the browser to initiate before executing the callback,
// passing in a reference to the socket connection
io.sockets.on("connection", function(socket) {

    // Send a message using the emit() method of the socket connection, passing some data to
    // any connected browser listening for the "new-data-on-server" event sent from the socket
    socket.emit("new-data-on-server", "Ready and waiting for messages");

    // When a message named "new-data-on-client" is received from the client, execute the
    // callback function, passing in the data passed along with the message
    socket.on("new-data-on-client", function(data) {

        // Immediate broadcast back out the received message wrapped in a simple JavaScript
        // object with a property named "received"
        socket.emit("new-data-on-server", {
            received: data
        });
    });
});

// Start listening for web requests on the given port number
server.listen(PORT);

// Output a message to the command line to instruct the user that the web server is running
console.log("Now try browsing http://127.0.0.1:" + PORT);
```

Before we run the code in Listing 14-9 as a Node.js application, we need to create our package.json file and install our dependencies. Run npm init on the command line in the folder containing this code listing to create a basic package.json file. Next install the dependencies with the following commands, which will also save the dependency version references within the package.json file:

```
npm install express --save
npm install socket.io --save
```

Now we can run our application on the command line with the following command (assuming that you saved the code listing to a file named Listing14-9.js):

```
npm Listing14-9.js
```

Next, we need the code for our HTML page, which is shown in Listing 14-10. The page will contain a form field, for inputting messages, and two display areas to reflect messages sent to the server and those received from the server. Because our Node.js web application has been configured to allow access to any file in the current folder through the web server, if we name this file Listing14-10.html and place it in the same folder as the code listing from Listing 14-9, we can access it through our web browser by navigating to http://127.0.0.1:400/Listing14-10.html. Note how the server automatically provides the JavaScript library required for communication to the Socket.IO web server via the URL path /socket.io/socket.io.js. This simplifies the task of writing the code to connect our HTML page to the web server.

Listing 14-10. HTML page for communicating real-time messages with a Socket.IO web server application

```
<!doctype html>
<html>
<head>
    <title>Socket.IO Example</title>
    <meta charset="utf-8">
</head>
<body>
    <h1>Socket.IO Example</h1>

    <!-- Create a form with a single text field, named "message-field". When the form is
        submitted, we want to send the field value to the server, and show the message
        in the <div id="messages-sent"> element below -->
    <form method="post" action="/" id="send-message-form">
        <input type="text" name="message-field" id="message-field">
        <input type="submit" value="Send message">
    </form>

    <!-- Create an element to present messages sent from the browser to the server -->
    <h2>Messages Sent From Browser</h2>
    <div id="messages-sent"></div>

    <!-- Create an element to present messages received from the server -->
    <h2>Messages Received From Server</h2>
    <div id="messages-received"></div>

    <!-- Load the Socket.IO JavaScript file provided by the server - this is automatically
        available at this location if Socket.IO is running on the server and provides the
        necessary web socket connection back to the server. It also supplies the fallback
        code in case web sockets are not supported by the current browser -->
    <script src="/socket.io/socket.io.js"></script>

    <!-- Load the script found in Listing 14-11 to connect the page up to the web socket
        connection -->
    <script src="Listing14-11.js"></script>
</body>
</html>
```

With our web server and our HTML page in place, all we need to do is connect the two together, which is the role of the code in Listing 14-11, referenced from the bottom of the HTML page in Listing 14-10.

Listing 14-11. Connect a HTML page to the Socket.IO web server to communicate and display messages

```
// This script has a dependency on the "/socket.io/socket.io.js" script provided by the
// Socket.IO framework when it is referenced from the web server, which surfaces the global
// variable "io"

// Establish the web socket connection to the server to enable sending and receiving of
// messages
var socket = io(),

    // Get references to the form element and text form field element from the page
    formElem = document.getElementById("send-message-form"),
    messageFormFieldElem = document.getElementById("message-field"),

    // Get references to the empty <div> tags on the page which we will populate with messages
    // sent to and received from the server
    messagesSentElem = document.getElementById("messages-sent"),
    messagesReceivedElem = document.getElementById("messages-received");

// Listen for the "new-data-on-server" event sent from the server over the web socket
// connection. The callback method will be executed immediately on reception of the message,
// passing along the message data sent with the event. We can then append this message to the
// current page within the <div id="messages-received"> element
socket.on("new-data-on-server", function(data) {

    // Create a new paragraph element
    var paragraphElem = document.createElement("p");

    // Populate the new <p> tag with the current time and the message received - use
    // JSON.stringify() to convert the message from its current type to a string for display
    paragraphElem.innerHTML = new Date().toUTCString() + " - " + JSON.stringify(data);

    // Add the message to the <div id="messages-received"> element on the page
    messagesReceivedElem.appendChild(paragraphElem);
});

// Connect a form handler to the "submit" event of the <form> element to send the message
// written in the form field to the server
formElem.addEventListener("submit", function(e) {

    // Define a variable for storing the message to send to the server when the form is
    // submitted, populating it with the value stored in the form field
    var message = {
            sent: messageFormFieldElem.value
        },

        // Create a new paragraph element
        paragraphElem = document.createElement("p");

    // Prevent the default submit behavior of the <form> element from occurring, to avoid
    // the page refreshing - we'll send the message data to the server manually
    e.preventDefault();
```

```
// Emit a web socket broadcast event to send the message to the server using the event
// name "new-data-on-client". The server can then react to this message type as it wishes
socket.emit("new-data-on-client", message);

// Populate the new <p> tag with the current time and a copy of the sent message - using
// JSON.stringify() to convert the message from its current object type to a string for
// display
paragraphElem.innerHTML = new Date().toUTCString() + " - " + JSON.stringify(message);

// Add the message to the <div id="messages-sent"> element on the page
messagesSentElem.appendChild(paragraphElem);

// Clear the form field text to allow a new message to be sent
messageFormFieldElem.value = "";
}, false);
```

Running the code in Listings 14-9 through 14-11 together produces the result shown in Figure 14-9. If you open up the page in multiple browser windows, you should discover that messages sent and received in one window are kept separate from those sent to or from another. This is ideal for the application we covered here; however, this is not the desired behavior for other types of applications, for example, a chat application or others requiring collaboration between multiple connected users.

The restrictions placed on messages sent from a Socket.IO server are wrapped up within the socket.emit() method, which was used in the web server application from Listing 14-9. Used as is, messages are localized to each individual browser-server connection. Should you wish, however, to transmit a message to be received by any connected browser, including the sending browser, you can use the io.emit() method instead, which is used in the same way:

```
io.emit("new-data-on-server", "Message Text");
```

If you wish to send a message to all connected browsers apart from a particular one, for example, the one sending the message, you can use the socket.broadcast.emit() method, which sends the message out to all sockets except that represented by the socket object:

```
socket.broadcast.emit("new-data-on-server", "Message Text");
```

By creating Socket.IO applications combining each type of emit() method, you are able to create real-time multiuser connected online applications with surprisingly little code.

To learn more about Socket.IO and how to build specific types of application using this framework, check out the documentation online via http://bit.ly/sockdoc.

Node.js Hosting

We've seen how to set up and run Node.js web server applications from a local machine, but in the real world we can't host our applications from our local machines. We need an online hosting solution capable of running our applications in the cloud. Joyent, the company behind the support of the Node.js application platform, manage an up-to-date list of known hosting providers online at http://bit.ly/node_hosting, which can be a good first point of reference when you have your application written and ready to go. A number support code deployments directly from a Git repository, and many offer free basic hosting packages. It's a resource worth checking out once you have an application ready to share with the world.

Summary

In this chapter, we have looked at Node.js, an application framework built to allow JavaScript developers the ability to write command line applications, web servers, and server-side applications. In addition, we've seen the Node Package Manager and associated npm tool, the importance of the package.json file, and seen how to import dependent code packages for use in our Node.js applications. Finally, we looked into some popular frameworks to help you write scalable web servers for standard HTTP applications as well as modern real-time web socket applications.

In the next chapter, we will look into a set of automated tools, built on a Node.js foundation, that you can apply to your development workflow to both make your day-to-day coding easier and also improve the quality of your JavaScript.

CHAPTER 15

■■■

Build Tools and Automation

The day-to-day workflow for web developers has remained largely unchanged for a number of years, and is largely a manual process of managing assets, writing code, and then testing that code in multiple browsers. Tools have existed for checking code quality and simplifying certain tasks, but these have been run manually and, as such, tend to get forgotten or run inconsistently, making it easy to ignore the results that such checks produce. Similarly, the management of third-party libraries has often been a case of copy-and-paste from project to project with little in the way of version control and management. Finally, the setting up of new projects often involves starting completely from scratch each time, despite the potential for reuse of code from other projects. In this chapter, I will look at the tools available to allow you to automate your development workflow and code release process, manage your third-party dependencies, and set up your projects with a reliable foundation each and every time.

Build Tools

Programmers of other languages are familiar with running a *build process* of some kind when they want to release code; as well as compiling their code for output, this process typically checks code quality against a predefined benchmark, runs unit tests against each of the functions in the code base, and runs other automated tasks as needed for the solution. It's time we, as JavaScript developers, simplify our development workflow, improve our code quality, and package up production-ready versions of our code by applying this same principle to our work by using a JavaScript build tool, or automated task runner.

Build tools serve any web developer who wants to run tasks automatically against their code base, such as JavaScript static code analysis, unit testing and minifcation, image compression, SASS (http://sass-lang.com) compilation to CSS, or specialist integration tasks with other systems. If you're working in a team, you can store your build configuration in a file with the rest of your code, allowing everyone to share the same set of tasks. Build tools are used by many companies and project teams globally, including Adobe, Twitter, and jQuery. Within the development team I lead at AKQA, we use the build tools covered in this chapter on every project we run.

Throughout the chapters we have come across a number of tools designed to aid the professional JavaScript developer—to simplify the onboarding of new developers, improve quality of their code, and reduce the size of their code. From the automatic code documentation generator in Chapter 2 and the code quality tools in Chapter 3, to the minification and obfuscation tools in Chapter 4, all served the purpose of ensuring that our code was the best it could be and the easiest to understand. In this section, we are going to look at how to bring all these types of tools together with task runners that will automate a typical development workflow and produce production-ready versions of your code files for public release.

A task runner is one that allows you to chain together a series of tasks, or actions, that can then run in sequence to perform certain actions against your code. Some popular command line task runners that you may have had experience with if you've come to JavaScript from other programming languages include Ant (http://bit.ly/ant-build), Gradle (http://bit.ly/gradle-build), Rake (http://bit.ly/rake-build), Make (http://bit.ly/make-build), and Maven (http://bit.ly/maven-build). For JavaScript-based projects, it makes sense to have a command line task runner that executes JavaScript-based tasks natively so that developers can easily write and adapt their own tasks for their specific needs. It also allows any JavaScript file in the project to be processed and executed natively, enabling profiling and code checks to be easily run. By basing such a build system on the Node.js application platform, we have the added benefit of cross-platform compatibility.

Grunt—The JavaScript Task Runner

The most popular build tool used by professional JavaScript developers at the time of writing is Grunt (`http://gruntjs.com`), which you may recall was mentioned briefly in Chapter 3. Grunt is an automated task runner, written in JavaScript and running via Node.js, which can be set up with any number of plugin tasks, configured to run as and when needed, either individually or in a defined sequence, to help you automate your JavaScript workflow—checking the quality of your code, concatenating files together, minifying them, and essentially producing the final JavaScript code you're most happy with releasing to the public. By automating a task sequence, you ensure that steps don't get missed and that tasks always run in the correct order, resulting in a consistent development workflow and build process.

Figure 15-1. *The Grunt homepage features a wealth of resources to help you get started running tasks*

At the time of writing, Grunt has over three thousand plugin tasks, listed at `http://bit.ly/grunt-plugins`, available for use in your task sequence, covering the most popular tasks you may wish to perform.

Installing Grunt

Before we start using Grunt, we need to install the Grunt Command Line Interface (CLI) tool, available via http://bit.ly/grunt-cli, which provides access to the Grunt command line tool globally across all the folders on your machine. The Grunt CLI tool allows you to run different versions of the Grunt task runner within different project folders, which is great news if you plan to have multiple projects installed on your machine.

To install the Grunt CLI tool, execute the following at the command prompt within any folder on your machine (Mac and Linux users may have to precede this command with sudo to authenticate as a super user):

```
npm install -g grunt-cli
```

The Grunt CLI tool, the Grunt task runner, and each of its plugin tasks are all Node.js packages, hosted in the NPM directory. To download the Grunt task runner tool for use with your project, execute the following command within your project directory (run npm init to set up a new package.json file if you don't already have one in this folder):

```
npm install grunt --save-dev
```

Note the use of the --save-dev command line parameter, which automatically saves a reference to the specific version of the downloaded Grunt package in the devDependencies section of the package.json file. This is to specifically denote that Grunt is a tool for use in development only, and is not a package required to run the project code itself. Similarly, all other tasks that we install will be placed within this devDependencies section. For example, to install the JSHint plugin task for Grunt to perform static code analysis on your JavaScript files, execute the following on the command line. More details about this plugin, named grunt-contrib-jshint, can be found via http://bit.ly/grunt_jshint—the contrib part of the plugin name indicates that it is an official plugin for Grunt developed by the same team as the task runner tool itself:

```
npm install grunt-contrib-jshint --save-dev
```

Configuring Grunt Tasks

With Grunt and its associated JSHint plugin installed in our project folder, the next step is to configure Grunt to execute our plugin task with our chosen settings. Grunt is configured through a configuration file, known as a *Gruntfile*, which must be named Gruntfile.js and should exist in the root folder of your project, in the same location as your package.json file.

The Gruntfile is a standard JavaScript file that will be run along with the Grunt tool via the Node.js application framework, and should be configured as a Node.js module—any code that we wish to make accessible outside the file, and therefore to Grunt itself, must be set to the module.exports property within the Gruntfile.

The Gruntfile.js file should be initialized with a wrapper function, providing access to the Grunt API through a grunt parameter, and then made publicly accessible through the module.exports property. All of our Grunt configuration settings will then exist within this function's body:

```
module.exports = function(grunt) {
    // Configuration goes here. The 'grunt' function parameter contains the Grunt API methods.
};
```

The next step is to load each of the plugin task packages that we wish Grunt to be able to run by using the API's loadNpmTasks() method. The following line of code should be repeated for each plugin, substituting the plugin name in the relevant place:

```
grunt.loadNpmTasks("grunt-contrib-jshint");
```

We can now configure our task settings using the initConfig() method of the Grunt API. We pass a JavaScript object to this method, with one property per task containing the settings to apply to that task. For the JSHint plugin task, the property name to use is jshint—the exact task name to use will be detailed in the documentation for any plugin you choose to reference. For the JSHint task this documentation is available online at http://bit.ly/grunt_jshint.

The JSHint plugin documentation details the settings that can be applied to this task, which include a src property for referencing the files to apply the task to, and an options property for specifying the exact rules to use to override the default settings. The full list of JSHint rule options can be viewed online at http://bit.ly/jshint_opts. If we wish to run the JSHint task against all the JavaScript files in a specific subdirectory of our project folder named scripts/, as well as against the Gruntile.js itself, we could use the following array value for the src property for this task:

```
src: ["Gruntfile.js", "scripts/*.js"]
```

Note how we can specify not only exact filenames but also use the asterisk (*) wildcard value to refer to all files matching a specific file name pattern. The "scripts/*.js" pattern, for example, matches any file with a .js extension directly within the scripts/ folder. A pattern containing double-asterisks (**), such "scripts/**/*.js", however, would match all files with a .js extension within not just the scripts/ directory, but any subdirectory of that folder also. The double-asterisk pattern can be very useful if you don't know the exact structure of the folder hierarchy you wish to apply the Grunt task to.

Updating our Gruntfile, therefore, to configure the JSHint task to perform static code analysis on these files, enforcing the use of the strict mode "use strict" statement in all files, is a simple case of passing the configuration object to the initConfig() method of the Grunt API, as shown:

```
grunt.initConfig({
    jshint: {
        options: {
            strict: true
        },
        src: ["Gruntfile.js", "scripts/**/*.js"]
    }
});
```

Any task can be run by specifying its name directly on the command line when executing Grunt; however, we need the ability to easily manage a list of tasks that will eventually run in sequence, which we can achieve by defining an *alias* task name and associating it with the list of tasks that we wish to execute. Passing this alias name to Grunt on the command line would then execute all the associated tasks in turn. For simplicity, Grunt will allow an alias task named default to execute without needing to pass its name on the command line. Alias tasks are registered in the Gruntfile using the registerTask() method of the Grunt API, as shown; we can add more tasks at a later stage by adding to the list of tasks in the array:

```
grunt.registerTask("default", ["jshint"]);
```

Listing 15-1 shows the final version of our basic Gruntfile. Name this file Gruntfile.js so it will be identified by Grunt.

Listing 15-1. A basic Gruntfile

```javascript
// Specify the wrapper function, which will be passed the Grunt API as a parameter, making this
// function externally available outside of this file by applying it to the module.exports
// property, as with any other Node.js modules
module.exports = function(grunt) {

    // Load the Grunt plugin tasks we have previously installed with the npm tool
    grunt.loadNpmTasks("grunt-contrib-jshint");

    // Configure the JSHint task loaded previously with options to apply to the listed files
    grunt.initConfig({
        jshint: {
            options: {
                strict: true
            },

            // The use of the ** and * wildcard values ensures all .js files within the
            // scripts/ folder and any subfolders are loaded for use with JSHint
            src: ["Gruntfile.js", "scripts/**/*.js"]
        }
    });

    // Register a task alias. The "default" task name ensures the listed tasks will load
    // simply by executing the "grunt" command on the command line
    grunt.registerTask("default", ["jshint"]);
};
```

Running Grunt

To run Grunt with its `default` task alias, simply execute the following on the command line:

```
grunt
```

If you wish to run a single task, or another named alias, you can specify the task or alias name directly on the command line, as shown:

```
grunt jshint
```

Using the Gruntfile from Listing 15-1, the output shown in Figure 15-2 is produced when Grunt is run, indicating that an error has occurred and giving details of that error. The build stops at this point until the error is fixed and Grunt is run again. The response indicates that the Gruntfile is missing a `"use strict"` statement, a condition we enforced in our task configuration.

```
○ ○ ○          15-Build Tools And Automation — bash — 78×13
den-macbook-pro:15-Build Tools And Automation dennis.odell$ grunt
Running "jshint:src" (jshint) task

  Gruntfile.js
    2 |    grunt.loadNpmTasks("grunt-contrib-jshint");
           ^ Missing "use strict" statement.

>> 1 error in 2 files
Warning: Task "jshint:src" failed. Use --force to continue.

Aborted due to warnings.
den-macbook-pro:15-Build Tools And Automation dennis.odell$ ▯
```

Figure 15-2. The command line output from Grunt, indicating that a warning has occurred

Adding a `"use strict"` statement into the top of the function in the Gruntfile and rerunning Grunt produces the response shown in Figure 15-3, indicating that the JSHint task has now succeeded and so the Grunt `default` alias task has completed without error.

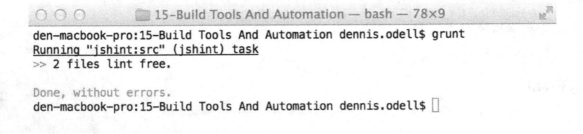

```
○ ○ ○          15-Build Tools And Automation — bash — 78×9
den-macbook-pro:15-Build Tools And Automation dennis.odell$ grunt
Running "jshint:src" (jshint) task
>> 2 files lint free.

Done, without errors.
den-macbook-pro:15-Build Tools And Automation dennis.odell$ ▯
```

Figure 15-3. The command line output from Grunt, indicating that all tasks have completed successfully

Extended Grunt Configuration

Grunt supports more features than those we've covered so far, including support for JSON data file importing, multitasks allowing alternative configuration settings for different requirements, and the ability to write your own custom plugins where there is no acceptable existing solution. The plugins directory can be found at `http://bit.ly/grunt-plugins`.

JSON File Importing

The Grunt API contains a series of methods for handling the reading, writing, and copying of external files. The most commonly used of these is the `file.readJSON()` method that allows the data stored in an external JSON-format file to be loaded into the Gruntfile, making its data available as a standard JavaScript object to be used in task configuration. Usually, the properties stored in the `package.json` file are imported to give access to project details such as name, version, description, and any other properties stored within.

■ **Note** A companion `file.readYAML()` method in the Grunt API allows YAML-formatted data files to be read into a Grunt configuration file. The YAML format is designed to be a more human-readable equivalent of JSON, better suited for cases in which data files need to be edited often by humans rather than machines. To read more about this data format, visit the project homepage at `http://yaml.org`.

Load the contents of the `package.json` file into a Gruntfile as shown, setting the return value to the `pkg` property in the configuration object used with the `initConfig()` method:

```
grunt.initConfig({
    pkg: grunt.file.readJSON("package.json")
});
```

Values can then be read out from the `pkg` object property, or any other named property in the configuration object for that matter, within string values surrounded by template delimiters `<%=` and `%>`. To read the `name` and `version` properties from the `package.json` file, for example, and use them within our JSHint task, we reference them as shown:

```
grunt.initConfig({
    pkg: grunt.file.readJSON("package.json"),
    jshint: {
        options: {
            strict: true
        },
        src: ["Gruntfile.js", "<%= pkg.name %>-<%= pkg.version %>.js"]
    }
});
```

Assuming that our `package.json` file contains the following properties, for example:

```
{
    "name": "my-project",
    "version": "0.0.1"
}
```

our JSHint configuration will effectively resolve to the following array value in its `src` configuration property:

```
src: ["Gruntfile.js", my-project-0.0.1.js"]
```

The values within the template strings are replaced with the designated values before Grunt runs, as if these values were hardcoded in the file. We can reference them in multiple places and a simple change to properties in our `package.json` file results in all the necessary changes being made to our task configuration wherever required in our Gruntfile without any extra effort on our part.

Multi-Tasks and Targets

Grunt supports the ability to split each task configuration into several separate configurations allowing different task options to accommodate different scenarios, such as appling different settings to different files, for example. This feature is known as *multitasks* and is achieved by adding an extra named object property beneath each task property name in the configuration section of the Gruntfile. Each of these multitask configuration objects is known as a *target*, and different targets can be run through Grunt one at a time, or all targets run together in the order that they are defined.

The code in Listing 15-2 shows a complete Gruntfile with two targets configured for the JSHint multitask, which are named grunt and project, respectively. The settings in the jshint.options property will apply to all targets but can be overridden on a per-target basis with an additional options object placed within each target's individual configuration property.

Listing 15-2. Gruntfile with multiple targets specified for a JSHint multitask

```
module.exports = function(grunt) {

    // Enable strict mode
    "use strict";

    grunt.loadNpmTasks("grunt-contrib-jshint");

    grunt.initConfig({

        // Load external data from another file for use within task configuration
        pkg: grunt.file.readJSON("package.json"),
        jshint: {

            // Apply a set of JSHint options to apply to all targets
            options: {
                strict: true
            },

            // Define a target with settings to apply in addition to those defined for all
            // JSHint tasks above, including which files to apply JSHint to
            grunt: {
                src: ["Gruntfile.js"]
            },

            // Define a second target, named "project"
            project: {

                // Apply extra options for this target, in addition to those options applied
                // for all JSHint tasks. In this case, both "strict" and "trailing" properties
                // will be set to "true". Settings at this level with the same name as those
                // previously defined will cause the setting to be overwritten
                options: {
                    trailing: true
                },

                // Use the settings from the package.json file, stored locally in the "pkg"
                // property to dynamically apply values to the Gruntfile configuration
                src: ["<%= pkg.name %>-<%= pkg.version %>.js"]
```

```
                }
            }
    });

    grunt.registerTask("default", ["jshint"]);
};
```

Running Grunt against the Gruntfile shown in Listing 15-2 produces the output shown in Figure 15-4, with each individual target in a multitask run in turn in the order specificed within the Gruntfile itself.

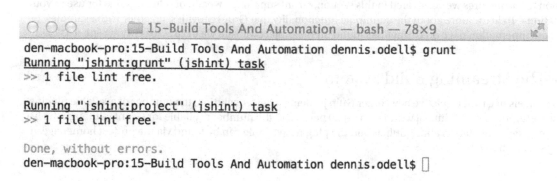

Figure 15-4. *Running Grunt with a JSHint multitask containing two separate targets*

Specific targets can be executed within an alias task, or directly on the command line, by specifying the task name followed by a colon character (:) and then the target name. To run the project target of the JSHint task on the command line, for example, execute the following command, which will produce the output shown in Figure 15-5:

```
grunt jshint:project
```

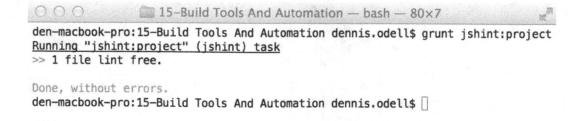

Figure 15-5. *Executing a single target of an individual Grunt multitask*

Multitasks are powerful and become more useful as your Gruntfile grows, allowing you to separate tasks into more specific targets tailored toward your exact requirements.

Writing Your Own Grunt Plugin

You may find as you develop in your experience with Grunt that the exact plugin you require is not present in the plugin directory. If this is the case, you'll be glad to hear you can write your own custom plugin in JavaScript to meet your specific project need. Review the documentation online via `http://bit.ly/grunt-write-plugin` to find out how to write your own Grunt plugin.

In addition to the features we've covered in this section, Grunt supports a wealth of other options for use in your task configurations. To learn more about the additional functionality that Grunt provides, together with examples, check out the documentation page on Grunt tasks found on the project website via `http://bit.ly/grunt-tasks`.

Gulp.js—The Streaming Build System

Snapping at the heels of Grunt is relative newcomer Gulp.js. Being a newer solution, the number of available plugins stands at over six hundred at the time of writing, about 20 percent of the number available for Grunt, although the list is growing by the week. Full details about Gulp.js and the plugins available can be found via the project homepage at `http://gulpjs.com`, shown in Figure 15-6.

Figure 15-6. *The Gulp.js project homepage*

The Gulp.js build system is built on Node.js and performs the ability to run tasks in a similar way to Grunt although with three distinct differences. First, it utilizes Node.js's *streams* functionality, which allows the output of one task to feed, or *pipe*, into the input of another without needing an intermediary step of writing temporary files to disk; this makes task running more efficient and, in most cases, faster. Second, configuration is moved away from a single, large configuration object in favor of a code-based, chained method-calling approach, with the relevant configuration passed into methods representing each task. Third, Gulp.js tasks are deliberately designed to be small—to do one thing and do that one thing well—meaning that large tasks perform multiple actions are shunned in favour of connecting together smaller tasks, with the output of one task feeding into the next.

Installing Gulp.js

To install Gulp.js for use in all your projects across any folder in your system, execute the following on the command line (Mac and Linux users may need to precede the command with sudo):

```
npm install -g gulp
```

Next, install the gulp package into your project folder, saving it to the devDependencies section of your package.json file—execute npm init to initialize a package.json file first if you don't already have one:

```
npm install gulp --save-dev
```

Just as with Grunt, plugin tasks are installed through the npm tool. To install the JSHint task for Gulp.js, we need to install the gulp-jshint task by executing the following on the command line, saving its reference to the devDependencies section of our package.json file:

```
npm install gulp-jshint --save-dev
```

Documentation for this task can be found online at http://bit.ly/gulp-jshint.

Configuring Gulp.js

As with Grunt, a JavaScript configuration file is required to set up the tasks to run and in which order. This file is known as a *gulpfile* and must be named gulpfile.js. Rather than creating a Node.js module, as with Grunt, the structure of this configuration file is actually a Node.js application in itself. To set up the file, therefore, we need to require() the "gulp" package and call the methods exposed from this, which represent the Gulp.js API.

Plugins are Node.js modules that expose methods representing their functionality, so they do not define task names directly as they do in Grunt. To define a task, therefore, the task() method of the Gulp.js API must be called, passing in a unique name for the new task and a function to execute when the task is run, executing any referenced plugin methods and returning the output.

The basic structure for a gulpfile is as follows:

```
var gulp = require("gulp");

gulp.task("default", function() {
    // Tasks get called here, with the output returned to the calling function
});
```

The Gulp.js API contains methods that we will use inside our gulpfile tasks, including src(), which lets us define the file list to apply to our plugin, dest(), which allows us to write the output of plugins and other methods to the file system, and pipe(), which passes the output of one plugin or method to the next. Each method is designed to be chained, resulting in tasks represented by a series of small constituent function calls.

Listing 15-3 shows a sample gulpfile defining a jshint task, which loads in a set of files before passing these to the JSHint plugin method to run static code analysis against those files. The results are then passed to a reporter function that displays the results of the code analysis in the command window—exactly the kind of division of tasks that Gulp.js is built on and that makes it so easy to configure. As with Grunt, alias tasks, including a default task, can be defined to group together other tasks into a series that should be executed in sequence.

Listing 15-3. A sample gulpfile

```javascript
// Reference the gulp package and JSHint plugin package
var gulp = require("gulp"),
    jshint = require("gulp-jshint");

// Define a Gulp.js task, naming it "jshint" - we can then execute it directly by name, or link
// it together with other tasks under an alias name, to be executed in sequence
gulp.task("jshint", function() {

    // Return the result of the operation to the calling function
    // Locate the files to use with this task - here, this gulpfile itself and any .js file
    // within the scripts/ folder and its subfolders
    return gulp.src(["gulpfile.js", "scripts/**/*.js"])

        // Pipe those files to the "jshint" plugin, specifying the options to apply - here, we
        // ensure strict mode is enforced in the selected files. This runs JSHint but does not
        // display its results
        .pipe(jshint({
            strict: true
        }))

        // Finally, pipe the output of JSHint to a reporter for displaying on the command line.
        // By splitting up JSHint into one part that performs the static code analysis and one
        // part that displays the results, we are capable of creating more functional tasks
        // that can take the direct results from JSHint and use them in any other way we
        // wish to. This is what makes Gulp.js so highly configurable.
        .pipe(jshint.reporter("default"));
});

// Define a default task - naming it "default" ensures it will be executed without the need to
// pass through a specific task name from the command line
gulp.task("default", ["jshint"]);
```

Running Gulp.js

Run the Gulp.js tool against the code in Listing 15-3, which should first be saved in a file named gulpfile.js, by executing the following on the command line:

```
gulp
```

The default task will be executed because no task name was provided, producing the result shown in Figure 15-7.

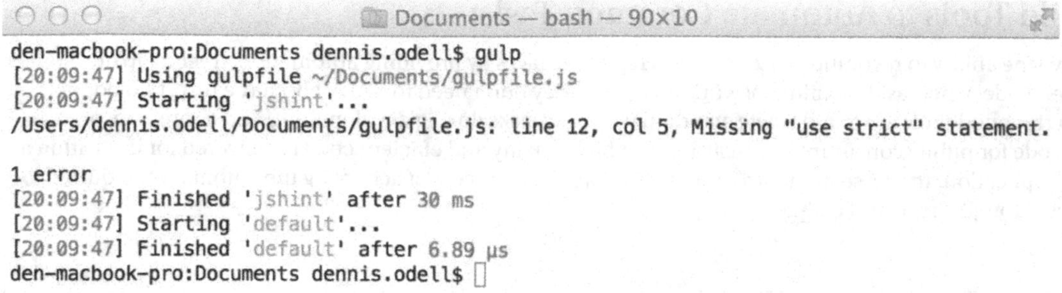

```
○ ○ ○                    📖 Documents — bash — 90×10                          ⤢
den-macbook-pro:Documents dennis.odell$ gulp
[20:09:47] Using gulpfile ~/Documents/gulpfile.js
[20:09:47] Starting 'jshint'...
/Users/dennis.odell/Documents/gulpfile.js: line 12, col 5, Missing "use strict" statement.

1 error
[20:09:47] Finished 'jshint' after 30 ms
[20:09:47] Starting 'default'...
[20:09:47] Finished 'default' after 6.89 µs
den-macbook-pro:Documents dennis.odell$ ▯
```

Figure 15-7. The command line output from Gulp.js, indicating that an error has occurred

The response indicates that the gulpfile.js file is missing a "use strict" statement. Adding this statement into the top of the function in the gulpfile and rerunning Gulp.js, produces the response shown in Figure 15-8, indicating that JSHint has run successfully and therefore the whole Gulp.js default alias task has completed without error.

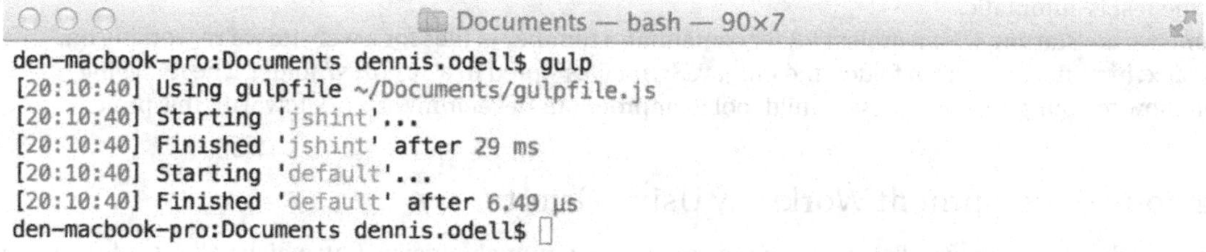

```
○ ○ ○                    📖 Documents — bash — 90×7                           ⤢
den-macbook-pro:Documents dennis.odell$ gulp
[20:10:40] Using gulpfile ~/Documents/gulpfile.js
[20:10:40] Starting 'jshint'...
[20:10:40] Finished 'jshint' after 29 ms
[20:10:40] Starting 'default'...
[20:10:40] Finished 'default' after 6.49 µs
den-macbook-pro:Documents dennis.odell$ ▯
```

Figure 15-8. The command line output from Gulp.js, indicating that all tasks have completed successfully

Extended Gulp.js Configuration

Because a gulpfile is simply a Node.js application, what required special API methods and template strings in Grunt configuration requires nothing of the sort here. To import the properties from a package.json file for use in your task setup, simply use the Node.js require() method and access the properties directly as a standard JavaScript object:

```
var pkg = require("package.json");
pkg.name;   // "my-project"
pkg.version; // "0.0.1"
```

Writing Your Own Gulp.js Plugin

You may find as you develop in your experience with Gulp.js that the exact plugin you require is not present in the plugin directory. If this is the case, you'll be glad to hear you can write your own custom plugin in JavaScript to meet your specific project need. Review the documentation online at http://bit.ly/gulp-write-plugin to find out how to write your own Gulp.js plugin.

In addition to the features we've covered in this section, Gulp.js supports a wealth of other options for use in your task configurations. To learn more about the additional functionality that Gulp.js provides, together with examples, check out the documentation page on the Gulp.js API found on the project website at http://bit.ly/gulp-api.

Using Build Tools to Automate Common Tasks

Build tools have the ability to revolutionize common repetitive tasks by providing automation, freeing up developers to focus on their code, whereas the build tool works to ensure they don't need to worry about the rest. Two popular uses for JavaScript build tools are to automate standard workflow tasks during development, and to prepare, or *build*, a set of code for public consumption, ensuring that high-quality and efficient code is delivered for use within a resulting web application. In this section, I will take you through the process of achieving the automation required to meet both uses through Grunt and Gulp.js.

Improving Your Development Workflow

Professional JavaScript developers want to spend their time working on their code, yet need to ensure that when they need to run their code in a browser that it is error-free, up to date, and doesn't involve a time-consuming setup process before seeing any results. In this section, we are going to configure both Grunt and Gulp.js to spin up a local web server to run our code and check our JavaScript files for potential errors using static code analysis. It will then wait for us to make changes to our files, rerunning the static code analysis when we do and dynamically reloading any open web browser connected to our local web server once the analysis is complete. We just need to start our chosen build tool and the rest is automatic.

Let's assume we are starting with a project folder containing a number of files for a website we're working on, including an `index.html` file in our root folder and our JavaScript files stored in a `scripts/` folder. The following sections explain how to configure your chosen build tool to improve our development workflow with this project.

Improving Your Development Workflow Using Grunt

We can improve our development workflow through the use of three Grunt plugins: JSHint, which will provide static code analysis, Connect (`http://bit.ly/grunt-connect`), which will spin up a local web server quickly and easily, and Watch (`http://bit.ly/grunt-watch`), which is a file-change observer—it will look for changes made to files in a specified folder, triggering static code analysis and reloading any open web page connected to the local web server when they are altered in any way.

Dynamic web page reloading is achieved through the Live Reload feature (`http://livereload.com`). The local web server injects a special JavaScript file reference into any HTML page it serves, opening and maintaining a web socket connection to the server. When changes are made to code files, the Watch task broadcasts a message over this socket connection, instructing the web browser to reload the page, causing it to load the changes made to the files that changed.

Start by installing Grunt and the three required plugins into your project directory (use `npm init` to setup a `package.json` file if none exists in this folder):

```
npm install grunt --save-dev
npm install grunt-contrib-jshint --save-dev
npm install grunt-contrib-connect --save-dev
npm install grunt-contrib-watch --save-dev
```

The code in Listing 15-4 shows a Gruntfile that can be used to improve your development workflow by spinning up a web server, running static code analysis using JSHint whenever a JavaScript file is changed, and automatically refreshing open browser windows connected to that server at the same time. Follow the inline code comments to understand how each task is configured.

Listing 15-4. Gruntfile to improve development workflow

```javascript
module.exports = function(grunt) {
    "use strict";

    // Define the location of the JavaScript files in our application that we wish to run our
    // tasks against - along with this Gruntfile, the use of wildcard (* and **) values means
    // that we're representing .js files within the scripts/ folder directly, as well as files
    // one level beneath that in the folder hierarchy
    var scriptFiles = ["Gruntfile.js", "scripts/**/*.js"];

    // Load the JSHint, Connect and Watch plugin tasks previously installed via npm
    grunt.loadNpmTasks("grunt-contrib-jshint");
    grunt.loadNpmTasks("grunt-contrib-connect");
    grunt.loadNpmTasks("grunt-contrib-watch");

    // Configure Grunt with the JSHint, Connect and Watch tasks
    grunt.initConfig({

        // Configure the JSHint task to perform static code analysis on the files in our
        // scripts/ folder and enforce strict mode in all
        jshint: {
            options: {
                strict: true
            },
            src: scriptFiles
        },

        // Configure the Connect task to start up a web server at http://localhost:3000 - by
        // default it will point to the files in the root of the project folder, so a file
        // named index.html in the root folder will be displayed when browser this new URL.
        // By enabling the "livereload" property, the server will inject a reference to a
        // Live Reload script into your HTML pages automatically - used in conjunction with
        // another task that will trigger the Live Reload in specific circumstances, such as
        // the Watch task, below
        connect: {
            server: {
                options: {
                    port: 3000,
                    livereload: true
                }
            }
        },

        // Configure the Watch task to observe changes made to any JavaScript file in our
        // scripts/ folder and trigger the JSHint task when those files are changed, ensuring
        // code quality standards are kept high throughout project development. Enabling the
        // "livereload" option ensures that any Live Reload script in a running web page is
        // notified once the JSHint task has run, causing it to be reloaded automatically,
        // saving us the task of manually refreshing the page. This option thus works in
        // conjunction with the Live Reload script injected into the page by the Connect task
        watch: {
```

```
        scripts: {
            files: scriptFiles,
            tasks: ["jshint"],
            options: {
                livereload: true
            }
        }
    }

    // Extra targets can be added in here for different file types, such as CSS or HTML
    // files, to allow specific tasks to be triggered when those file types are changed
    }
});

// Configure the default Grunt task to run JSHint, Connect and Watch tasks in sequence.
// The Watch plugin will continue to monitor for changes and, together with the LiveReload
// capability, will ensure that the web site hosted on our new web server will be kept
// up to date automatically as we change the JavaScript files in our project - no need to
// even press Refresh in our browsers!
grunt.registerTask("default", ["jshint", "connect", "watch"]);
};
```

Running Grunt against the code in Listing 15-4, saved to a file named Gruntfile.js, will execute JSHint against the JavaScript files in the scripts/ folder and then cause a web server to spin up on http://localhost:3000, pointing to the files in our project folder. The Grunt process will remain active in the command window as it watches for changes made to JavaScript files. When it detects a change is made, it will rerun JSHint against the updated files, reloading any open browser window viewing the index.html page, or any other HTML page in our web application. If you wish to stop the Grunt process, use the Ctrl+C (Windows, Linux) or Cmd+C (Mac) keyboard shortcuts to terminate the command.

Improving Your Development Workflow Using Gulp.js

We can achieve this automated development workflow through Gulp.js by taking advantage of the JSHint and Connect (http://bit.ly/gulp-connect) plugins. There is no separate Watch plugin, as there is with Grunt, as file-change observing functionality is built directly into the Gulp.js API through its watch() method. Although this method does not support Live Reload directly, we can configure a custom Watch task to execute this method followed by a call to the reload() method of the Connect plugin, which will procuce the result that we require.

Start by installing Gulp.js and the two required plugins into your project directory (use npm init to setup a package.json file if none exists in this folder):

```
npm install gulp --save-dev
npm install gulp-jshint --save-dev
npm install gulp-connect --save-dev
```

The code in Listing 15-5 shows a gulpfile that can be used to improve your development workflow by spinning up a web server, running static code analysis using JSHint whenever a JavaScript file is changed, and automatically refreshing open browser windows connected to that server at the same time. Follow the inline code comments to understand how each task is configured.

Listing 15-5. Gulpfile to improve development workflow

```javascript
// Load the Gulp package, along with the JSHint and Connect plugins for Gulp, all of which
// have previously been installed through npm
var gulp = require("gulp"),
    jshint = require("gulp-jshint"),
    connect = require("gulp-connect"),

    // Define the location of the JavaScript files in our application that we wish to run our
    // tasks against - this gulpfile and any .js file within the scripts/ folder and its
    // sub directories
    scriptFiles = ["gulpfile.js", "scripts/**/*.js"];

// Define a Connect task, which will start up a web server at http://localhost:3000, pointing
// to the files stored in the project root folder. Enabling the "livereload" property injects
// a Live Reload script into any running HTML page so that, if a message is received to reload
// the page, or any files within, the browser will do so - we will trigger this message in the
// JSHint task below
gulp.task("connect", function() {
    "use strict";

    connect.server({
        port: 3000,
        livereload: true
    });
});

// Define the JSHint task to perform static code analysis on our code files, ensuring that
// strict mode is enabled for all our functions. This is similar to the JSHint task from
// Listing 15-3 with an additional command at the end of the function chain to force a Live
// Reload of any running HTML page through the web server spun up in the Connect task previously
gulp.task("jshint", function() {
    "use strict";

    return gulp.src(scriptFiles)
        .pipe(jshint({
            strict: true
        }))
        .pipe(jshint.reporter("default"))

        // Send the message through the web server to perform a Live Reload of any HTML pages
        // running from the server in any connected web browser
        .pipe(connect.reload());
});

// Define a Watch task to execute the JSHint task when any of the predefined JavaScript files
// are altered. Gulp.js features its own built-in watch() method - no external plugin required
gulp.task("watch", function() {
    "use strict";

    gulp.watch(scriptFiles, ["jshint"]);
});
```

```
// Configure the default Grunt task to run JSHint, Connect and Watch tasks in sequence, ensuring
// high code quality whilst hosting our application and reloading the browser when changes are
// made to JavaScript files
gulp.task("default", ["jshint", "connect", "watch"]);
```

Running the Gulp.js tool against the code in Listing 15-5, saved to a file named gulpfile.js, will execute JSHint against the JavaScript files in the scripts/ folder and then cause a web server to spin up on http://localhost:3000, pointing to the files in our project folder. The Gulp.js process will remain active in the command window as it watches for changes made to JavaScript files. When it detects a change is made, it will rerun JSHint against the updated files, reloading any open browser window viewing the index.html page, or any other HTML page in our web application. If you wish to stop the Gulp.js process, use the Ctrl+C (Windows, Linux) or Cmd+C (Mac) keyboard shortcuts to terminate the command.

Creating Production-Ready Code

The JavaScript code that developers prefer to work with is often split over several files, providing logical division of the application's structure and allowing simpler collobration between several members of a project team. The ideal JavaScript code for public consumption, however, should be spread over as few files as necessary, to reduce HTTP requests, and minified to reduce file size and improve download times. Rather than have to compromise, choosing one structure over the other, the professional JavaScript developer turns to build tools to automate the generation of this form of production-ready code from their original development files, ensuring that only high-quality code is released by combining this with static code analysis and running unit tests, generating reports on code coverage and even having the ability to automatically generate a documentation website based on specially formatted code comments in their original JavaScript files.

So as to provide a good separation between development code and release code, many developers choose to perform their development work within a single folder, often named src/, which forms the basis of the original set of files to apply to the build tool. The build will typically then generate a separate folder, often named dist/, into which the production-ready version of all the application files will be placed. Using this structure, there can be little confusion as to which files should be used for development and which are automatically generated through the build process, and providing a single output folder for use when deploying the application code to a live web server for public consumption.

Let's assume that we are starting with a src/ folder within our project folder, containing a number of files for a web site we're working on, including an index.html file and our JavaScript files stored in a scripts/ subfolder. The following sections explain how to configure your chosen build tool to create production-ready code.

Creating Production-Ready Code Using Grunt

We can add to our code to improve our development workflow to create production-ready code through the use of seven additional Grunt plugins: Clean (http://bit.ly/grunt-clean), which will empty the contents of a folder (in this case the dist/ folder, ensuring that it is emptied each time the build is run), Copy (http://bit.ly/grunt-copy), which will copy over selected static non-JavaScript files from the src/ directory to the dist/ directory, Jasmine (http://bit.ly/grunt-jasmine), and an associated Istanbul plugin (http://bit.ly/grunt-istanbul), to run unit tests and produce code coverage reports, Concat (http://bit.ly/grunt-concat), which we will use to combine the contents of several JavaScript files together into one, Uglify (http://bit.ly/grunt-uglify), which will minify this single JavaScript file, reducing its size, and YUIDoc (http://bit.ly/grunt-yuidoc), which will generate a documentation site using specially formatted JavaScript code comments.

Start by installing Grunt and the required plugins into your project directory (use `npm init` to setup a package.json file if none exists in this folder):

```
npm install grunt --save-dev
npm install grunt-contrib-jshint --save-dev
npm install grunt-contrib-connect --save-dev
npm install grunt-contrib-watch --save-dev
npm install grunt-contrib-clean --save-dev
npm install grunt-contrib-copy --save-dev
npm install grunt-contrib-jasmine --save-dev
npm install grunt-template-jasmine-istanbul --save-dev
npm install grunt-contrib-concat --save-dev
npm install grunt-contrib-uglify --save-dev
npm install grunt-contrib-yuidoc --save-dev
```

The code in Listing 15-6 shows a complete Gruntfile that, in addition to improving your development workflow, can be used to produce a production-ready version of JavaScript code stored in a `src/scripts/` folder. Follow the inline code comments to understand how each task is configured.

Listing 15-6. Gruntfile with separate development and build tasks

```
module.exports = function(grunt) {
    "use strict";

    // Define variables to represent the folder and file locations required for task
    // configuration - saves repetition

    // The "src/" folder contains the code we will work on during development, including
    // "scripts/" and "tests/" folders containing our JavaScript code and Jasmine test spec
    // scripts, respectively
    var srcFolder = "src/",
        scriptFolder = srcFolder + "scripts/",
        scriptFiles = scriptFolder + "**/*.js",
        unitTestFolder = srcFolder + "tests/",
        unitTestFiles = unitTestFolder + "**/*.js",

        // The "dist/" folder will be generated automatically by this Gruntfile when run, and
        // populated with the release version of our application files
        outputFolder = "dist/",
        outputScriptFolder = outputFolder + "scripts/",

        // Define the name and location of a single script file into which all others will
        // be concatenated into, becoming the main JavaScript file of our application
        outputScriptFile = outputScriptFolder + "main.js",

        // Define the name and location for a minified version of our single application script
        outputScriptFileMinified = outputScriptFolder + "main.min.js",

        // Define output folders for generated Istanbul reports and YUIDoc documentation files
        outputReportFolder = outputFolder + "report/",
        outputDocsFolder = outputFolder + "docs/";
```

```
// Load the JSHint, Connect and Watch tasks, which will be used for local development
grunt.loadNpmTasks("grunt-contrib-jshint");
grunt.loadNpmTasks("grunt-contrib-connect");
grunt.loadNpmTasks("grunt-contrib-watch");

// Load the Clean, Copy, Jasmine, Concat, Uglify and YUIDoc tasks, which will be used
// together with JSHint (loaded previously) to form our release build, preparing all
// files for public consumption
grunt.loadNpmTasks("grunt-contrib-clean");
grunt.loadNpmTasks("grunt-contrib-copy");
grunt.loadNpmTasks("grunt-contrib-jasmine");
grunt.loadNpmTasks("grunt-contrib-concat");
grunt.loadNpmTasks("grunt-contrib-uglify");
grunt.loadNpmTasks("grunt-contrib-yuidoc");

// Configure Grunt for all tasks
grunt.initConfig({

    // Load the properties from the package.json file into a property for use in task
    // configuration
    pkg: grunt.file.readJSON("package.json"),

    // Configure JSHint as in Listing 15-4
    jshint: {
        options: {
            strict: true
        },
        src: scriptFiles
    },

    // Configure Connect as in Listing 15-4
    connect: {
        server: {
            options: {
                port: 3000,
                livereload: true,

                // Now we're working within the "src/" folder, use this as the location
                // to find the files to host on this web server
                base: srcFolder
            }
        }
    },

    // Configure Watch as in Listing 15-4
    watch: {
        scripts: {
            files: scriptFiles,
            tasks: ["jshint"],
            options: {
                livereload: true
```

```
            }
        }
    },

    // Probably the simplest Grunt plugin to configure, the Clean task empties the contents
    // of a given folder - here we wish to ensure the "dist/" folder is empty each time
    // we wish to regenerate our production-ready files
    clean: [outputFolder],

    // We'll use the Copy task to duplicate static files from the "src/" folder that need
    // no extra processing, placing them into the "dist/" folder. In this case, we copy
    // over everything except the contents of the "scripts/" and "tests/" folders
    copy: {
        all: {
            files: [{

                // The use of the exclamation point (!) before a folder or file name
                // causes it to be excluded from the list of files. Here we wish to copy
                // all files witin "src/", except those in the "scripts/" and "tests/"
                // folders, over to the "dist/" output folder
                cwd: srcFolder,
                src: ["**", "!scripts/**", "!tests/**"],
                dest: outputFolder,

                // The "expand" property ensures the orginal folder structure is kept
                // intact when the files are copied over
                expand: true
            }]
        }
    },

    // Configure Jasmine to run together with Istanbul to ensure unit tests pass and to
    // generate a code coverage report which will be placed in the "dist/report" output
    // folder for review. We saw this Jasmine task first in Listing 3-13.
    jasmine: {
        coverage: {
            src: scriptFiles,
            options: {

                // Point to the location of the unit test spec files
                specs: unitTestFiles,

                // Import the Istanbul template plugin for the Jasmine plugin task
                template: require("grunt-template-jasmine-istanbul"),

                // Configure the output folder and file for Istanbul's code coverage
                // reports
                templateOptions: {
                    coverage: outputReportFolder + "coverage.json",
                    report: outputReportFolder
```

```
                    }
                }
            }
        },

        // Instruct the Concat task to combine all the JavaScript files located in the
        // "src/scripts/" folder into a single file, which we'll call "main.js". We can
        // then separate our development across separate JavaScript files and combine them
        // in this stage to avoid the need for an excessive number of HTTP requests to load
        // all our scripts on our page
        concat: {
            scripts: {
                src: scriptFiles,
                dest: outputScriptFile
            }
        },

        // The Uglify task will minify our concatenated JavaScript file, reducing its file
        // size without removing any functionality
        uglify: {

            // The "banner" option allows us to add a comment to the top of the generated
            // minified file, in which we can display the name and version of our project, as
            // taken from our package.json file
            options: {
                banner: "/*! <%= pkg.name %> - version <%= pkg.version %> */\n"
            },
            scripts: {

                // Execute a function to dynamically create the name of the destination file
                // from the variable names above. This is equivalent of an object of the
                // following structure, which will minify the "dist/scripts/main.js" file,
                // storing the result in "dist/scripts/main.min.js", ready for use in our
                // HTML page:
                // {
                //     "dist/scripts/main.min.js": "dist/scripts/main.js"
                // }
                files: (function() {
                    var files = {};

                    files[outputScriptFileMinified] = outputScriptFile;

                    return files;
                }())
            }
        },

        // The YUIDoc task will generate a separate static web site derived from specially
        // formatted comments placed in our JavaScript files, allowing new developers to get
        // up to speed with the structure of the project code without needing to comb through
        // each line of code
```

```
    yuidoc: {
        docs: {

            // The generated site will feature the name and version number, taken directly
            // from the project package.json file
            name: "<%= pkg.name %>",
            version: "<%= pkg.version %>",

            // Tell YUIDoc where to find the JavaScript files for this project, and where
            // to place the generated web site files
            options: {
                paths: scriptFolder,
                outdir: outputDocsFolder
            }
        }
    }
});

// Define the default task to run JSHint, Connect and Watch, for local development
grunt.registerTask("default", ["jshint", "connect", "watch"]);

// Define a new "build" task to empty the "dist/" folder, copy over site files, run JSHint
// and Jasmine to check code quality, generate code coverage reports through Istanbul,
// concatenate the JavaScript files into a single application file, minify the contents of
// that file, and finally generate a documentation site based on the YUIDoc-formatted code
// comments in the original JavaScript files
grunt.registerTask("build", ["clean", "copy", "jshint", "jasmine", "concat", "uglify",
"yuidoc"]);
};
```

Running Grunt against the code in Listing 15-6, saved to a file named Gruntfile.js, will execute either the default task to improve your development workflow, or the separate build task to generate a production-ready version of your JavaScript application code files, depending on which task name is passed to the Grunt tool on the command line when executed. Running the latter task will automatically create or empty out a dist/ folder within your project root folder, copy over static files, such as HTML, image, and stylesheet files (but not JavaScript files) into this new folder, maintaining the same folder structure as exists within the original src/ folder, perform static code analysis and unit test your JavaScript code, generating code coverage reports, before combining the JavaScript files together into a single main.js file which is placed in the dist/scripts/ folder. This file is then minified and saved into the same location under the name main.min.js, from where it can be referenced from your HTML page. Finally, the task creates a documentation website based on specially formatted code comments found in your original JavaScript files.

Creating Production-Ready Code Using Gulp.js

We can add to our code to improve our development workflow to create production-ready code through the use of eight additional Gulp.js plugins: Clean (http://bit.ly/gulp-clean), Jasmine (http://bit.ly/gulp-jasmine), Istanbul (http://bit.ly/gulp-istanbul), Concat (http://bit.ly/gulp-concat), Uglify (http://bit.ly/gulp-uglify), and YUIDoc (http://bit.ly/gulp-yuidoc), which perform similar tasks to their Grunt counterparts, along with Rename (http://bit.ly/gulp-rename), which allows a Gulp.js task to save out a file with a different name than its input file, ideal for giving our minified JavaScript file a .min.js file suffix, and Header (http://bit.ly/gulp-header), which allows an extra text string to be inserted at the start of any file, perfect for adding a comment to the start of our minified JavaScript file detailing the project name and version number – something that was provided automatically by Grunt's Uglify plugin.

Start by installing Gulp.js and the required plugins into your project directory (use `npm init` to set up a `package.json` file if none exists in this folder):

```
npm install gulp --save-dev
npm install gulp-jshint --save-dev
npm install gulp-connect --save-dev
npm install gulp-clean --save-dev
npm install gulp-jasmine --save-dev
npm install gulp-istanbul --save-dev
npm install gulp-concat --save-dev
npm install gulp-uglify --save-dev
npm install gulp-yuidoc --save-dev
npm install gulp-rename --save-dev
npm install gulp-header --save-dev
```

The code in Listing 15-7 shows a complete gulpfile that, in addition to improving your development workflow, can be used to produce a production-ready version of JavaScript code stored in a `src/scripts/` folder. Follow the inline code comments to understand how each task is configured.

Listing 15-7. Gulpfile with separate development and build tasks

```
// Load the Gulp.js package
var gulp = require("gulp"),

    // Load the JSHint, Connect, Clean, Jasmine, Istanbul, Concat, Uglify, YUIDoc, Rename and
    // Header plugin tasks
    jshint = require("gulp-jshint"),
    connect = require("gulp-connect"),
    clean = require("gulp-clean"),
    jasmine = require("gulp-jasmine"),
    istanbul = require("gulp-istanbul"),
    concat = require("gulp-concat"),
    uglify = require("gulp-uglify"),
    yuidoc = require("gulp-yuidoc"),
    rename = require("gulp-rename"),

    // The Header task adds a given string of text to the top of a file, useful for adding
    // dynamic comments at the start of a file
    header = require("gulp-header"),

    // Load the properties from the package.json file into a variable for use in task
    // configuration
    pkg = require("./package.json"),

    // Define variables to represent the folder and file locations required for task
    // configuration - saves repetition

    // The "src/" folder contains the code we will work on during development, including
    // "scripts/" and "tests/" folders containing our JavaScript code and Jasmine test spec
    // scripts, respectively
    srcFolder = "src/",
    scriptFolder = srcFolder + "scripts/",
```

```
        scriptFiles = scriptFolder + "**/*.js",
        unitTestFolder = srcFolder + "tests/",
        unitTestFiles = unitTestFolder + "**/*.js",

        // The "dist/" folder will be generated automatically by this Gruntfile when run, and
        // populated with the release version of our application files
        outputFolder = "dist/",
        outputScriptFolder = outputFolder + "scripts/",

        // Define the name and location of a single script file into which all others will
        // be concatenated into, becoming the main JavaScript file of our application
        outputScriptFileName = "main.js",
        outputScriptFile = outputScriptFolder + outputScriptFileName,

        // Define the file suffix to apply to the minified version of our single application script
        outputScriptFileMinifiedSuffix = ".min",

        // Define output folders for generated Istanbul reports and YUIDoc documentation files
        outputReportFolder = outputFolder + "report/",
        outputDocsFolder = outputFolder + "docs/";

// Configure Connect as in Listing 15-5
gulp.task("connect", function() {
    "use strict";

    connect.server({
        port: 3000,
        livereload: true
    });
});

// Configure JSHint as in Listing 15-5
gulp.task("jshint", function() {
    "use strict";

    return gulp.src(scriptFiles)
        .pipe(jshint({
            strict: true
        }))
        .pipe(jshint.reporter("default"))
        .pipe(connect.reload());
});

// Configure a Watch task as in Listing 15-5
gulp.task("watch", function() {
    "use strict";

    gulp.watch(scriptFiles, ["jshint"]);
});
```

```
// Define a Clean task to empty the contents of the "dist/" output folder each time we prepare
// our production-ready release code
gulp.task("clean", function() {
    "use strict";

    return gulp.src(outputFolder, {

            // Setting the "read" option to false with gulp.src() causes Gulp.js to ignore the
            // contents of the input files, resulting in a faster task
            read: false
        });

            // Pipe the output folder through the clean() task method, erasing it from the file
            // system
            .pipe(clean());
});

// Define a Copy task to duplicate static files that we wish to bundle with our release code
// into our output "dist/" folder
gulp.task("copy", function() {
    "use strict";

    // Copy all files witin "src/", except those in the "scripts/" and "tests/" folders, over
    // to the "dist/" output folder. There is no need for a special plugin to perform file
    // copying, it is handled directly through the Gulp.js API methods src() and dest()
    return gulp.src(["**", "!scripts/**", "!tests/**"], {
            cwd: srcFolder
        })
        .pipe(gulp.dest(outputFolder));
});

// Define a task to perform unit testing through Jasmine and code coverage report generation
// via Istanbul. To save running two tasks, which will effectively end up running the unit
// tests twice, we combine the two together into one task
gulp.task("jasmine-istanbul", function() {
    "use strict";

    // Pipe the files from the "src/scripts/" directory into Istanbul, which "instruments" the
    // files, ensuring that code coverage reports can be generated later. No files are actually
    // saved to the file system, they are kept in memory while they are being used, and are
    // then destroyed when the task is complete
    return gulp.src(scriptFiles)
        .pipe(istanbul())

        // When the script files have been instrumented, execute Jasmine against the unit
        // test specs, piping the code coverage reports generated by Istanbul when these tests
        // are run into the "dist/reports" folder
        .on("finish", function() {

            // Run the unit test files through Jasmine. Due to the nature of the gulp-jasmine
            // plugin, the unit test files must be Node.js application files, meaning that
            // before the tests can be run, we need to include a line at the top of the test
```

```
            // script to require() the original script file we are testing - this means that
            // the script file we're testing needs to have a "module.exports = " line to
            // expose the functions to test for the unit test script. A few extra hoops to jump
            // through compared to when testing with Grunt, however it's not too unfamiliar
            // territory!
            gulp.src(unitTestFiles)
                .pipe(jasmine())

                // Create the Istanbul code coverage reports now the unit tests have been run
                // against the instrumented code
                .pipe(istanbul.writeReports({
                    dir: outputReportFolder,
                    reporters: ['lcov'],
                    reportOpts: {
                        dir: outputReportFolder
                    }
                }));
        });
});

// Define a Concat task to combine the files in the "src/scripts/" folder into a single
// JavaScript application file
gulp.task("concat", function() {
    "use strict";

    return gulp.src(scriptFiles)

        // Pass the name of the new script file to create to the concat() function
        .pipe(concat(outputScriptFileName))

        // Place the new file into the "dist/scripts/" output folder
        .pipe(gulp.dest(outputScriptFolder));
});

// Define an Uglify task to minify the contents of our concatenated JavaScript file to reduce
// its size without removing its functionality, before adding a header comment to the minified
// file, renaming it to add a ".min" suffix to the resulting file, and then placing the new
// file in the "dist/scripts/" output folder
gulp.task("uglify", function() {
    "use strict";

    // Run the "dist/scripts/main.js" file through the uglify() task method to produce a
    // minified version of that file
    return gulp.src(outputScriptFile)
        .pipe(uglify())

        // Add a comment header to the minified JavaScript file, including the name and
        // version details from the package.json file
        .pipe(header("/*! " + pkg.name + " - version " + pkg.version + " */\n"))
```

417

```
            // Rename the minified file to add the ".min" suffix, the resulting file name will
            // then be "main.min.js"
            .pipe(rename({suffix: outputScriptFileMinifiedSuffix}))

            // Place the minified file into the "dist/scripts/" output folder
            .pipe(gulp.dest(outputScriptFolder));
});

// Define a YUIDoc task to generate a separate static web site derived from specially formatted
// comments placed in our JavaScript files, allowing new developers to get up to speed with the
// structure of the project code without needing to comb through each line of code
gulp.task("yuidoc", function() {
    "use strict";

    // Load the JavaScript files from the "src/scripts/" folder and run these through YUIDoc,
    // passing in the name and version number of the project from the package.json file to
    // include in the resulting static documentation web site
    return gulp.src(scriptFiles)
        .pipe(yuidoc({
            project: {
                "name": pkg.name,
                "version": pkg.version
            }
        }))

        // Place the resulting static web site files in the "dist/docs/" output folder
        .pipe(gulp.dest(outputDocsFolder));
});

// Define a default task to run JSHint, Connect and Watch, for local development
gulp.task("default", ["jshint", "connect", "watch"]);

// Define a new "build" task to empty the "dist/" folder, copy over site files, run JSHint
// and Jasmine to check code quality, generating code coverage reports with Istanbul,
// concatenate the JavaScript files into a single application file, minify the contents of that
// file, and finally generate a documentation site based on the YUIDoc-formatted code comments
// in the original JavaScript files
gulp.task("build", ["clean", "copy", "jshint", "jasmine-istanbul", "concat", "uglify", "yuidoc"]);
```

Running Gulp.js against the code in Listing 15-7, saved to a file named gulpfile.js, will execute either the default task to improve your development workflow, or the separate build task to generate a production-ready version of your JavaScript application code files, depending on which task name is passed to the Gulp.js tool on the command line when executed. Running the latter task will automatically create or empty out a dist/ folder within your project root folder, copy over static files, such as HTML, image, and stylesheet files (but not JavaScript files) into this new folder, maintaining the same folder structure as exists within the original src/ folder, perform static code analysis and unit test your JavaScript code, generating code coverage reports, before combining the JavaScript files together into a single main.js file, which is placed in the dist/scripts/ folder. This file is then minified and saved into the same location under the name main.min.js, from where it can be referenced from your HTML page. Finally, the task creates a documentation website based on specially formatted code comments found in your original JavaScript files.

Both Grunt and Gulp.js perform these automation tasks particularly well, although Gulp.js has the edge on speed, whereas Grunt has the best plugin support. You should choose your build tool as appropriate with this, and the requirements of your project, in mind.

Managing Third-Party Libraries and Frameworks

As your web application grows, you may find that your code is dependent on a number of third-party libraries, frameworks, and plugin scripts that you need to store and manage locally within your project. Some of these scripts will be best used with specific versions of others that you reference, and ensuring that you have the correct version of each installed can be a maintenance chore. Inspired by the Node.js package.json file approach, a number of front-end *package manager* tools have sprung up, allowing third-party libraries and frameworks, together with their exact version numbers, to be defined in a configuration file. The package manager can then install these library dependencies within your project using this configuration, and this process can be automated using Grunt and Gulp.js, meaning that you don't need to commit your third-party dependency files to your project source code control system, the correct version of each can be dynamically installed each time with your chosen build tool.

One of the most common front-end package managers is Bower (http://bower.io), developed by Twitter. Through its package directory, which is similar to the NPM directory, developers have access to over fifteen thousand JavaScript libraries and frameworks for inclusion in their projects, including jQuery, RequireJS, AngularJS, Backbone, and a host of other popular scripts and plugins. Bower, like Grunt and Gulp.js, is built on Node.js, so installing the tool for use across all folders on your machine involves executing the following on the command line (Mac and Linux users may need to precede the command with sudo):

```
npm install -g bower
```

Much like the package.json file commonly used with Node.js for managing packages and specific versions of dependencies, a bower.json file is required for use with the Bower package manager, which contains general project details along with a list of the front-end library and framework dependencies. In addition to main project dependencies, development-only dependencies can be specified, which define those libraries required for development only that should not be present in the production version of the code, such as debugging scripts and unit test frameworks.

Installing packages with Bower is very similar to installing packages using the npm tool—the name of the package is provided on the command line, taken from the online directory at http://bower.io/search/, along with the --save option used to add the package to a dependencies section of the bower.json file, and a --save-dev option allowing the package to be added to a devDependencies section of the file, indicating that the package should not a part of the main application and is required for development only. To install the jQuery package, therefore, execute the following on the command line in your project's root folder:

```
bower install jquery --save
```

All packages are installed in a bower_components/ folder by default, which you should ensure does not get committed to your source code control system, as the specific versions of the defined packages should be installed dynamically to each developer's machine using Bower. Your code can then reference the files from this directory in your application.

Listing 15-8 shows an example bower.json file, defining three third-party library dependencies for a JavaScript application—jQuery, AngularJS, and RequireJS, along with the Firebug Lite (http://bit.ly/firebug-lite) script for use in development only.

Listing 15-8. An example bower.json file

```
{
    "name": "my-project",
    "version": "0.0.1",
    "dependencies": {
        "jquery": "~2.1.1",
        "angular": "~1.2.17",
        "requirejs": "~2.1.14"
    },
    "devDependencies": {
        "firebug-lite": "~1.5.1"
    }
}
```

Once your project has a defined bower.json file in place, installation of all packages for new developers is a simple case of executing the following on the command line, which will install all of the defined packages into the project folder:

```
bower install
```

Dependency installation with Bower can be automated using Grunt or Gulp.js through the use of the grunt-bowercopy (http://bit.ly/grunt-bowercopy) and gulp-bower (http://bit.ly/gulp-bower) plugins, respectively, both of which will install packages defined in a local bower.json file before copying the resulting files from the local bower_components/ directory to a defined output directory, such as the dist/ folder structure we saw in the previous automation section.

Bower, and other package managers of its ilk—including spm (http://spmjs.io), component (http://component.io), and Jam (http://jamjs.org), all of which are configured and work in a similar way—allow the simple but effective management of specific versions of third-party dependencies in your front-end web applications, ensuring that errors are less likely to occur and only the exact dependencies required are ever installed for your project.

Project Setup and Scaffolding

The process of starting and setting up a new project is often time-consuming, involving lots of decisions about the best folder and file structure, the most appropriate frameworks, and the best approach to automation and dependency management. In the spirit of allowing developers more time to focus on development, a team at Google created an automated tool called Yeoman (http://yeoman.io) designed to be used to set up new projects, configuring folder structures, creating intial files, and installing and configuring build tools, allowing you, the developer, to get started on development in the quickest possible time.

Yeoman incorporates Grunt, for automated task running, Bower, for web package management, and *yo*, the core of Yeoamn—the glue that connects both Grunt and Bower tools together with the correct configuration, and creates default folders and files on your behalf. Because different types of project require different configuration, structures, and files, Yeoman plugins, known as *generators*, provide the specific settings required to set up and initialize different types of project.

Yo is a Node.js tool and can be installed by executing the following on the command line, which will also install Grunt and Bower if these are not already installed (Mac and Linux users may need to precede the command with sudo):

```
npm install -g yo
```

Next, you'll need to select an appropriate generator to use as the foundation for a new project that you wish to create. A directory of over twenty official supported generators, tailored specificially for AngularJS, Backbone, jQuery, and other frameworks, is available online at `http://bit.ly/yeoman-official`, and a list of over nine hundred unofficial community generators is available via `http://bit.ly/yeoman-community`. If you're just getting started with Yeoman and need to generate a simple website optionally using HTML5 Boilerplate (`http://html5boilerplate.com`), jQuery, Modernizr (`http://modernizr.com`) and Bootstrap (`http://getbootstrap.com`), then the generator-webapp plugin (`http://bit.ly/yeoman-webapp`) is recommended. To install this generator for use across any folder on your machine, simply execute the following on the command line in any folder:

```
npm install -g generator-webapp
```

To use a generator to set up a new project, create a new folder and navigate into that folder on the command line, then execute the yo tool, passing in the name of the generator, which is always the part after the hyphen (-) in its name. For example, to use the generator-webapp generator to initialize a new project folder, execute the following on the command line within that new folder:

```
yo webapp
```

Executing this command produces the response shown in Figure 15-9, showing an introduction graphic, and asking a question of the user regarding which extra libraries they would like to install, the answer of which will determine which folders and files are created in the resulting structure, and how configuration files are set up. Answering the question then triggers the installation and configuration of project files in the directory. The resulting folder and file structure produced when selecting the default option on the command line, which takes only a few seconds to generate, is shown in Figure 15-10.

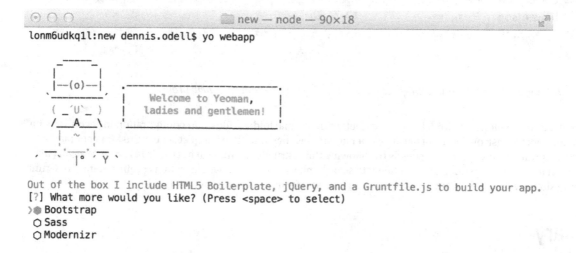

Figure 15-9. Yeoman running on the command line, helping lay the foundation for a new project

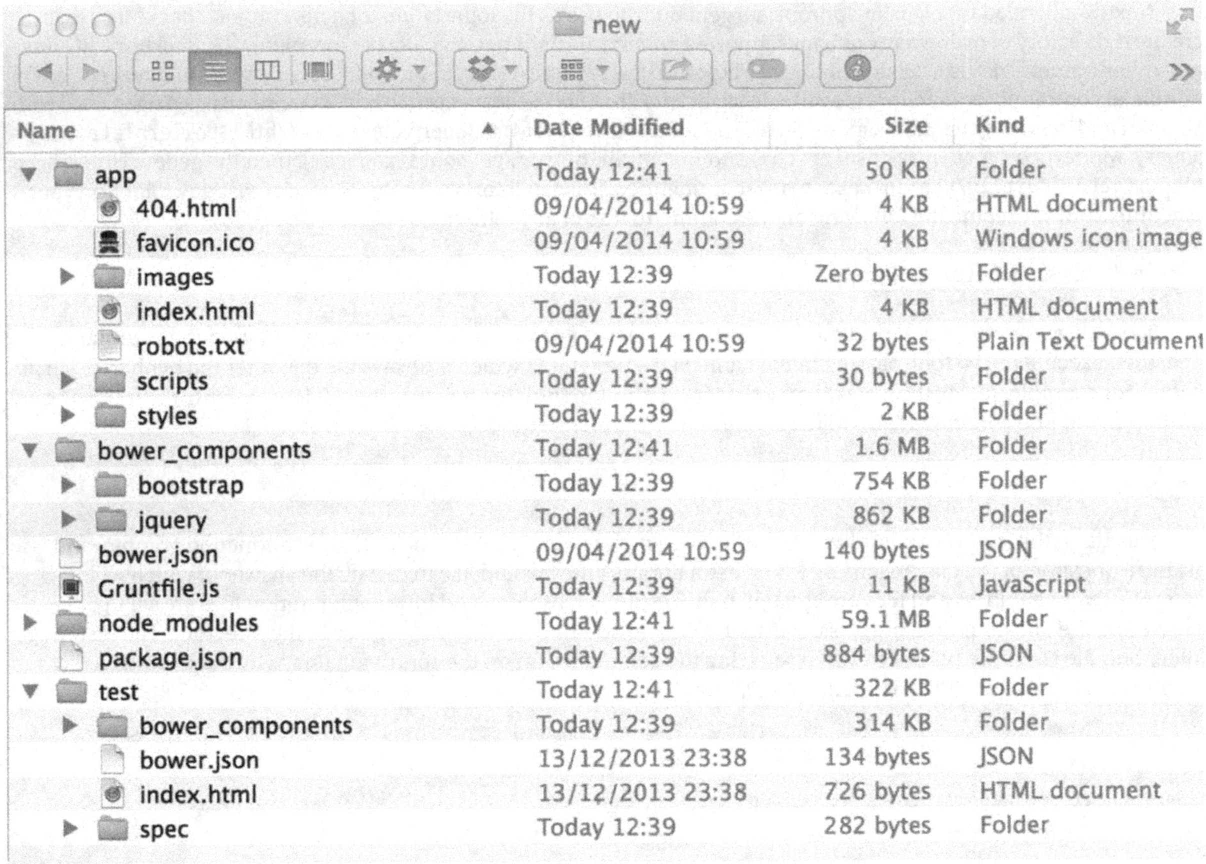

Figure 15-10. *Yeoman generates and configures folders and files for use with your new project*

Yeoman allows developers to initialize new projects with optimal folders, files, and configuration in seconds using prebuilt generators that ask questions of the developer about how they want their project set up. Custom generators can be built according to specific project needs by following the instructions online at http://bit.ly/yeoman-create. Utilize Yeoman to drastically reduce the time taken to set up a new project, and benefit from its preinstallation of Grunt and Bower to simplify your development workflow and help you focus on writing your best code.

Summary

In this chapter, we have looked into JavaScript build tools and automation of repetitive and time-consuming tasks to improve your development workflow and ensure the quality of the code you release to the public. We've seen how web package managers can better define third-party front-end dependencies for your project code, and how to create an initial setup for your project files, providing a solid foundation for further development. Professional JavaScript developers use build tools to allow them more time to focus on writing and improving their code and less time worrying about their workflow and managing their release process. Experiment with the tools that I've covered in this chapter and find the tools and plugins that work best for your specific project needs and benefit from them in your day-to-day work.

In the next chapter, we will look at the development tools built into today's web browsers that can help you to debug and profile your JavaScript code while running in a real-world environment.

CHAPTER 16

■ ■ ■

Browser Developer Tools

Throughout this book, I have explained how professional JavaScript developers use advanced coding techniques, take advantage of language and browser capabilities, and apply tooling to their workflow and their code in order to produce high-quality, maintainable JavaScript code for the benefit of the end users of their applications and other developers working alongside them. The main frontier of web development is the browser, the platform for running our applications in the wild for the general public to access. While we can run a plethora of tools against our code to check its quality in advance, there really is no substitiute for running that code within a web browser to ensure not only that it runs correctly but also that it is performant and memory-efficient. We can measure and debug our code within the browser environment using the sets of developer tools built into all the major browsers for an under-the-hood look at what's happening while our code is executed. We can use the data gleaned from these tools to improve our code, adding the final polish to our JavaScript to ensure it will perform efficiently for our end users. In this chapter, I will take you through the browser developer tools that will help ensure that your code is performant and accurate.

One of the earliest popular browser developer tools was Firebug (`https://getfirebug.com`), an extension to Mozilla's Firefox browser released in 2006, which allowed developers to perform tasks against the current running web page, including inspecting DOM elements and attributes in a live representation of the current page structure, observing the CSS style rules applied to any element, following a list of all network requests made to render the current page, and a JavaScript developer console for executing commands against the page code run in memory. Due to its ease of use and powerful, accurate toolset, it was quickly adopted by professional web developers around the world and ensured that Firefox became the browser of choice for developers at that time.

Since 2006, every major browser manufacturer has incorporated their own set of equivalent developer tools into their products, with many features inspired by or derived from Firebug, and today's web developers are now split as to which is the best overall in-browser toolset. In this chapter, I will introduce you to the developer tools featured in each major browser and detail the functionality that they share that will help you debug and improve the efficiency of your JavaScript code.

Locating the Hidden Browser Developer Tools

Recent versions of Microsoft Internet Explorer, Google Chrome, Apple Safari, Opera, and Mozilla Firefox browsers on desktop devices all contain a set of hidden developer tools that can be accessed in the following ways:

- In Internet Explorer, simply hit the F12 key on the keyboard; alternatively, select "F12 Developer Tools" from the browser's settings menu.

- In Chrome, use the key combination *Ctrl + Shift + I* in Windows or *Option (⌥) + Command (⌘) + I* in Mac OS X, alternatively select *Tools\Developer Tools* from the menu.

- In Safari, open the *Preferences...* menu, select the *Advanced* tab, and check the *Show Develop menu in menu bar* option. The key combination *Option (⌥) + Command (⌘) + I* then opens the developer tools. Alternatively, in the new *Develop* menu that appears in the menu bar on selecting this option, choose the *Show Web Inspector* menu item.

- In Opera, which is based on Google Chrome under the hood, use the same key combination, *Ctrl + Shift + I* in Windows or *Option (⌥) + Command (⌘) + I* in Mac OS X. Alternatively, select the *View\Show Developer Menu* option in the menu bar.

- To open the standard developer tools in Firefox, use the key combination *Ctrl + Shift + C* in Windows or *Option (⌥) + Command (⌘) + C* in Mac OS X. Alternatively, select *Tools\Web Developer\Inspector* from the menu bar.

- To open the Firebug development tool for Firefox, first install the browser extension from `https://getfirebug.com` and then select the *Tools\Web Developer\Firebug\Show Firebug* option from the menu bar.

Alternatively, many browsers allow you to right-click any element on the current page and select the *Inspect Element* context menu item to bring up the developer toolbar showing a default view of the current state of the page DOM.

Figure 16-1 shows the browser developer tools running against a web page in the Safari browser. Note the ability to see the live DOM structure of the running page, on the left of the toolbar, along with the CSS style rules applied to each element, along the right edge of the toolbar. Hovering over an element in the DOM structure highlights that element on the running web page to aid debugging. You can click to edit the DOM and CSS attributes to update the page contents live in the browser window.

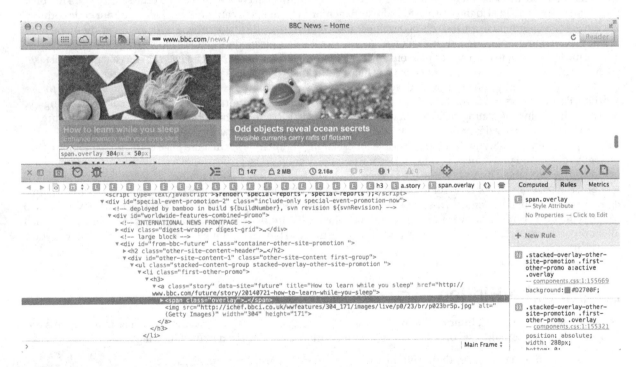

Figure 16-1. *The browser developer tools running against a web page in the Safari browser*

The developer tools in all major browsers share much of the same data views. In this chapter, we will focus on those that apply best to JavaScript development; however, I encourage you to experiment yourself with the features within each, to discover how these can assist you with more than just your JavaScript development.

The JavaScript Console

The primary tab of the browser developer tools for JavaScript developers is known as the *console*. This allows you not only to execute JavaScript commands that run against the code loaded into memory from the current running page but also to output debug information from your code using a `console` JavaScript object, provided by the developer tools. We saw this same object in Chapter 14, where it was used to output messages to the command line of running Node.js applications. Here it outputs messages to the JavaScript console window in the browser developer tools instead.

Outputting Messages to the Console Window

Should you wish to output the value of a variable, or write a message to the console window to help you debug an issue in your running JavaScript code, use the `console.log()` method instead of the standard browser `alert()` dialog. You can write to the console as often as you need to in order to display the desired information; you can even pass multiple parameters to this method to write these out side-by-side on the same line on the console. Any variable passed to the function will be displayed in an appropriate way depending on its value type, including objects, which will display with a clickable handle to allow you to navigate its hierarchy to view the contents of its properties and methods within, and functions, which will display as a string to allow you to view the contents of the code within. Listing 16-1 shows some possible uses for the `console.log()` method, and Figure 16-2 shows the output in the Chrome browser developer tools console when the code is run within the context of the web page in the browser.

Listing 16-1. Outputting values and variables to the JavaScript developer tools console

```
console.log("Code executed at this point");
console.log("The <body> element:", document.body);
console.log("<body> element class name:", document.body.className);
console.log("The window object:", window);
```

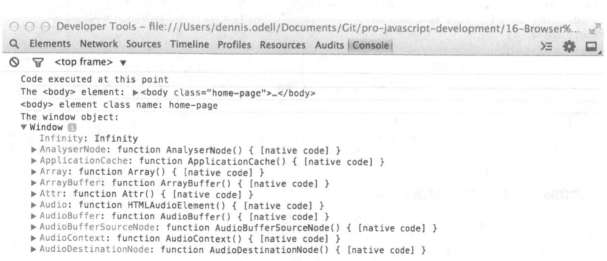

Figure 16-2. The console output of running Listing 16-1 within a web page

You can denote particular console messages and variable values as having different types using four variant methods of the console.log() method:

- console.info(), which denotes the message is informational only

- console.debug(), which denotes the message is intended to help debug errors

- console.warn(), which denotes an issue may have occurred in the code and that the message indicates the details of that potential problem

- console.error(), which denotes that an error has occurred and that the accompanying message contains details of that error

Each is highlighted within the developer console in different ways, and a filter control at the top of the console window allows messages to be hidden and shown according to their type denoted by the different methods used to display them.

Should you wish to highlight your console messages using your own color schemes, you can provide CSS style information as the second parameter to a console.log() method call, provided that you begin the string-based message contained in the first parameter with the %c control code sequence.

Listing 16-2 shows the different category levels of message that can be applied to a message sent to the console window, and also how to apply your own custom style to your messages. Figure 16-3 shows the output in the Chrome browser developer tools console when the code in Listing 16-2 is run within the context of the web page in the browser. Note how the different categories of messages are displayed in different ways to identify them.

Listing 16-2. Outputting different category levels and message styles to the JavaScript developer tools console

```
console.info("info(): Code executed at this point");
console.debug("debug(): The <body> element:", document.body);
console.warn("warn(): <body> element class name:", document.body.className);
console.error("error(): The window object:", window);
console.log("%clog(): This is a custom-styled message", "font-weight: bold; background: black;
color: white;");
```

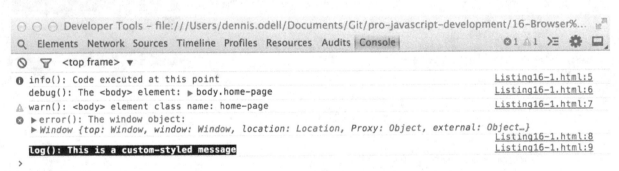

Figure 16-3. *The console window output in Google Chrome when running Listing 16-2 within a web page*

The info(), debug(), warn() and error() methods of the console object are very useful for larger JavaScript applications that may require a great deal of debugging during development to identify and fix potential issues before they are released to the public. You should use them as much as necessary to understand how your code is running, taking advantage of the console window's message filtering ability to only flag up those messages of the type that you need at any one time.

Using the Console for Performance Measurement

The console object contains two methods, time() and timeEnd(), for dealing with the passing of time, which we can use to create a basic form of code performance measurement. Executing console.time(), passing it a unique identifier label string as an argument, starts a timer running in the browser associated with that given identifier. Calling the same method using different identifiers allows multiple timers to be started without interfering with each other. To stop the timer running, execute console.timeEnd(), passing it the same identifier value used to begin the timer you wish to stop. At this point, the number of milliseconds passed between the timer starting and it ending will be written out to the JavaScript console along with the name of the identifier associated with that timer. This allows basic performance measurement to be run against sections of your code, which can help you ascertain performance bottlenecks in your code and aid you rewrite your code to streamline any comparatively slow operations.

The code in Listing 16-3 demonstrates the use of the time() and timeEnd() methods of the console object to measure the performance of a particular code loop.

Listing 16-3. Measuring the time taken to run a section of code using the JavaScript developer console

```javascript
function counter(length) {
    var output = 0,
        index = 0;

    console.time("Loop timer " + length);

    for (; index < length; index++) {
        output = output + index;
    }

    console.timeEnd("Loop timer " + length);
}

counter(10000);
counter(100000);
counter(1000000);
```

Running the code in Listing 16-3 within the context of a web page in the browser produces the JavaScript console output shown in Figure 16-4. Observe the durations between each time() and timeEnd() method call are written to the console alongside the unique identifier name associated with each call of the counter() method. We'll take a further look at JavaScript performance profiling later in this chapter.

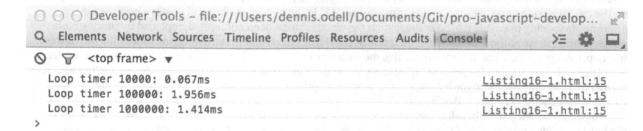

Figure 16-4. The console output of running Listing 16-3 within the context of a web page

Remove Code References to the Console Object for Release

Before you release your final public code, ensure that you remove your references to the console object from your JavaScript files as this object is only present in browsers with developer tools currently installed and enabled, which is likely not the case in the majority of your users' browsers. If you are using an automated Grunt build process, you can use the grunt-strip plugin task (http://bit.ly/grunt-strip) to do this for you. For Gulp.js task runner users, the gulp-strip-debug package (http://bit.ly/gulp-strip) is the plugin you need to remove this object's method calls before release.

The JavaScript console is an incredibly useful tool for developers to output messages as their code is running, to examine the state of variables and to establish which code branches are executing and how long certain operations are taking to complete. To learn more about the JavaScript console, check out the article "Mastering The Developer Tools Console" by Matt West on Treehouse Blog at http://bit.ly/js-console.

Debugging Running JavaScript Code

Along with the JavaScript console, the browser developer tools allow the ability to observe and debug running code, to stop it in its tracks, step through line-by-line, and resume it running at any point. Minified code is not a problem for the developer tools as we have the means to either convert it to unminified code with the press of a button, or to introduce a link to an unminified version of each JavaScript file that the browser tools substitute for the running code when displayed in the tool window.

Working with Minified Code

Whereas the JavaScript developer console is ideal for debugging and following code during development, occasionally we need to debug code that has already been minified and is running from a web server other than on our local development machine. Thankfully, there are two options available for working with minified JavaScript files within the browser developer tools: *pretty-printing* and *source maps*.

Pretty Printing

The first option for working with minified code in the browser developer tools is *pretty-printing*, whereby the spacing removed from the JavaScript file during the minification process is added back into the file by following a standard pattern of tabs and spaces to nest functions, objects, and other code blocks in an attempt to make the minified file readable again.

Enabling pretty-print in the Firefox developer tools is a simple case of selecting its *Debugger* tab to show the JavaScript files currently loaded in memory by the displayed web page. Select a minified file from the list in the panel on the left-hand side, then click the icon button marked "{}" in the bottom toolbar and observe how the file is given appropriate spacing to enable it to be easily read. If the variables have been obfuscated, replaced by shorter, more obtuse names, these will still be shown in their obfuscated form, which may make debugging more difficult; however, pretty-printing may help you to better recognize the structure of the original file in order to debug it in the browser.

The Firebug extension supports pretty-printing through an identical button displayed in the top toolbar within its *Script* tab. Selecting any file in the left-hand panel after this option is enabled shows a pretty-print version of that file, whether the original was minified or not.

In Safari's developer tools, select the *Resources* tab, locate a minified JavaScript file from the list in the panel on the left-hand side and click the "{}" button in the top right toolbar above the file text to pretty-print its contents.

Similarly in Chrome and Opera developer tools, which share the same underlying code base, select the *Sources* tab and identify a minified file; clicking the "{}" button below the file will pretty-print its contents.

In Internet Explorer, open the developer tools and select the *Debugger* tab, locate a minified file, and click the "{}" button in the top toolbar to pretty-print the selected file's contents.

Pretty-printing is a very quick and simple method for viewing minified files in the browser developer tools, although for simpler debugging, and access to the original names of obfuscated variables and functions names, *source maps* are the preferable option.

Source Maps

The second option for working with minified code in the browser developer tools is known as *source maps*, where a minified file is encoded with a reference to a full, unminified version of the same JavaScript code, even if the original code was spread across multiple files. Source map files use a .map extension and feature a JSON structure describing the mapping between the original and minified files, including their variable and function names if these were obfuscated during the minification process.

Linking a minified file to an associated source map file is as simple as appending a specially formatted comment to the end of the JavaScript file referencing the location of the source map. To connect a minified file named scripts.min.js to a JSON-format source map file named /scripts/scripts.js.map, for example, add the following comment to the end of the minified file:

```
//# sourceMappingURL=/scripts/scripts.js.map
```

Alternatively, if you have access to your web server, you can add the following HTTP header to the response of the minified file, although many choose to use the specially formatted comment for its simplicity:

```
X-SourceMap: /scripts/scripts/js.map
```

Generate the source map file at the same time as you minifiy your JavaScript files. Both the UglifyJS (http://bit.ly/uglify_js) and Google Closure Compiler (http://bit.ly/closure_compile—use the create_source_map option) tools featured in Chapter 4 have the ability to generate a source map file automatically and will automatically include the specially formatted commend reference at the bottom of the minified file.

In the Chrome developer tools, you will have to enable the ability to recognize source maps. Click the *Settings* menu icon within the toolbar and select *Enable Source Maps* within the *General* options section. Other browsers' developer tools will have the feature enabled by default. Selecting the *Sources* tab in the Chrome developer tools shows you a hierarchical folder view of the files loaded that make up the current web page. Any files linked to from the data structure of a source map show up in this hierarchy as if they had been loaded via a direct link from the HTML page itself.

Similarly, in the Firefox developer tools, selecting the *Debugger* tab produces a list of JavaScript source files in a panel on the left-hand side. Included in this list automatically are the full, unminified versions of each of the files linked to from any source maps. At the time of writing, Firebug does not support source maps, so you should resort to the builtin Firefox developer tools to take advantage of this feature.

The Safari developer tools display minified files with associated source maps as an extra item in the hierarchy of loaded files in the left-hand panel within the *Resources* tab. The files linked via source maps are then shown beneath the minified file's name in the hierarchy, as shown in Figure 16-5, which has a minified file named scripts.js that links to a number of original, unminified files.

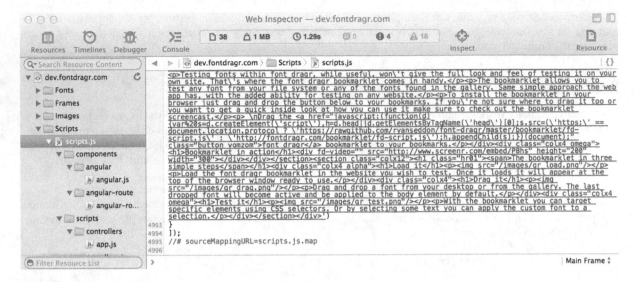

Figure 16-5. *Unminified files from source maps are shown one level beneath the original minified file in Safari*

The Internet Explorer developer tools provide access to the source maps feature through the *Debugger* tab. When a JavaScript file is selected that references a source map, an extra button appears on the toolbar above the file contents, which, when pressed, loads and displays the unminified version of the file in the main panel, replacing the minified file.

Pause and Observe Running JavaScript Code

The browser developer tools feature additional functionality for observing how your JavaScript code is running in the browser up close, even allowing each line of code to be executed one at a time, with the changes in variable values being observed as each line executes.

To stop your JavaScript code from executing when it reaches a certain line in a particular code file, insert a *breakpoint* on this line using one of the two techniques outlined later in this chapter. Once the page is loaded or refreshed and the code line reached, the page pauses and puts you in control of the running of the JavaScript code from this point.

The first technique for inserting a breakpoint into your code is to add a line of code to force execution to pause at that point in your file. To do this, add the following line to your JavaScript file at the point at which you want execution to pause:

```
debugger;
```

When executed, the developer tools will pause at this point, putting you in control of the execution flow and allowing you to observe the values of any global or local variables at that instant in code execution. Ensure that you remove any reference to this command from your code before release, however, as, like the `console` object, this is a custom JavaScript command for use with the browser developer tools only.

The second technique for inserting a breakpoint is simply to click on the code line number that you wish to pause execution on when viewing a JavaScript file within the browser developer tools. A marker will appear beside the code line to indicate a breakpoint has been set, which can be removed by clicking a second time. Refreshing the page will persist any breakpoints and the code will pause once it reaches the first breakpoint, awaiting your next action.

Once set, most browser developer tools allow you to right-click on a breakpoint and edit the conditions that apply to it, allowing you to specify the exact state the application should be in before that particular breakpoint is fired. This is particularly useful if you wish to put a breakpoint within a loop but only want the breakpoint to stop the code execution when it reaches a specific iteration of that loop.

When paused at a breakpoint, you can inspect the values of any variables set by that point in the code surrounding the breakpoint by simply hovering the mouse over any variable name (unfortunately, this is not supported in Firefox developer tools, so use Firebug to take advantage of this feature). A tooltip will show the value within the highlighted variable and allow you to expand objects to reveal the values within their properties as well. You may also open up the JavaScript console while paused and use the data entry field to execute additional code, or to query the values of specific variables, all within the current scope of the breakpoint. This is useful for forcing different return values from functions, or ensuring that specific conditional statements execute in the flow of the code.

Regardless of the browser developer tools used, when paused at a breakpoint a panel on the right-hand side reveals the details of the execution call stack, including the function names called leading into the function currently paused within, and a list of global variables and local scope variables, together with their current values. When paused within a function, for example, you have access to all the variables declared within that function, as well as special variables such as arguments, showing all the arguments passed to that function on execution. This provides you, the developer, with an at-a-glance view of the state of the variables in your application to allow you to ascertain whether they are as they should be or not, allowing you to debug further if needed.

Once paused, you will notice that a *continue* button is accessible within the toolbar above the displayed JavaScript code in the toolbar, reminiscent of a video play button. When this is pressed, the code will resume execution until the next breakpoint is hit. Notice also the presence of a set of three *step* action buttons beside the *continue* button in the toolbar. These allow you to continue execution of the code one statement at a time without needing to set another breakpoint, allowing you to see the operations performed on your variables and the flow taken through the application by the browser's JavaScript interpreter without needing to know in advance what course it will take. One of these step buttons will execute the next statement in the current file without entering any called function if it comes across one. This is useful if you are more interested in the returned values from called functions rather than the code within those functions. Another of these buttons will execute the next statement, entering a called function if one is present and pausing again at the first statement within that function. The final button allows you to execute the rest of the function currently being executed and pausing again at the next statement after the function call that took the program flow into that function. Using these buttons, you are able to track the flow of your code, observing the values stored in local and global variables along the way, to help you locate and debug issues within your code within the context of the running web page in the current browser.

Figure 16-6 shows an example of the Safari developer tools, paused on reaching a breakpoint denoted in the line number column beside the code in the central area. The left-hand panel shows the *continue* and *step* buttons, the execution call stack, including function names executed before reaching the current breakpoint, and a list of all breakpoints in all running files. The right-hand panel shows the current variables declared in the local scope, in the current function closure, and in the global scope. Other browser developer tools show the same information in similar layouts.

Figure 16-6. *Using breakpoints to pause code execution in order to observe the values in local variables*

Profiling JavaScript Code

The browser developer tools allow you to profile both the memory usage of your web application, as well as the runtime performance of your individual JavaScript functions. Using this data, you can update your code to make it more efficient for your users, removing memory leaks and freeing up any potential performance bottlenecks.

Locating Memory Leaks

As your code creates and initializes variables within functions, these values consume a certain amount of memory within the browser, dependent on their type and value. As the execution of their scope concludes, the variables are internally marked for deletion. A *garbage collector* process in the browser disposes of these variables, and any others that it deems are no longer required as they have no active reference from any other object in the running code, freeing up their memory. A memory leak is where, over the course of time, certain variables that are no longer required are not disposed of, meaning that slowly the memory left available for the rest of the browser diminishes until such point that there is none left and the browser process is forced to crash. There are three primary causes of memory leaks in JavaScript-based web applications.

First, memory leaks can occur through the use of the `console` object to log the value of an object to the JavaScript console in the browser developer tools. This keeps a reference to the object "alive" in memory though the rest of the code base may no longer need access to it. This may cause memory leak issues in development that won't be present in your final code once these logging method calls have been removed, so be wary of this.

Second, references to JavaScript function closures are another common source of memory leaks in web applications. Imagine an event handler closure that references a property of an object somewhere else within your code. Even if that object is no longer required or used after a certain point in your code, the fact that the closure could potentially be executed, and thus reference that object, means that the object will be kept in memory for as long as that event handler is still active. Make sure, therefore, that you use the `removeEventListener()` method on DOM elements to ensure that references to objects no longer required are removed and their memory freed up.

Finally, memory leaks can occur due to stored references between two or more objects that keep the memory allocated by one of those objects reserved despite it no longer being needed by the application. It may seem counterintuitive, but often the best way to reduce the chance of memory leakage is to store data referenced from other objects as a copy of that data in a separate local variable.

The browser developer tools in Chrome, Opera, and Internet Explorer 11 feature the ability to profile the memory usage of your JavaScript code as it runs in the context of your web application.

Memory Profiling in Chrome and Opera

To see how much memory JavaScript is consuming within the Chrome browser, open the *Task Manager* window through the *Window\Task Manager* menu bar option. Right-click in the open tab list header and select to display *JavaScript Memory* within the table. You will then see how much memory the JavaScript-portion of your web application is consuming. If you have multiple open tabs, you will see the memory consumption of those apps also, allowing you to make comparisons to other web applications.

If you need to observe the exact memory usage of your application at any point, you can use the *Heap Snapshot* feature within the *Profiles* tab of the Chrome or Opera developer tools. To get an instant snapshot of memory usage by object, select the *Take Heap Snapshot* radio button and click the *Start* button. The snapshot taken will be visible in the left-hand panel, which you can select to show you a summary of objects created organized by the constructor function, or builtin type, used to instantiate it, and showing the memory size consumed by each. You can then drill down to find out which objects are consuming more memory than expected to allow you to fix specific issues that might be present in those objects.

If you want to compare how the entire memory usage of your web application changes over a specific time period, use the *Record Heap Allocations* radio option within the *Profiles* tab of the developer tools and click the *Start* button. A red indicator will appear in the top left of the developer tools to indicate that the memory usage is being recorded. Click this indicator to stop recording when you are ready. The memory usage between the point you started recording and the point you stopped will be plotted on a graph in the main panel of the developer tools, with spikes indicating memory usage changes. Beneath the graph is the list of objects whose memory usage has changed over the duration of recording. A range selector above the graph allows you to filter down the memory usage events to a narrow range, helping you focus on exactly which object changes provoked large memory changes so that you can look into ways of improving excessive memory usage in your application.

The *Timeline* tab in the browser's developer tools reveals a *Memory* timeline tool in the left-side panel. To run a memory timeline check, simply keep the Timeline tab selected when you refresh your page to start the measurement. A graph should appear showing the amount of memory consumed by your running page until the page load event is reached. Beneath the graph is a list of records showing each event that took place that had an effect on the application's memory usage, complete with details of the type of event, the file name, and line number of the operation that affected the memory usage. Selecting a time range using the sliders above the graph allows you to filter the list of records down to those within a specific range—perhaps where you notice a large spike in memory usage that does not get freed up later on—that will help debug which operations are causing memory to be consumed by your application when it initializes and runs. Figure 16-7 shows the Memory timeline tool in action, complete with a graph of memory usage over time, a list of events that caused changes to memory allocation, and a counter of active DOM nodes and event listeners, which can often be the cause of memory leaks in web applications.

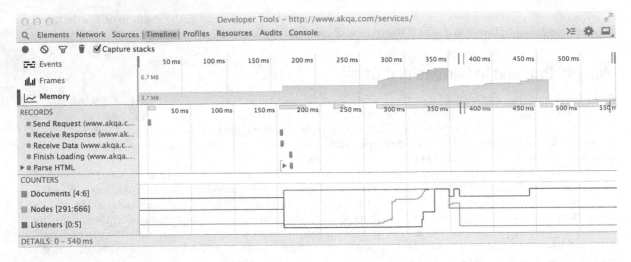

Figure 16-7. *The Memory timeline tool active in Chrome and Opera browser developer tools*

To learn more about the memory profile capabilities of the Chrome browser developer tools, and by extension Opera's developer tools, check out the following online resource at `http://bit.ly/chrome-memory`.

Memory Profiling in Internet Explorer 11

Inspired by the memory profiling abilities of the Chrome browser developer tools, Microsoft added a similar yet refined version of the same functionality in version 11 of their Internet Explorer browser. Clicking the *Memory* tab in the IE11 developer tools brings up a panel with an option to begin memory profiling. Select the *play* button in the toolbar, or follow the link in the center of the panel, to begin profiling memory usage in the browser; a graph will appear detailing the memory usage as time passes. To take a snapshot of the memory usage at any given point, select the *Take heap snapshot* button beneath the graph. Details of the memory usage at that point will appear in a box below the graph. Clicking on the memory size shown within the box will present a list of the objects in memory and their individual memory size, allowing you to see which objects may be causing memory issues in your application. Creating a second snapshot will show the details of the size of memory and object count changes between the new snapshot and the previous one. Selecting the link on either piece of information shows a comparison between the memory usage and object list between the two snapshots.

Figure 16-8 shows the Memory tool in action within the Internet Explorer browser developer tools, showing a graph of memory usage over time, and two memory snapshots taken within a few seconds of each other, with the difference in memory size and object count between the two snapshots highlighted within the details box of the second snapshot.

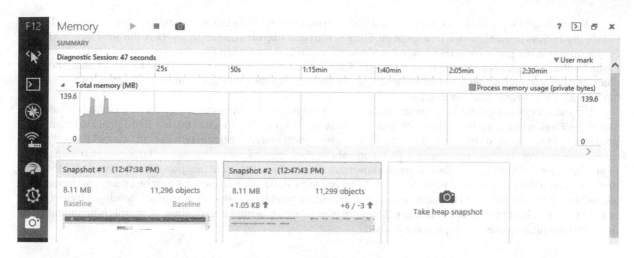

Figure 16-8. *The Memory tab in IE11 developer tools provides a simple UI for investigating memory usage*

The memory profiling tools in Internet Explorer largely match those of the Chrome and Opera developer tools; however, they are contained within a single tab with what is, in my opinion, an easier-to-use interface for debugging memory usage within your web application.

To learn more about the IE11 Memory tool, look at the following online resource on the subject at `http://bit.ly/ie-memory`.

Identifying Performance Bottlenecks

Sometimes you'll notice when testing your web applications that at certain points when JavaScript is executing the browser will seem to lock up or freeze for a split second. This occurs when the browser is forced to give priority to the JavaScript interpreter over its renderer due to a series of operations taking place that leave no space for the renderer to catch up with itself. This is often the result of `for` or `while` loops executing too many iterations, swamping the browser. In such a case, or to ensure that there is no chance of such a case occurring in your code, utilize the performance profiling features of the browser developer tools to measure and improve your JavaScript code.

In Chrome and Opera developer tools, the *Profiles* tab allows you to profile your JavaScript with the *Collect JavaScript CPU Profile* radio option. Click *Start* to begin profiling and *Stop* when you no longer wish to collect any more data. You will be presented with a list of named function calls arranged in order of the time spent within them, with links provided to the file and line number from where they were executed. A "%" toggle button in the top toolbar allows you to switch between a display of the absolute time taken to execute each function, in milliseconds, and the percentage of the total profiled time that was spent within the function. If any particular function executed other functions internally, these are shown with an arrow beside them, allowing you to filter the time spent within each individual subfunction. This view alone should allow you to locate where any performance bottlenecks are occurring in the running of your code, but a separate Chart view, accessible through a selection box in the toolbar, shows a graphical view of performance over the profiled time, with spikes indicating activity. The lower graph also allows you to view the time taken within each file and function, by hovering the mouse over the spikes. A range slider above the chart allows you to narrow down the displayed data to a certain time range within the profiled period, allowing you to focus on a specific region of activity to track down any performance issues in your code. To learn more about the JavaScript profiling capabilities of the Chrome developer tools, read about it in more detail online at `http://bit.ly/chrome-profile`.

The Safari developer tools has a very similar feature within its *Timelines* tab. A button in the left-hand panel beside the *Profiles* heading allows JavaScript profiling to start and stop on demand by selecing the *Start JavaScript Profile* option in the popup selection box. A list of function calls and time taken for each is produced with a "%" button in the toolbar to switch between time units displayed, resembling that in Chrome's developer tools, although the charting ability is missing here. To learn more about the profiling abilities of Safari in more detail, check out `http://bit.ly/safari-profile` online.

The browser developer tools in Firefox contain the same profiling feature implemented in a very similar way. Select the *Profiles* tab in the developer tools and select the *time* icon in the top left of the left-hand panel to begin profiling, clicking again to stop collecting data. The similar view of hierarchical function calls in order of execution duration is displayed in the main panel, with a graph above showing performance peaks and troughs, as shown in Figure 16-9. Selecting an area in the top graph allows you to filter down the list of function calls shown to only those that occurred within the selected time range, enabling you to establish which functions may be causing performance issues and need addressing. To learn more about the JavaScript profiling abilities of the Firefox developer tools, check out `http://bit.ly/firefox-profile`. Note that there is no similar tool built into Firebug, so for this functionality, defer to the builtin Firefox developer tools instead.

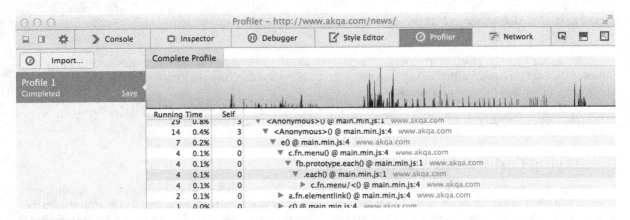

Figure 16-9. *The Profiler tab in Firefox developer tools allow you to drill down to locate poor performing functions*

The Internet Explorer 11 developer tools feature a similar profiling ability through its *Profiler* tab. To start profiling JavaScript, click the green *play* button in the top toolbar, clicking the red *stop* button it is replaced with to cease collecting data. The list of executed functions is then displayed in the main panel area, with toggles to take you between a *Functions* and *Call Tree* view, the former of which shows a flat view of each function called with the longest performing function at the top of the list, and the latter of which shows a hierarchical view of the called functions, based on which functions called which others internally. As with the Safari developer tools, there is no graph view of the data allowing you to filter by time; however, the list itself contains enough information to debug performance issues as it points to the files and line numbers of the functions that took the longest time to execute, showing you exactly where to focus your debugging efforts. To learn more about the JavaScript profiling capabilities of the IE11 developer tools, check out `http://bit.ly/ie-profile`.

Using the profiling abilities of the browser developer tools, you can drill right down into the running code to discover which functions are taking the longest time to execute, allowing you to check over your code for those functions to attempt to find more efficient ways of performing the same operations with the same results.

Summary

In this chapter, we have seen how to use the browsers' in-built developer tools to debug and monitor our JavaScript code in the context of a real, live, running application environment, using the data provided by these tools to improve our code for the benefit of our users, making it more performant, memory-efficient, and less prone to runtime errors. To learn even more about the features of the browser developer tools, including which features are present in which browser, check out Andi Smith's fantastic online resource, "Dev Tool Secrets," at `http://devtoolsecrets.com`.

Throughout the course of this book, I have explained how professional JavaScript developers use advanced coding techniques, take advantage of language and browser capabilities, and apply tooling to their workflow and their code in order to produce high-quality, maintainable JavaScript code for the benefit of the end users of their applications and other developers working alongside them. I trust you've picked up a number of ideas, techniques, and skills that you can now apply to your own projects, allowing you gain more experience and more confidence, to excel as a professional JavaScript developer. Thank you for reading, and happy coding!

Index

A

Abstract factory pattern, 122–126
Adapter pattern, 137–139
Apply and call methods, 15–16
Architectural patterns
    MVC (*see* Model-View-Controller (MVC))
    MVP (*see* Model-View-Presenter (MVP) pattern)
    MVVM (*see* Model-View-ViewModel
        (MVVM) pattern)
Arrays
    creation, 110
    functions within loops, 112
    looping, 110–111

B

Behavioral design patterns
    chain of responsibility, 163–166
    command, 166–169
    description, 163
    interator, 169–172
    mediator, 177–181
    memento, 181–183
    observer, 172–176
    promises, 183–187
    strategy, 194–198
Browser developer tools
    DOM, 424
    Internet Explorer and Chrome, 423
    JavaScript (*see* JavaScript)
    Mozilla's Firefox browser, 423
    Safari browser, 424
Build automation and tools
    benchmark, 391
    bower.json, 419
    code quality, 391
    development workflow, 391
    dynamic web page, 404
    front-end package manager, 419
    grunt-bowercopy, 420
    Gruntfile.js, 406
    Gulp.js, 400–403, 406, 408
    index.html page, 406
    JavaScript task runner (*see* JavaScript
        task runner, grants)
    Node.js application platform, 392
    NPM directory, 419
    production-ready code
        (*see* Production-ready code)
    repetitive tasks, 404
    scaffolding, 420–421
    task runner, 391
    time-consuming, 404
    web applications, 404, 420
    web server, 404
Builder pattern, 127–129

C

Canvas API
    basic drawing operations, 261–262, 264
    building Frogger game
        (*see* Frogger game, Canvas API)
    building games
        animation, 267
        collision detection, 269–270
        drawImage() method, 265–266
        game control, 268–269
        layering canvases, 272
        procedures and structures, 265
        sprite map, drawing individual image, 266
    game loop
        at fixed frame rate, setInterval() function, 270
        requestAnimationFrame, 271
    high-definition (retina) graphics, 264
    three-dimensional graphics, 261
    two-dimensional drawing context, 261

Chain of responsibility pattern, 163–166
Client-side templates
    array item, 357
    conditional sections, 349
    custom helpers, 358–360
    DOM, 341
    EJS, 365–366
    Handlebars.js, 353–356
    HTML, 341–343
    if helper, 357
    Inverted sections, 350–351
    Iterator sections, 349
    JavaScript data, 342
    library, 344–345
    log Helper, 358
    Mustache.js, 345–346, 348
    partial templates, 352–353
    precompiling templates, 360, 362–364
    registerPartial() method, 356
    text string, 343
    Underscore.js, 366–367
    variables, 348
CLI tool (see Command line interface (CLI) tool)
Code file dependencies management
    aliases, 230
    BBC, 229
    content delivery networks and fallbacks, 230
    modules, 228–230
    modules creation, 231–232
    RequireJS
        alternatives, 235
        code optimizer tool, 234CSS style rules, 224, 226
        definition, 223
        folder structure, 228
        homepage, 227
        HTML code, 224
        library, 223
        newsletter sign-up form, 226
        plugins, 234
    scripts loading, 232–233
Code quality measurement
    code coverage, 83
    complex code, 86
    Grunt command line interface, 84
    Gruntfile.js, 85
    Istanbul, 84
    LCOV, 85–86
    Mac and Linux users, 87
    metrics, 87
    NPM, 84
    Plato tool, 86, 88
    running tools, 83
Coding conventions and naming
    camel-case, word divisions, 25
    description, 23

descriptive names, 24
function block, 26
lowercase letter, 24–25
uppercase characters, 25
variable and function name hoisting
    code blocks and scope, 26–27
    hoisting of functions, 28
    variables, 27
Command line interface (CLI) tool, 393
Command pattern, 166–169
Composite pattern, 140–141
Content delivery networks (CDN), 230
Context and this keyword
    constructor function
        initializing properties, 10
        literal object input, 10–11
        this keyword within, 8
    dot notation, 7
    efficient constructor, 9
    storing value into variable, 7
Creational design patterns
    abstract factory, 122–126
    builder, 127–129
    description, 119
    factory, 120–122
    prototype, 129–131
    singleton, 132–133, 135

■ D

Debugging running, JavaScript
    breakpoint, 430
    Chrome developer tools, 429
    conditional statements, 431
    console object, 430
    continue button, 431
    Firefox developer tools, 429
    Internet Explorer developer tools, 430
    JSON-format, 429
    left-hand panel, 431
    local variables, 432
    pretty printing, 428–429
    Safari developer tools, 429
    source maps, 429
    unminified code, 428
    web server, 428
Decorator pattern, 141–143
Documentation
    inline and block comments, 37
    Markdown (see Markdown)
    structured, 38
    website creation, YUIDoc
        "classes" and modules, 62
        documented code uses, 58
        HTML site, documented JavaScript code, 62

JavaScript application, 58
JSON-formatted file, 58
node, 58
NPM, 58
packages, 58
YUIDoc format (*see* YUIDoc documentation format)
Document Object Model (DOM), 341
DOM. *See* Document Object Model (DOM)

■ **E**

ECMAScript 5
array methods
description, 31
Each method, 31
every and some methods, 32
filter method, 33
map method, 32
function binding, 30
JSON Data Format Parsing, 28
object methods
description, 33
object create method, 35–36
object freeze method, 34
Object getOwnPropertyDescriptor method, 34
object keys method, 35
property definitions, 34–35
strict mode, 29–30
EJS. *See* Embedded JavaScript (EJS)
Embedded JavaScript (EJS)
JavaScript templating language, 364
Mustache.js and Handlebars.js, 365
render() method, 365
Ruby language developers, 364
update() method, 366
Encapsulation, 14

■ **F**

Façade pattern, 144–145
Factory pattern, 120–122
Flyweight pattern, 145–148, 150–151
Frogger game, Canvas API
arcade classic, 273
core game logic, 276–278
HTML page, 273
namespace, key properties and methods, 274–276
purpose, 272

■ **G**

Gulp.js
gulpfile.js., 401
gulp-jshint, 401
Node.js, 401

Node.js require() method, 403
package.json, 401
streams functionality, 401
task() method, 401
use strict statement, 403

■ **H**

Handlebars.js
Handlebars.compile() method, 354
HTML, 355
JavaScript data hash, 354
Mustache format, 353
High-quality JavaScript
code quality measurement
(*see* Code quality measurement)
runtime errors, 79
static code analysis (*see* Static code analysis, JS)
unit testing frameworks
input combination, 72
Jasmine project, 72–75, 77
matchers, 78–79
web browsers, 65
HTML. *See* HyperText Markup Language (HTML)
HTML5 application cache, 256–257
http module
API documentation, 374
local web server, 372
web server frameworks, 373
HyperText Markup Language (HTML)
Ajax, 342
server-side, 342
superfluous information, 343

■ **I**

ICE framework. *See* Interactive Connectivity Establishment (ICE) framework
Interactive Connectivity Establishment (ICE) framework, 325
Iterator pattern, 169–172

■ **J, K, L**

Jasmine unit testing framework
add() function, 73
expect() function, 74
extensive documentation, 73
HTML, 75
non-numeric inputs, 75
spec runner, 74–76
string concatenation, 76
suites, 72
toEqual() function, 74
unit testing frameworks, 77

JavaScript
  bottlenecks, 435
  Chrome and Opera developer tools, 435
  code references, 428
  console.debug(), 426
  console.error(), 426
  console.info(), 426
  console.log() method, 425
  console.timeEnd(), 427
  console.warn(), 426
  debugging running (*see* JavaScript:Debugging
      running, JavaScript)
  Firefox developer tools, 436
  Google Chrome, 426
  memory leaks, 432
  Node.js applications, 425
  performance measurement, 427
JavaScript applications
  arrays uses (*see* Arrays)
  Document Object Manipulation
    CSS style, 100–101
    existing elements closing, 99–100
    minimise access to
        page elements, 98–99
    offline DOM, 100
  DOM event performance
    event delegation, 101–102
    rapid-fire events, 103
    websites and applications, 101
  function performance
    function return values storing, 104
    generic memoization
        to function, 106
    memoization technique, 105
  page loading time
    compilation, 92
    global variables, 96–97
    Google Closure Compiler,
        for code compilation, 95–96
    GZip encode delivery, 91
    HTML tag order matters, 91
    JSMin for code minification, 93–94
    lazy loading JavaScript Files, 97–98
    minification, 92
    obfuscation, 92
    UglifyJS for code obfuscation, 94–95
  performance measurements, 117–118
  regular expressions
    characters, 107
    character sequence, 109
    definition, 106
    modifiers, 108
    RegExp constructor, 107
    string replace() method, 108

    string replace() method call, 109
    String type methods, 108
  Web workers, offload intensive tasks
    configuration, 114
    creation, 113
    image data processing, 114–117
    terminate() method, 114
    user interface, 113
    W3C standardized version, 113
JavaScript applications (*see* Architectural patterns)
JavaScript lint (JSLint)
  alert method, 67
  C language, 65
  Class object, 68
  computer's processor, 65
  directive, 67
  frameworks, 69
  function keyword, 66
  NPM tool, 69
  running code, 67
JavaScript task runner, grunts
  API, 394
  CLI tool, 393
  command line, 395
  devDependencies, 393
  file.readJSON() method, 396
  file.readYAML() method, 397
  Gruntfile.js, 393
  initConfig() method, 394, 397
  JSHint, 394, 398
  loadNpmTasks() method, 394
  module.exports, 393
  multitasks, 398
  Node.js packages, 393
  package.json, 393, 397
  plugin directory, 400
  registerTask() method, 394
  static code analysis, 394
  targets, 399
  template strings, 397
  use strict statement, 396
  wealth of resources, 392
JSHint, 69–70

■ **M**

Markdown
  backslash uses, 57
  breaking lines and
      creating paragraphs, 49
  code display, 54
  content grouping under headings, 49
  emphasized text, 53
  horizontal rules creation, 56

HTML, 57
images insertion, 56
linking to URLs, 55
lists creation, 50
quotes addition, 54
YUIDoc support, 48
Mediator pattern, 177–181
Memento pattern, 181–183
Memory leaks, JavaScript
garbage collector, 432
heap Snapshot, 433
Internet Explorer 11, 434–435
profiles tab, 433
removeEventListener() method, 432
timeline tab, 433–434
web applications, 432
Mixin pattern, 152–155
Mobile JavaScript
mobile device sensors
event framing, sensor data, 250
geolocation sensor, 240–243
in-built, 240
missing sensors, 249
motion sensors, 248–249
orientation and
direction sensors, 245–248
touch sensor, 243–245
mobile web development
battery life, 237
network bandwidth
speeds and latency, 238
on-board memory size, 238
operating system responsiveness, 239
network connection failures
and offline states
detection, 252–253
HTML5 application cache, 256–257
inconvenient experiences, 251
Web Storage API, 253–254, 256
Responsive Web Design, 258
Model-View-Controller (MVC)
data structure, 199
email addresses management, 199–201
JavaScript applications, 199
View code, user interface, 201–205
Model-View-Presenter (MVP) pattern
email address list application, 209–213
observer pattern, 214
Model-View-ViewModel (MVVM) pattern
data-submit attributes, 215
email system, 216–218
internal business logic, 214
observer pattern, 219–220

Module pattern, 155–158
Mustache.js
data hash, 345
Google Templates, 345
Mustache.render() method, 346
script tag, 345

■ N

Network Address Translation (NAT), 321
Node.js application platform
API documentation, 371
command-line applications, 369
command line arguments, 371
devDependencies, 378
Hello World, 370
hosting solution, 389
http Module, 372–374
JavaScript, 369
loading modules, 372
log() method, 371
module.exports property, 380
npm, 369, 375–376
package.json, 376, 378
packages, 374
process.argv array, 372
require() method, 379–380
web applications, 382–384
yuidoc application, 376
Node Package Manager (NPM), 58, 69
NPM. See Node Package Manager (NPM)

■ O

Object-oriented JavaScript
apply and call methods, 15–16
arguments object, 16–18
assigning properties and methods
prototype, 4, 6
scope, 6
base "class" creator, 22–23
chaining methods, 11–12
classes, 2
coding conventions and naming
(see Coding conventions and naming)
context and this keyword
(see Context and this keyword)
custom objects, 1–2
ECMAScript 5 (see ECMAScript 5)
encapsulation, 14
inheritance, 12–14
object's constructor, detection, 3–4
polymorphism, 14–15

Object-oriented JavaScript (*cont.*)
    public, private, and protected
        properties and methods, 18–20
    simplifying inheritance, 20, 22
Observer pattern, 172–176

■ P, Q

Polymorphism, 14–15
Precompiling templates
    Handlebars.js compile() method, 360
    Mustache library, 360
    NPM, 361
    templatefile.handlebars, 361
    web applications, 364
Production-ready code
    build tasks, 409
    development workflow, 408
    Gruntfile.js, 413
    Gulp.js, 413, 415–418
    main.js file, 413
    public consumption, 408
Promises pattern, 183–187
Prototype pattern, 129–131
Proxy pattern, 159–161

■ R

Responsive Web Design, 258
Runtime errors, JS
    code quality, 79
    custom error, 82–83
    error type, 81
    eval error, 80
    range error, 80
    reference error, 80
    syntax error, 79
    URI error, 80
    wrap code, 80–81

■ S

Scaffolding
    generators, 420
    time-consuming, 420
    Yeoman, 421
Session Description Protocol (SDP), 325
Session Traversal Utilities for NAT (STUN), 325
Singleton pattern, 40, 132–134
Socket.IO
    HTML, 388
    HTTP methods, 384
    JavaScript library, 387

package.json, 386
real-time, 384, 387
socket.broadcast.emit() method, 389
socket.emit() method, 389
W3C WebSocket API, 384
Static code analysis, JS
    bugs, 65
    closure compiler, 70
    compiled code, 70
    documentation site, 71
    JSHint, 69–70
    JSLint, 65, 67–69
    operating system, 71
    potential errors, 65
Strategy pattern, 194–198
Structural design patterns
    adapter, 137–139
    composite, 140–141
    decorator, 141–143
    description, 137
    façade, 143–145
    flyweight, 145–148, 150
    mixin, 152–155
    module, 155–158
    proxy, 159–161
STUN. *See* Session Traversal
        Utilities for NAT (STUN)

■ T, U

Traversal Using Relays around NAT (TURN), 325
TURN. *See* Traversal Using
        Relays around NAT (TURN)

■ V

Video chat client
    class, 331–334
    HTML page, 329–330
    JavaScript files, 329
    video call, 328–329
Video chat web application
    connection and signaling
        Ajax, 326
        ICE framework, 325
        NAT, 325
        RTCPeerConnection class interface, 325–326
        STUN and TURN, 325
    firebase service for simple signaling
        data-access API, 327
        pseudo-JSON format, 327–328
        WebSocket connections, 326
    getUserMedia() API method, 325

■ W, X

Web applications
    API documentation, 384
    express framework, 382
    package.json file, 384
Webcam and microphone
    browser's window.URL.createObjectURL()
        method, 323–324
    callback function, 322
    getUserMedia() method
        accessing the webcam and microphone, 323
        onSuccess() callback method, 323
        polyfills, 322
Web Real Time Communication (WebRTC) API
    specification, 321
    video chat client, 328–334
    video chat web application, 325–328
    webcam and microphone, 322–324
WebRTC. *See* Web Real Time
        Communication (WebRTC) API

■ Y, Z

YUIDoc documentation format
    block comments, 38
    chained methods, 47
    "classes", constructors,
        properties and methods
        Accommodation, 39
        fully-documented
          JavaScript "class", 41
        property documentation, 40
        public variable name, 40
        singleton, 40
        static "class" documentation, 40
        variables and
          functions uses, 40
Code editors, 38
code examples, 48
constant value,
    property containing, 43
events, 47
grouping, related "classes", 47
inherited "classes", 46
inputs parameters and
    methods return values
    dot notation, 42
    inputs and outputs, 42
optional method
    input parameters, 43
private, protected and public
    methods and properties, 44
tags, 39, 48

Get the eBook for only $10!

Now you can take the weightless companion with you anywhere, anytime. Your purchase of this book entitles you to 3 electronic versions for only $10.

This Apress title will prove so indispensible that you'll want to carry it with you everywhere, which is why we are offering the eBook in 3 formats for only $10 if you have already purchased the print book.

Convenient and fully searchable, the PDF version enables you to easily find and copy code—or perform examples by quickly toggling between instructions and applications. The MOBI format is ideal for your Kindle, while the ePUB can be utilized on a variety of mobile devices.

Go to www.apress.com/promo/tendollars to purchase your companion eBook.